Helena Gomm

Simon Clarke
Gina Cuciniello
Paul Dummett
Paul Emmerson
Jon Hird
Mark Powell
Nicholas Sheard
Jeremy Taylor
Jon Wright

in company

Pre-intermediate
Teacher's Book

MACMILLAN

Contents

Spring has arrived, judging by the number of tourists that have appeared in the streets. Phil has an hour free before his next lesson. Picking out a nice café, he chooses a window table and orders a coffee. After spending a few minutes people-watching, he starts to think about the lesson he's just come out of: his first class with a new group of students at the central offices of a pharmaceutical company. Half the lesson was spent in an informal chat based on the needs analysis, and there seem to be some potential problems. Phil opens his briefcase and takes out his notes.

> Jean Claude Duval, Purchasing Manager. Pre-int. Has been studying English for 'many years'. Uses English at work most days in e-mails and phone calls to suppliers, though these tend to follow the same pattern most of the time. Also has occasional face-to-face meetings: wants to improve general communication for these. Has difficulty just chatting during breaks in meetings or over lunch.

> Anton Brun, IT Systems Manager. Int. Did three years' English at school. Doesn't currently use English at work but thinks it will be 'useful for the future'. Mainly interested in social English. Fairly fluent, but some grammar problems.

> Marie Nöelle Rousillon, Chief Financial Officer. Pre-int. Studied English at school and university, but didn't use it for years. Has now had to start using English regularly in monthly meetings with the new American shareholders and feels 'completely lost'. And it isn't just the meetings – says she goes to hide in her office during breaks to avoid having to engage in any conversation. Also receives occasional phone calls, mainly to check financial information, but her bilingual secretary deals with e-mails.

Phil knows the company well. There's no way he can move Anton to another group at a higher level: the other classes are all in the research labs outside the city. And, anyway, Anton's warmth and interest in people helped the group to gel and work more productively together. But will he get bored working at a lower level? As long as the topics are interesting enough, perhaps he'll stay focused. And Phil could give him extra grammar and vocabulary work, which he'd really benefit from.

Marie Nöelle's needs are certainly the most urgent, but also the most specialised, and will probably involve lexis the others have no need for. Still, terminology is probably not her main problem. The real challenge is coping with complex interactions. The skills she needs – getting her point of view across, understanding different opinions, dealing with telephone calls, handling social situations – are useful for just about everyone.

Jean Claude's most immediate need is probably to develop self-confidence. Lots of tasks with concrete outcomes, guided conversation on different topics and vocabulary building activities would suit him.

As he thinks things through, Phil begins to feel more confident. Now, what about writing skills?

In Company is Macmillan's skills-based Business English series, aimed at professional, adult learners seeking to realise their full potential as speakers of English at work – both in and out of the office – and in social settings. It aims to provide learners with the language and skills they need using motivating and engaging material. Authentic and realistic business stories and situations form the basis for texts, dialogues and speaking activities.

In Company Pre-intermediate takes students through twenty progressively more challenging units which include describing your work and company, obtaining and sharing information, networking and travelling on business. The course reflects the need for students at this level to develop their grammatical competence, increase their lexical range and, above all, acquire strategies to communicate effectively in both professional and social situations.

Ten key observations on the teaching of English to professional learners underpin the course:

1 Professionals like to be regularly reminded why they are studying and what's in it for them.
2 They are used to goal-setting and time constraints and tend to welcome a fairly fast pace.
3 They are motivated by topics which directly relate to their own personal experiences.
4 They expect to see an immediate, practical payoff of some kind at the end of each lesson.
5 It is English, not business, they have come to you for help with (but see 7).
6 They want to be able to actually *do* business with their English rather than just talk about it.
7 They appreciate texts and tasks which reflect what they have to do in their job.
8 They also appreciate texts and tasks which allow them to escape what they have to do in their job.
9 They don't regard having fun as incompatible with 'serious learning' (but see 1 and 4).
10 They like to see an overall plan and method behind the classes they attend.

Practical approach

In Company Pre-intermediate is a practical course in *how* to do business in English. With target language selectively introduced on a need-to-know basis, each unit is a fast track to competence in a particular business skill. Recognising that people need more than just phrase lists and useful language boxes to operate effectively in real-life business situations, each unit provides a substantial amount of guided skills work to give students the chance to fully assimilate the target language and 'make it their own', before going on to tackle fluency activities.

Topics and skills developed at this level include:
- describing your work and company
- using the telephone
- discussing pros and cons
- making comparisons
- telling anecdotes
- writing e-mails and reports
- obtaining and giving information
- dealing with social situations
- making requests
- discussing consequences
- making plans

Having something to say

In Company Pre-intermediate taps into students' emotions, with the assumption that by focusing on areas which have some human interest or twist, they will have more to say. The classroom is an artificial environment in which imagination plays an essential role. It is unlikely that students will have to use their English in a situation in which they are approached by an executive headhunter (Unit 11, page 53), or discover that a job candidate is a fraud (Unit 14, page 65). Yet situations like these have a dramatic impact which makes the target language memorable.

Why are the units divided into categories?

In Company Pre-intermediate contains four types of unit: *Conversation skills, Work issues, Connecting* and *Company life.*

Conversation skills

Acquiring communication strategies for a variety of work-related and social contexts is the main emphasis of these units. Functional language is presented and practised through dialogues. There is some lexical input but no grammar focus.

Work issues

These units are built around themes which are common to all working situations such as work-related stress, business travel, time management, office gossip and working from home. The approach taken ensures that these topics are brought to life. For example, in *Unit 14 Hiring and firing*, the themes of sacking and labour conflicts have been included because topics like these are likely to generate strong opinion and interest in the classroom.

Connecting

The focus of these units is the world of communication and travel. Particular importance has been given to the Internet and the role of information technology in present-day business practice. Not only does this reflect the reality of the IT revolution in the workplace over recent years, but it also gives students the opportunity to look at the conventions and language of this world.

Company life

These units include tense work to enable learners to discuss their routines, past experiences, achievements and future plans in relation to their work and their company. Students are also encouraged to think outside the realms of their own experience and use their imagination, for example, by inventing their own dot.com (Unit 1, page 9), or writing a report on a company with problems (Unit 10, page 48).

Categorising the units in this way helps teachers to identify more easily the areas which are of interest to their students. It also helps students to keep track of their progress.

Lexical syllabus

In Company Pre-intermediate devotes a lot of attention to lexis, which is presented through both written and recorded texts. Students are encouraged to take note of common collocations and word building, and this is reinforced by the optional Lexis links (at the back of the Student's Book), which can either be set for homework or made the basis of vocabulary-building lessons.

Grammar syllabus

At pre-intermediate level, although students have met some of the major structures previously, they are meeting others for the first time. The approach in *In Company Pre-intermediate* is to highlight the grammar as it naturally emerges in the activities. Meaning and concept are made clear through context and example, and provision is made for adequate controlled practice before students attempt to use the language in a more ambitious context. Throughout the course, there is a strong, progressive grammar syllabus, which learners particularly appreciate at this level. This is backed up by fifteen Grammar links (at the back of the Student's Book), cross-linked to the fifteen main skills-based units, which provide more explicit explanation and practice exercises.

Controlled practice

For pre-intermediate students, the most appreciated parts of the lesson are often those moments when they are asked to produce stretches of accurate English in a controlled context. *In Company Pre-intermediate* places special emphasis on controlled practice as part of the build-up for fluency-based work. For example, students listen to a conversation and then reconstruct it from prompts before going on to act out their own dialogues.

Class cassettes and CDs

Throughout the course, substantial use is made of audio recordings to input business expressions and grammatical structures. Indeed, very little of the language work is not either presented or recycled in a recording.

The recordings feature both native and non-native speaker accents, providing the students with extensive exposure to real spoken English. There is frequently an element of humour in the recordings which, besides entertaining the students, motivates them to listen again for things they missed the first time round. The target language in the units is in bold in the recordings (at the back of the Student's Book and in the Teacher's Book with the accompanying lesson notes).

How can I exploit the dialogues further?

Distinguish between different types of listening skills practice. The exercises are initially task-based activities which focus on comprehension. However, it is also important to give learners the opportunity to listen to texts again in a more detailed way. In other words, having understood *what* was said, you should then give some attention to *how* things are said. Try the following intensive listening techniques:

- allow the students to listen to the recording again in a relaxed way while they follow the script at the back of the Student's Book.
- pause the recording after questions for students to recall or predict the response (if they write these down as they go, you can ask them to recall all the questions at the end).
- pause the recording after responses to questions and ask students to think of other possible responses.
- pause the recording in the middle of lexical chunks (collocations, fixed expressions) for students to complete them either orally or by writing them down.
- ask students to write down a recording as you play it, line by line. If they miss a word, encourage them to look at the words around it and imagine what could go in the gap. Ask students to compare their transcripts to the original. Focus on common errors and spelling problems.

- ask students to listen to a conversation and repeat it line by line. Then build up the conversation on the board using word prompts. Ask students to re-create the conversation from the prompts.
- looking at the recording line by line, ask students to 'play' each line in their heads without actually speaking, and then listen and compare to how it actually sounds.

Reading texts

The reading texts in *In Company Pre-intermediate* have been chosen to involve, entertain and provoke students into lively discussion, as well as to contextualise key target vocabulary. Squeezing a text completely dry of all useful language usually demotivates a class, but many of the longer texts in *In Company Pre-intermediate* are informationally and lexically rich and can usefully be revisited.

How can I exploit the texts further?

Try some of the following:
- ask students to set each other questions on the text.
- ask students set you questions on the text, and vice versa.
- give students several figures from the text and ask them to recall the context in which they were mentioned.
- read the text aloud but slur certain words/phrases and get students to ask you for repetition/clarification.
- give students the first half of 8–10 collocations and a time limit in which to search for the collocates in the text.
- give students a set of miscollocates and ask them to correct them by referring to the text.
- read out the text pausing in the middle of collocations / fixed expressions / idioms for students to predict the completions either by shouting out or writing down the answer.
- read out the text pausing at specific vocabulary items and ask questions like: *What's the opposite of X? What's the word we learned the other day which is like X? X is a noun: what's the verb form / adjective? X often goes with the word Y: what other words can go with Y? Give me another sentence using X.*
- ask students to read the text aloud as a pronunciation exercise. Don't look at the text yourself as they read: this will force you to concentrate on the comprehensibility of their output. Ask them to do this in pairs.
- write key words on the board relating to the main ideas in the text and ask students to reconstruct the text orally.

Fluency work

In Company Pre-intermediate includes two types of fluency activity which draw on both the specific language presented in a unit and the wider linguistic resources of the students. These are:
- roleplays and simulations, where the students are given a scenario and perhaps some kind of 'personal agenda'.
- 'framework' activities, where the students decide on the content for an interview, report or phone call and the Student's Book provides them with a linguistic framework to help deliver that information.

In order to avoid learner and teacher frustration, sufficient preparation for both types of activity is essential, and it may sometimes be advisable to carry out the actual fluency activity in a subsequent lesson to ensure plenty of time for preparation and feedback.

Teacher's Book

In this book you'll find comprehensive teacher's notes which give an overview of each unit, detailed procedural instructions for all the exercises and an *If you're short of time* section at the end of each unit. These are interleaved with the Student's Book pages and contain the recording scripts which relate to the Student's Book page opposite. The Student's Book pages themselves are faded slightly so that the overprinted answer key stands out clearly, helping teachers to locate the answers easily. Suggested answers for longer tasks are provided in the teacher's notes. The Grammar and Lexis links pages may be photocopied and given to students to check their answers.

The book also features a Resource materials section containing thirty photocopiable worksheets which extend and/or revise elements in the Student's Book. These were written by nine practising business English teachers and provide approximately twenty extra hours of material to supplement the Student's Book.

Ten 'rules of thumb' teaching tips

- Avoid saying *Let's turn to page …* when starting a new lesson. Instead, try to generate interest in the subject matter while students still have their books closed.
- Always do the first item of an exercise with the whole class to make sure that students know what they have to do.
- When doing written exercises in pairs, don't let students write to begin with. This will encourage them to speak and to remember their answers for a subsequent feedback session. Allow them to write the answers after the feedback so that they have a written record to refer to at a later date.
- Use drills to give students the opportunity to get their tongues round new language. Most students enjoy well-executed drills (and it's also a way to pick up a flagging lesson).
- Students sometimes complain about not being corrected enough, but rarely about being corrected too much.
- Always revise something from a previous class during the lesson.
- Arrange the classroom to suit your class. In small classes, encourage students to sit near you.
- Avoid asking questions which are impossible to answer. For example, for students to answer *What does X mean?* often requires more complicated language than you're actually trying to teach.
- Plan your lesson backwards. Decide what you want the students to be doing at the end of the lesson and work out how to get there.
- Keep a note of ad-hoc items which crop up and common mistakes that students make. Use these as the basis for informal revision and warm-up activities.

Simon Clarke
July 2003
(with thanks to Mark Powell)

Helena Gomm

Simon Clarke
Gina Cuciniello
Paul Dummett
Paul Emmerson
Jon Hird
Mark Powell
Nicholas Sheard
Jeremy Taylor
Jon Wright

in company

Pre-intermediate
Teacher's Book

MACMILLAN

Contents: Student's Book

2

3

First salesman: I made some very valuable contacts today.
Second salesman: I didn't get any orders either. *Anon*

1   The words on the left are from a business presentation. Match them to the definitions on the right.

a	website	**1**	money you spend on rent, equipment, salaries, etc.
b	potential market	**2**	companies who put money into new businesses
c	average	**3**	people who you can sell to
d	costs	**4**	pay someone to do a job
e	investment	**5**	a group of web pages on the Internet
f	employ	**6**	publicity you send to people's homes by post
g	direct mail campaign	**7**	money you need to establish or expand a business
h	venture capitalists	**8**	the sum of, for example, ten different numbers divided by ten

a	5	b	3	c	8	d	1	e	7	f	4	g	6	h	2

> **elevator pitch:** a concise, carefully planned description about your company that your mother could understand in the time it takes to ride up an elevator. A good elevator pitch is less than 60 seconds long.

2   Use the words in 1 to talk about an idea for a new business.

For example: *Millions of people are learning English. The **potential market** for the new electronic dictionary is enormous.*

3   Read this extract from the web page of a venture capitalist.

Company life

1 Selling your company

This unit is about promoting a company (or a business idea) to potential investors. Students look at some useful vocabulary from a business presentation and then read an extract from the web page of a venture capitalist. Then they listen to a pitch by a businessman who is keen to find investors for his business and read a report on this company, written by a business analyst. They comment on what they think about the business idea and then examine the tenses used in the report.

Work on collocations which are useful when talking about companies and investment follows and students use these to complete sentences. An amusing web page from an imaginary dog food company with an innovative approach to sales provides a fun reading text and practice in making sentences with some of the vocabulary from the unit.

In the final section, students think of their own dot.com start-up company. They work in pairs to make investment pitches and then write descriptions of each other's companies.

The grammatical focus is on the Present Simple and Present Continuous, and the lexical focus is on business and the Internet.

In this first section, students begin by matching definitions to some useful words which they will encounter in this unit. They also look at the website of a venture capitalist which invites people to make an 'elevator pitch' – a quick presentation of their company that can be understood in the time it takes to ride up an elevator (or *lift* in British English).

Warm-up

Particularly if this is a new class and students are unknown to you and to each other, you might like to begin by finding out what type of company each student works for. If they all work for the same company, ask them to say what it is that they do for the company. If they are not yet employed, ask what kind of business they hope to get into.

1 Students do the matching individually at first and then compare their answers in pairs.

2 Give students plenty of time to formulate sentences using the words in exercise 1.

3 Focus students' attention on the definition for *elevator pitch* before they read the text on the web page. Ask them to brainstorm the kinds of information that they think should be included in an elevator pitch. Remind them that they only have 60 seconds for the pitch!

If you have time, you might like to ask students if they know of any other meanings of the word *pitch* (to throw something, such as a ball; the ground where sports such as football, rugby, cricket and hockey are played). The term may have come from the fact that the person doing the pitching is in a way throwing their presentation to someone else in the hope that they will catch it or pick it up and act on it.

Give students time to read the web page and ask them whether the questions on it will produce the kind of information they suggested earlier should be included in an elevator pitch.

4 It may not be immediately obvious from the pictures what Nick Jenkins' business is, so encourage students to come up with a range of ideas. Write them on the board, but do not confirm or deny anything at this stage.

5 📼 **1.1** Play the recording for the first time just to establish the answer to the question in exercise 4. (He runs an on-line greeting card company.) Then play it again for students to complete the answers to the questions.

Ask students if they have ever used a company like Nick's or if they have ever received an on-line card. Don't ask them what they think of his business idea yet because this will be discussed in exercise 7.

6 Students attempt to complete the text before they listen to the recording. Allow them to compare and discuss their answers in pairs or small groups before you play the recording for them to check.

📼 **1.1**

Hello, my name is Nick Jenkins, and the name of my company is Moonpig. We operate a website that allows users to select and personalise greetings cards, which we print and post within 24 hours. Customers can choose from more than 650 cards and can customise the captions on the cover as well as the greeting.
I have an MBA and previous experience setting up sugar and grain trading operations in the former Soviet Union. I employ 12 people at Moonpig.

Our competitive advantage is that this is one of the few times that you can buy something from the Internet that's actually better than a similar product that you can buy in a shop. We have a £750,000 digital printing system that allows us to print and laminate cards. Our running costs are low and we are making a profit of £1.20 on each card sold, which is a margin of 60%.
Our potential market is enormous. 92% of the British population buy an average of 12 cards each a year. The greetings card business is worth more than £1 billion a year in the UK and £10 billion worldwide.

We're very successful. At the moment we have 15,000 registered users. Our turnover is increasing by 50% a month and we are expecting to be profitable within six months. Our target is to get 300,000 customers in the UK and 750,000 worldwide in five years. We are looking for between two million and three million pounds of investment to finance marketing in the UK and the US. Our direct mail campaigns are proving particularly successful, and I am talking to venture capitalists in the US about setting up a website there.

4 Nick Jenkins phoned The Investment Hour with his business idea. Look at the three pictures on this page. What do you think his business is?

5 🔊 **1.1** Listen to Nick Jenkins' elevator pitch. What are his answers to the questions on the web page in 3?

a We operate a website that allows users to select and personalise greetings cards, which we print and post within 24 hours.

b I have an MBA and previous experience setting up sugar and grain trading operations in the former Soviet Union.

c Our product is something you can buy from the Internet that is actually better than a similar product you can buy from a shop.

d The 92% of the British population who buy around 12 cards a year plus the worldwide greetings card market, worth £10 billion.

e We have 15,000 registered users and our turnover is increasing by 50% a month. We expect to be profitable within 6 months.

f Between two and three million pounds.

6 After listening to Nick Jenkins' elevator pitch, Jon Day, the investment analyst, wrote the following report. Complete it using the figures in the box. Then listen again and check your answers.

750,000	£1 billion	24	60%	92%	650	300,000
£2 million and £3 million	50%	£1.20	£750,000	12	15,000

Moonpig

Moonpig operates a website that allows users to personalise, print and send greetings cards within (a) __24__ hours. Users can choose from more than (b) __650__ cards and can customise the captions on the cover as well as the greeting.

5   The founder, Nick Jenkins, has an MBA and previous experience setting up businesses in the former Soviet Union. He employs (c) __12__ people at Moonpig.

He says their competitive advantage is that this is one of the few times that you can buy something from the Internet that's actually better than a similar product
10   that you can buy in a shop. They have a (d) __£750,000__ digital printing system. Their running costs are low and they make a profit of (e) __£1.20__ on each card sold, a margin of (f) __60%__.

Their potential market is enormous. (g) __92%__ of the British population buy an average of 12 cards each a year. The greetings card
15   business is worth more than (h) __£1 billion__ a year in the UK alone and £10 billion worldwide.

At the moment they have (i) __15,000__ users and more and more people are registering each month. Turnover is increasing by (j) __50%__ a month and they are expecting to be profitable
20   within six months. Their target is to get (k) __300,000__ customers in the UK and (l) __750,000__ worldwide in five years.

They are looking for between (m) __£2 million and £3 million__ of investment to finance marketing in the UK and the US. Their direct mail campaigns are proving very successful, and they are talking to venture capitalists in the US
25   about setting up a website there.

Adapted from *Customised Greetings Cards Win Stamp of Approval* from The Times, London 16.12.00

7 What do you think of Nick Jenkins' business idea? Look at page 124 to see what Jon Day, the investment analyst, thought.

Grammar link

for more on the Present Simple and Continuous see page 94

Present Simple vs Present Continuous

8 Complete the chart as in the example. Find two more examples in the report in 6 and add them to the chart.

	Present Simple	Present Continuous	Stable situation	Current situation /activity	Situation of change
92% of the British population buy an average of 12 cards each a year.	✓		✓		
Turnover is increasing by 50% a month.		✓			✓
He employs 12 people at Moonpig.	✓		✓		
They are looking for between £2 million and £3 million of investment.		✓		✓	

Talking business

Collocations

1 Combine the verbs in A with the words in B. Make as many different combinations as possible. For example: *make a profit*

> **A** make   have   hire   run   set up
>
> **B** a company   a business   a profit   staff   a website   previous experience

have a company	run a company
have a business	run a business
have a website	set up a company
have previous experience	set up a business
hire staff	set up a website

2 Use the collocations in 1 to complete the sentences below. You may need to change the form of the verb.

a Our investors are happy because we _are making a profit_.

b We _set up a website_ so that people can get information about our products online.

c They use a recruiting agency to _hire staff_.

d Giovanni Bianchi _runs a company_ which his family owns in Milan.

e He has the right qualifications for the job but _does_ he _have previous experience_?

3 Choose three collocations from 1 and make your own examples.

Word building

4 The words in brackets are from the report on page 5. They are all important business words. Use the correct form of each to complete the sentences.

7 Ask students to discuss this question in pairs or groups and get feedback from them on their own ideas before they turn to page 124 to read what Jon Day thought. Then ask them to report back to the class on whether they agreed with him or not.

Present Simple vs Present Continuous

8 Allow students to work in pairs to complete the chart.

Direct students' attention to the Grammar link on page 94 where they will find more information about the uses of the Present Simple and Present Continuous and practice exercises to help them use these tenses correctly.

Other examples from the text that students could add to the chart are as follows:

Moonpig operates a website that allows users to ...
(Present Simple; Stable situation)

The founder, Nick Jenkins, has an MBA and previous experience ...
(Present Simple; Stable situation)

He says their competitive advantage is that ...
(Present Simple; Stable situation)

They have a £750,000 digital printing system.
(Present Simple; Stable situation)

Their running costs are low and they make a profit of ...
(Present Simple; Stable situation)

Their potential market is enormous.
(Present Simple; Stable situation)

The greetings card business is worth ...
(Present Simple; Stable situation)

At the moment they have 15,000 users ...
(Present Simple; Stable situation)

... and more and more people are registering each month.
(Present Continuous; Situation of change)

... they are expecting to be profitable within six months.
(Present Continuous; Current situation/activity)

Their target is to get 300,000 customers in the UK ...
(Present Simple; Stable situation)

Their direct mail campaigns are proving very successful ...
(Present Continuous; Current situation/activity)

... and they are talking to venture capitalists in the US ...
(Present Continuous; Current situation/activity)

Talking business

In this section, students do more work on the kind of vocabulary which can be used to talk about companies and the business they engage in. They look at some common collocations, using them to complete sentences and then practise word building and using the correct form of a word in a sentence.

Collocations

1 You could do this as a team game with teams competing to find as many different combinations as possible. Have the teams read their collocations out to the class so that everyone gets a chance to hear them. Teams could challenge each other to produce a sentence if they disagree with any of the combinations suggested.

2 To make this more interactive and to check the answers, you could ask one student to read out the sentence stem and another student to provide the missing collocation.

3 Using these collocations in sentences of their own will help to give students a context for them, which may make it easier to memorise them. Have students read their sentences to the class and make sure that a new sentence is provided for each collocation.

Word building

4 Students often think that it is sufficient to know one form of a word, and they may make mistakes such as *My business is succeed*. Emphasise the importance of using words in their correct form. When students learn a new word, it is a good idea for them to write it down together with its other forms. From time to time, give them an adjective and ask them what the noun form is, or vice versa. This recycles vocabulary and is a good way of improving the accuracy of their vocabulary use.

Direct students' attention to the Lexis link on page 95 where they will find a practice exercise with more useful words connected to running a business, and a crossword using computer and Internet-related vocabulary, which will be a useful follow-up for the next section.

The company web page

In this section, students will read the web page of betterdogfood.com, a company which claims to ensure a thriving market for its product by supplying people with hungry dogs and then selling dog food to them! The web page is used to practise vocabulary related to computers and the Internet, as well as another example of a company pitch.

Warm-up

Ask students to tell the class about the most interesting websites they have ever visited. Encourage them to say whose website it was, what the aim of the website was and why they found it so interesting.

1 Give students plenty of time to read the web page and elicit their reactions to it before they scan the text to find the matching words. This site does actually exist, though of course the dogs you can download are not real! If you have access to computers, students might like to go on-line and have a look at it. It has many amusing pages which will give them excellent practice in English. You could even download a class dog or get students to work in teams to write quiz questions on the site for other teams to answer.

When checking the answers, encourage students to produce their own sentences, using the words in a meaningful context.

Lexis link

for more on the
vocabulary of business
and the Internet see
page 95

a His new business is a great ___success___. (successful)

b We have good ideas, but we need to convince our ___investors___. (investment)

c As the market grows, they are increasing ___productivity___. (product)

d It's a very ___profitable___ business. (profit)

e Every day I read the ___financial___ newspapers. (finance)

f We are looking for ___capital___ to start up a new business. (capitalist)

The company web page

1 You are surfing the Internet and you see the web page below. Find words which mean the same as the following:

a move information to a computer from the Internet (para 1) ___download___

b take to a specific place (para 1) ___deliver___

c growth (para 2) ___expansion___

d goods or money that a company owns (para 3) ___stock___

e without competition (para 3) ___unrivalled___

f original (para 4) ___innovative___

g running after (para 6) ___chasing___

h maintain (para 7) ___sustain___

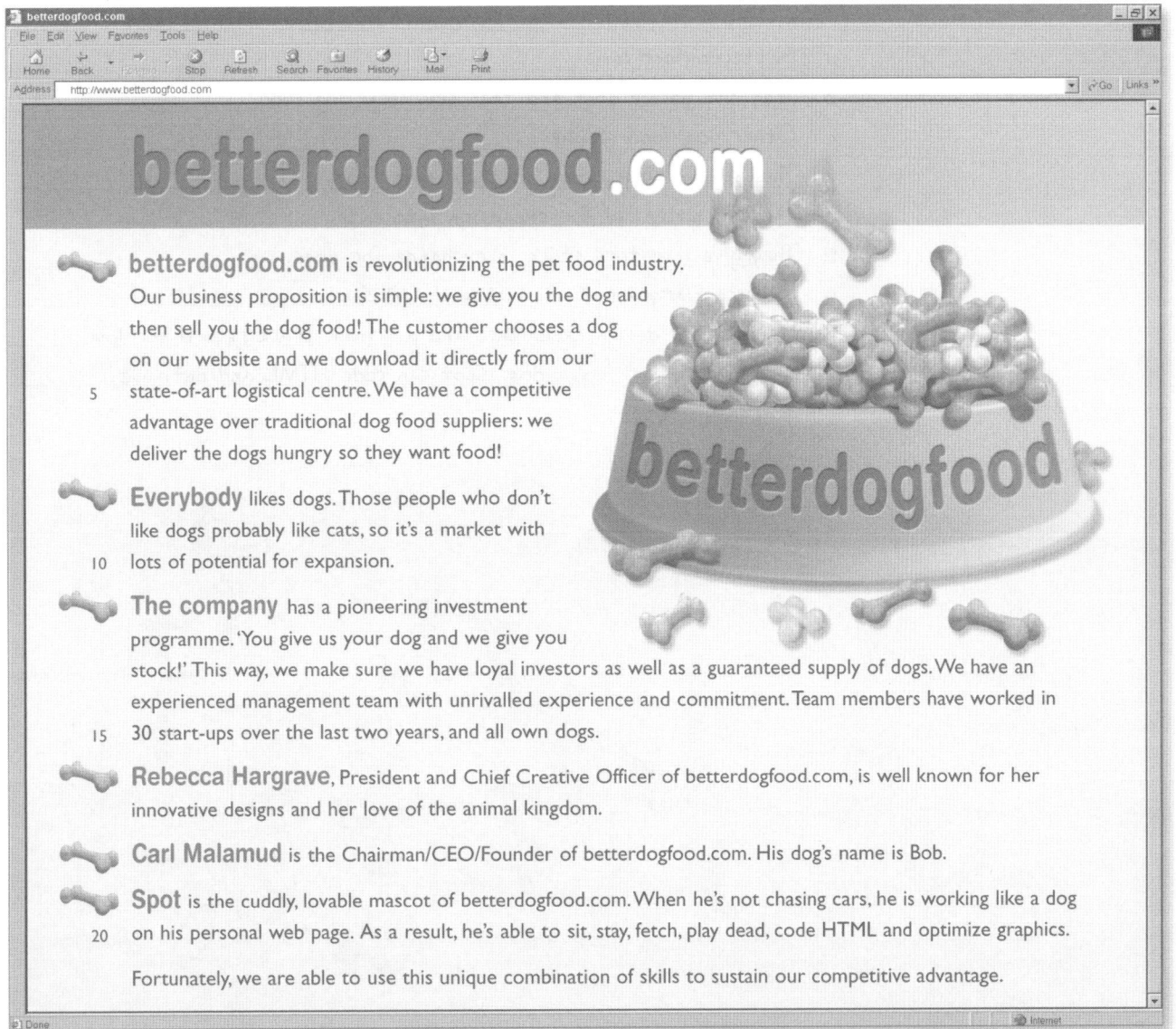

2 Reorganise the words to form questions.

a company's the what's name

<u>What's the company's name?</u>

b exactly they do what do

<u>What exactly do they do? / What do they do exactly?</u>

c of competition what is kind there

<u>What kind of competition is there?</u>

d their advantage what competitive is

<u>What is their competitive advantage?</u>

e their is market what potential

<u>What is their potential market?</u>

f for do they investment how the business get

<u>How do they get investment for the business?</u>

g behind people company the who are the

<u>Who are the people behind the company?</u>

h experience previous they what do have

<u>What previous experience do they have?</u>

3 Answer the questions in 2 with information about betterdogfood.com.

a <u>Betterdogfood.com</u>

b <u>They give people dogs and then sell them dog food.</u>

c <u>Other dog food suppliers.</u>

d <u>They supply hungry dogs so they want food.</u>

e <u>There is potential for expansion into cats.</u>

f <u>They give investors stock in exchange for dogs.</u>

g <u>Rebecca Hargrave, Carl Malamud and Spot.</u>

h <u>Rebecca has design experience and a proven track record for love of animals. Carl has a dog. Spot can code HTML and optimise graphics.</u>

"Whatever you're selling, they're buying."

2,3 You could check the answers to these two exercises by asking one student to form a question and nominate another student to answer it. Alternatively, check that all the questions have been formed first and then ask students to read the web page on page 7 again and write the answers.

Your dot.com start-up

In this section, students invent their own company and write and present a pitch for it. They then write a description of a company whose pitch they have listened to.

Warm-up

Brainstorm some ideas for companies which could be used in this section. Students may want to devise humorous ideas in the style of the betterdogfood site, or they may want to do something more serious.

Fluency

1 Students work in pairs to devise their own dot.com start-up. Give them time to complete all the sections of the first column of the table and to discuss how best to pitch their idea. Then they change partners, make their pitch and listen to their new partner's pitch, making notes about this in the second column of the table.

   If you have time, you could get students to listen to a variety of pitches around the class, nominate the best ones they heard and have a class vote on which is the most interesting.

2 Students write up their new partner's company using the framework provided. Encourage them to refer back to the betterdogfood.com web page for help if necessary.

   You could display the finished descriptions on the wall to allow everyone in the class to read them. As there should be two descriptions of each company, you could put them side by side so that students can compare the different treatments.

If you're short of time

Have students complete exercise 6 on page 5 for homework and then play the recording again at the beginning of the next class for them to check their answers.

The preparation for *Your dot.com start-up* exercise 1 could be done at home and the pitches made in the next lesson. Exercise 2 could be set for homework.

Set the *Grammar and Lexis links* exercises for homework and check the answers at the beginning of the next class.

Your dot.com start-up

Fluency   **1**   Work with a partner. Discuss your ideas for your own dot.com. It can be either serious or humorous. Complete the 'Your dot.com start-up' column in the table below. Then change partner and pitch your idea to your new partner. Listen to your new partner's pitch and take notes.

	Your dot.com start-up	Your new partner's dot.com start-up
Name of company		
Product or service		
Potential market		
How you make money		
Management team		
Competition		
Competitive advantage		
Investment needed		

2   Use the framework below to write a web page describing your new partner's company.

_____ (*name of company*)

is a _____ (*type of company*)

The main activity of the company is _____

Their potential market is _____

_____

It makes money by _____

The management team _____

_____

The competition _____

_____

Their competitive advantage is _____

_____

_____

They are looking for investment to _____

_____

_____

 Company life

2 Women in business

Women now represent 50% of university graduates. To get the best brains, it's obvious to me that we need more women. *Eivind Reiten, CEO of Norske Hydro*

Fortune 500 = the 500 biggest companies in the USA

Board of Directors = the group of individuals responsible for the running of the entire company

CEO = Chief Executive Officer, the highest level director in the company

1 Complete the statistics using the numbers in the box. Compare your answers with a partner.

> 4.1%   12.5%   46.5%   two   11.7%

a __46.5%__ of all workers in the USA are women.

b __12.5%__ of senior managers in the Fortune 500 are women.

c Women represent __4.1%__ of top earners.

d Women comprise __11.7%__ of individuals serving on Boards of Directors.

e However, there are only __two__ women CEOs in the Fortune 500.

Discussion **2** Look at page 124 to check the statistics in 1. Then discuss the questions.

a Is the situation similar in your country?

b Do you think this situation will change in the future?

3 Careers&women.com is a website aimed at women who work in – or would like to work in – technology-related jobs. Read the extract from their site and answer the questions on page 11.

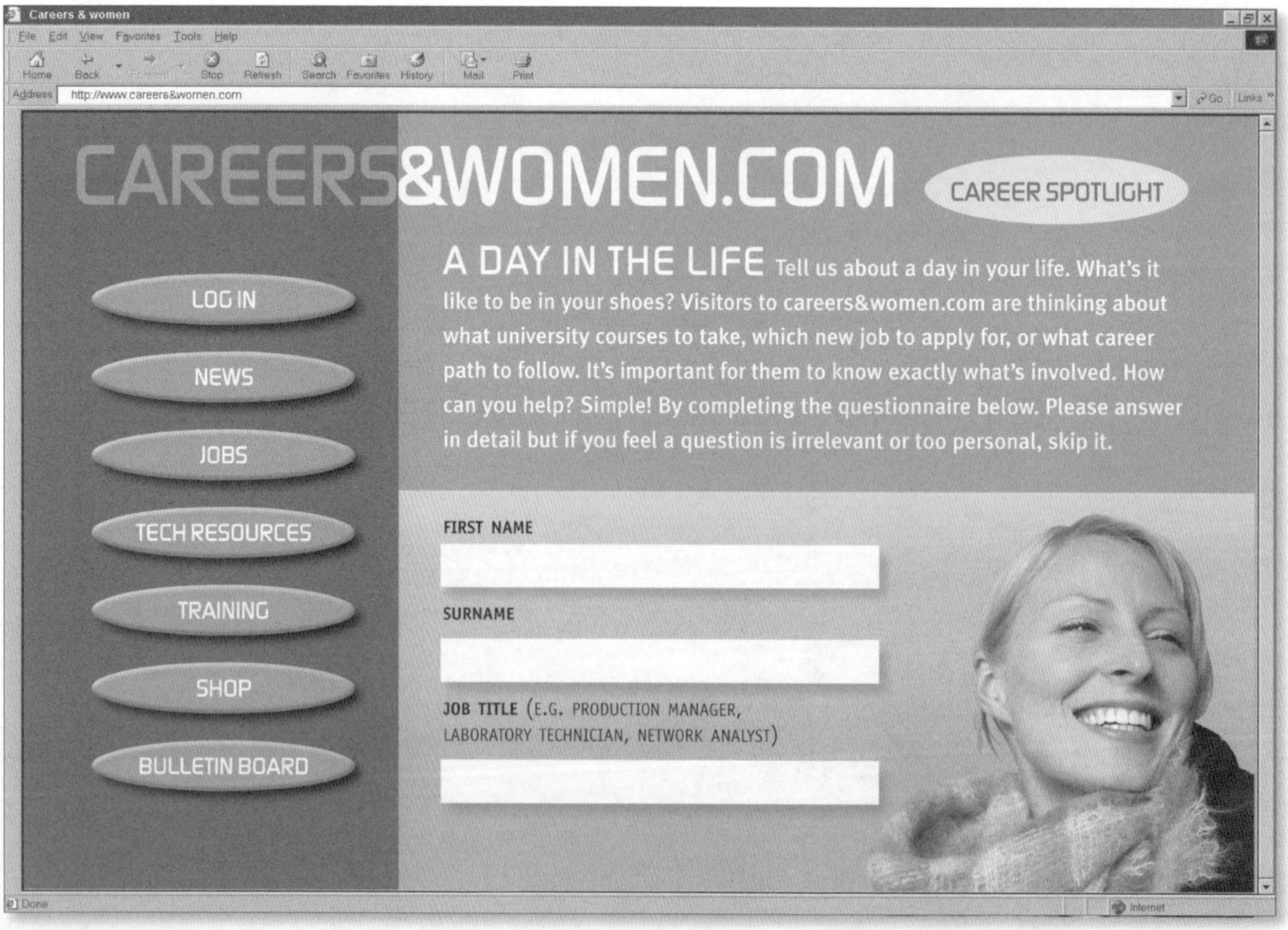

Careers & women

File Edit View Favorites Tools Help

Home Back Forward Stop Refresh Search Favorites History Mail Print

Address http://www.careers&women.com   Go Links

CAREERS&WOMEN.COM   CAREER SPOTLIGHT

- LOG IN
- NEWS
- JOBS
- TECH RESOURCES
- TRAINING
- SHOP
- BULLETIN BOARD

A DAY IN THE LIFE Tell us about a day in your life. What's it like to be in your shoes? Visitors to careers&women.com are thinking about what university courses to take, which new job to apply for, or what career path to follow. It's important for them to know exactly what's involved. How can you help? Simple! By completing the questionnaire below. Please answer in detail but if you feel a question is irrelevant or too personal, skip it.

FIRST NAME

SURNAME

JOB TITLE (E.G. PRODUCTION MANAGER, LABORATORY TECHNICIAN, NETWORK ANALYST)

Done   Internet

Company Life

2 Women in business

This unit is mainly about opportunities for women in business. It begins by looking at a range of statistics about women in the workplace and presents a website aimed at attracting women to technology-related jobs. It does this by publishing information supplied by women who already work in the industry about their jobs.

Recognising that one of the things that keeps women back is the need to combine a career with family life, the unit then goes on to examine how people can balance work and leisure and ensure that they reduce the amount of stress in their lives.

The grammatical focus is on expressing frequency, and the lexical focus is on work and routines.

In this first section, students begin by completing some statistics about women in business. They check their answers and then discuss the situation in their own country. They then practise asking and answering questions about jobs, looking at a website which offers information about careers in technology and listening to people talk about it.

Warm-up

Focus students' attention on the quotation from Eivind Reiten at the top of the page and ask for reactions. Ask them whether they think that we have now moved on from the old arguments about a woman's place being in the home to a recognition, similar to this CEO's, that if a company wants the best people, it had better start recruiting more women to top jobs.

1   Remind students that the tint boxes in the margin are there to help them with difficult vocabulary.

Discussion

2   Make sure that students have completed all the gaps in exercise 1 and compared their answers with a partner before they turn to page 124 to check their answers.

Before they answer the two questions, elicit their reactions to the statistics. Was there anything there that surprised them?

3   If you have any women in your class, find out how many of them either work in technology-related jobs or would like to. Ask them if the careers advice they received when they were at school tended to steer them towards industries traditionally favoured by women or whether they were encouraged to look at a wide spectrum of opportunities.

Focus students' attention on the web page and elicit what image they think the website is trying to convey. (The bright colours and happy smiling face of the attractive young woman pictured are probably meant to give the impression that jobs in the technology industry are exciting, and enjoyable and will be attractive to young women.)

When they have answered the questions on page 11, ask students to say what they think of this website. Is it a good idea? Would they be happy to supply details of their own jobs to encourage other people to enter their field? Are there any questions about their job that they would not want to answer? Do they think the website should be extended to cover all jobs, and not just technology-related ones? Would such a website be useful for men as well as women?

4 You could allow students to work in pairs and do this as a race with the first pair to match all the answers to the questions as the winner. To check the answers, ask one student in the winning pair to ask the questions, and the other to give the woman's answers.

For homework, you might like to ask students to answer the questions about themselves.

a Who is the questionnaire for? __Women who already work in technology-related jobs.__

b Why does Careers&women.com want this information? __To pass it on to women who are thinking about working in technology-related jobs.__

c Do women who respond have to answer all the questions? __No.__

4 Read the replies of one woman who answered the questions. Match the questions below to her answers.

- How much holiday do you get?
- What sort of company do you work for?
- What do you enjoy most about your work?
- What does your job involve?
- What do you do?
- Have you got any advice for women that are interested in going into your field?
- How much travel does your job involve?
- How many hours a week do you work?
- Do you work late or at the weekend?
- What is the female to male ratio in your position/field?

a __What do you do?__

In my company they call me a Regional Marketing Manager, that's my job title.

b __What sort of company do you work for?__

We're a multinational with offices in 15 different countries around the world.

c __What does your job involve?__

I'm in charge of sales support for my country, and I'm also involved in developing new marketing strategies.

d __How many hours a week do you work?__

35 hours. I'm based in France and officially that's the maximum number of hours you can work.

e __Do you work late or at the weekend?__

No, I never work later than six. We have a couple of hours off for lunch as well. I usually have a sandwich at my desk, though, and then I like to go for a walk to clear my head.

f __How much travel does your job involve?__

Quite a lot. It's mainly within France and occasionally other European countries. Once or twice a year I go back to the States for a meeting at our central office.

g __How much holiday do you get?__

In France we get five weeks a year. It's quite generous compared to the USA.

h __What is the female to male ratio in your position/field?__

I'd say that marketing departments usually have more women than men. At least, that's usually the case in the USA and France, which are the countries I've worked in.

i __What do you enjoy most about your work?__

I love my independence. It's hard work but usually very interesting.

j __Have you got any advice for women that are interested in going into your field?__

Get some work experience while you're a student, even if you have to do it for free. Companies are more interested in experience than qualifications. Obviously, you need a degree if you want to be something like an engineer, but it's easier to find a job if you've got some practical experience.

5  **2.1** Two friends are looking at the Careers&women.com website. They are discussing how a woman called Joanne answered the questionnaire. Listen and make notes about how she answered the questions in 4.

6 Complete the conversation between the two friends in 5 with suitable questions. Then listen again and compare your questions with what the speaker says.

A Oh, look, here's something in our field.

B _What's the position?_

A Design Team Co-ordinator.

B Yes, but _what kind of company is it?_

A They produce computer games software.

B So, _what does the job involve, then?_

A Well, her name's Joanne, and she says that she's responsible for anything design-related in the company. And that it's very rewarding.

B What does she most enjoy about the work?

A She has a huge amount of responsibility, opportunities to learn, and it never gets boring because the job is always changing.

B _How many hours a week does she work?_

A Up to sixty hours a week.

B Sixty hours a week!

A Yes, eleven hours on weekdays and a half-day over the weekend.

B That's sounds an awful lot.

A Yes, but hang on. That's only during development stages. It's usually forty to forty-five hours.

B _Does she have to work evenings?_

A It doesn't say. She doesn't start that early, though. Most days she gets in at around nine thirty, it says.

B _What's the ratio of women to men in this job?_

A Let's see. Three out of the fourteen in her company are women, which she says is unusually balanced for the computer games industry.

B Balanced! Why?

A Because on the whole these companies only employ women as decoration for their stands at conferences.

B Well, that doesn't sound very positive. _How much travel does she get?_

A None at all. She never travels because she can do everything from the office. Travelling is for holidays.

B And _how much holiday do they give her?_

A Five weeks a year. Sounds quite generous.

B Yes, it's more than most companies offer.

A Hmm. It's just the kind of job I'm looking for. I wonder how she got into it.

B Be assertive without being rude and stick up for yourself when you're right. That's her advice.

Fluency　**7** Work with a partner. Speaker A look at the chart on page 126. Speaker B look at the chart on page 130. Ask questions as in 6 to complete the charts.

8 Ask your partner similar questions and write down the answers.

5 ▣ **2.1** Ask students to keep their books open at page 11 as they listen so that they can see the questions but not read the gapped tapescript which is given in exercise 6 on page 12. They should make notes of what the speakers say about how Joanne answered the questions. Ask them to compare their notes in pairs or small groups.

6 Students could work in pairs to complete the questions. Then play the recording again for them to check their questions. Emphasise that their questions are correct if they make sense in the context, even if they are not exactly the same as those on the recording.

As this is a real website, if you have access to computers, you might like to get your students to go on-line and have a look at it. They could devise a quiz for each other on any of the responses to the questionnaire they find.

Fluency

7 This is an information-gap activity in which students have to ask each other questions about two women to complete forms. Ensure that they don't look at each other's pages, and encourage them to use similar questions to those in exercise 6.

8 Students interview each other about their own jobs. If you set the homework suggested in exercise 4, they will already have thought about their answers to the kind of questions they are likely to be asked, so they should be reasonably fluent. Don't, however, allow them to read out any written answers that they have produced.

▣ **2.1**

A: Oh, look, here's something in our field.
B: **What's the position?**
A: Design Team Co-ordinator.
B: Yes, but **what kind of company is it?**
A: They produce computer games software.
B: So, **what does the job involve, then?**
A: Well, her name's Joanne, and she says that she's responsible for anything design-related in the company. And that it's very rewarding.
B: **What does she most enjoy about the work?**
A: She has a huge amount of responsibility, opportunities to learn, and it never gets boring because the job is always changing.
B: **How many hours a week does she work?**

A: Up to sixty hours a week.
B: Sixty hours a week!
A: Yes, eleven hours on weekdays and a half-day over the weekend.
B: That's sounds an awful lot.
A: Yes, but hang on. That's only during development stages. It's usually forty to forty-five hours.
B: **Does she have to work evenings?**
A: It doesn't say. She doesn't start that early, though. Most days she gets in at around nine thirty, it says.
B: **What's the ratio of women to men in this job?**
A: Let's see. Three out of the fourteen in her company are women, which she says is unusually balanced for the computer games industry.

B: Balanced! Why?
A: Because on the whole these companies only employ women as decoration for their stands at conferences.
B: Well, that doesn't sound very positive. **How much travel does she get?**
A: None at all. She never travels because she can do everything from the office. Travelling is for holidays.
B: And **how much holiday do they give her?**
A: Five weeks a year. Sounds quite generous.
B: Yes, it's more than most companies offer.
A: Hmm. It's just the kind of job I'm looking for. I wonder how she got into it.
B: Be assertive without being rude and stick up for yourself when you're right. That's her advice.

How often do you ...?

In this section, the focus changes slightly away from a concentration on women in the workplace to the responsibilities and stresses felt by all workers. Students use frequency expressions to talk about their own working lives.

Warm-up

Put the frequency expressions in the box in exercise 1 in two columns on the board. In the first column put *often, not often, always, hardly ever, sometimes, usually* and *never*. In the second column put *every day, twice a year, every week* and *once a month*. Ask students to put the two columns in order from the most frequent to the least frequent.

Expressing frequency

1   When students have completed the sentences, ask them to compare them with a partner or in small groups. Ask a variety of students to read out their sentences to check that they are putting the frequency expressions in the right place in the sentence.

Direct students' attention to the Grammar link on page 96 where they will find more information about the position of frequency expressions and a practice exercise to help students put them in the right place.

2   Students will all put different things in the action column, so there should be a variety of questions being asked around the class. In a feedback session, find out what questions were asked and what some of the replies were. Ask students if they are surprised by anything they have found out about their colleagues or classmates.

Taking things easy

In this section, the focus is on taking exercise – and its opposite, relaxing. Students complete a questionnaire about taking exercise and health. They then read an article in which a scientist has come to an unusual conclusion about the benefits of not taking any exercise.

Warm-up

Find out how many of the class belong to a gym. Ask them why they go, how often they go and what they do when they are there. Find out what other forms of exercise members of the class take.

1   Students work in pairs to complete the questionnaire, which is about attitudes and beliefs about exercise. Encourage them to compare their answers with other pairs to see if there is any consensus.

How often do you ...?

Expressing
frequency

1 Add a frequency expression to each sentence so that it is true for you.

| always | usually | sometimes | often | every day | every week |
| twice a year | once a month | not often | hardly ever | never |

Grammar link

for more on expressing
frequency see page 96

a I go to work by car.
b I get home late.
c I work at the weekend.
d I have a holiday.
e I feel bored with my job.

f My boss gives me a hard time.
g My computer crashes.
h I find time to relax and enjoy myself.
i I have arguments with people at work.
j I read the financial papers.

2 Complete the 'Action' and 'You' columns in the chart below. Then ask questions to complete the 'Your partner' column.

Action	You	Your partner
eat out	once a week	

How often do you ...?
Do you ... much?
Do you ever ...?

Taking things easy

1 Do you take regular exercise? Do you think it's important? Work with a partner and complete the questionnaire below.

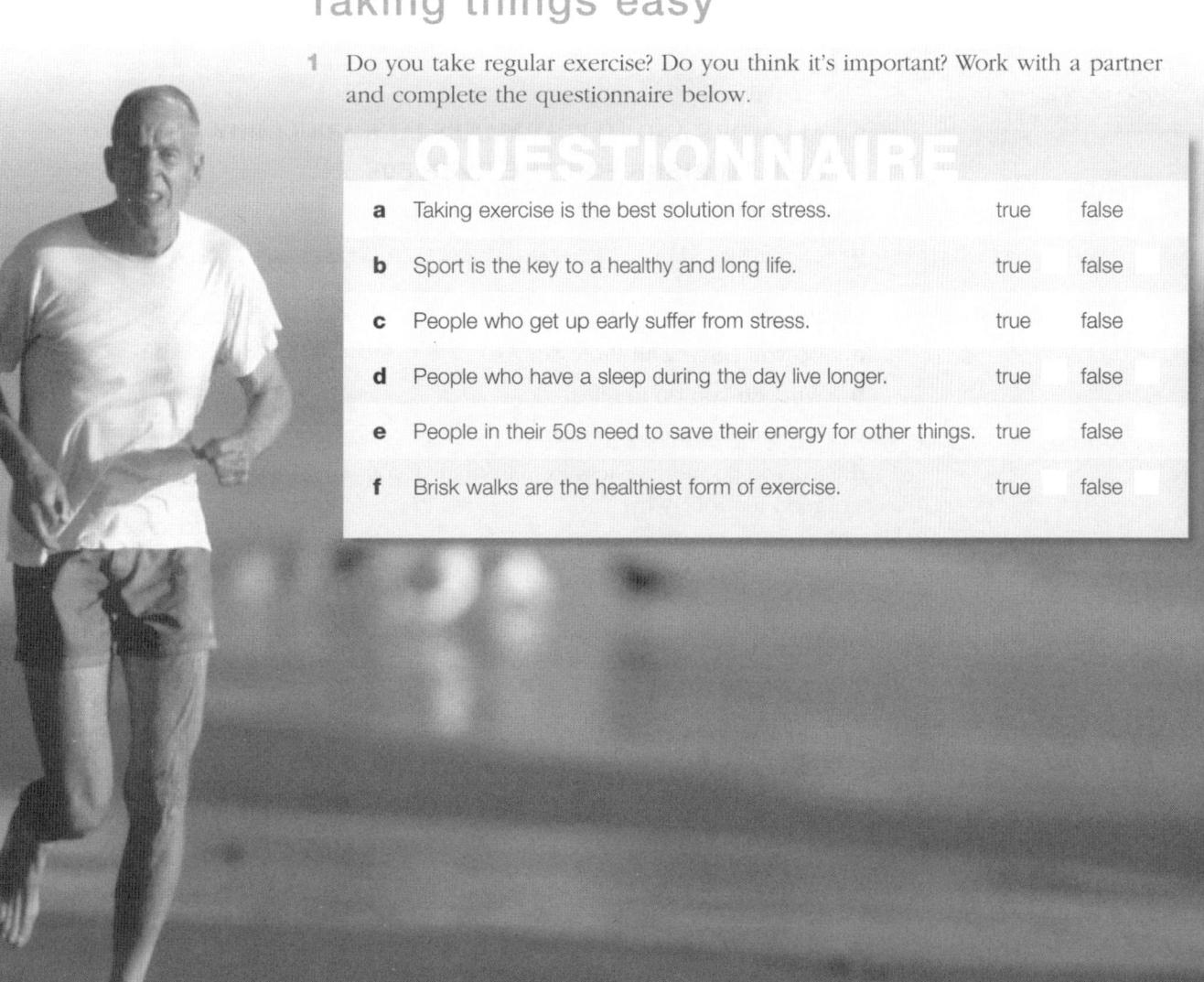

QUESTIONNAIRE

a	Taking exercise is the best solution for stress.	true	false
b	Sport is the key to a healthy and long life.	true	false
c	People who get up early suffer from stress.	true	false
d	People who have a sleep during the day live longer.	true	false
e	People in their 50s need to save their energy for other things.	true	false
f	Brisk walks are the healthiest form of exercise.	true	false

2 Now read the article to see if you are correct.

They say that a healthy body is a healthy mind, but according to a German expert it is lazy people who lead longer and healthier lives. Professor Peter Axt recommends avoiding strenuous activity like aerobics or working out in a gym. 'People who prefer <u>to laze</u> in a hammock instead of running a marathon or who
5   <u>take a midday nap</u> instead of playing squash have a better chance of living into old age,' says this scientist. They are also less likely to suffer from professional stress.

He cowrote *On the Joy of Laziness* with his daughter, who is also a doctor. In the book he advises people to 'waste half your time. Just enjoy lazing
10   around.' Those who get up early in the morning usually feel stressed for the rest of the day, so his advice is <u>to take it easy</u>.

However, Professor Axt stresses that laziness in only one of the keys to a longer life. In fact, the subtitle of his book is *How best to use your energies*. He argues that if you are too fat, you need more energy to maintain body functions,
15   and is in favour of moderate exercise like 'meditative' jogging or brisk walks to 'relax body and spirit at the same time'.

On the other hand, any exertion is not recommended, especially for middle-aged people who should be particularly careful about doing too much sport. Professor Axt believes we have only a limited amount of energy, and people who
20   use up their supply more quickly live shorter lives. 'Research shows that people who run long distances into their 50s are using up energy they need for other purposes.'

Lexis link

for more on the vocabulary of work and routines see page 97

3 Underline three expressions which mean 'to relax' or 'to rest'.

4 Choose the best title for the article.

   a   **ALL WORK AND NO PLAY MAKES JACK A DULL BOY**

   b   **HEALTH RISKS FOR THE OVER 50s**

   c   SIESTA OR MARATHON?

   d   _____ (*your own idea*)

Discussion   **5** Discuss the following questions with other people in the class.

   a   Do you agree with Professor Axt?

   b   What do you do to relax?

   c   Do you find it easy to relax?

   d   Do you do more or less exercise than **1** you would like to? **2** you think is good for you? Why?

2   The article presents the rather unconventional conclusions reached by a German scientist on the benefits of being lazy rather than energetic. Give students plenty of time to read the text and ask one of them to give a brief summary of the ideas in it. Elicit their reactions to the text and answer any questions they may have on vocabulary.

3   Students read the text again more carefully to find and underline the three expressions.

Direct students' attention to the Lexis link on page 97 where they will find more on the vocabulary of work and routines.

4   Give students time to devise their own titles, then ask for suggestions and write them on the board. Ask students to choose the title that they think fits the article best, either one of those given in the Student's Book or one of their own suggestions. Ask them to justify their choices.

Discussion

5   Students should discuss the questions in groups and be prepared to give feedback on their discussions to the rest of the class. You could appoint a secretary in each group to take notes and report back to the class at the end on what was said.

If you're short of time

Omit exercises 7 and 8 on page 12 and have students answer the questions in exercise 4 on page 11 for homework.

Students could read the text on page 14 at home and come to class prepared to discuss it.

Set the *Grammar and Lexis links* exercises for homework and check the answers at the beginning of the next class.

Connecting 3 Telephone talk

This unit is about telephones in business. It begins with some practice in saying numbers and presents an interesting text on how much money companies lose because their staff are bad at handling calls.

Examples of telephone skills and appropriate language are given which are followed by a section on customer frustration and what makes customers most angry when they telephone a company.

A section on using indirect questions to sound more polite follows and more useful telephone expressions are given and practised.

In the final section, students listen to a telephone conversation and complete a form before roleplaying their own telephone conversations.

The grammatical focus is on indirect questions, and the lexical focus is on the telephone.

In this first section, the focus is on the pronunciation of numbers. Students practise saying various types of numbers and dictate them to each other. They then read a text about the cost to companies of bad telephone handling and identify the significance of various numbers within the text. They then discuss policies on phone use within their own company and look at some useful language to use on the phone and ways of describing different telephone skills.

Warm-up

Put a few numbers that are of significance in your life on the board, e.g. the number of children you have, the number of years you have been teaching, your telephone number, the numbers in your car registration, etc., but don't say what they represent. Ask students to read them out and guess what they are. They can then work in pairs to write down their own significant numbers and ask and answer about what they represent.

Numbers

1   **▭ 3.1** Go round the class asking students to read out the numbers in the box. Then play the recording for students to check.

Play the recording again and encourage students to read out the numbers at the same time as the speaker, copying the pronunciation and intonation. If your students have difficulty with numbers, you might like to turn to the Lexis link on page 98 and do the practice exercise on writing out the full form of numbers and figures before you move on to the next exercise.

2   To make this even more interactive, divide the class into two teams and have them take turns to call out different calculations. Allow the opposing team five seconds to produce the answer (longer if the teams come up with some complicated sums).

3   Encourage students to compare their answers in pairs or small groups before they look at the text to check. Ask students if any of the information in the text surprised them and whether they think their own company has a similar problem with bad telephone handling. Encourage anyone who has had the experience of calling a company and having their call badly handled to tell the class what happened and how they felt.

▭ 3.1

1 Twenty-five per cent.
2 Six hundred and thirty-two thousand, two hundred and thirty-three.
3 Two million dollars.
4 Four point three million pounds.
5 Six euros twenty-five.
6 Five point six two three four.
7 Three thousand and twenty-two pounds.
8 Six million, five hundred and seventy-six thousand, three hundred and fifty-eight.
9 Two plus two equals four.
10 Eight minus two equals six.
11 Five times three equals fifteen.
12 Twelve divided by three equals four.

3 Telephone talk

No, I don't know his telephone number. But it was up in the high numbers.
John Maynard Keynes, British economist

Numbers

1 How do you say the following in English?

25%	632,233	$2,000,000	£4.3 m	€6.25	5.6234
£3,022	6,576,358	2 + 2 = 4	8 − 2 = 6	5 x 3 = 15	12 ÷ 3 = 4

3.1 Now listen and check your answers.

2 Write down eight different figures or calculations. Dictate them to your partner.

3 You are going to read an article about using the telephone in business. Before you read, guess the answers to the following questions. Then read the article to see if you are correct.

a In a survey, companies failed to answer ___20%___ of calls within ten rings.
  1 10% **2** 20% **3** 50%

b ___90%___ of all sales enquiries begin on the telephone.
  1 50% **2** 70% **3** 90%

c A telephonist could answer ___300,000___ calls in a year.
  1 30,000 **2** 300,000 **3** 3,000,000

RINGING IN THE

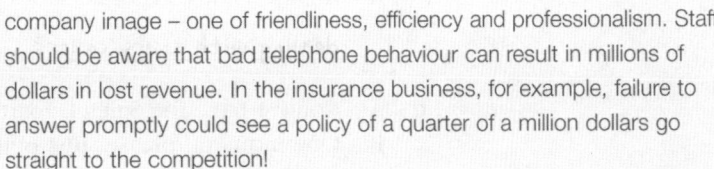

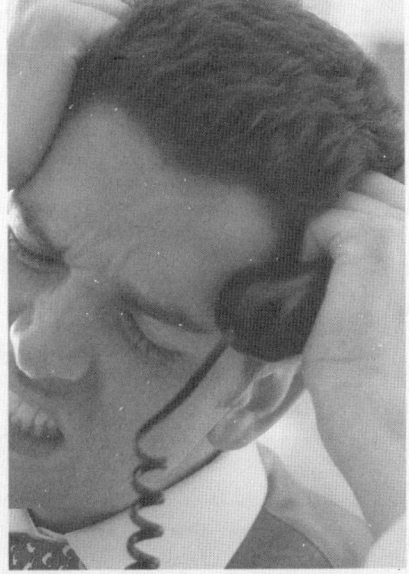

COMPANIES lose millions of dollars of business through bad telephone handling. A survey found that company switchboards failed to answer one out of five calls within ten rings, or reply to 10% of calls within 20 rings. Ninety percent of all sales enquiries begin on the telephone, so this is the opportunity to project a healthy company image – one of friendliness, efficiency and professionalism. Staff should be aware that bad telephone behaviour can result in millions of
10 dollars in lost revenue. In the insurance business, for example, failure to answer promptly could see a policy of a quarter of a million dollars go straight to the competition!

A single telephone receptionist can answer as many as 300,000 calls a year. Companies should train personnel in the skills of transferring a call,
15 placing calls on hold, dealing with angry callers, answering correspondence by phone, using a caller's name, and taking messages correctly. Callers should not hear expressions like 'she's just gone out' or 'he's not with us anymore'. Surveys show that customers want a prompt response by a real person (not a machine) who can make a decision.
20 For a great many of a firm's customers, the first – and often the only – impression they carry in their minds is the one generated by the people they talk to on the phone. The quality of a firm's response to a call is one of the chief factors in creating a perception of good or bad service. And remember, more business is lost through poor service than by poor product performance.

Adapted from *Ringing up the Millions* by Brendan Walsh

4 The following figures appear in the article on page 15. Can you remember what they refer to?

    a one out of five _the number of calls companies fail to answer within ten rings_

    b millions of dollars _amount lost by companies through bad telephone handling_

    c a quarter of a million dollars _the value of an insurance policy that could be lost because a call is not answered promptly_

    d first _the impression of a company that stays in a customer's mind_

Discussion

5 Discuss the following questions with a partner.

    a Does your company have any policies on phone use? Does it provide training?

    b What functions does your phone have? Do you know how to use them all?

    c Do you prefer to use a mobile or a landline?

6 'More business is lost through bad service than by poor product performance.' Do you agree?

Telephone skills

7 Match the six telephone skills listed in paragraph 2 of _Ringing in the millions_ to the following examples of telephone language.

    a A Can I have extension 305, please?
        B I'm afraid the line is engaged. Will you hold?

        placing calls on hold

    b A Could I just check that? You need 50 units by Friday, and Mr Johansson can contact you on 943 694726.
        B Yes, that's correct.
        A Right, Mr Smith. I'll give him the message as soon as he's free.

        taking messages correctly

    c A ... and it really isn't good enough.
        B Yes, Mr Wright. I understand what you're saying and I do apologise for the error. As soon as Mr Downs is back I'll ask him to get in contact with you. I'm really sorry about this.
        A Right, thank you. I realise it's not your fault.

        dealing with angry callers

    d A Could I have the Sales Department, please?
        B One moment, please. Just putting you through now.

        transferring a call

    e A Shonagh Clark speaking.
        B Hello, I'm phoning you about your letter of 12th June.

        answering correspondence by phone

    f A This is Jorgen Bode here. Could I speak to Jean Simmons, please?
        B Oh, I'm sorry, Mr Bode, but Ms Simmons isn't in the office right now. Can I ask her to call you back? Or I can contact her on her mobile if it's urgent.

        using a caller's name

4   Encourage students to try to remember what the figures refer to without looking back at the text first, before they look back and check.

Discussion

5   If any of your students have brought their mobiles to class, you could exploit this fact by asking them to demonstrate the good features of their particular model, having them explain to the others how to send a text message, etc.

6   If your students have differing views on this question, you might like to ask them to prepare arguments on one side or the other to present to the class in a mini debate in the next lesson. Encourage them to cite personal experience to back up their arguments.

Telephone skills

7   After they have matched the mini dialogues with the correct telephone skills, students could practise them in pairs.

Customer frustration

In this section, students look at the kinds of things which make callers most frustrated when they telephone a company. Students complete items in a questionnaire and then decide how they feel about each one.

Warm-up

Focus students' attention on the three pictures on this page. Ask them to describe the expressions on the people's faces and to say how they think they feel. Ask students to work in pairs to write a speech bubble for each person. Have a class vote on the best/funniest suggestion.

1   Before they do the exercise, elicit from students what kind of things make them feel frustrated at work or in their personal lives. You could compile a class list of the most frustrating things.

When they have finished completing the questionnaire and before they move on to exercise 2, have a feedback session to determine which of the items students personally find most frustrating. Do they have any useful tactics either for dealing with their frustration or dealing with the person or company that is causing it?

2   Ask students if they agree with Brendan Walsh's conclusions on page 124 of the Student's Book.

Customer frustration

1 Complete the list of telephone frustrations using the verbs in the box. Then put ticks in the columns according to your level of frustration for each one.

> get play put get listen return take get transfer repeat call get

QUESTIONNAIRE

		NOT PLEASED	UNHAPPY	HOPPING MAD

a They __play__ irritating music when you're put on hold.

b You __get__ cut off in the middle of your call.

c People you call __take__ a long time to answer.

d They __put__ you on hold and forget about you.

e You __get__ an answer phone.

f They __transfer__ you to another person and you have to __repeat__ your enquiry.

g They don't __listen__ properly to what you are saying.

h You continually __get__ an engaged tone when you __call__ someone.

i People don't __return__ your calls.

j You __get__ through to a voicemail system.

2 Look on page 124 to see what the five most frustrating problems are according to Brendan Walsh.

Could you tell me ...?

Indirect questions

1 🔊 3.2 You use indirect questions to sound more polite. Complete the dialogue below. Then listen to see if you are correct.

A InterAir, can I help you?

B Yes, please. I'd like some information about a flight arriving from Munich.

A Yes. Do you _know what the flight number is?_

B The flight number? I'm not sure. I know it leaves Munich at 1730.

A Oh, yes, that's IA 345.

B Yes, that's it. Could _you tell me what time it_ gets in?

A Yes, the arrival time is 1910.

B 1910. Do you _know if there's_ any delay?

A No, the flight is on time.

B Right, thank you very much.

A You're welcome. Goodbye.

2 Look at the prompts on page 124 and practise the conversation with a partner.

3 Look at the chart below. Then rephrase the questions using *Do you know ...?* or *Could you tell me ...?*

Do you know ... Could you tell me ...	how long it takes? where the airport is?
	if she got my message? if you'll finish the order on time?

Grammar link

for more on indirect
questions see page 98

a What time does the flight leave?

Do you know what time the flight leaves?

b Which terminal does it leave from?

Could you tell me which terminal it leaves from?

c How far is the factory from the airport?

Do you know how far the factory is from the airport?

d Which car hire company is it?

Could you tell me which car hire company it is?

e Which models do they have available?

Do you know which models they have available?

f Do I need an international driving licence?

Could you tell me if I need an international driving licence?

g Where are we staying?

Do you know where we are staying?

h Is it a nice place?

Could you tell me if it is a nice place?

i Have they booked a meeting room?

Do you know if they have booked a meeting room?

Could you tell me ...?

One way to avoid conflict on the phone is to sound polite and friendly. This section focuses on indirect questions as a way of sounding more polite.

Warm-up

Focus students' attention on the title of this section and elicit various ways of completing the question.

Indirect questions

1   **3.2** Before students complete the dialogue, elicit from one student an example of a direct question and then ask another to turn it into an indirect question. Establish that indirect questions make people sound more polite.

2   The prompts on page 124 of the Student's Book are there to help students to construct the same conversation that they heard and read in exercise 1, but without reading it straight off the page. The more you can get students' eyes off the page and looking at each other when they practise conversations, the better they will sound and the more fluent they will become. When students write their own conversations to practise in class, it is a good idea to encourage them to write prompts only rather than the full text.

3   When you check the answers, you could have one student read out the direct question, sounding deliberately abrupt and another provide the indirect question, sounding excessively polite. This is quite fun to do and the more they exaggerate their intonation, the more likely they are to appreciate and remember the difference between the two types of question.

Direct students' attention to the Grammar link on page 98 where they will find more information about forming and using indirect questions.

3.2

A: InterAir, can I help you?
B: Yes, please. I'd like some information about a flight arriving from Munich.
A: Yes. **Do you know what the flight number is?**

B: The flight number? I'm not sure. I know it leaves Munich at 1730.
A: Oh, yes, that's IA 345.
B: Yes, that's it. **Could you tell me what time it gets in?**
A: Yes, the arrival time is 1910.

B: 1910. **Do you know if there's any delay?**
A: No, the flight is on time.
B: Right, thank you very much.
A: You're welcome. Goodbye.

4 Student B has all the information to answer the questions in the previous exercise. Make sure Student A explains the situation with the non-functioning datalink to Student B so that it is clear why all the information must be given over the phone.

Telephone phrases

In this section, students are provided with some language that they will find very useful when they make their own telephone calls in English.

To make this exercise more interactive, you could get one student to say the correct question or statement and another student to provide a suitable reply.

Direct students' attention to the Lexis link on page 98 where they will find more on telephone vocabulary. When they have completed the telephone conversations in the exercises in the Lexis link, they could practise them in pairs. Practice of telephone conversations is often best done with students sitting back to back so they can't see each other's faces and have to listen carefully to what their partner says.

Sales contacts

In this section, students practise taking down information from phone calls.

1 📼 **3.3** You could begin by focusing attention on the form and finding out if the students' companies use similar forms. What kind of information do their own forms require?

Make sure students read the form thoroughly so that they know what kind of information they are listening for. Then play the recording for students to complete the form.

Roleplay

2 Give students plenty of time to read the situations and decide what they are going to say. Remind them of all the useful telephone language they have studied in this unit and encourage them to put it into practice. Discourage them from writing out a script of what they are going to say.

This is another situation where it is a good idea to have students sitting back to back. They will then have to concentrate on their own form and what is being said to them and will be unable to glance at their partner's information for help.

If you're short of time

Ask students to read the text on page 15 and do exercise 4 at home.

The exercise in the *Telephone phrases* section could also be set for homework.

Set the *Grammar and Lexis links* exercises for homework and check the answers at the beginning of the next class.

📼 **3.3**

A: Hello, could I speak to Mr White, please?
B: Speaking. How can I help you?
A: Hello, Mr White. My name is Clarkson, from Bellstone & Smith, the elevator manufacturers.
B: Yes, I think I've heard of you.
A: I'm in charge of the customer support department. I'm phoning to ask for an estimate. It's for a service manual we're preparing.
B: Oh, yes. I don't think we've done anything for you before.
A: No, that's right. We're in the process of updating all our manuals. If the price is right, it will mean quite a lot of work.
B: I see. Well, could you give me the details, then?
A: Yes, it's for a manual of just over 100 pages.

B: 100 pages. Could you tell me what size?
A: It's in A5. We want to print 20,000. But I'd like estimates for 10,000 and 30,000 as well.
B: I see. Is it in colour?
A: No, it's in black and white. Mainly text. The cover is in colour, though. I can put it all on a CD for you. Is that all right?
B: Yes, that would be perfect. Could I just read my notes back?
A: Yes, go ahead.
B: You want quotes for print runs of 10,000, 20,000 and 30,000 of an A5 100-page manual in black and white. The cover is in colour and you'll be presenting the material on disk or CD.
A: That's right.
B: Would you like me to visit you with some samples?

A: Yes, okay.
B: Would tomorrow morning suit you?
A: No, I'm out of the office tomorrow. How about Friday? About ten o'clock?
B: Friday ... the 16th ... at ten. That's fine. I'll bring the estimates with me and we can discuss the details then.
A: Fine.
B: Oh, could you give me the address?
A: Yes, it's 14, Clapham Road, London SW14.
B: And your telephone number?
A: 0207 839 4216.
B: 0207 839 4216. Right. Oh, do you have e-mail?
A: Yes, it's clarkson.bellstone@lineone.com.
B: Can I just check that? clarkson, dot, bellstone at lineone, dot, com.
A: Okay, then, Mr White. See you on Friday.
B: Yes. Goodbye, then.
A: Goodbye.

---

4   Work with a partner. Speaker B see page 132.

Speaker A You are travelling on business in the UK. When you finish there you are going straight to the USA for a special sales conference. You expected to receive information about this trip from your office, but the datalink in your hotel doesn't work, and you don't have access to your e-mail account. Ring your office to get the necessary information. Ask the questions in 3. Make a note of all the information.

Telephone phrases

Match the following to make telephone expressions.

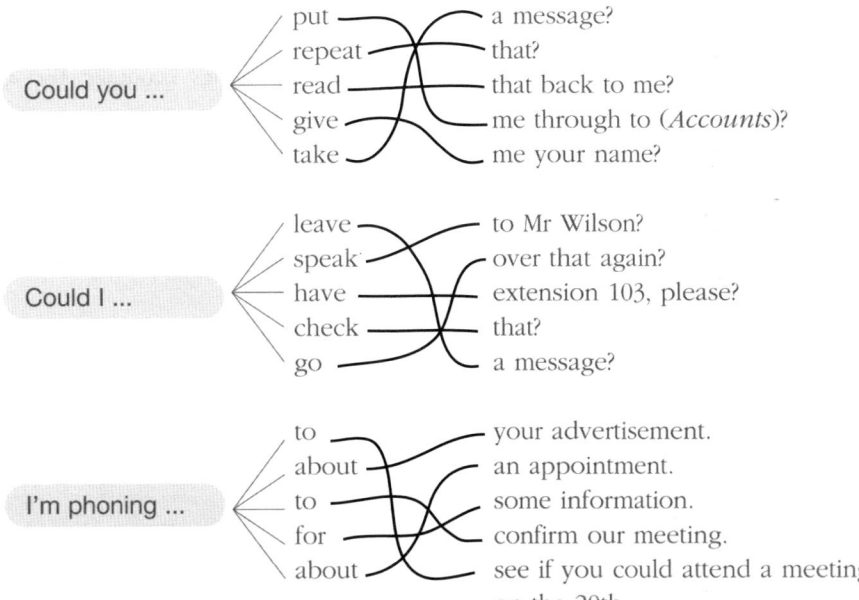

Could you ...
put — a message?
repeat — that?
read — that back to me?
give — me through to (Accounts)?
take — me your name?

Could I ...
leave — to Mr Wilson?
speak — over that again?
have — extension 103, please?
check — that?
go — a message?

I'm phoning ...
to — your advertisement.
about — an appointment.
to — some information.
for — confirm our meeting.
about — see if you could attend a meeting on the 20th.

Lexis link

for more on telephone vocabulary see page 98

Sales contacts

1   ▭ 3.3 The sales team at *ADH Graphics* uses the form below to record the details of all phone calls with potential clients. Listen to the conversation and complete the form.

Phone Contact Form ADH Graphics

Date: Wednesday 14th May
Call initiated by: Client
Call handler: B. White

Client: Bellstone + Smith

Address: (a) __14__, Clapham Rd, London SW14

Contact: Mr Clarkson

Position: (b) Head of __Customer Support__

Tel: (c) __0207 839 4216__

E-mail: clarkson.bellstone@lineone.com

Nature of business: Elevator manufacturer

Purpose of call:

Wants estimate for printing a (d) __manual__ of (e) __100__ pages. Copies: (f) __20,000__. Estimates also for (g) __10,000__ and (h) __30,000__ copies. Size: (i) __A5__ in black + white. Cover in colour. Will supply material on disk or CD.

Comments:

They are updating all their manuals, so could give us more work if the price is right.

Action required: Visit client with (j) __samples__
By whom: B. White
Date and time: (k) __Friday__ __16th__ May at 10 am

Roleplay   2   Work with a partner and practise telephoning for information and taking notes. Speaker A see page 126. Speaker B see page 130.

4 Networking

A gossip talks about others, a bore talks about himself – and a brilliant conversationalist talks about you. *Anon*

1 **▄▄** 4.1 Rick Van Looy and Florent Rondele meet in a hotel bar after dinner. Listen to **Conversation 1** and answer the questions.

a What does Florent do? ___marketing for a leisure goods retail company___

b What does Rick do? ___sales manager for a Dutch clothing firm___

c Do they know each other? ___no___

Now listen to **Conversation 2** and answer the questions.

a Where are the speakers? ___on a plane___

b One of the speakers asks 'Does this belong to you?' What do you think 'this' is? ___a pen___

c Where are the speakers going? ___Bangkok___

d Why? ___One lives there, the other is on a business trip.___

2 Listen again and complete the questions that are asked in the conversations.

	Question word	Auxiliary	Subject	Verb	etc.
a		Do	you	mind	if I join you?
b		Are	you		from around here, then?
c	What	do	you	do?	
d		Do	you	mean	sports equipment?
e	How many stores	have	you	got?	
f	What line of business	are	you		in?
g		Do	you	know	it?
h		Are	you	opening	a store here, then?
i		Do	you	fancy	something to drink?
j		Does	this	belong	to you?
k		Have	you	got	the time?
l		Do	we	land	soon?
m		Do	you	know	Bangkok?
n		Is	this		your first trip there?

3 How are questions b, f, and n in 2 different to the others?

___The verb 'to be' goes in place of the auxiliary and there is no 'main verb'.___

4 Networking

This unit is about networking, the skill of making useful business contacts by socialising at conferences, meetings, parties and the like. Students practise the kinds of questions that people ask when they are making small talk and they learn how to describe other people.

In this first section, students listen to two people making small talk in a hotel bar. They answer questions about what is said and complete the questions that are asked in the conversation. They then practise making their own questions to find out information about the person sitting next to them.

Warm-up

Stand the students in a line and whisper a piece of gossip to the first person in the line. That person whispers it to the next person and so on until it has reached the end of the line. No one is allowed to ask for a repetition of what has been said. The final person tells the others what he/she has heard. Usually the facts will have changed substantially and students can have fun seeing how gossip and rumours can move further and further away from the truth the more people are involved in the telling of them.

Focus students' attention on the quotation at the top of the page. Do they agree with it?

1 **4.1** Set the scene by focusing students' attention on the picture and eliciting ideas about the kinds of things the two men in the bar might be talking about.

Make sure students have read the questions before you play the recording so that they know exactly what information they are listening for.

2 Before listening again, ask students to look through the table of questions and try to complete the gaps. Then play the recording again. You may need to play it several times and pause it between conversations to give students time to fill in the gaps.

After checking the answers, ask students to suggest a suitable response to each question.

3 Elicit further examples of questions that follow the same pattern as b, f and n.

4.1

Conversation 1
A: Hello, **do you mind if I join you?**
B: Er, no, not at all.
A: How do you do? My name's Rick Van Looy.
B: Hi. Pleased to meet you. I'm Florent Rondele.
A: **Are you from around here, then?**
B: No, but my company has a store in town. Actually, I live in France.
A: So, **what do you do**, Florent?
B: I'm in marketing. I work for a retail company. We deal mainly in leisure goods.
A: **Do you mean sports equipment?**
B: Well, both sports and casual wear. Clothes, shoes, accessories, stuff like that. We have stores in several countries.

A: Sounds like a big operation. How many stores have you got?
B: Nearly fifty in total. And **what line of business are you in, Rick?**
A: Well, quite similar really. I'm a sales manager for a large Dutch clothing firm, Verweij Fashion – do you know it?
B: Yes, of course. Are you opening a store here, then?
A: Yes, we're looking at possible sites at the moment.
B: Hm. That can be a slow process. Rick, **do you fancy something to drink?**
A: Erm, yeah, thanks.
B: Come on, then. **There's a table free over there.**

Conversation 2
A: Excuse me, does this belong to you?
B: Oh, thank you very much.
A: It was on the floor.
B: Yes, I was looking for it just now. I wanted to finish this crossword. I'm feeling a bit groggy, actually.
A: Yes, it's a long flight.
B: Oh, isn't it? **Have you got the time?**
A: Yes, it's ... erm ... just after midnight.
B: So, do we land soon?
A: Yes, in about half an hour.
B: Oh, good. **Do you know Bangkok?**
A: Yes, I live there. **Is this your first trip there?**
B: Yes, it is actually.
A: On business, I suppose?
B: Yes, I'm visiting a supplier.
A: Oh, really? I wonder if I ...

4 Allow students to work in pairs to write the questions.

After checking the answers, have one student read out a question and another provide the answer. In this way, students will hear the questions and answers in the context of a conversation and it should make the structures easier to remember.

You could ask students to follow this up by taking turns to ask each other the questions and give answers which are true for them.

5 In this exercise, students get the chance to put into practice what they have learned. See who can find out the most information about their partner in the time allowed, but emphasise to students that the art of small talk does not lie in grilling people about their backgrounds. Questions need to be put gently and answers responded to with polite interest and reciprocal information about oneself.

Talking about other people

Conversations which focus solely on the exchange of personal information between two people are unlikely to be sustained for long. This section introduces students to talking about other people. They first put a dialogue in order, then they examine some of the language used in it and some alternative expressions which can be used. Finally, they practise talking about other people using business cards to provide the core information.

Warm-up

Focus students' attention on the title of this unit, *Networking*. Elicit that *networking* means making useful business contacts by talking to people at meetings, conferences, etc. A network is a collection of things that are connected, and networking often involves introducing people to each other or getting introductions to people through contacts you have already made. Find out from students if they have ever got an introduction to someone they wanted to meet from someone else. Was the introduction successful?

1 📼 **4.2** Allow students to work in pairs to order the conversation. When students have listened and checked their answers, ask one pair to perform the conversation for the class.

📼 **4.2**

A: **Do you know Jan Nowacki?**
B: Yes, isn't he Director of Business Development at Guinness?

A: Not any longer. Now he's the Public Relations Manager at the National Bank of Poland.
B: The National Bank of Poland, that's interesting. **Do you have any contact with him in your work?**

A: Not really, but I occasionally play golf with him.
B: **What's he like?**
A: He's a nice chap. You'd like him.

4 Write questions for the answers in **bold**.

a Who do you work for?   **IBM**.

b Where is your company
   based?   **Berlin**. Our offices are in the city centre.

c Where are you staying?   **In the Royal**. It's a great hotel.

d Do you speak (German)?   **No**, only French.

e Who is (Alex) talking to?   He's talking **to a client**.

f What do you do? / What's
   your job?   I'm an **accountant**.

g Have you got any children?   **Yes**, two boys aged seven and ten.

h Where are you from?   **Portugal**. I was born in Lisbon.

i Are you married?   **Yes**, I am – in fact, this is my wife, Yuki.

j Do you play golf?   **No**, I don't. There's no golf course near
                                  where I live. I play squash.

k Do you know (Adriana   **Yes**. I met her last year at a conference
   Bellini)?   in Vienna.

Answers on page 124

5 Your company has sent you to an international meeting. It starts in five minutes.
You don't know the person sitting next to you. Use the chart below to make
conversation and to find out about them.

Question word	Auxiliary	Subject	Verb	etc.
			live	
			work	here
Where	do		do	English
What	does	you	doing	at the moment
How	are	your company	have	any other languages
Why	has	he	got	your job
When	do	she	like	this book
How many employees	are	they	go	any children
	have		travel	to work
			studying	much in your work
			speak	

Talking about other people

1 ▭ 4.2 Look at the conversation below. Number the lines in the correct order.
Then listen and check your answers.

[6] What's he like?

[2] Yes, isn't he Director of Business Development at Guinness?

[1] Do you know Jan Nowacki?

[4] The National Bank of Poland, that's interesting. Do you have any contact
with him in your work?

[3] Not any longer. Now he's the Public Relations Manager at the National Bank
of Poland.

[7] He's a nice chap. You'd like him.

[5] Not really, but I occasionally play golf with him.

2 Which parts of the conversation could you replace with the expressions below?

a Have you ever met <u>Do you know</u>

b doesn't he work for <u>isn't he Director of Business Development at</u>

c bump into him at conferences <u>play golf with him</u>

d I don't like him much really. <u>He's a nice chap.</u>

e I don't anymore. <u>Not any longer.</u>

f What do you think of him? <u>What's he like?</u>

g You'd get on well. <u>You'd like him.</u>

3 Look at the business cards below which show the jobs five people did before and what they do now. (One of them is retired). Work with a partner. Using the conversation in 1 as a model, have conversations about the people on the cards. Add comments about their personalities and talents using the phrases in the box.

> He/She's an interesting person.   He/She's rather reserved.
> He/She's a good laugh.   He/She's a bit arrogant.
> He/She's a bit of a bore.   He/She always has the latest gossip.

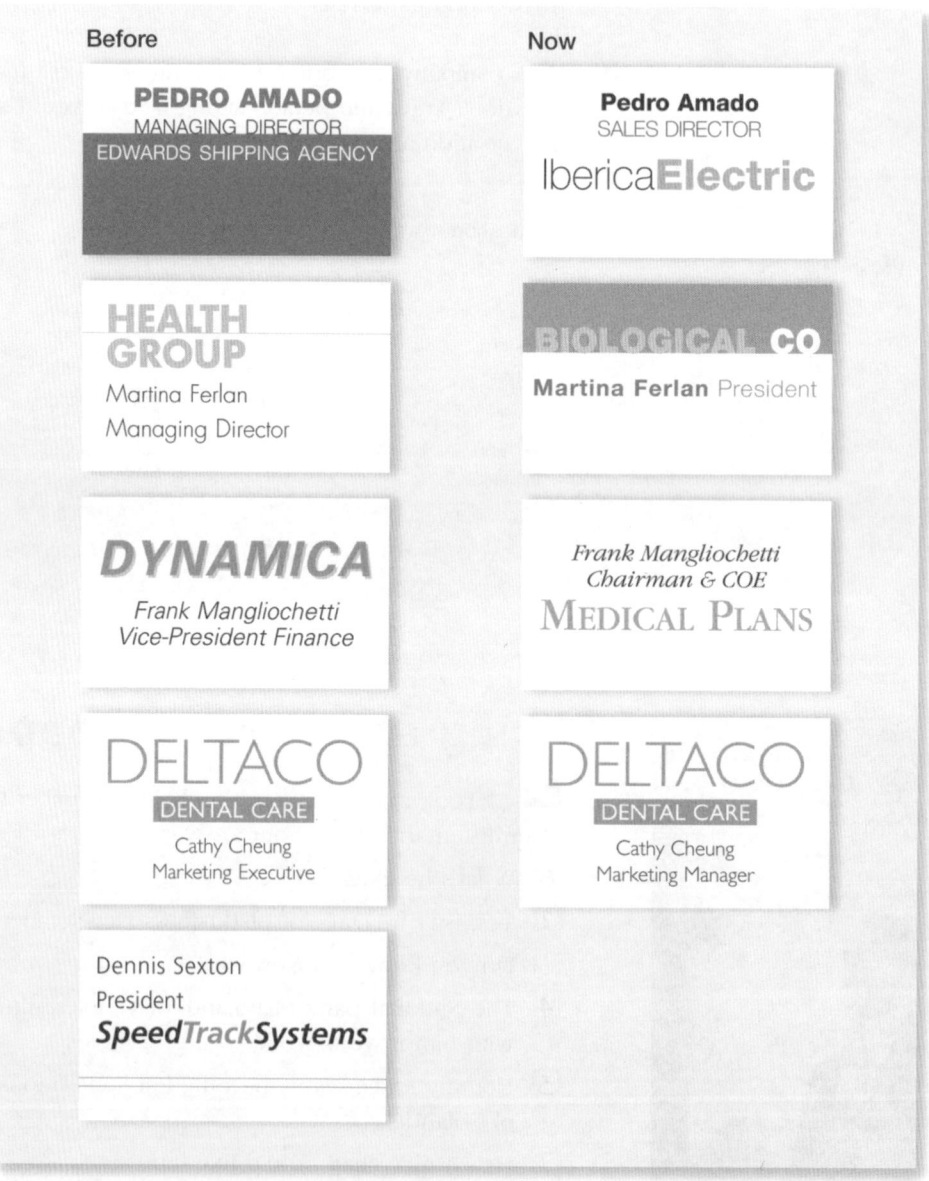

4 Now think about some people you know and have similar conversations about them.

2   Students identify the parts of the conversation in exercise 1 that could be replaced with the given expressions. If you have time, ask them to roleplay the conversation in pairs using the new expressions where appropriate.

3   Go through the instructions with the class and make sure they understand that the jobs the people used to do are represented by the business cards on the left and their present positions by those on the right. Establish that one person has retired and elicit who it is (Dennis Sexton). Check that students understand the phrases in the box.

As students practise their conversations, go round offering help and encouragement and make a note of any particularly good conversations which could be performed to the class later.

4   Again, make a note of any interesting conversations which could be performed in front of the whole class.

If you're short of time

In *Talking about other people* exercise 3, ask students to choose only one or two people to talk about.

Company life

5 Company histories

This unit is about how to describe the history of a company. It starts by looking at the history of Nintendo, the successful Japanese interactive entertainment company. Students then listen to a radio documentary on the history of the Internet and complete an article about it. They do more work on the structure of questions and finally write the text for a web page on the history of a company that they know.

The grammatical focus is on the Past Simple and time expressions, and the lexical focus is on business verbs.

In this first section, students complete a text on Nintendo which uses the Present Simple to list the dates and events in the company's history. They then practise writing a description which uses the Past Simple.

Warm-up

Find out from your students how much they know about their company's history. Do they know when the company was founded and by whom? Has it always been involved in the same kind of business? What major events have taken place over the years?

Focus students' attention on the quotation from Henry Ford at the top of the page. Do they agree with him?

1 This exercise uses a lot of business verbs which students will find useful to describe companies and what they do. There are even more verbs in the Lexis link on page 101, where a gap-fill exercise puts them in context.

Before students start the exercise, find out how much they already know about Nintendo and whether they possess or are familiar with any of its products.

Allow students to compare their answers to the exercise in pairs or small groups before checking with the class.

5 Company histories

History is more or less bunk. It's tradition. We don't want tradition. We want to live in the present and the only history that is worth a tinker's damn is the history we make today. *Henry Ford, American car manufacturer*

1 Read the history of Nintendo below. Complete the text using the words and phrases in the box.

> sales of   microprocessor   subsidiary   one billionth game pack
> hand-held game system   more than 500,000   a breakthrough game concept
> manufacturing games   sales records   corporate headquarters
> first playing cards   anniversaries of

NINTENDO Co. Ltd, of Kyoto, Japan, is the worldwide leader in the creation of interactive entertainment. Nintendo manufactures and markets hardware and software for its popular home video game systems, including the Nintendo 64 and GameBoy, the world's best-selling video game system.

1902 Fusajiro Yamauchi, great grandfather of the present president, **manufactures** the <u>first playing cards</u> in Japan.

1933 Mr Yamauchi **founds** Yamauchi Nintendo & Co.

1963 The company **changes** its name to Nintendo Co. Ltd. and starts <u>manufacturing games</u> in addition to playing cards.

1970 Nintendo **reconstructs** and **enlarges** its <u>corporate headquarters</u>.

1975 The company **develops** a video game system.

1976 It **uses** a <u>microprocessor</u> in a video game system for the first time.

1980 Nintendo **establishes** a <u>subsidiary</u>, Nintendo of America Inc.

1985 The company **starts** <u>sales of</u> the Nintendo Entertainment System (NES) in America.

1987 NES **reaches** number one selling toy status in America.

1989 Nintendo **introduces** GameBoy, the first portable <u>hand-held game system</u> with interchangeable game packs.

1995 The company **celebrates** the sale of the <u>one billionth game pack</u>.

1996 They **launch** Nintendo 64 in Japan on June 23, selling <u>more than 500,000</u> systems the first day.

1998 Nintendo **releases** Pokemon, <u>a breakthrough game concept</u> for GameBoy, which generates a worldwide collecting craze.

1999 The company **expands** the Pokemon franchise.

2001 With the 20th <u>anniversaries of</u> Nintendo characters Mario and Donkey Kong, GameBoy Advanced and the Nintendo Game Cube home video game console hit the market. The US launch of Game Cube on November 18 smashes previous US <u>sales records</u>.

2 The fifteen verbs in **bold** in 1 have regular forms in the Past Simple: infinitive + **-ed / -d.**

For example: *start → start**ed*** *release → release**d***

The pronunciation of **-ed** can be /d/, /t/, or /ɪd/. Write the Past Simple of the verbs in **bold** in 1 in the table below, according to their pronunciation.

Group 1	Group 2	Group 3
/d/	/t/	/ɪd/
used	released	started
manufactured	developed	founded
changed	established	reconstructed
enlarged	reached	celebrated
	introduced	expanded
	launched	

Lexis link

for more on business verbs see page 101

3 🔊 **5.1** Listen to someone talking about the history of Nintendo. Check your answers in 2.

4 Write five questions about Nintendo's history. Use the Past Simple.

(example answers)   When did Mr Yamauchi found the company?

What did Nintendo do in 1975?

How many units of Nintendo 64 did they sell on the first day?

What was the most significant event in Nintendo's recent history?

Why did the company change its name?

5 Write five sentences about Nintendo using the Past Simple. They can be true or false. Work with a partner. Close your books and test each other on the history of Nintendo by reading out your sentences and saying if the other person's sentences are true. If they are false, correct them. Who can remember the most?

Who really invented the Internet?

1 🔊 **5.2** You are going to listen to a radio documentary on the history of the Internet. First, do the quiz below. Then listen to see if you are correct.

Leonard Kleinrock, a computer scientist at UCLA, stands next to the refrigerator-sized computer that made the first-ever connection to what was to become the Internet.

The internet

a In which year did Leonard Kleinrock connect the first two computers?
1 1969   **2** 1975   **3** 1983

b What was the first message sent on the Internet?
1 'hello'   **2** 'lo'   **3** 'log in'

c What did the first version of the Internet connect?
1 military installations   **2** government buildings   **3** universities

d In which year was the first international computer connection made?
1 1969   **2** 1973   **3** 1983

e What is the 'universal language' of the Internet?
1 English   **2** Java Script   **3** TCP/IP

f What was the name of the first browser?
1 Netscape   **2** Mosaic   **3** Gopher

Past Simple: regular verbs

2 This exercise focuses on the Past Simple of the regular verbs used in the text in exercise 1. Students have to group them according to their pronunciation. When they are doing this, encourage them to say the Past Simple forms aloud so that they get a feel for what sounds right.

Direct students' attention to the Lexis link on page 101 where they will find more on business verbs.

3 ▣ **5.1** Check the answers with the class again after they have listened to the recording to make sure that they have put the verbs in the right columns in exercise 2.

4 Do a couple of example questions first with the class to check that students are using the Past Simple correctly. Then give them time to write their five questions and compare them with a partner. You could ask a few students to ask their questions and nominate other students to provide the answers.

5 Encourage students to write a mixture of true and false sentences. They then test each other in pairs.

Who really invented the Internet?

In this section, students do a quiz on the early years of the Internet and then listen to a documentary about it. They continue their work on the Past Simple by completing a text on the birth of the Internet and by asking and answering questions on it. This develops into more work on the formation of questions, particularly those which have no subject.

Warm-up

Find out how important the Internet is in your students' lives and whether they mainly use it for business or for pleasure. Ask them if they can remember sending their first e-mail. When was it and who did they send it to?

1 ▣ **5.2** Encourage students to do the quiz individually before comparing their answers in pairs or small groups. See how much consensus there is about the answers before you play the recording and check the answers.

▣ **5.1**

The Japanese company, Nintendo, is the world leader in interactive entertainment systems. To date, Nintendo has sold more than one billion video games worldwide, including Nintendo 64 and GameBoy, the world's best-selling video game.
The history of Nintendo goes back to 1902, when Fusajiro Yamauchi, the great grandfather of the present day president, **manufactured** the first playing cards in Japan. Although they were originally for export, the cards became popular in Japan as well as abroad.
Yamauchi **founded** an unlimited partnership, Yamauchi Nintendo & Company, in 1933. Thirty years later, in 1963, the company **changed** its name to Nintendo Co. Ltd., and started to manufacture games in addition to playing cards.
In 1970 Nintendo **reconstructed** and **enlarged** its corporate headquarters, and introduced electronic technology into its products. It **developed** the first video game in 1975, and the following year **used** a microprocessor in a game system for the first time.
A key year in the company's history was 1980, when Nintendo **established** a subsidiary in the USA, Nintendo of America, Inc. Five years passed before it **started** sales in the States of NES, the Nintendo Entertainment System, which **reached** number one selling toy status in just two years.
Perhaps the most significant event in Nintendo's recent history was in 1989 when it **introduced** the first portable hand-held game system with interchangeable game packs, GameBoy. GameBoy was a tremendous success and in 1995 the company **celebrated** the sales of its one billionth game pack.
When Nintendo **launched** Nintendo 64 in Japan on June 23 1996, it sold more than 500,000 units on the first day. Two years later it **released** Pokemon, a breakthrough game concept for GameBoy which generated a worldwide craze and, in 1999, the company **expanded** the Pokemon franchise, which was by then an international social phenomenon.
GameBoy Advanced, which introduced improvements and additional features to the original GameBoy, hit the market in 2001, continuing Nintendo's commitment to constant innovation and quality in its game systems.

▣ **5.2**

Was the Internet born in 1969 or in 1983? It all depends on who you talk to.
In 1965, the Advanced Research Projects Agency under the US Department of Defense, **began** work on a system to connect computers. They **called** the project ARPANET.
On September 2nd, 1969, Professor Leonard Kleinrock connected the first two machines. Twenty people **watched** in a laboratory at the University of California as meaningless data flowed between two computers along a 15 foot grey cable. For many people, that day **marked** the birth of today's Internet. The next month they sent the first message on the Net to a computer at Stanford University. The message was 'lo'. They **wanted** to send the words 'log in' but when they typed 'g' the system **crashed**. In fact the first word was quite appropriate, as a phonetic version of 'hello'.

By January 1970 ARPANET **linked** computers in four American universities, and by the following year there were 23 hosts in the system, connecting different universities and research institutes.
In 1973 Ray Tomlinson **sent** the first e-mail via ARPANET. In the same year it also went international, connecting hosts in England and Norway.
Another landmark was in 1979 when two graduate students at Duke University **established** the first USENET newsgroups. Users from all over the world **joined** these discussion groups to talk about the Net, politics, religion and thousands of other subjects.
In 1974 Bob Kahn and Vincent Cerf **invented** a software that allowed ARPANET to connect to other networks using different operating systems. The software, called TCP/IP, **became** the universal language of the Internet on January 1st, 1983. Some people say that this was the true birth of the Net.
More and more networks joined the system and the number of hosts **increased** dramatically: from 10,000 in 1984 to 100,000 in 1987.
By the early 1990s the World Wide Web was the most popular way of browsing the web, and the network was accessible to anyone in the world with a computer. In 1992 the number of hosts **reached** 1,000,000.
In 1993, Mosaic **became** available. This was the first graphics-based browser of the type we all use today. The growth rate of the Internet was an incredible 341% and by 1998 there were over 30,000,000 hosts.

2 If your students are confident, you could encourage them to see how much of the recording they understood the first time round by trying to number the events before they listen again. Then play the recording for them to check their answers.

3 If your students have difficulty with the past forms of verbs, you could go through the verbs in the box with them and elicit the past form of each verb before they use them to complete the article.

4 Play the recording again for students to check their answers and then answer any questions they may have about difficult vocabulary in the text. Ask them how much of the information in the text they already knew.

2 Listen again and number the events below in the correct order.

|6| Bob Kahn and Vincent Cerf invent a software for connecting computers on the Internet.

|2| Professor Kleinrock connects two computers.

|4| Ray Tomlinson sends the first e-mail.

|3| The first version of the Internet links four American universities.

|5| Users join the first USENET newsgroups.

|8| The first Internet browser becomes available.

|1| The Advanced Research Projects Agency starts work on ARPANET.

|9| The number of hosts (computers providing Internet services) reaches 30,000,000.

|7| An 'official language' of the Internet is established.

3 Complete the article with the verbs in the box in the Past Simple. Some of them are irregular.

> join   link   send   become   increase   mark   begin   crash   watch
> establish   invent   become   reach   call   want

BIRTH
OF THE
INTERNET

Was the Internet born in 1969 or in 1983? It all depends on who you talk to. In 1965, the Advanced Research Projects Agency under the US Department of Defense (a) __began__ work on a system to connect computers. They (b) __called__ the project ARPANET.

5   On September 2nd, 1969, Professor Leonard Kleinrock connected the first two machines. Twenty people (c) __watched__ in a laboratory at the University of California as meaningless data flowed between two computers along a 15 foot grey cable. For many people, that day (d) __marked__ the birth of today's Internet.

10   The next month they sent the first message on the Net to a computer at Stanford University. The message was 'lo'. They (e) __wanted__ to send the words 'log in' but when they typed 'g' the system (f) __crashed__. In fact the first word was quite appropriate, as a phonetic version of 'hello'.

     By January 1970 ARPANET (g) __linked__ computers in four American
15 universities, and by the following year there were 23 hosts in the system, connecting different universities and research institutes.

     In 1973 Ray Tomlinson (h) __sent__ the first e-mail via ARPANET. In the same year it also went international, connecting hosts in England and Norway.

     Another landmark was in 1979 when two graduate students at Duke
20 University (i) __established__ the first USENET newsgroups. Users from all over the world (j) __joined__ these discussion groups to talk about the Net, politics, religion and thousands of other subjects.

     In 1974 Bob Kahn and Vincent Cerf (k) __invented__ a software that allowed ARPANET to connect to other networks using different operating systems. The
25 software, called TCP/IP, (l) __became__ the universal language of the Internet on January 1st, 1983. Some people say that this was the true birth of the Net.

     More and more networks joined the system and the number of hosts (m) __increased__ dramatically: from 10,000 in 1984 to 100,000 in 1987.

     By the early 1990s the World Wide Web was the most popular way of
30 browsing the web, and the network was accessible to anyone in the world with a computer. In 1992 the number of hosts (n) __reached__ 1,000,000.

     In 1993, Mosaic (o) __became__ available. This was the first graphics-based browser of the type we all use today. The growth rate of the Internet was an incredible 341% and by 1998 there were over 30,000,000 hosts.

4 Listen again and check your answers.

5 In pairs, ask and answer questions about the history of the Internet using the word prompts.

a When / Professor Kleinrock / connect / first two computers?

When did Professor Kleinrock connect the first two computers? (1969)

b Where / send / first message?

Where did they send the first message? (to a computer at Stanford University)

c What / Ray Tomlinson / send / 1973?

What did Ray Tomlinson send in 1973? (the first e-mail)

d Why / users / join / USENET groups?

Why did users join USENET groups? (to talk about the Net, politics, religion, etc.)

e When / TCP/IP / become / official language?

When did TCP/IP become the official language? (1983)

f How much / the Internet / grow / 1993?

How much did the Internet grow in 1993? (341%)

6 The questions in 5 use the following structure:

Question word	did	Subject	Infinitive	etc.
When	did	Professor Kleinrock	connect	two computers?

When you do not know the subject, you use the following structure:

	Who/What	Verb in Past Simple	etc.
~~Who did send the first e-mail?~~	Who	sent	the first e-mail?
~~What did happen?~~	What	happened?	

This usually only happens with 'who' and 'what'.

7 Look at the chart below and practise asking and answering questions like this. *Who did Sarah fax? Jack. Who phoned Jack? Jane.*

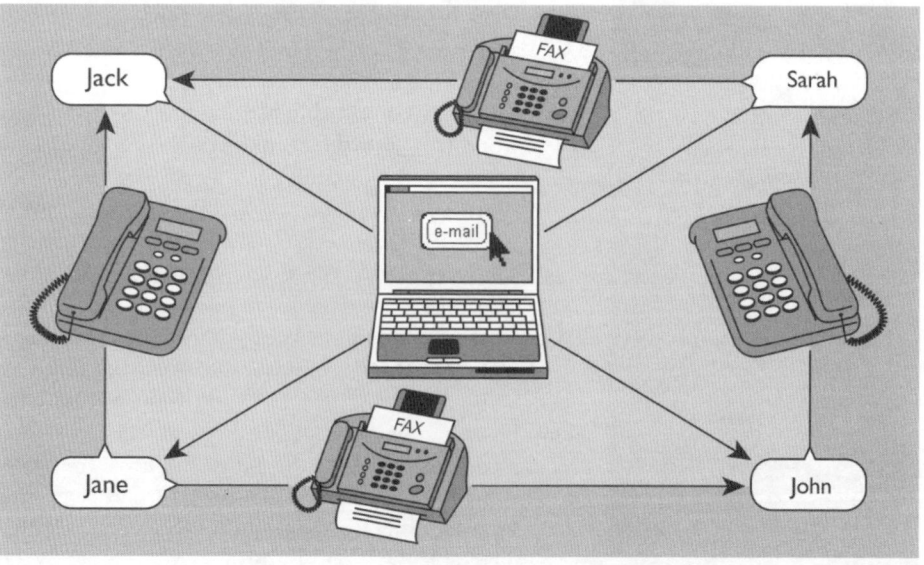

Grammar link

for more on the Past Simple see page 100

8 Write five questions using both structures in 6 about either the history of the Internet or the history of your company.

Asking questions

5   Working in pairs, students use the prompts to ask and answer questions about the history of the Internet. You could ask them to add two extra questions of their own at the end of the exercise.

6   Look at the two structure boxes with the class and elicit two more examples of questions using these different structures.

Questions with no subject

7   Students should work in pairs and take turns asking and answering questions based on the chart.

8   Encourage students to use their questions to quiz each other about the history of the Internet or their own company's history.

Direct students' attention to the Grammar link on page 100 where they will find more information on the formation and use of the Past Simple and practice exercises to help them use the tense correctly, including one on the formation of questions.

When was the last time you ...?

9   Go through the example with the class, perhaps asking a pair of students to read it aloud. Emphasise the importance of follow-up questions which are used to keep a conversation going (but remind them also that one shouldn't grill people with a barrage of questions and that it is important to listen and respond to what is said in answer to a question).

With weaker students, you could check that they have matched up the verbs and phrases correctly and can put all the verbs into the Past Simple before they work in pairs to ask and answer the questions.

Company history

In this section, students get the opportunity to put into practice everything they have learned in this unit by producing their own company history to put on a web page. Reassure them that they can make up the details if they are unfamiliar with the history of a real company.

Fluency

Check that students understand the meaning of the verbs in the box. Go through the items in the list with the class and then give them time to prepare their texts. If your students work for the same company, you could brainstorm some facts about the company with the whole class before allowing students to work in pairs to write the web page.

You could display the web pages on the wall to allow everyone in the class to read them.

Focus students' attention on the cartoon and make sure that students understand the meaning of *uncanny* (extraordinary; not easily explained) and that they get the joke.

If you're short of time

You could omit *Who really invented the Internet?* exercise 2, and exercise 3 could be done for homework.

Students could write the web page text for *Company history* for homework.

Set the *Grammar and Lexis links* exercises for homework and check the answers at the beginning of the next class.

9 Use the verbs on the left with the words and phrases on the right to ask your
partner questions beginning *When was the last time you ...?* Then ask follow-up
questions. For example:

A **When was the last time you** sent an e-mail?

B This morning.

A Who did you send it to?

B To a customer.

A What was it about?

Use the phrases in the box, if you like.

> I never do / have.   I really can't remember.   It was a long time ago.
> I'm not sure.

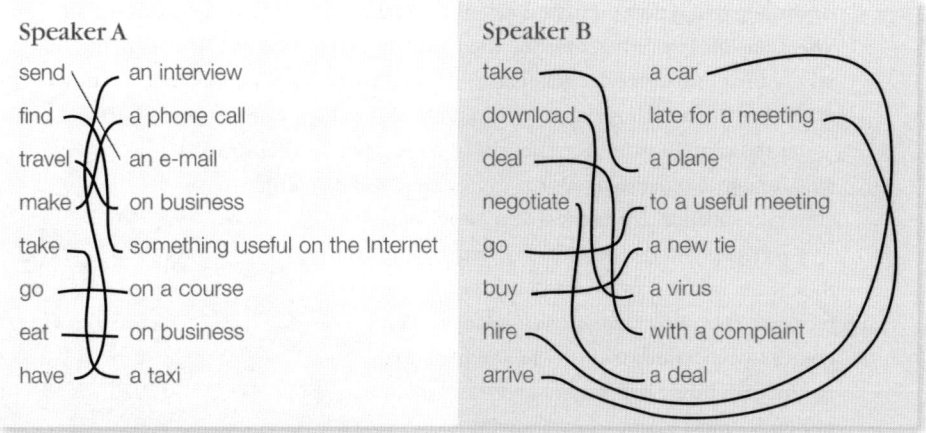

Speaker A

send — an interview
find — a phone call
travel — an e-mail
make — on business
take — something useful on the Internet
go — on a course
eat — on business
have — a taxi

Speaker B

take — a car
download — late for a meeting
deal — a plane
negotiate — to a useful meeting
go — a new tie
buy — a virus
hire — with a complaint
arrive — a deal

Company history

Write a web page giving the history of a company you know about or one you have
invented. You may find some of the words in the box useful.

> found   establish   begin   manufacture   develop   achieve   reach   launch
> expand   produce   want   increase

Include information about the following:

- the origins of the company, who
  founded it and when
- key dates in its history
- the opening of new offices or factories
- important orders or contracts it
  obtained
- periods of important growth
- introduction of new products or
  services
- establishment of subsidiaries
- appointment of key personalities in its
  management
- significant recent events

*"Well, that's just uncanny! How did
you know that we formed the
company in the early '70s?"*

6 Correspondence

Unless one is a genius, it is best to aim at being intelligible.

Anthony Hope (Sir Anthony Hope Hawkins), British novelist

1   Read the following article from a business magazine and discuss the questions with a partner.

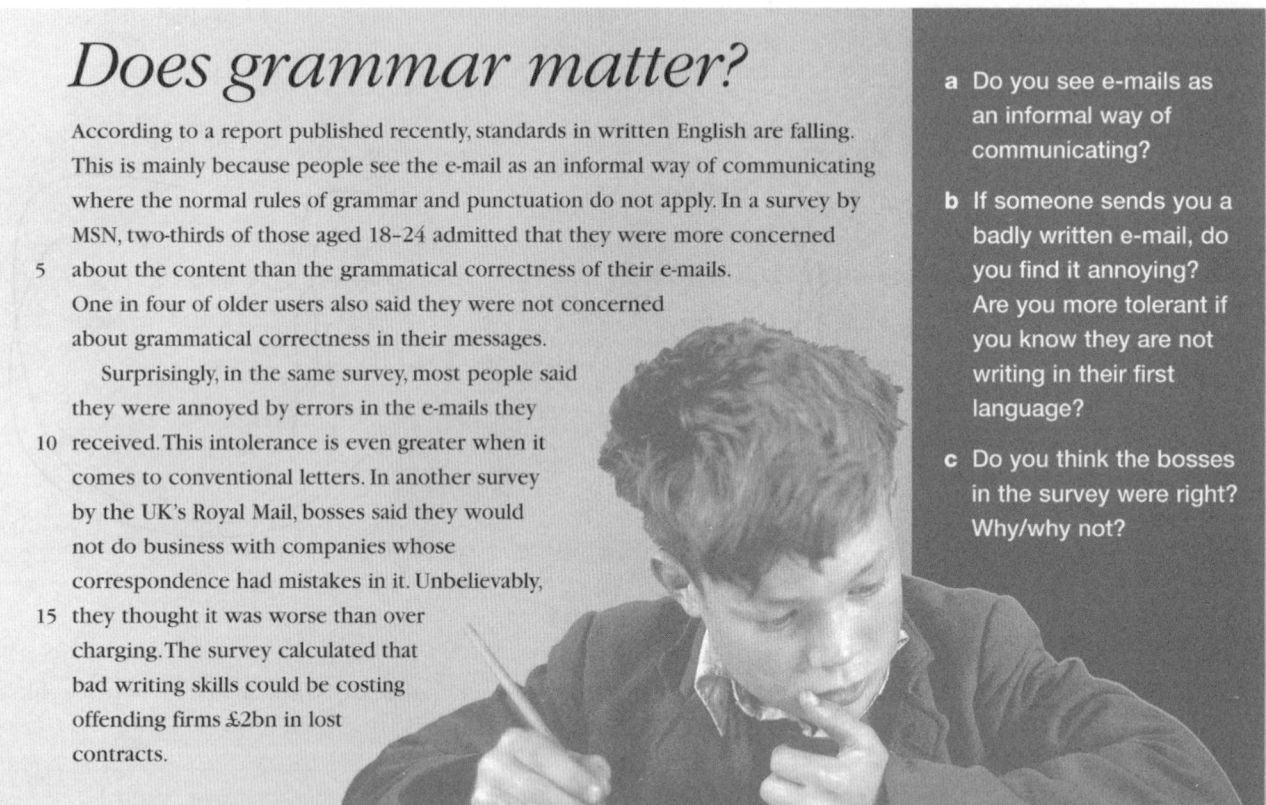

Does grammar matter?

According to a report published recently, standards in written English are falling. This is mainly because people see the e-mail as an informal way of communicating where the normal rules of grammar and punctuation do not apply. In a survey by MSN, two-thirds of those aged 18–24 admitted that they were more concerned
5   about the content than the grammatical correctness of their e-mails. One in four of older users also said they were not concerned about grammatical correctness in their messages.

   Surprisingly, in the same survey, most people said they were annoyed by errors in the e-mails they
10   received. This intolerance is even greater when it comes to conventional letters. In another survey by the UK's Royal Mail, bosses said they would not do business with companies whose correspondence had mistakes in it. Unbelievably,
15   they thought it was worse than over charging. The survey calculated that bad writing skills could be costing offending firms £2bn in lost contracts.

a   Do you see e-mails as an informal way of communicating?

b   If someone sends you a badly written e-mail, do you find it annoying? Are you more tolerant if you know they are not writing in their first language?

c   Do you think the bosses in the survey were right? Why/why not?

Discussion   2   Answer the questions. Then discuss your results with people in the class.

QUESTIONNAIRE

How often do you ...	every hour	every day	every week	not often	other
a use the telephone?	☐	☐	☐	☐	☐
b send and receive faxes?	☐	☐	☐	☐	☐
c look at your e-mail?	☐	☐	☐	☐	☐
d send things by courier?	☐	☐	☐	☐	☐
e use internal mail?	☐	☐	☐	☐	☐
f use the postal service?	☐	☐	☐	☐	☐
g have face to face meetings?	☐	☐	☐	☐	☐

Connecting # 6 Correspondence

This unit is about business correspondence and includes work on different types of correspondence such as letters, faxes and e-mails. With the growth of e-mail and the decline in letter writing, many native speakers of English have relaxed their writing style and with increased informality has come an increased tendency towards inaccuracy and an apparent tolerance of grammatical errors. However, this unit begins with a warning about the financial consequences of bad writing skills in the workplace, which may not be tolerated as much as people may think.

The grammatical focus is on *will* for unplanned decisions, and the lexical focus is on business communication.

In this first section, students read an article on the implications to a company of its employees not being able to write well and then go on to discuss the importance of accuracy in writing. They then move on to a discussion of the advantages and disadvantages of different methods of communication and say how frequently they use each one.

Warm-up

Focus students' attention on the quotation from Anthony Hope at the top of the page and the title of the article. Ask students if grammar matters in their own language. Are standards of writing in their own language declining and, if so, do they think the development of e-mail has contributed to this decline? Find out if formal grammar is still taught in schools in their country.

1   Give students plenty of time to read and discuss the article. When they have finished, you could ask them to try to summarise the main point in one sentence. Alternatively, write a gapped version of this summary on the board and ask students to complete it: *While people are not too [concerned] about mistakes in the e-mails they [send out], they are intolerant of [mistakes] in messages they [receive] and this could be costing companies a lot of [business].*

Discussion

2   Students should work individually at first to complete the questionnaire, then discuss their answers with others in the class. Ask students who reported particularly frequent (or infrequent) use of any of the items to give their reasons for this.

3 Go through the expressions in the box with the class and make sure everyone understands them. You could put the items from the questionnaire in exercise 2 on the board as headings and invite students to write the appropriate words under each heading, indicating whether each is an advantage or disadvantage by putting a tick or cross next to it.

4 Ask a student to read out the example summary. They then prepare their own summaries of the conclusions they came to in exercises 2 and 3.

On-the-spot decisions

In this section, students listen to a telephone conversation in which an on-the-spot decision is made. They look at the use of *will* + infinitive for decisions made at the time of speaking. They then practise dialogues in which one person offers a problem and the other an on-the-spot solution.

Warm-up

In the dialogue in exercise 1, students will hear someone dictating his e-mail address over the phone. It might be a good idea to make sure at this point that students can give their own e-mail addresses correctly, spelling out any difficult words and pointing out anything that is spelled as one word. You could write your own e-mail address on the board first and read it out to the class to demonstrate how it is done.

1 📟 **6.1** Make sure students have read the questions before you play the recording so that they know exactly what information they are listening for. You may need to play the recording a second time so that they can note down any answers they missed the first time round.

Taking decisions

2 You could point out to students that none of the options here is grammatically incorrect, but only one structure (*will* + infinitive) is appropriate for expressing an on-the-spot decision. There are more exercises practising this use of *will* in the Grammar link on page 102.

3 When students have completed the conversation, ask them to compare their answers with a partner and then practise reading it aloud in pairs to check that it makes sense.

4 📟 **6.2** Play the recording for students to check their answers. Ask if anyone has a different version, which they think makes sense – there may be other possible answers, particularly for the last two gaps.

📟 **6.1**

A: JFA Fabrics, can I help you?
B: Yes, I'm phoning from Natural Furnishings in Chelsea. Could I speak to Peter Simpson, please?
A: I'm afraid he's out of the office right now. Can I help you?
B: Well, it's about a fax I sent him. I'm waiting for a reply and it's quite urgent.
A: What's it about exactly?
B: It's a bit complicated to explain on the phone. I need a copy of a certificate for customs. Maybe he didn't get my fax. Can I just check your fax number – 0208 530 6370?
A: Yes, that's right. Listen, **why don't you send the details to me by e-mail and I'll**

send you a copy of the certificate as an attached Acrobat file.
B: Yes, that's a good idea. What's your e-mail address?
A: Jim, dot. That's J-I-M, dot, J-F-A, at lineone, dot, net. Lineone is all one word.
B: Can I just check that? Jim, dot, JFA, at lineone, dot, net.
A: Yes, that's right.
B: Okay, **I'll deal with the e-mail straight away**. By the way, my name's Cathy, Cathy Slater. You must be Jim.
A: Yes, Jim Kutz. Don't worry about the certificate. You'll have it by this afternoon.
B: Okay, thanks for your help.
A: You're welcome. Bye.

📟 **6.2**

A: Have we got a decision from Jim about the Mason contract?
B: No, don't worry. **I'll call him about it this afternoon**.
A: I tried – there's no answer.
B: Well, **I'll send him an e-mail**, then.
A: You can't – our intranet is down.
B: Never mind – **I'll send him a fax**.
A: I don't think we have their fax number.
B: Well, in that case, **I'll write him a letter** before I leave the office.
A: Oh, come on, that'll take far too long.
B: So, **we'll have to fly out to see him!**
A: Oh, that's a bit expensive …

3 What are the advantages and disadvantages of the different methods of communication in 2? Think about the following:

> bulk and weight   signatures   reliability   confidentiality   convenience   training   technology   image   handwriting   artwork and photographs   cost   speed   quality

4 Write a summary of your conclusions in 2 and 3. For example:

All of us use internal mail about twice a week. It's reliable, cheaper than the postal service and you can send packages of all sizes. Some people use fax to send documents which need a signature.

On-the-spot decisions

1 ▣ **6.1** Listen to the telephone conversation between Cathy Slater, the caller, and Jim Kutz, who answers the call. Answer the questions.

  a Who does Cathy want to speak to? <u>Peter Simpson</u>

  b Why? <u>She sent him an urgent fax but he didn't reply.</u>

  c Why did she send him a fax? <u>She needs a copy of a certificate for customs.</u>

  d What solution does Jim offer? <u>If Cathy sends him the details by</u>
    <u>e-mail, he will send the certificate as an attached file.</u>

  e What is Jim's e-mail address? <u>Jim.JFA@lineone.net</u>

Taking decisions   **2** Some situations require on-the-spot decisions. What did the speakers in 1 say? Circle the correct answers.

I'll send you I'm going to send I'm sending	a copy of the certificate.	
Don't worry,	I'll deal I'm going to deal I'm dealing	with the e-mail straight away.

You use *will* + infinitive to show that you are making an on-the-spot decision and to promise action.

3 Complete the conversation below using *will* + infinitive.

  A Have we got a decision from Jim about the Mason contract?

  B No, don't worry, I<u>'ll call him about it this afternoon.</u>

  A I tried – there's no answer.

  B Well, I<u>'ll send him an e-mail, then.</u>

  A You can't – our intranet is down.

  B Never mind – I<u>'ll send him a fax.</u>

  A I don't think we have their fax number.

  B Well, in that case, I<u>'ll write him a letter before I leave the office.</u>

  A Oh, come on, that'll take far too long.

  B So, we<u>'ll have to fly out to see him!</u>

  A Oh, that's a bit expensive.

4 ▣ **6.2** Listen and compare your answer to 3.

5 Work with a partner. Speaker A look at the chart below. Speaker B look at the chart on page 132.

Speaker A Choose a problem from the table and tell Speaker B. Begin *I've got a problem* ... Speaker B will offer a solution and then tell you about a problem. React using one of the solutions below. Say *Don't worry, I'll* ...

For example:

A I've got a problem, the battery in my mobile's flat.

B Don't worry, I'll lend you mine.

Grammar link

for more on *will* for unplanned decisions see page 102

Problems	Solutions
I've got a headache.	... take you to the airport.
We didn't get your fax.	... fax the details to you instead.
This report has lots of errors in it.	... show you how it works.
I can't remember his phone number.	... explain them to you.
I haven't booked my flight to Berlin.	... call the IT technician.
I need three copies of this proposal.	... phone you this afternoon.
I don't know anything about this company.	... change the ink cartridge.

Answers on page 131

An important order

1 ▄▄ **6.3** Look at the fax below. It confirms the details of an order made on the telephone. Listen to the conversation and complete the missing information.

FAX

STERNHydraulics

Limmatstrasse 450
8030 ZÜRICH
Tel. 01 360 4464

Dear John,

Further to our phone conversation today, I would like to confirm the following order:

Hydraulic pump ref: (a) _SG 94321_

Number of units: (b) _5_

To be delivered no later than (c) _June 22nd_ .

Please let us know of any problems in processing this order. We are especially concerned about receiving the parts on time as it is for a (d) _new_ customer.

Best regards,

Elena Moretti

Stern Hydraulics

5 Students take turns to present their problems and their solutions. They can check their answers on page 131.

Direct students' attention to the Grammar link on page 102 where they will find more information about *will* for unplanned decisions and practice exercises to help them use this form correctly.

An important order

In this section, students listen to a telephone conversation and complete a letter of confirmation for an order. Further exercises explore what happens when something goes wrong with this order and how the people involved deal with the problem.

Warm-up

Ask students if they have any experience of taking orders by telephone and if anything has ever gone wrong with the order. Encourage them to tell the class what happened and how they dealt with it. Find out what the procedure is in their company for accepting orders by phone. Is a confirmation letter needed? Do they have to fill out a particular form?

1 ▣ **6.3** Focus students' attention on the letter and make sure students have read it before you play the recording. This will help them to understand what the conversation is about and will ensure that they know exactly what information they are listening for.

▣ **6.3**

A: S-A-G, can I help you?

B: Yes, could I speak to John Bird?

A: I'm afraid he's not in the office right now. Can I take a message?

B: Oh, dear! It's an urgent order – we need five hydraulic pumps by June the 22nd.

A: Just a minute. Could you tell me your name, please?

B: Yes, I'm sorry. It's Elena Moretti from Stern Hydraulics in Switzerland.

A: Right, I'll take down the details and get John to contact you. Did you say five units?

B: Yes, the reference is SG 94321.

A: SG 94321 – five units.

B: Yes, that's right. But the important thing is the delivery date – June the 22nd.

A: I don't think that will be a problem.

B: Good, it's for a new customer.

A: I see. Right, when John comes in, I'll tell him immediately. Could you confirm the order in writing?

B: Yes, of course. Thanks very much.

A: You're welcome. Goodbye.

B: Goodbye.

2 The use of prompts here is designed to help students to construct the same conversation that they heard in exercise 1, but without reading it straight off the page. The more you can get students' eyes off the page and looking at each other when they practise conversations, the better they will sound and the more fluent they will become. Encourage them to look at each other as much as possible when they speak and to listen carefully to what their partner says.

Check the answers by having one confident pair perform their conversation for the class and asking others to put their hands up if they disagree with a particular sentence.

3 When students have completed the conversation, they should practise saying it aloud in their pairs.

4 ▭ **6.4** Play the recording for students to check their answers.

5 When students have identified the error in the order confirmation, ask them to speculate on how Elena felt when she received this document and why. What do they think she will do next? For homework you could ask them to write a short telephone conversation or e-mail from Elena to John Bird telling him about the mistake.

▭ **6.4**
A: Could I speak to Elena Moretti, please?
B: Speaking. Is that John?
A: Yes. Hello, Elena. I'm phoning back about your order.
B: Yes, it's quite urgent.
A: Don't worry. I've got all the details in your fax. No problem.
B: That's good. I was worried about it.
A: Well, can I help you with anything else?
B: No, but I hope we get more business from this customer.
A: Yes, of course. Okay, I'll be in touch. Bye for now.
B: Goodbye.

2 Work with a partner. Practise the conversation using the prompts.

A S-A-G / help?

B Yes / speak / John Bird?

A afraid / not / office / now / can / message?

B Oh, dear! / urgent order / we / five hydraulic pumps / June 22nd

A Just / minute / tell / name please?

B sorry / Elena Moretti / Stern Hydraulics / Switzerland

A Right / take down / details / get John / contact / say five units?

B Yes / reference / SG 94321

A SG 94321 / five units

B yes / right / important thing / delivery date / June 22nd

A not think / a problem

B good / for / new customer

A I see / when John comes / tell him immediately / confirm / order / writing?

B yes / course / thanks / much

A you / welcome / goodbye

B goodbye

3 Later that day John Bird phoned back. Work with a partner. Try to complete the conversation using the words and phrases in the box.

> is that   more business   help you   could I speak to   in touch
> phoning   it's quite   good   all the details   worry   worried

John __Could I speak to__ Elena Moretti, please?

Elena Speaking. __Is that__ John?

John Yes. Hello, Elena. I'm __phoning__ back about your order.

Elena Yes, __it's quite__ urgent.

John Don't __worry__. I've got __all the details__ in your fax. No problem.

Elena That's __good__. I was __worried__ about it.

John Well, can I __help you__ with anything else?

Elena No, but I hope we get __more business__ from this customer.

John Yes, of course. Okay, I'll be __in touch__. Bye for now.

Elena Goodbye.

4 ▭ 6.4 Now listen to the conversation in 3 to see if you are correct.

5 Later, Elena received this confirmation of her order. What is the mistake?

> ### SAG
>
> CONFIRMATION OF ORDER DH010601 June 1st
>
> Order received: May 23rd
>
> Part Ref. Number: SG 94321
>
> No. of units: 5
>
> Delivery required: (July 7th) ⟵ June 22nd
>
> Processed by:
>
> John Bird

6 ▶️ **6.5** Elena phoned SAG to tell John Bird about the mistake. Number the lines of the conversation in the correct order. Then listen and check.

1. S-A-G, can I help you?

10. No, it's not your fault. Just ask John to phone me.

9. Right, Elena, leave it with me. I'm terribly sorry about this.

3. Oh, hello, Elena. I'm afraid John isn't here at the moment. Can I take a message?

6. Yes, it says July 7th, but the agreed delivery date was June 22nd. It's really important.

2. Yes, this is Elena Moretti from Stern Hydraulics. Could I speak to John Bird, please?

5. Oh, dear. Can you give me the details?

11. All right, then. Bye for now.

8. Thank you. I'm not at all happy about this. A lot depends on this order.

7. I see. Well, I'll tell him as soon as he comes in.

4. Yes, he sent me an order confirmation – the reference is DH010601 – but the delivery date is wrong.

12. Goodbye.

Answers on page 125

Fluency **7** When John Bird got back to the office, he tried to phone Elena but couldn't get through. He decided to send an e-mail. Write his e-mail using the prompts below.

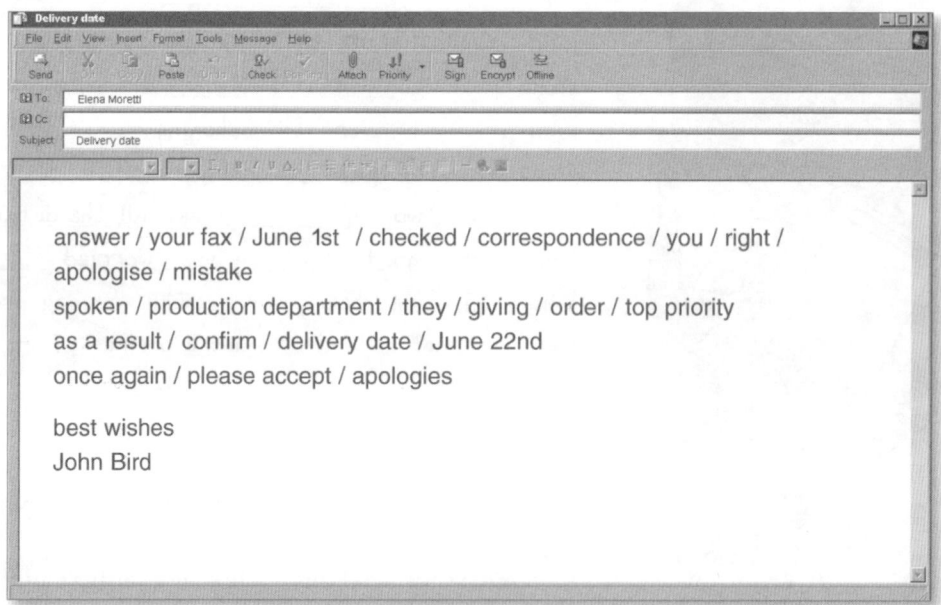

answer / your fax / June 1st / checked / correspondence / you / right / apologise / mistake
spoken / production department / they / giving / order / top priority
as a result / confirm / delivery date / June 22nd
once again / please accept / apologies

best wishes
John Bird

Lexis link

for more on the vocabulary of business communication see page 102

Fluency **8** On June 22nd the parts didn't arrive. They didn't arrive until June 30th. Elena phoned John again. Work with a partner and act out the conversation. Speaker A see below. Speaker B see page 132.

Speaker A
You are Elena Moretti. You are furious with John Bird. The order arrived late and as a result you will get no more orders from your customer. SAG let you down and you think John Bird is responsible. You are also angry about the fact that he never returns your calls and always makes mistakes. Unless he offers you some compensation (such as heavy discounts on future orders), tell him you will take your business elsewhere.

6 ▭ **6.5** If students did the homework suggested in exercise 5, ask them to compare their work with what Elena actually said in her telephone conversation with John Bird. When students have put the conversation in order, play the recording for them to check their answers. They can also look at page 125 to check and then they can use the script there to practise the conversation in pairs.

Fluency

7 When students have written their e-mails, ask them to compare them in pairs or small groups.

Suggested answer

> Dear Elena
>
> I got your message and tried to phone you today, but couldn't get through. I have looked back at your original fax and my notes of our conversation on June 1st and having checked our correspondence, I agree that you are absolutely right about the delivery date. I apologise for the mistake.
>
> I have spoken to our production department and they are giving your order top priority. As a result, I can confirm that the delivery date will be June 22nd.
>
> Once again, please accept my apologies for the mistake.
>
> Best wishes
>
> John Bird

Direct students' attention to the Lexis link on page 102 where they will find a practice activity with more useful words connected to the vocabulary of business communication, and a crossword using vocabulary from this unit.

Fluency

8 Go through the situation with the class before students divide into pairs to do the roleplay. Ask them for some words to describe how they think Elena feels and how they think John feels. Elicit if this kind of thing has ever happened to them.

Students then divide into pairs and follow their instructions. Go round offering help and encouragement where necessary. Note down any particularly successful exchanges and ask those students to demonstrate their conversation to the class.

If you're short of time

Ask students to complete the questionnaire in exercise 2 on page 28 for homework and report their answers to the class in the next lesson.

Students could also write the e-mail in *An important order* exercise 7 for homework.

Set the *Grammar and Lexis links* exercises for homework and check the answers at the beginning of the next class.

▭ **6.5**

A: S-A-G, can I help you?

B: Yes, this is Elena Moretti from Stern Hydraulics. Could I speak to John Bird, please?

A: Oh, hello, Elena, I'm afraid John isn't here at the moment. Can I take a message?

B: Yes, he sent me an order confirmation – the reference is DH010601 – but the delivery date is wrong.

A: Oh, dear. Can you give me the details?

B: Yes, it says July the 7th, but the agreed delivery date was June the 22nd. It's really important.

A: I see. Well, I'll tell him as soon as he comes in.

B: Thank you. I'm not at all happy about this. A lot depends on this order.

A: Right, Elena, leave it with me. I'm terribly sorry about this.

B: No, it's not your fault. Just ask John to phone me.

A: All right, then. Bye for now.

B: Goodbye.

Company life   7 Making comparisons

This unit is about comparing things. This work is set in the context of talking about hotels and cars and introduces some useful vocabulary for talking about business travel and checking into a hotel.

The grammatical focus is on comparatives and superlatives, and the lexical focus is on hotel services.

In this first section, students discuss what features make a good hotel, and then look at the service offered by one hotel through a dialogue in which a jetlagged traveller checks in. Students then practise the conversation between the traveller and the hotel receptionist.

Warm-up

Focus students' attention on the pictures on page 33 and ask them to predict what the unit is about and what significance the pictures have.

Ask students how often they have to stay in a hotel on business. Do they have any favourite hotels? If so, which are they and why do they like them? Do they think the standard of service in hotels is good, and is good service a factor for them when they are choosing where to stay?

1   When students have ticked the features they expect a good hotel to provide and added any ideas of their own, you could have a class discussion on what the most important features are (number them in order of importance) and ask students to say which ones would be a factor which would influence them when they were choosing a hotel.

2   ▭ 7.1 Make sure students have read the questions before you play the recording so that they know exactly what information they are listening for, and that they have understood what time of day this conversation takes place. You might like to ask them to predict the answers before they hear the conversation.

When you have checked the answers, ask if students find it surprising that the guest was offered breakfast at two o'clock in the afternoon. Have any of them had a similar experience? Would they want to eat a meal which was relevant to the time zone they had just left or do they prefer to try to fit into the new time zone as quickly as possible?

3   The use of prompts here is designed to help students to construct the same conversation that they heard in exercise 2, but without reading it straight off the page. Encourage students to look at each other as they speak, using the prompts only as reminders.

Global hotels

In this section, students read a text about the implications of globalisation in the hotel industry and are introduced to some useful vocabulary for talking about hotels and travel.

1   Encourage students to work individually at first to make their predictions and then to compare them in pairs or small groups. They should then read the article on page 34 to see if their predictions were correct. Find out if anyone has stayed in an InterContinental Hotel and if their recollection of their stay matches the information in the text.

▭ 7.1

A: Good afternoon.
B: Good afternoon. I have a reservation in the name of Wilson.
A: Er … yes, that's right. Did you have a good flight, sir?
B: Yes, not too bad. It was a bit long.
A: Could I see your passport, please?
B: Yes, of course. Here you are.
A: Thank you, your room is 301. Would you like some breakfast sent up to your room?
B: Breakfast? Em … yes, that would be nice.
A: Would you like tea or coffee?
B: Coffee, please. Oh, em, I need to send an e-mail.
A: That's no problem. You'll find a terminal in your room.
B: Right, thanks.
A: You're welcome. Have a good stay.

7 Making comparisons

Shall I compare thee to a summer's day? William Shakespeare, Sonnet 18, III:5, 1599

1 What features do you expect a good hotel to provide? Tick the features you expect. Add your own ideas to the list.

- [ ] widescreen television
- [ ] high-speed Internet connections
- [ ] 24-hour room service
- [ ] historic architecture
- [ ] beautiful surroundings
- [ ] convenient location
- [ ] swimming pool
- [ ] fitness rooms
- [ ] sauna

2 🔊 **7.1** It's two o'clock in the afternoon. A guest arrives at a hotel and checks in. Listen to the conversation and answer the questions.

a What does the receptionist offer the guest? Why? <u>breakfast – the guest has just flown in from a different time zone where it is time for breakfast</u>

b What does the guest need to do? <u>send an e-mail</u>

3 Practise the conversation with a partner using the prompts below.

Receptionist afternoon
Guest afternoon / reservation / name of
Receptionist yes / right / have / flight?
Guest yes / too bad / bit long
Receptionist see / passport?
Guest course / here
Receptionist thank / room / 301 / like / breakfast sent / room?
Guest breakfast? / yes / nice
Receptionist tea or coffee?
Guest coffee please / need / send / e-mail
Receptionist no problem / find / terminal / room
Guest right / thanks
Receptionist welcome / good stay

Global hotels

1 Before you read the article on page 34, decide if the following statements are true or false. Then read to see if you are correct.

		True	False
a	InterContinental Hotels keep worldwide records on client preferences.	✓	
b	Most independent hotels can't afford sufficient staff to provide the services of a multinational hotel chain.	✓	
c	Hotels make most of their money from food and drink.		✓
d	American clients are more used to 'brand name' hotel chains.	✓	
e	In Europe it is more difficult to build hotels than in the USA.	✓	
f	A seventeenth century castle is an ideal site for a multinational chain hotel.		✓

HOTEL CHAIN TAKEOVER

Any place, any time, anywhere, the chances are the bathroom will be on the left of your room.

Adapted from *Hotels play the global brand game* by Andrew Clark © The Guardian 2001

Travellers get off long-haul flights and receive a carefully prepared welcome at the InterContinental Hotel in Sydney. Receptionists offer refreshments suitable for the time zone which guests have just
5 come from. It is early afternoon in Sydney's high summer, but they greet British businessmen suffering from jetlag with a breakfast of toast, marmalade and cornflakes.

The hotel chain even checks its worldwide
10 database of guests to anticipate which newspaper each customer takes, in order to offer a 'local equivalent'.

The hotel industry is becoming more and more globalised. International chains are encircling the
15 world, taking over local operators. In the US, 75% of hotels have a well-known brand, compared with just 25% in Europe. Size is becoming more important as customer expectations rise. International business travellers want Internet connections, widescreen
20 televisions and push-button blinds in every room. They want faxes delivered to their rooms at all hours of the night and the ability to order *foie gras* at four o'clock in the morning. This means employing more staff than most independent operators can afford.
25 Between a third and half of hotels' revenue

comes from food and drink, but these only contribute 20% to 30% of profit. The real profits come from the rooms, so for most operators the principle objective is to improve occupancy. Loyalty
30 card schemes are becoming increasingly elaborate. They can record guests' preferences for well-cooked steak, ground-floor rooms or feather-free pillows.

However, there are limits to the internationalisation of European hotels. It's much
35 simpler to build hotels in the US than in Europe because there is so much space in the US. If you want a hotel, you can just build it. In Europe there are fewer opportunities for construction, so there are more conversions. Converted buildings aren't as easy
40 to adapt to the US chain model as new buildings because the rooms are different shapes and sizes, so the standard 'template' doesn't work.

It is difficult to turn a seventeenth century castle into a Holiday Inn, so some independent
45 operators still prosper. That is bad news for the ideal guest of a multinational chain. He likes to wake up anywhere in the world in the knowledge that the bathroom is on the left, the blinds are blue and the phone is on the wall, six and a half inches above
50 the bedside table.

---

2 Find words in the article which mean:

a long distance journey by plane _long-haul flight_

b area of the world with the same time _time zone_

c tiredness caused by travelling long distances by plane _jetlag_

d be able to pay for _afford_

e income _revenue_

f do well economically _prosper_

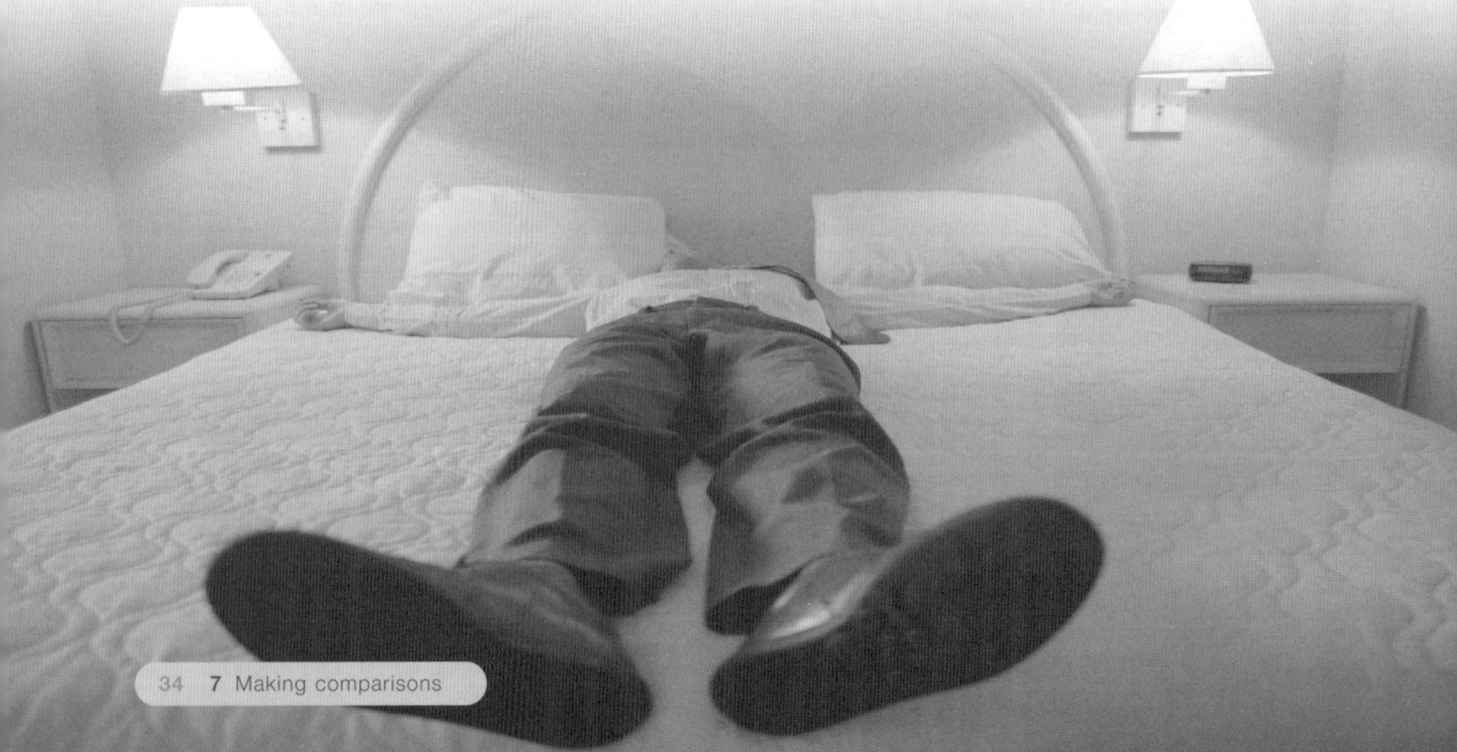

2 Students should scan the text quickly to find the matching words. Find out what experience they have of any of these things, particularly jetlag. Do they have any advice to offer on the best way to overcome it?

Elicit reactions to the text. Do students prefer to stay in hotels which are almost indistinguishable from those in different cities, but which are part of the same chain? Or would they rather stay in a hotel that had some local character and individuality? How important are convenience and familiarity when they are staying in a hotel on business?

3   When students have completed the sentences, ask them to read them aloud when you check the answers to ensure that they can pronounce all the words correctly.

4   Students decide if the statements in exercise 3 are true for their country and change any that are not.

Comparatives

5   Focus students' attention on the example sentence and point out that the words in bold are used to make a comparison between two things. Ask if anyone can remember why it is simpler to build hotels in the US than in Europe (because there is more space there).

When students have underlined the sentences in the text which compare things, ask them to read them aloud. The underlined sentences demonstrate different ways of comparing things. Ask students to say what the sentences are comparing.

Answers

> (line 13) *The hotel industry is becoming ...* compares the situation in the hotel industry before with the situation now.
>
> (line 15) *In the US, 75% of hotels ...* compares the percentages of hotels with a well-known brand in the US and Europe.
>
> (line 23) *This means employing more staff than ...* compares the hotel chains' ability to employ staff with that of independent operators.
>
> (line 37) *In Europe there are fewer opportunities ...* compares the opportunities for construction in the US with those in Europe and the number of hotel conversions in the US with those in Europe.
>
> (line 39) *Converted buildings aren't as easy ...* compares converted buildings with new buildings.

If students are having difficulty with comparative forms, you could turn to the Grammar link on page 104 and do the practice exercises there which relate to comparatives. Work on superlatives follows later in this unit.

Road test

In this section, the focus turns from hotels to cars and students are invited to compare different models of luxury car. They then discuss their own cars and how they compare with other similar models on the market and go on to talk about their dream car.

Warm-up

Focus students' attention on the two pictures of cars. Ask them if they have ever owned or driven one of these cars and which one they think they would prefer to own.

1   Check that students understand the meaning of the words in the box. Go through the example sentences with the class and then give them time to read the information in the table and make comparisons. You could do this as a team game with teams competing to finish all their comparisons as quickly as possible. Some of the comparisons can be made from the table, others are a matter of personal opinion. The answers to the factual ones can be found on page 128.

Discussion

2   Encourage students to use language for making comparisons when they talk about these questions. When they have had their discussion in pairs, ask them to compare notes with other pairs and then report back to the class on what has been said.

Have a class vote on what their dream car would be. Would it be a model that is in existence now, or would they like to combine different features from different models in order to achieve the perfect car?

3 Complete the sentences with the words in 2.

a When travellers arrive here from the USA, they often suffer from _jetlag_ .

b Most families can _afford_ two cars.

c To get here from the UK you have to take a _long-haul flight_ .

d The _revenue_ from tourism is important for the economy.

e We are in the same _time zone_ as Prague.

f The agricultural and food processing industries _prosper_ because of the good climate.

4 Are the sentences in 3 true for your country? Change the sentences which are not true.

Comparatives 5 Look at this sentence from the article on page 34.

*It's much **simpler** to build hotels in the US **than** in Europe.*

Find five other examples of how things are compared in the article. Underline them.

Road test

1 Compare the two cars below using the information in the table and the adjectives in the box. You may need to use some adjectives more than once.

*The Maserati is **more expensive than** the Chevrolet.*
*The Chevrolet has a **longer** guarantee **than** the Maserati.*

| powerful | good | expensive | economical | attractive | fast | long |
| high | wide | heavy | light | big | small | stylish | sexy |

	Maserati 3200 GT	Chevrolet Corvette
Price	89,401 euros	59,997 euros
Guarantee	2 years	3 years or 100,000 km
Motor	3,217 cc	5,665 cc
Power	370 brake horse power	344 brake horse power
Top speed	280 km/hr	274 km/hr
Consumption	15.07 litres/100kms	13.19 litres/100kms
Length	4.51 m	4.56 m
Width	1.82 m	1.87 m
Height	1.31 m	1.21 m
Size of boot	220 litres	320 litres
Fuel tank	90 litres	70 litres
Weight	1,620 kg	1,455 kg

Maserati 3200 GT

Chevrolet Corvette

Answers on page 128

Discussion 2 Work with a partner and discuss the following questions.

a Do you have a car? What make and model is it? How does it compare to other cars in the same price range? Will you buy the same car again or something different?

b Have you had other cars in the past? If you have, what were they? How did they compare with the car you have now?

c Do you have a dream car? What is it?

World leaders

Superlatives

1 Speaker A look at the instructions below. Speaker B look at the instructions on page 131.

Speaker A

Look at the tables below. Your partner has the missing information. Ask questions to complete the tables. For example, *Which is **the second biggest** hotel chain / car manufacturer in the world? Where is it based? How many rooms does it have / cars does it sell?*

The six biggest hotel chains ranked by number of rooms	Company	Country	Number of rooms
	1 Cendant Corporation	USA	542,630
	2 Bass Hotels and Resorts	UK	471,680
	3 Marriott International	USA	355,900
	4 Accor	France	354,652
	5 Choice Hotels	USA	338,254
	6 Best Western	USA	313,247

Top six car manufacturers in the world ranked by sales	Company	Country	Sales (in millions)
	1 General Motors	USA	6.60
	2 Ford Group	USA	4.83
	3 VW Group	Germany	4.00
	4 Toyota	Japan	3.87
	5 Daimler Chrysler	Germany	2.83
	6 Fiat Group	Italy	2.61

Grammar link

for more on comparatives and superlatives see page 104

2 Now make your own sentences. For example,

*Microsoft is based in Seattle. It is **the largest** software company in the world.*

*My company is based in Berlin. Locally, we are **the second largest** provider of Internet services.*

Discussion

3 Work in groups to talk about your hotel experiences. What's the best hotel you have ever stayed in? And the worst? What was good or bad about it?

Acquiring a hotel

Fluency

1 You work for MundiHotel, a global hotel organisation which has an interest in acquiring a hotel in the Milan area of Italy for its European chain. There are two existing hotels for sale – the Marco Polo and the Canova – or you could build a new hotel. Look at the table on page 37. Work with a partner and decide which is the best option for your company. Fill in the details for the new hotel, if necessary. Before you begin think about the arguments in favour of each option.

2 Then write a report about your decision. Use the framework below to help you.

The three options we looked at were ...   However, ...
The advantages of the Marco Polo are ...   The third option is ...
On the other hand, ...   In conclusion, ...
The Canova ...

World leaders

In this section, the focus is on both cars and hotels. It begins with an information gap activity in which students work together to complete a table comparing different international hotel chains and different car manufacturers. They then make sentences based on the table and go on to talk about their own experiences of staying in hotels.

Warm-up

Go quickly down the list of hotel chains in the table and ask students to raise their hands if they have stayed in any of their hotels. Do the same with the car manufacturers and find out who has owned a car made by any of them.

Superlatives

1 Before students work in their pairs, draw their attention to the example of a superlative in the instructions for Student A on page 36. They should then spend a few minutes deciding what questions they will need to ask their partners before they begin.

Students can check the answers by comparing their completed charts.

2 Encourage students to come up with a variety of superlative sentences about their own companies or ones that they know about. Go round the class asking for examples to check that they are forming their sentences correctly.

Direct students' attention to the Grammar link on page 104 where they will find more information on comparatives and superlatives and practice exercises to help them use these forms correctly.

Discussion

3 If the discussion brings out any interesting or funny stories about staying in hotels, encourage the relevant students to share them with the whole class.

Acquiring a hotel

In this section, students use the language they have used for comparing things to make a choice between buying one of two existing hotels and the option of building a new one. They discuss the options and think about the arguments in favour of each one. They then go on to write a report on their decision, using a framework to guide them.

Fluency

1 Go through the instructions with the class to make sure everyone understands the situation and what they have to do. Encourage students to use comparatives and superlatives to talk about the options and make their decision. Remind them that they can fill in the details about the new hotel in any way they wish.

2 The framework should help students to write a coherent report detailing the advantages and disadvantages of each option and outlining their decision. Ask some students to read their reports to the class or collect them in and display them on the wall for the others to read.

Room service

In this section, students practise some of the language they are likely to need when staying in a hotel. First they complete a dialogue between a hotel guest and room service and then they make up their own dialogues using this as a model.

Warm-up

Focus students' attention on the title of this section and ask them what room service is. Has anyone ever used it? What did they ask for?

1   🔲 **7.2** Students should try to complete the dialogue before they listen to the recording. Then play the recording for them to compare their answers.

Direct students' attention to the Lexis link on page 105 where they will find more on the vocabulary of hotel services and another example dialogue between a guest and room service for them to put in order.

2   Students practise the dialogue in pairs. When they have finished, encourage them to do it again, making minor changes to the words, for example, changing the time of the early morning call or the items the guest wants for breakfast. This will prepare them for the next exercise in which they have to devise their own dialogues.

Fluency

3   This exercise gives students the opportunity to put into practice some of the language they have learned in this unit. They can make the dialogues as simple or as complicated as they wish, but make sure that they are giving enough detail. For example, Student B should say exactly what it is he/she would like to eat, rather than just ordering 'something to eat'. The room service clerk in each dialogue should ask questions to clarify exactly what is required.

If you're short of time

You could omit *Global hotels* exercise 4.

Set exercise 1 of *Road test* and exercise 2 of *Acquiring a hotel* for homework.

Set the *Grammar and Lexis links* exercises for homework and check the answers at the beginning of the next class.

🔲 **7.2**

A: Room service. My name is Johan. Can I help you?
B: Yes, this is room 301. Could I have an early morning call, please?
A: Certainly, sir. What time would you like the call?
B: At half past six.
A: 6.30. No problem. Would you like breakfast sent up to your room?
B: No, thanks. I'll have it in the dining room.
A: The dining room opens for breakfast at 7.30.
B: Oh, in that case I will have it in my room. Just coffee and a croissant.
A: Coffee and a croissant. Anything else?
B: No, that's all.
A: Okay. Good night, sir.
B: Thank you. Good night.

Name of hotel	Marco Polo	Canova	(new hotel)
Total investment	$23,000,000	$15,000,000	$17-23,000,000
Description	Luxury accommodation. Modern building situated in city centre.	Restored castle dating from Roman times set in 5000m² of countryside with golf course nearby. 10kms from airport.	Land to build a hotel 2kms from airport. Possibly an excellent opportunity.
Annual revenue	$3,700,000	$2,700,000	$3,700,000 (?)
Number of rooms	178	124	approx 200
Average occupancy rate	55%	65%	_____
Swimming pool	No	Yes	_____
Meeting rooms	Yes	Yes	_____
Laundry rooms	Yes	Yes	_____
Spa/sauna	No	Yes	_____
Restaurant	Yes	Yes	_____
Exercise facilities	No	Yes	_____
Car park	Yes	Yes	_____

Room service

1   7.2 It is ten o'clock at night. A guest calls room service to ask for something. Complete the conversation below. Then listen and compare your answers.

Room Service Room service. My name is Johan. Can I help you?

Guest Yes, this is room 301. _Could I have_ an early morning call, please?

Room Service Certainly, sir. What time _would you like_ the call?

Guest At half past six.

Room Service 6.30. No problem. _Would you like_ breakfast sent up to your room?

Guest No, thanks. I _'ll have_ it in the dining room.

Room Service The dining room opens for breakfast at 7.30.

Guest Oh, in that case I _will have it_ in my room. Just coffee and a croissant.

Room Service Coffee and a croissant. _Anything else_ ?

Guest No, that's all.

Room Service Okay. _Good night_ , sir.

Guest Thank you. Good night.

Lexis link

for more on the vocabulary of hotel services see page 105

2 Practise the conversation in 1 with a partner.

Fluency   3 Work with a partner.

Speaker A You are the room service clerk.

Speaker B Phone room service to make requests for:

- something to eat
- someone to fix the air conditioning
- tomorrow's weather forecast
- someone to dry-clean a tie or a skirt
- help with the modem/data port
- (*your own request*)

Now change roles. Speaker B, you are the room service clerk. Speaker A see page 128.

8 Did I ever tell you ...?

The trouble with telling a good story is that it invariably reminds the other fellow of a bad one. *Sid Caesar*

anecdote /ˈænɪkˌdəʊt/
noun [C] a story that you tell people about something interesting or funny that has happened to you

from Macmillan English Dictionary

1 ▭ **8.1** Complete the anecdote below with suitable words. Then listen and compare your answers.

A   Look at that car!

B   Yes, it's a real beauty. Porsche 911.

A   Did I ever tell you about the time I had a __ride__ in a Porsche?

B   No, I don't think so.

A   It was when I __was__ a student. I was __hitch-hiking__ in Europe and this chap in a Porsche stopped. He took me all the way across Austria. We __went__ about 220 kilometres an hour all the way.

B   What about the __police__ ?

A   Well, they __stopped__ us about four times, but this chap just showed some identity card and they waved us on.

B   Was he someone __important__ , then?

A   I don't know, I didn't ask. I __suppose__ he was some sort of high-ranking official. He didn't talk much, but we *did* get there very quickly.

2 ▭ **8.2** Look at these sentences from the anecdote in 1.

It was when I was a student. I was hitch-hiking in Europe.

Make similar sentences using the prompts below. There are several alternatives. Then listen and compare your answers.

It was ...

a   while / live / Italy __It was while I was living in Italy.__

b   before / start / work / here __It was before I started working here.__

c   after / leave / university __It was after I left university.__

d   when / work / ICL __It was when I was working at ICL.__

e   before / get / married __It was before I got married.__

f   just after / children / born __It was just after my children were born.__

I was ...

g   look / job __I was looking for a job.__

h   do / Masters / the States __I was doing my Masters in the States.__

Conversation skills 8 Did I ever tell you ...?

This unit is about telling anecdotes or short stories about events in your own experience which are often funny or interesting and which may provoke someone else to reply with a story about a similar experience. As such, they are a useful way of maintaining a conversation and fostering good relationships between people.

The unit starts with a recording of someone telling an anecdote about an incident that happened when he was a student. Students examine some of the language used for telling stories and learn some useful ways of finishing off a story. They then work in pairs to tell anecdotes to each other.

Warm-up

Focus students' attention on the quotation from Sid Caesar at the top of the page. Ask them if they agree. Is it customary in their culture to respond to the telling of a story by telling one of your own? Do they enjoy listening to other people's stories or do they find it boring?

1 **8.1** Focus students' attention on the definition of *anecdote* in the margin. Tell them that they are going to listen to an anecdote and that they should first read the dialogue and see if they can predict what the missing words are. Allow students to compare their answers in pairs or small groups before playing the recording for them to check.

Point out that the person telling the story first asks whether he has ever told the story to his friend before. The friend replies that he doesn't think he has. Ask students if they would say that they hadn't heard the story before, even if they had, just to be polite.

2 **8.2** Go through the example sentences with the class and point out that these structures are very common when people are telling stories. Their function is to set the scene and establish the background to a story. The structure *It was ...* is immediately recognisable to native speakers of English as the beginning of a story and they are likely to sit back and listen with enjoyment to what follows.

Students make similar sentences using the prompts. Ensure that they realise that several alternatives are possible. Then play the recording for them to compare their answers. The material on the recording sets each sentence in a natural context and gives some idea of what the speaker is going to go on to say.

8.1

A: Look at that car!
B: Yes, it's a real beauty. Porsche 911.
A: Did I ever tell you about the time I had a ride in a Porsche?
B: No, I don't think so.
A: **It was when I was a student. I was hitch-hiking in Europe** and this chap in a Porsche stopped. He took me all the way across Austria. We went about 220 kilometres an hour all the way.
B: What about the police?
A: Well, they stopped us about four times, but this chap just showed some identity card and they waved us on.
B: Was he someone important, then?
A: I don't know, I didn't ask. I suppose he was some sort of high-ranking official. **He didn't talk much, but we *did* get there very quickly**.

8.2

a Yes, that was a long time ago. **It was while I was living in Italy**. I had this apartment in the centre of Milan ...
b I can remember what happened. **It was before I started working here**. I was working on a temporary basis ...
c No, it wasn't until much later. **It was after I left university**. I'd got my degree ...
d Oh, yes, that reminds me. **It was when I was working at ICL**. I was in the marketing department ...
e I had more time in those days. **It was before I got married**. In fact, I hadn't even met Mary ...
f The timing was awful. **It was just after my children were born**. And there I was without ...

g I'd just arrived in London. **I was looking for a job**. I bought the paper every day ...
h Yes, I was still studying at the time. **I was doing my Masters in the States**. At the Harvard Business School, in fact ...
i I was nineteen. **I was studying at Cambridge**. Things weren't going very well ...
j No, it was with a different set-up. **I was working for a small company north of here**. One day the boss walked into ...
k I was having a gap year after university. **I was travelling through Asia**. I'd just arrived in Saigon and ...
l It happened last March. **I was staying at the Continental Hotel in Prague**. Lovely hotel, I recommend it.

3 **8.3** You could play the end of the recording again to demonstrate the correct intonation in the example sentence. Make sure that students understand that *did* is simply there to add emphasis and normally we would say *We got there very quickly*.

Students make emphatic comments using the prompts. Encourage them to read them aloud to a partner using appropriate stress on the word *did* before playing the recording for them to check their answers.

Note: for the answers to this exercise, see the tapescript below.

4,5 The answers given here are examples only. There are many different ways in which students could complete these sentences. Allow them to compare their answers in pairs and encourage them to share any particularly interesting sentences with the class.

6 The prompts here should enable students to come up with an anecdote to tell their partner, but you may need to give them plenty of time to prepare. This preparation could be done for homework. Students may wish to tell anecdotes unconnected to those suggested in the book and they should be encouraged to do so. As they tell their anecdotes, go round offering help and encouragement, and make a note of any interesting stories that could be repeated for the whole class.

If you're short of time

Students could do exercises 4 and 5 and the preparation for exercise 6 for homework.

8.3

a We had a good time, but it *did* cost a fortune!

b He got the job, but he *did* have to marry the boss's daughter!

c We got there in the end, but we *did* sit on a bus all day.

d I got a good job, but I *did* have to leave the country to find one.

e She made a success of her business, but her husband *did* leave her.

f He sold more than anyone else, but he *did* have a heart attack.

I was ...

 i study / at Cambridge <u>I was studying at Cambridge.</u>

 j work / small company / north <u>I was working for a small</u>
  <u>company north of here.</u>

 k travel / Asia <u>I was travelling through Asia.</u>

 l stay / Continental Hotel / Prague <u>I was staying at the</u>
  <u>Continental Hotel in Prague.</u>

3 🔊 8.3 The speaker ends the anecdote in 1 with a comment:

*He didn't talk much, but we **did** get there very quickly.*
*... we **did** get there very quickly is similar to we **certainly** got there very quickly.*

Did adds emphasis to the verb *get.* ***Did*** is stressed when you speak.

Make similar comments using the following prompts, then listen and compare your answers.

 a we / have a good time / cost a fortune
 b he / get the job / have to marry the boss's daughter
 c we / get there in the end / sit on a bus all day
 d I / get a good job / have to leave the country / find one
 e she / make a success / business / her husband / leave her
 f he / sell more than anyone else / have a heart attack

4 Complete the sentences below. Use *did* for emphasis. (example answers)

 a It was a good car, <u>but it did cost a lot of money.</u>

 b I enjoyed the meal, <u>but I did have to listen to my boss for two hours.</u>

 c The conference wasn't very good, <u>but I did have a chance to do some sightseeing.</u>

 d They managed to find a hotel, <u>but it did take a long time.</u>

5 Complete the sentences below so that they make sense. (example answers)

 a <u>We took the boss's car for a drive</u>, but we did ask first.

 b <u>I couldn't get through on the phone</u>, but I did send him an e-mail.

 c <u>He gave her a lot of extra work</u>, but he did take her out to dinner.

 d <u>He was rather late for the interview</u>, but she did give him the job.

6 Work with a partner and each tell an anecdote based on the questions below. Help your partner by asking more questions.

Speaker A
Have you ever been stopped by the police when you were driving? Where were you going? Why did they stop you? Were they right or wrong? What was the outcome? Did it change your attitude either to driving or to the police, or did it confirm what you already thought?

Speaker B
Who was your least favourite teacher at school or lecturer at university? Why didn't you like them? Can you remember an incident that was typical of that person? Who was involved? What happened? What was the outcome? Did it change your point of view in any way or did it confirm what you already thought?

9 Spirit of enterprise

Beware of all enterprises that require new clothes. *Henry David Thoreau, US writer*

1   Look at the pictures below. They are elements from a story about a successful business. What do you think the business is?

2   🔊 **9.1** Listen to a conversation between Simon Taylor, a young entrepreneur, and his bank manager, and see if you are correct.

3   Listen to the conversation again and answer the questions.

a   What does Simon Taylor want to do? _borrow money to start a worm farm_

b   How does his bank manager react? _He is surprised._

c   How would you react if you were the bank manager?

4   🔊 **9.2** Read the introduction to an article about this story. Before writing the article, the journalist interviewed Simon Taylor about his worm farm. Listen to the interview and answer the questions below.

a   Was the worm farm Simon's first idea? _No. First he thought of fish farming or maggots for fishermen._

b   Why did he decide to set up a worm farm? _The start-up costs were low._

c   What does he mainly feed the worms? _salad waste from supermarkets and restaurants_

d   Has he tried any other types of food? What? _Yes, toxic waste from the paper industry._

e   Has it been successful? _Yes._

f   Is his business ecological? _Yes. Recycling toxic waste with worms is good for the environment._

5   Listen again. Prepare to explain the connections between the following words and phrases.

a   fish farming   investment

Simon thought about fish farming at first, but decided that the initial investment was too high.

b   worm farming   start-up costs

Simon decided to go into worm farming because the start-up costs were relatively low.

THE WORM MAN

Picture the scene. You go to your bank manager and ask him for money to develop a great business idea – a worm farm. Not surprisingly, the bank manager finds it difficult to keep a straight face. But this isn't an imaginary tale. It's the true story of a business success ...

Company life **9 Spirit of enterprise**

This unit is about successful businesses (enterprises) that have been built up by people who saw a gap in the market and worked hard to fill it. Two case histories are studied, that of a man who started a worm farm to supply anglers with bait, and that of a group which has diversified within the fashion industry and made use of innovative and flexible management policies to develop and thrive within a competitive market.

The grammatical focus is on the Present Perfect versus the Past Simple, and the lexical focus is on word building.

In this first section, students listen to a conversation between Simon Taylor, a man who wants to start a new business providing worms for anglers, and his bank manager. They then listen to a journalist interviewing Simon about his successful worm farm and practise using the Present Perfect and Past Simple tenses to describe the events in the development of Simon's business. Finally they reconstruct the conversation between Simon and the journalist.

Warm-up

Focus students' attention on the quotation from Henry David Thoreau at the top of the page and elicit some opinions about what it means. (Suggested answer: The enterprises that are most likely to succeed are those in which you get your clothes dirty, i.e. those that require hard manual labour.)

1 Ask students to describe what they can see in the pictures first and then have them speculate on what the business is. Do not confirm any answers at this stage.

2 ▭ **9.1** Tell students that the first time they listen to the recording all they need to find out is whether they were correct in their predictions in exercise 1. They will have further opportunities for more detailed listening later. Play the recording and see if anyone correctly predicted the nature of the business (a worm farm supplying bait for anglers).

3 Make sure students have read the questions before you play the recording so that they know exactly what information they are listening for.

When you have checked the answers, elicit students' reactions to what they have heard. Are they surprised that the bank manager is surprised by Simon's proposal? Do they think the idea has any chance of succeeding?

4 ▭ **9.2** Go through the introduction to the article with the class. Elicit that *finds it difficult to keep a straight face* means *finds it hard not to laugh*. The bank manager's expression is clearly shown in the picture on the right.

Make sure students have read the questions before you play the recording so that they know exactly what information they are listening for.

Play the recording. Then allow students to compare their answers in pairs before you check the answers with the class.

5 With stronger students, see if anyone can explain the connections before they listen to the interview again.

Play the recording again. Then give students time to formulate proper sentences explaining the connections.

▭ **9.1**

A: Good morning. Please sit down.
B: Good morning. Thank you for seeing me.
A: Let's see, then. How can I help you, Simon?
B: Well, I'd like to borrow some money to set up a business.
A: What kind of business were you thinking of?
B: Well, em, I know it sounds strange, but I have this idea for setting up a worm farm.
A: A what?
B: A worm farm ... a farm to produce worms for fishing bait.
A: Is there really a market for it?
B: Yes, but apart from fishing bait, worms can recycle food waste.
A: I see.
B: And, in Holland, they use worms to produce a special kind of soil which is ideal for growing organic tomatoes.
A: Well, could I see your business plan ...?

▭ **9.2**

A: Simon, where did you get the idea for a worm farm?
B: Well, my family owns a farm, and some of the land wasn't being used.
A: So, you had the land available. Was this your first idea for a business?
B: No, at first I thought of fish farming or maggots for fishermen.
A: Why did you change your mind?
B: I decided the investment was too big. I didn't want to take a risk.
A: So, why did you decide to set up a worm farm?
B: Because the start-up costs were relatively low.
A: How did you start, then?
B: I began by packing worms in pots for fishermen.
A: What do you feed them?
B: I mainly feed them salad waste from supermarkets and restaurants, but as demand has grown, we've tried other food sources.

A: For example?
B: Well, we've fed them with toxic waste from the paper industry.
A: Really? Does it work?
B: Yes, the results have been very positive. They can recycle the waste. It's cheaper than burying it in expensive dumps. And it's good for the environment.
A: It sounds amazing. How much do you produce?
B: This year we've produced ten tons of worms, and next year we hope to double production to twenty.
A: There's a market for all these worms, then.
B: Oh, yes. In the UK, fisherman use around 250 tons of worms every year, so there's a healthy demand. But we're also looking at other uses.
A: Well, Simon, that's all very interesting. Thanks very much and good luck for the future.
B: Thank you. You're welcome.

6 You could do this exercise as a class discussion.

Present Perfect & Past Simple

7 Ask students to work individually to order the summary and then compare their answers in pairs. They should then turn to page 128 and read the full article.

8 Elicit one example of each tense with the class to ensure that everyone understands the two forms. When they have found and underlined the examples of the tenses, elicit answers to the two questions about usage.

9 Students reconstruct the conversation from the prompts. Encourage them to look at their partner as they speak and to listen carefully to what is said to them rather than just concentrating on constructing their next line of the dialogue.

Direct students' attention to the Grammar link on page 106 where they will find more information on the form and use of the Present Perfect and Past Simple and practice exercises to help them use these tenses correctly.

c growing demand   toxic waste from the paper industry

Growing demand for his worms has made Simon try new food sources such as toxic waste from the paper industry.

d 10 tons   20 tons   250 tons

This year he produced 10 tons of worms; next year he hopes to produce 20 tons. In the UK fishermen use 250 tons a year.

6 What other unusual ways of making money have you heard of?

Present Perfect &
Past Simple

7 Number the parts of the summary of Simon's story in the correct order. Check your answers by comparing it with the full article on page 128.

1   Four years ago, Simon …

3   … thought about fish farming but the investment …

10   … to double production next year. UK fishermen use around 250 tons of worms a year, so …

8   … has started to experiment with industrial waste from the paper industry. This year he …

2   … acquired some land on his family's farm. At first he …

4   … was too high, so he …

9   … has produced over ten tons of worms but he expects …

5   … opted for a worm farm. He feeds the worms on salad waste from supermarkets but demand …

6   … has grown and he …

7   … has experimented with other possibilities. For example, he …

11   … there is plenty of demand. But he is also looking at other uses.

8 Underline four examples of the Past Simple and four examples of the Present Perfect in 7. Which structure is used to show that:

- a stage in Simon's project is completely finished? *Past Simple*
- an event is part of a continuing stage in the project? *Present Perfect*

9 Use the word prompts to reconstruct the conversation between Simon and the journalist. Think carefully about which tense you should use.

Journalist this / first idea / for / business?

Simon no / first / think / fish farming

Journalist why / change / mind

Simon decide / investment too big / not want / take / risk

Journalist why / decide / set up / worm farm?

Simon because / start-up costs / relatively low

Journalist how / start?

Simon begin / packing worms / pots / fishermen

Journalist what / feed / worms?

Simon feed / waste / supermarkets & restaurants / demand / grow / we / try other food sources

Journalist example?

Simon we / feed / waste / paper industry

Journalist really / work?

Simon yes / results / very positive / they / recycle / waste / cheaper / burying it / expensive dumps / good / environment

Journalist sound / amazing / how much / produce?

Simon this year / produce / 10 tons / next year / hope / double production / 20

Journalist market / all these worms?

Simon in the UK fishermen use / 250 tons / year / also / look / at other uses

Grammar link

for more on the Present Perfect and Past Simple see page 106

Change

1 Label each graph with two verbs from the box which describe change.

| go up   fall   remain stable   go down   increase   not change |

a

go up, increase

b

remain stable, not change

c

fall, go down

2 Work in groups. Using the verbs in 1, describe what has happened recently in your country or region, and in the company you work for. Use the topics below to help you. For example: *Interest rates **have fallen** in the last six months. The number of people working in my team at work **has increased** recently.*

in your country or region
house prices	taxes
rate of inflation	interest rates
unemployment	population
economic growth	traffic

in your company
number of staff
revenues
profits
amount of work

Has anything else important happened in your country, region or company?

3 Read the information below about a successful Spanish company, Inditex, and answer the questions.

a Who is the founder of the Inditex Group? _Amancio Ortega_

b Where and when did it start? _1975 in La Coruña, Spain_

c What business is it in? _fashion – textile design, production and distribution_

d What is the secret of its success? _innovation and flexibility in management_

e How many companies are there in the group? _almost a hundred_

Lexis link

for work on word building see page 107

BUSINESS BRIEFING

INDITEX

The founder of Inditex, Amancio Ortega, has a catch phrase: 'Don't explain
5   how we're going to make money today. Tell me how we're going to make it in five years' time.' The Inditex Group's first Zara shop opened its doors in 1975 in La Coruña, Spain. Today, the Group's stores can be seen in places such as New York's 5th Avenue, Paris' Champs-Elysées, London's Regent Street, and Tokyo's Shibuya Shopping Quarters. Its unique management
10 methods, based on innovation and flexibility, have turned Inditex into one of the world's largest fashion groups, made up of almost a hundred companies dealing with activities related to textile design, production and distribution.

4 Work with a partner. Speaker A look at the instructions below. Speaker B look at the instructions on page 133.

Speaker A Look at the information in the table on page 43. Work with your partner to complete the missing information and find out how Inditex has changed over the last four years.

Change

In this section, the focus changes to another successful enterprise, this time in the fashion industry. Students begin by looking at ways to talk about change. They then read a text about a successful Spanish company. They answer questions on the text and then do an information gap activity to find out more about the company and how it has changed over the last four years. Finally, they complete a report on changes in the company and then write one on a company they know.

Warm-up

Find out how many sayings or expressions the students know which involve the word *change* or the concept of changing. Allow them to cite examples in their own language if they don't know any in English. You might like to teach them the sayings *A change is as good as a rest* and *A leopard can't change his spots*. Expressions they already know may include *changing room, spare change, a change for the better, change money / a battery / a tyre / one's clothes*, etc.

1 Focus students' attention on the three graphs and the words in the box. Ask students to identify which verbs go with which graphs (there are two for each graph). You could also elicit that *go up, not change* and *go down* are all more informal than *increase, fall* and *remain stable*.

2 Before students start talking about what has happened in their country, region or company, you could go through the words in the box in exercise 1 and elicit what the Present Perfect forms are (*has/have gone up*, etc.).

Working in groups, students make sentences about recent changes. Remind them that they don't have to restrict themselves to the suggestions in the book – they can talk about anything important which has happened recently.

3 Go through the questions with the class and then ask students to read the text quickly to find the answers.

Direct students' attention to the Lexis link on page 107 where the word building exercise will show them the other possible forms of several of the words in this text. Remind students that whenever they record new vocabulary, it is a good idea to note down any other forms of the same word.

4 This information exchange activity will give students practice in asking questions, and will provide more information about Inditex and the way it has changed over the last four years. They will use this information in the next exercise.

5   Students use the information they found out in exercise 4 to complete the report. Remind them of the use of the Present Perfect tense to show that events are part of a continuing process.

Ask one or two students to read their reports aloud. Check that the tenses have been used correctly.

6   This writing exercise could be set for homework.

If you're short of time

Set *Change* exercise 6 for homework.

Set the *Grammar and Lexis links* exercises for homework and check the answers at the beginning of the next class.

Inditex	four years ago	now
Shops worldwide	748	1,377
Shops in Spain	489	818
Shops in rest of world	259	559
Countries where the group operates	21	39
Chains in group	Zara, Pull & Bear Massimo Dutti	Zara, Pull & Bear, Massimo Dutti, Bershka, Stradivarius, Oysho
Net revenues	€1,615 million	€3,249 million
Net profits	€153 million	€345 million
Headquarters	Arteixo, La Coruña, Spain	New building in Arteixo, La Coruña

5 Complete the report using information from 4 and the verbs in the box in either the Past Simple or Present Perfect.

> open   increase   make   move   reach   grow   launch

The recent history of Inditex is a tremendous success story. Over the last four years the group (a) __has grown__ enormously. It now operates in (b) __39__ countries, and the number of shops worldwide (c) __has increased__ from (d) __748__ to (e) __1,377__. In this time the group (f) __has launched__ (g) __three__ new chains, and (h) __has opened__ 329 new shops in Spain and 300 in the rest of the world. This year net revenues (i) __have reached__ a level of (j) __€3,249 million__, and the group (k) __has made__ profits of (l) __€345 million__. All Inditex's activities are controlled from Arteixo, La Coruña, where the group recently (m) __moved__ into new headquarters.

6 Write a similar report about the changes in a company you know about.

10 Stressed to the limit

Stress is like having one foot on the accelerator of a car, with the other foot on the brake. We wind up stripping our gears. The chronic build-up of stress takes an enormous toll on our bodies in terms of wear and tear. *Dr Reed C Moskowitz*

Discussion 1 Work with a partner. Which of these factors produce the most stress? Add your own ideas.

> dealing with the public   working long hours   meeting deadlines
> travelling   making phone calls   learning to use new technology
> being promoted   looking after children   doing boring, repetitive tasks
> dealing with big sums of money   being responsible for people's lives
> waiting for other people to do things

2 📼 10.1 An interviewer for the radio programme *Work Today* spoke to four people in the street about stress. Listen to the interviews and answer the questions.

		Interview 1	Interview 2	Interview 3	Interview 4
a	What does the speaker do?	accountant	works in shop	teacher	self-employed architect
b	Does the speaker suffer from stress?	yes	yes	yes	no
c	What causes the stress, according to the speaker?	the boss	family	working with teenagers	–
d	Does the speaker mention any of the reasons in 1? Which?	meeting deadlines	looking after children	no	–

3 The last speaker says that stress is more a problem of mental attitude than what you do. Do you agree?

4 In your opinion, what are the three most stressful jobs? Use the list below to help you.

> middle manager   chief executive   teacher   taxi driver   telephonist
> secretary   police officer   factory worker   pilot   air traffic controller
> stockbroker   doctor   lawyer   shop assistant   accountant   waiter
> computer programmer   firefighter   miner   architect   journalist

Now compare your ideas with the list on page 129. Are you surprised? What do you think are the least stressful jobs?

have to 5 For each set of prompts a–g, make at least two sentences with *has to/have to/doesn't have to/don't have to*. For example:

> air traffic controller   factory worker   take decisions   be creative

An air traffic controller ***has to*** *take decisions very quickly.* (It's necessary)

A factory worker ***doesn't have to*** *be creative.* (It's not necessary)

Work issues # 10 Stressed to the limit

The focus of this unit is on stress and the effect it has on working people. It begins with a discussion of what things cause stress and presents an interview with four people talking about stress in their lives. Students then talk about which jobs they regard as most stressful and compare their opinions with some statistics. They then do some work on the use of *have to* to talk about what people's jobs entail. Avoidance and reduction of stress are the focus of a reading text which provides an opportunity for more work on word formation. Students then use *should* and *shouldn't* to talk about managers' and workers' responsibilities in the workplace. Finally they do an extended roleplay activity concerning stress in the workplace and write a report on a company's problems in this area.

The grammatical focus is on *have to* and *should(n't)*, and the lexical focus is on stress at work.

In this first section, there is a discussion on the causes of stress and the factors in people's jobs which make one job more stressful than another. Students practise using *have to* to describe people's job responsibilities and *should* and *shouldn't* to talk about how people can reduce stress.

Warm-up

Focus students' attention on the quotation from Dr Reed C Moskowitz at the top of the page. Find out what the students' attitude to stress is. Is it a problem in their lives? Do they see it as a positive factor in increasing productivity at work? What is the most stressful thing they have ever had to do at work? How do they cope with stress?

Discussion

1 Make sure students understand the items in the box. You could ask them to list them in order of the amount of stress they produce. Can they suggest any other factors?

2 ▭ **10.1** Make sure students have read the questions in the table before you play the recording so that they know exactly what information they are listening for.

After playing the recording, allow students to compare notes before checking the answers with the class.

3 Have a class discussion to find out how many students agree with the last speaker.

4 Ask students to work in small groups to discuss and decide on an order for the jobs. Tell them to give reasons why they think one particular job is more stressful than another. Encourage them to use *have to* to talk about what each job entails.

Find out how much agreement there is among the groups before they turn to page 129 and compare their answers with the statistics there. Elicit students' reactions to the information.

have to

5 Make sure that students know that *doesn't have to* means that something is not necessary. It is not a prohibition and doesn't mean the same as *mustn't* or *shouldn't*. Early finishers could compare the other jobs in exercise 4.

Ask various students to read out their sentences and ask the others if they agree with them. There is more information on the use of *have to* and *don't have to* in the Grammar link on page 108.

▭ **10.1**

Interview 1

A: According to statistics, around 75% of all visits to the doctor are the result of work-related stress. Do you think you suffer from stress? That's the question we're asking in the streets of Edinburgh. Excuse me, I'm from the radio programme *Work Today*. We're doing a survey on stress. Would you mind answering some questions?

B: Eh, well, actually, I'm in a bit of a hurry, but … em … go on, then.

A: Thank you. What's your job?

B: I'm an accountant.

A: Do you suffer from stress in your work?

B: Eh, yes, I do, I think.

A: What symptoms do you notice?

B: Em, I get a lot of headaches and I sleep very badly.

A: And what causes your stress?

B: It's my boss. He's a real … well, let's just say he doesn't exactly make life easy. He always wants things done for yesterday.

A: Thank you very much.

Interview 2

A: … and what do you do?

C: I work in a shop.

A: Do you suffer from stress?

C: No, not at work, I don't. I find being at home more stressful.

A: Why's that?

C: Well, I've got three children and my mother's ill. She lives with us. And my husband …well, he doesn't help much.

A: And do you have any physical symptoms?

C: Well, I get a bit on edge at times and then I get this horrible rash on my neck.

A: So, stress is a problem in your life.

C: Yes, definitely.

Interview 3

A: … and you, sir. Do you suffer from stress?

D: Well, to tell the truth, I'm off work at the moment because of it.

A: Really, what do you do?

D: I'm a teacher. I work with teenagers and I don't know why but every year they seem to get worse.

A: Yes, that does sound stressful.

D: Everyone thinks teaching's an easy option because of the holidays, but you get to a point where you just can't handle it any longer. You lose control. I almost hit a lad with a spanner, so I went to the doctor and he said it was stress.

A: Well, I hope things get better for you.

D: Thanks, but I think that basically the solution is probably to change jobs. Fortunately, I'm still young enough to do that.

A: Right. Good luck, then.

Interview 4

A: Can I ask you if you suffer from stress?

E: Who? Me? No, not at all. I don't really understand what it is, really.

A: And what do you do for a living?

E: I'm a self-employed architect. I work for myself.

A: I see, and what's your secret?

E: I'm sorry?

A: I mean, how do you avoid getting stressed?

E: I think it's all down to a philosophy of life. I just take each day as it comes. I don't worry about things. What I say is that if you've got a problem, solve it. And if you can't because there's no solution, there's no point in worrying because that won't help.

A: So, you think avoiding stress is to do with mental attitude, not what you do?

E: Yes, that's basically it.

A: Well, thanks very much.

E: Not at all.

6 Students take turns to interview each other about the responsibilities of their own jobs. When they have finished, ask them to change partners and tell their new partner about their original partner's job.

a lawyer   secretary   wear a suit   type letters   (example answers)

A lawyer has to wear a suit. A secretary has to type letters.

_____

b middle managers   chief executives   solve day-to-day problems
take strategic decisions

_Middle managers have to solve day-to-day problems. Chief executives have
to take strategic decisions._

c shop assistant   computer programmer   deal with the public
know computer languages

A shop assistant doesn't have to know computer languages.
A computer programmer doesn't have to deal with the public.

d lorry driver   taxi driver   drive long distances   memorise street maps

_A lorry driver has to drive long distances. A taxi driver has to memorise
street maps._

e nurse   factory worker   wear special clothes   work at night

_A nurse has to wear special clothes and work at night. A factory worker
has to wear special clothes and work at night._

f accountant   telephonist   use a computer   be honest

_An accountant has to use a computer and be honest. A telephonist doesn't
have to use a computer._

g teacher   engineer   tell people what to do   wear a tie

_A teacher doesn't have to wear a tie. An engineer has to tell people
what to do._

Make sentences about the other jobs in 4.

6 Now interview someone about their job like this:

In your job do you have to ...?   No, but I have to ... / Yes, and I also have to ...

Lexis link

for more on the
vocabulary of stress at
work see page 109

7 You are going to read an article about stress. All the words and phrases on the left are in the article. Match them to the definitions on the right.

a   linked to
b   root cause of
c   overwork
d   staff turnover
e   makes business sense
f   performance-related pay
g   morale

1   doing too much work
2   is good for the company
3   principal reason for
4   connected to
5   money for getting better results
6   people joining and leaving a company
7   positive or negative attitude

a	4	b	3	c	1	d	6	e	2	f	5	g	7

8 In your opinion, are the sentences below true or false?   True   False

a   Stress is always a bad thing.   ☐   ✓

b   Work-related stress can cause health problems.   ✓   ☐

c   Bad management is the main cause of stress.   ✓   ☐

d   Reducing stress costs companies money.   ☐   ✓

e   It's easy for companies to reduce stress.   ☐   ✓

(writer's opinion)

9 Read the article below. Does the writer agree with your opinions in 8?

Stressed to the limit

File Edit View Favorites Tools Help

Home Back Forward Stop Refresh Search Favorites History Mail Print

Address http://www.stressss.com

STRESSED
TO THE LIMIT

Deborah Houlding of BMG online magazine explores the problem of work-related stress and examines ways in which it can be avoided.

Stress is not an illness or a negative condition.
5 A certain amount of pressure brings out the best in our work. In the initial stages of stress there is a sensation of excitement and increased mental concentration.

However, too much stress is negative. It is bad
10 for the individual. It is also bad for the employing organisation. In the UK, for example, stress-related illness is the cause of half of lost working days.

The negative impact of stress is linked to heart disease, alcoholism, nervous breakdowns, job
15 dissatisfaction, certain forms of cancer, migraines, asthma, hay fever, insomnia, depression, eczema and many other medical and social problems.

Many surveys confirm the root cause of work-related stress to be bad management and
20 overwork. Too much pressure, long hours and poor communication are the main factors. Reports and studies have identified the principal cause of stress as 'new management techniques' designed to 'improve performance'. Policies such as
25 'performance-related pay' increase stress and demotivate a work force.

Many legal and medical experts are advising companies to consider the costs and legal implications of stress-related illness. They
30 emphasise the benefits of reducing stress as:
• better health
• reduced sickness absence
• increased performance and output
• better relationships with clients and colleagues
35 • lower staff turnover

Taking the decision to reduce stress makes sound business sense. It's better for profits and better for staff morale.

Managers should learn to motivate but not
40 exhaust employees. There is a balance between obtaining maximum efficiency, and a worker's need to rest and recuperate their creative energies.

Done   Internet

7   Matching up the words from the article and their definitions will help students when they come to read the full text. Allow students to compare their answers in pairs before checking with the class.

Direct students' attention to the Lexis link on page 109 where they will find more useful vocabulary connected with stress at work.

8   You could have a class vote on whether the sentences are true or false. Encourage students with strong opinions to give reasons for their answers.

9   Ask students to read the article quickly to find out if the writer agrees with their conclusions in exercise 8. (The writer appears to think that a, d and e are false, and that b and c are true. It isn't clear whether she thinks it's easy for companies to reduce stress or not, though she certainly believes it is beneficial to do so.)

Ask students to read the article again more carefully and elicit their reactions to it. Does anything in the article surprise them? Do they agree or disagree with any of it?

10 Allow students to compare their answers to the exercise in pairs before checking with the class.

Encourage students to use charts like this whenever they record new vocabulary in their notebooks. Knowledge of a word is greatly enhanced if you also know other forms of it and can use them all correctly.

11 Check the answers by asking various students to read the sentences aloud.

12 Students should work individually to write sentences about their own company and then show them to a partner. Partners should ask for more information where appropriate.

Should/shouldn't

13 Read the example sentences with the class and elicit further sentences using *should* and *shouldn't*.

Allow students to compare their answers to the exercise in pairs before checking with the class.

Direct students' attention to the Grammar link on page 108 where they will find more information and practice in the form and use of *should* and *shouldn't*.

10 Complete the chart with the correct form of the word.

noun	verb	adjective
stress	stress	<u>stressful</u> /stressed
motivation	<u>motivate</u>	motivating/<u>motivated</u>
creation/ <u>creativity</u>	create	<u>creative</u>
<u>excitement</u>	excite	<u>exciting</u> /excited

11 Complete each sentence with one of the words from above.

a Working with the public can be very <u>stressful</u> .

b When the new boss arrived, staff morale was very low and nobody was very <u>motivated</u> .

c I'm a graphic designer so my job requires a lot of <u>creativity</u> .

d I don't find the new project very <u>exciting</u> .

12 Make similar sentences about your own company.

Should/shouldn't

13 Look at these sentences.

*Managers **should** recognise their mistakes.* (It's a good idea.)
*Employees **shouldn't** work under unnecessary pressure.* (It's not a good idea.)

Make sentences that are true for you using *should/shouldn't* and the prompts below. For example, work well / have a certain amount of pressure
To work well you should have a certain amount of pressure.

a companies / try / reduce the level of stress

<u>Companies should try to reduce the level of stress.</u>

b workers / work very long hours

<u>Workers shouldn't have to work very long hours.</u>

c managers / communicate / ideas

<u>Managers should communicate ideas clearly.</u>

d companies / invest money / improve conditions

<u>Companies should invest money to improve conditions for workers.</u>

e managers / learn / motivate workers

<u>Managers should learn how to motivate workers.</u>

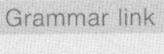

Grammar link

for more on *have to* and *should* see page 108

f workers / have time / rest

<u>Workers should have time to rest.</u>

14 Make sentences about your company like this:

In my company ... should / shouldn't ... but often / in fact they/he/she/we ...

Include the ideas below and add your own.
- distribution of work
- communications
- performance-related pay
- sufficient training
- new technology

The consultant's report

You are going to write a report on a company with problems. Follow steps 1–4 below.

Step 1

Work with a partner. Create your own company.
a What line of business is the company in?
b What's the name of the company?
c Where is it located?
d Is it an old-fashioned or a modern company?
e How long has it existed?

Step 2

You are going to perform a roleplay with a new partner. First, with your original partner, decide who is the employee and who is the consultant. Then find a new partner who is playing a different role to you.

Employee You work for the company you invented. You are completely negative about every aspect of your job and company. Criticise everything and everybody.

Consultant You are a management consultant hired to interview the staff of the employee's company to assess the levels of stress and morale. Interview the employee and note down the answers. Ask questions about

- working hours
- training provided
- internal communication
- company organisation
- holidays
- pay
- *(your own ideas)*

Step 3

Work with your original partner from Step 1. Write a report of the management consultant's interview. Use the framework below or adapt it to suit the interview.

- According to ... the main cause/s of stress in his/her work is/are ...
- Communications in the company are ...
- The system of payment is ...
- With regard to training, the situation is ...
- Other causes of problems are ...
- To reduce the level of stress the company should ...
- In conclusion, ...

MQSC consulting

Interview report

Company:

_____

Name of Interviewee:

_____

Interviewer:

_____

Date:

_____

Step 4

Work with your partner from Step 2 again. Check that the report of your interview is accurate.

14 This exercise could be set for homework. Ask students to bring their sentences to the next lesson and report back to the class about what they think their company should and shouldn't do.

The consultant's report

In this section, students continue their examination of stress in the workplace and work together to create and write a report on a company which has problems with stress management.

Read the instructions step by step with the class and make sure everyone understands what they have to do in each stage. Monitor the stages carefully, giving help and encouragement where necessary. Set a time limit for each stage and don't allow students to move on to the next stage until the whole class is ready, otherwise you may have some students rushing through to the end when some students are still working on step 2.

You could display the finished reports on the wall to allow everyone in the class to read them.

If you're short of time

Set exercise 5 on page 44 and exercise 14 on page 48 for homework.

Set the writing of the final report on page 48 for homework and have students present it in the next class.

Set the *Grammar and Lexis links* exercises for homework and check the answers at the beginning of the next class.

Company life

11 Top jobs

This unit is about high profile jobs. It begins with a description of a successful Japanese bicycle manufacturer. Students use this text to work on the Present Perfect with *for* and *since* and practise asking questions with *How long ...?* They then read profiles of two of the most successful men in the American software industry and learn some more useful vocabulary for talking about business life and people's jobs and responsibilities.

Finally, the focus shifts to the art of headhunting, luring top executives away from their present jobs with promises of better money or working conditions. Students listen to a phone call from a headhunter and then they interview each other and write profiles about their partner's career history to date for a headhunter's data base.

The grammatical focus is on the Present Perfect for the unfinished past and time expressions with *for* and *since*, and the lexical focus is on company news.

In this first section, students are presented with an account of the activities of the Japanese bicycle manufacturer Shimano which is then used to teach the use of the Present Perfect for talking about the unfinished past and time expressions with *for* and *since*.

Warm-up

Focus students' attention on the quotation from Darryl F Zanuck at the top of the page. Ask students if they agree with him. Find out if any student has had an experience of a work colleague either agreeing or disagreeing with them all the time, and what happened.

Brainstorm all the information about bicycles that students know. Find out if they can name the bicycle parts visible in the pictures on page 49 (wheels, handlebars, brakes, gears, pedals, mudguard, tyres, saddle) and whether they know the names of any famous bicycle manufacturers (Raleigh, Shimano).

Present Perfect for unfinished past

1   Students have worked on company histories before, so this exercise should be relatively easy for them. The words in the box are in the Present Simple which is appropriate for listing the events in a company's history. Students will go on to see how other tenses, including the Present Perfect are more suited to continuous descriptive text.

2   Allow students to work in pairs to discuss the sentences and complete the gaps.

11 Top jobs

> If two men on the same job agree all the time, then one is useless. If they disagree all the time, then both are useless. *Darryl F Zanuck, US film producer*

Present Perfect for unfinished past

1 Read the information about Shimano. Complete it using the words in the box.

opens   enters   incorporates   manufactures   sets up   celebrates   moves   founds

BRIEF HISTORY

SHIMANO

1921 Shozaburo Shimano __founds__ the Shimano Iron Works to produce bicycle components.

1936 Shimano __moves__ to present-day headquarters in Sakai City, Osaka.

1957 __Manufactures__ first bicycle gears.

1971 __Opens__ factory in Düsseldorf. Produces first Dura-Ace components for racing bikes.

1972 __Enters__ market for fishing equipment. Launches first specific components for mountain biking – Shimano Deore XT.

1997 __Sets up__ Action Sports Division to produce new products for snowboarding.

1999 Launches first products for golf market under the name Ultegra.

2001 __Celebrates__ 80th anniversary.

2002 __Incorporates__ hydraulic brake system in the XTR top mountain bike range.

2 Complete the sentences about Shimano using the verbs in the boxes.

still produces   has produced   started to produce

    a Shimano __started to produce__ bicycle components in 1921.

\+ **b** It __still produces__ bicycle components today.

\= **c** It __has produced__ bicycle components since 1921.

has had   still has   opened

    d Shimano __opened__ a factory in Düsseldorf over 30 years ago.

\+ **e** It __still has__ a factory in Düsseldorf today.

\= **f** It __has had__ a factory in Düsseldorf for over 30 years.

3 Match the sentences in 2 to the tenses below.

a d Past Simple   b e Present Simple   c f Present Perfect

4 Make similar sentences about Shimano with these prompts using the Present Perfect, *since* and *for*.

a have / headquarters / Sakai City   (example answers)

Shimano has had its headquarters in Sakai City since 1936.

b manufacture / bicycle gears

It has manufactured bicycle gears for over 40 years.

c make / fishing equipment

It has made fishing equipment since 1972.

d produce / components / mountain bikes

It has produced components for mountain bikes for over 30 years.

e have / snowboarding / products division

It has had a snowboarding products division since 1997.

f be / in the golf equipment market

It has been in the golf equipment market for over three years.

Since & for **5** Put the following time expressions in the correct column.

| five minutes   last year   1945   20 years   a long time   I was born   yesterday |
| he arrived   months   a few years   5 o'clock   this morning   a couple of days |

Grammar link

for more on the Present Perfect see page 110

since	for
last year 1945 I was born yesterday	five minutes 20 years a long time
he arrived 5 o'clock this morning	months a few years a couple of days

6 Write sentences which are true for you. Use the Present Perfect, *since* and *for*.

Tell me more

How long **1** Make questions with 'you' using the prompts. Use the Present Simple, Past Simple and Present Perfect, as appropriate.

a What kind of car / have? How long / have / it? Why / choose it?

What kind of car do you have? How long have you had it? Why did you choose it?

b have / a mobile phone? How long / have / it? use it / a lot?

Do you have a mobile phone? How long have you had it? Do you use it a lot?

c Where / live? How long / live / there?

Where do you live? How long have you lived there?

d Where / work? How long / work / there? What / job?

Where do you work? How long have you worked there? What's your job?

e How long / have / present job? Like / it?

How long have you had your present job? Do you like it?

f know

How long have you known (your best friend)?

g be interested in

Are you interested in (football)? How long have you been interested in it?

3   Do the matching exercise with the whole class and elicit that we use the Past Simple for actions in the past that are now completed, the Present Simple for present situations, and the Present Perfect for the unfinished past, to talk about when present situations began or how long they have continued. Point out the use of *since* in sentence c to talk about a point in time (1921) and *for* in sentence f to talk about a period of time (30 years).

4   Students use the prompts to make further sentences about Shimano. Go round making sure they are using the Present Perfect and *for* and *since* correctly.

Check the answers with the class by asking various students to read out the sentences.

Since & for

5   Allow students to compare their answers to the exercise in pairs before checking with the class.

Check the answers by reading out the words in the box and having students put up their right hand if the word goes with *since* and their left hand if it goes with *for*.

Direct students' attention to the Grammar link on page 110 where they will find more information about the use of the Present Perfect, and practice exercises to help them use this tense correctly.

6   Students write sentences which are true for them. Ask them to show their sentences to a partner and check that the Present Perfect, *for* and *since* are used correctly.

You might like to ask various students to read out their sentences to the class.

Tell me more

In this section, students continue to work on the Present Perfect tense and look at the difference between it and the Present Simple and Past Simple. The exercises here personalise the subject for the students, who are encouraged to talk about their own possessions and experiences.

How long

1   Work through the prompts for the first item in the activity with the class. Ask which question is about an action in the past which is now completed (Why / choose it?) and elicit that this requires the Past Simple. Ask one of the students to supply the correct question.

Then ask which question is about a present situation (What kind of car / have?) and elicit that this requires the Present Simple. Again, ask one of the students to supply the correct question.

Finally, ask which question is about a situation that began in the past but is still continuing (How long / have / it?). Elicit that this requires the Present Perfect and ask a third student to supply the correct question.

The final two questions (f and g) give students more flexibility to form their own questions about subjects which interest them.

2 In pairs, students ask and answer the questions they formed in exercise 1. Encourage students to ask follow-up questions to find out more details. Allow students to take notes of their partner's answers if they wish as these will be useful for the next exercise.

3 Students use what they remember of their partner's replies to their questions in exercise 2 or the notes they made to tell a new partner what they have learned about their original partner.

Bill's friend

In this section, students listen to and read a text about Steve Ballmer, a close friend of Bill Gates, who is now the CEO of Microsoft, the world's leading software company. The text tells how the transfer of the management of the company from Bill Gates to Steve Ballmer occurred and gives further examples of the Present Perfect in action. Students then do some work on some of the useful vocabulary in the text and use it to complete sentences.

1 💼 **11.1** Focus student's attention on the words and phrases they have to listen out for. The listening text is quite long, so reassure them that all they have to do as they listen is to number the items in the order they hear them. You could ask students to put their hands up as soon as they hear an item. In this way, weaker students will be helped by stronger students alerting them to the fact that one of the target items has just been mentioned.

Allow students to check their answers as they read the script in the next exercise.

2 Make sure students realise that there are ten mistakes in the script and that these are factual rather than grammatical errors. Ask them to read it carefully and underline any information that they think is different from what they heard in exercise 1. Allow them to compare notes in pairs or small groups before playing the recording again for them to check.

3 Allow students to do this in pairs if they wish. Then check the answers with the class.

💼 **11.1**

Who is the boss of the world's leading manufacturer of personal and business computing software? Ask most people and they will say the mega rich Bill Gates. But no, the planet's wealthiest man stepped down from the top job in January 2000 to take on a new appointment and pursue what he claims is his real passion. Apparently this is not making money, but designing software. **Since then, the chief executive of Microsoft Corporation has been his old university chum, Steve Ballmer.**
History tells us that Gates dropped out of Harvard to set up Microsoft with Paul Allen in 1975. Meanwhile, his other friend Steve, who lived down the hall, graduated with a degree in mathematics and economics. He

then went on to work for two years at Proctor and Gamble, and attend the Stanford University Graduate School of Business. **Ballmer has worked for Microsoft since 1980**, when Gates remembered his college mate and hired him as the company's first business manager. **Over the last 20 years Ballmer has been in charge of several Microsoft divisions**, including operations, operation system development, and sales and support. In July 1998 he was promoted to president, a role that gave him day-to-day responsibility for running the company. However, **since Gates became 'Chief Software Architect', Ballmer has assumed full management control of Microsoft**. (Just in case, Bill has retained some power as Chairman.)
Legend has it that in spring 1986, soon after

hiring Ballmer, Gates called him into his office. Microsoft's deadline to produce Windows was getting behind schedule, and Gates reportedly threatened to fire his friend if the software wasn't on the shelves by the end of the year. Needless to say, Windows was ready by the end of the year, and **they have remained the best of friends**. Proof of this is that Steve was best man at Bill's wedding.
Ballmer has influenced Microsoft with his own brand of energy and discipline.
He says, 'I want everyone to share my passion for our products and services. I want people to understand the amazing, positive way our software can make leisure time more enjoyable, and businesses more successful.' Ballmer jogs daily and loves basketball.

---

2 Work with a partner. Ask and answer the questions in 1. Try to get more information about each subject, if you can.

3 Change partners. Tell each other about your previous partner. For example: *Lucien lives just outside Toulouse. He has lived there for three years. He works as a research scientist at the university. He's worked there since last June.*

Bill's friend

1 📼 **11.1** The words and phrases below are from a radio profile of Steve Ballmer, the CEO of Microsoft. Listen to the profile and number the words in the order you hear them.

7 deadline	5 sales and support	3 Proctor and Gamble
2 chief executive	6 chairman	1 wealthiest man
4 first business manager	8 wedding	9 basketball

2 Read the script of the radio profile and correct the ten mistakes. Then listen again and check your answers.

BILL AND STEVE – two men and a destiny

Who is the boss of the world's leading manufacturer of personal and business computing software? Ask most people and they will say the mega rich Bill Gates. But no,
5 the planet's wealthiest man stepped down from the top job in January 2000 to take on a new appointment and pursue what he claims is his real passion. Apparently this is not making money, but ~~his art collection~~ [designing software]. Since then, the chief executive of
10 Microsoft Corporation has been his old university chum, Steve Ballmer.

History tells us that Gates dropped out of ~~Yale~~ [Harvard] to set up Microsoft with Paul Allen in 1975. Meanwhile, his other friend Steve, who lived down
15 the hall, graduated with a degree in ~~social science~~ [mathematics and economics]. He then went on to work for two years at Proctor and Gamble, and attend the ~~Manchester~~ [Stanford] University Graduate School of Business.

Ballmer has worked for Microsoft since
20 1980, when Gates remembered his college mate and hired him as the company's first business manager. Over the last 20 years Ballmer has been in charge of several Microsoft divisions, including operations, ~~marketing~~ [operation system development], and
25 sales and support. In July 1998 he was promoted to ~~managing director~~ [president], a role that gave him day-to-day responsibility for running the company. However, since
30 Gates became 'Chief Software Architect', Ballmer has assumed full management control of Microsoft. (Just in case, Bill has retained some power as Chairman.)

Legend has it that in spring 1986, soon after
35 hiring Ballmer, Gates called him into his office. Microsoft's deadline to produce ~~Office 97~~ [Windows] was getting behind schedule, and Gates reportedly threatened to fire his friend if the software wasn't on the shelves by the end of the year. Needless to
40 say, Windows was ready by the end of the year, and they have remained the best of friends. Proof of this is that Steve was ~~godfather~~ [best man] at Bill's wedding.

Ballmer has influenced Microsoft with his own brand of energy and discipline. He says, 'I want
45 everyone to share my passion for ~~cats and dogs~~ [our products and services]. I want people to understand the amazing, positive way our software can make leisure time more enjoyable, and businesses more successful.' Ballmer ~~plays squash~~ [jogs daily] and loves basketball.

3 Underline three examples of the Present Perfect in the script which tell us when a present situation started.

4 How much of the script can you remember without looking? Use the words in 1 to reconstruct the story with a partner.

Vocabulary **5** Find words and phrases in the script in 2 which mean the same as the following:

a resign/leave a job _step down_

b found/establish _set up_

c finish a university course _graduate_

d university qualification _degree_

e employ _hire_

f responsible for _in charge of_

g give someone a better job _promote_

h dismiss or sack _fire_

i spare time _leisure time_

6 Use the words and phrases in 5 to complete the following sentences.

a If they _promote_ you, you'll get more money.

b He _set up_ the company with the money he got from his family.

c Who is _in charge of_ marketing at the company?

d Last year the company _hired_ 350 new production line workers.

e John _graduated_ from Oxford with a degree in economics.

f She has an MBA as well as a _degree_ in law.

g They _fired_ her because she wasn't doing her job properly.

h The managing director _stepped down_ after the financial scandal.

i With this new job I don't have much _leisure time_, and I miss being able to do sport.

7 Write sentences which are true for you using the words and phrases in 6.

Lexis link

for more on the vocabulary of company news see page 111

Headhunters

4 Students should cover the script in exercise 2 as they try to reconstruct the story from the words in exercise 1. Alternatively, ask students in pairs to reconstruct half of the story each. The student who is not speaking at any one time can look at the script and give help by prompting if his/her partner gets stuck.

Vocabulary

5 Allow students to work in pairs to find the words. You could make this a race between pairs to see who can find all the words first. The winning pair should read out their answers and the others should fill in any gaps they have.

6, 7 Students use the words they have just learned to complete sentences and write sentences of their own.

Direct students' attention to the Lexis link on page 111 where they will find more on the vocabulary of company news.

Headhunters

In this section, students look at the practice of tempting top executives to move jobs by promising them a better salary or a better position. This is done by professional companies called *headhunters* who act on behalf of a client who is looking for someone to fill a vacant post. Headhunters discreetly contact suitably qualified people who may be interested in moving jobs and applying for this post. Students listen to a phone call from a headhunter, answer questions about what is said and then discuss whether they think it is an ethical way to behave. They then interview each other about their present jobs and write short texts which would be useful to a headhunter.

Warm-up

Focus students' attention on the rather grisly photo at the bottom of page 52 and tell students that *headhunters* originally referred to primitive tribes who cut off their enemies' heads as battle trophies. Ask what students think a headhunter is in the context of the business world (see above).

1 📼 **11.2** Focus students' attention on the picture at the top of the page. Find out if they work in open-plan offices where everyone can hear everybody else's phone calls. What are the advantages of this? What problems can it create? What do they do if they receive a personal phone call at work?

Make sure students have read the questions before you play the recording so that they know exactly what information they are listening for.

Allow students to compare their answers in pairs or small groups before checking the answers or playing the recording again.

Discussion

2 This could be done as a class discussion or a discussion in small groups. Ask students to tell each other if they have any personal experience of being contacted by a headhunter. What was their reaction? Does anyone hold their present position because they were headhunted?

Fluency

3 Elicit a few example questions from the class to make sure that they are forming them properly before they divide into pairs and start their interviews.

Writing

4 This writing exercise could be set for homework. You could display the finished descriptions on the wall to allow everyone in the class to read them.

If you're short of time

Omit the section *Tell me more* on pages 50 and 51.

Set the writing task in *Headhunters* exercise 4 for homework.

Set the *Grammar and Lexis links* exercises for homework and check the answers at the beginning of the next class.

📼 **11.2**

A: Good morning. Could I speak to Peter Davis, please?
B: Speaking.
A: Oh, hello, Mr Davis. My name is John Lindsay.
B: What can I do for you, Mr Lindsay?
A: It's more a case of what I can do for you ... Em, **how long have you worked for Blueprint International**, Mr Davis?
B: **For about six years**. Why do you ask?
A: And before that you worked for Navigate for three years.
B: Yes, I joined them as a trainee manager when I left university. But ... what is this about?
A: And you were made head of the International Division a year ago. How is it going?
B: Very well, thank you. Now, could you tell me what you want, Mr Lindsay?
A: I'd like to talk to you about an extremely interesting career opportunity. I work for

People Search, the management consultants. **We've been approached by a client** who's looking for someone with just your professional profile.
B: Oh, I see. So that's what it's about. Listen, Mr Lindsay, I'm really quite busy and ...
A: Yes, I understand that but you should know I'm talking about a considerable salary increase. **You've been married for a couple of years now** and recently became a father, I believe.
B: What's that got to do with it?
A: Well, think about your family and the financial possibilities of an advantageous career move at this moment in your life. I think you should at least talk to me.
B: Em, well, I suppose so. What's the name of the company?
A: I'd rather not say over the phone. Perhaps we could meet to discuss things further?
B: I'm not sure I'm that interested ... **Blueprint International have been very good to me**.

A: Oh, come on, Peter! What are the real prospects in your present post? **You've got as far as you can in Blueprint**. Do you want to be in the same place ten years from now? At least find the time to talk to us.
B: I'd like to think about it. Can I phone you back?
A: No, I'd prefer to phone you back myself in a couple of days. In the meantime, **think about what I've said**. A more stimulating work situation, not to mention a considerable rise in salary ... Talk it over with your wife.
B: Fair enough.
A: Oh, and one more thing, Peter. I'd appreciate it if you didn't mention this call to anyone in your company, okay?
B: Yes, yes, all right. So, you'll call me, then?
A: That's right. In a couple of days. We'll arrange a meeting somewhere. Bye for now, then.
B: Bye.

1 ⊡ 11.2 Peter Davis is in the office when he receives an unexpected call from John Lindsay. Listen to the conversation and answer the questions.

a Why does John Lindsay call Peter Davis?

He wants to headhunt him for another job.

b When did Peter Davis start work for Blueprint International?

about six years ago

c What did he do before?

He was a trainee manager for Navigate.

d How long has he been in charge of the international division?

a year

e When did he get married?

a couple of years ago

f Has he got any children?

Yes, he's just had his first child.

g Is he interested in what the caller has to say?

He is slightly interested.

Discussion 2 Discuss the following questions with other people in the class.

a What type of management consultants does John Lindsay work for?

a headhunting company

b Do you think what he does is ethical?

c How would you react in this situation?

Fluency 3 Interview your partner about his/her career history and make notes. Ask questions about work, education, home, family and possessions. Use the prompts in the box to help you.

> How long have you ...?   When / Where did you ... before?
> When did you start / leave / finish ...?

Writing 4 Using your notes, write a report for *People Search* on your partner. Use the model below.

> Peter Davis has worked for Blueprint International since 1997 where he has been head of their International Division for one year. Before Blueprint International he was at Navigate for three years. This was his first job after university where he studied engineering. He graduated from Nottingham University in 1993. He has been married for two years and has one child.

12 Conversation gambits

The things most people want to know about are usually none of their business.
George Bernard Shaw

gambit /ˈɡæmbɪt/ noun [C]
something you say or do
in an attempt to gain an
advantage

from *Macmillan English Dictionary*

1 Read the article about a type of bar and think about the following questions. Then discuss them with a partner.

a Do you think the Remote Lounge is a good idea?
b Are there bars like this where you live?
c Do you express yourself better by e-mail/on the Internet or face to face?
d If you were travelling alone, would you go to a bar like this?

REMOTELOUNGE

The Remote Lounge, located in the heart of downtown Manhattan, helps its clients to break the ice. For those who find it hard to take the first step, the Remote Lounge provides an innovative solution. Customers can 'spy' on other customers, as well as be 'spied' on themselves. The Remote Lounge offers its clients sixty cameras and
5 a hundred video screens. Individual consoles allow the customer to see who else is in the bar, order a drink, or send a message to another stranger, all without being seen. They can also take pictures which later appear on the bar's website.

According to the owners, in this situation their customers feel less shy about talking to someone they don't know. The person on the receiving end of a message can reject it, of
10 course, but they usually choose to continue the conversation using the console's telephone handset. The owners say that people using the Internet have learned to express themselves with greater freedom, using e-mail and chat rooms. They claim to have applied the same concept to their bar.

In the Remote Lounge, which officially opened on October 9th 2001, and is now open
15 seven days a week from 6 pm to 4 am, it's difficult to spend an evening staring at your glass of beer.

Conversation skills 12 Conversation gambits

In this unit, students learn some useful language and tips for starting up, continuing and ending conversations with strangers. Business people travelling on their own can feel isolated if they don't have anyone to talk to and a casual conversation at the conference bar has often led to a good business contact and even increased business for a company.

The unit begins with a text describing an innovative idea for helping people travelling on their own to start up conversations with people in a similar situation. Students then listen to and complete some conversations between strangers at a conference and learn some good ways of starting up a conversation. They then discuss suitable and unsuitable topics of conversation and polite ways to end a conversation.

In this first section, students read about the Remote Lounge, a bar in Manhattan where customers can send messages to each other and talk on the phone without seeing each other. Students discuss this idea and then listen and complete some conversations in which people who have never met before introduce themselves. They then look at techniques for starting up a conversation with a stranger.

Warm-up

Focus students' attention on the general definition of *gambit* in the margin. Ask students what they think *gambit* means in the expression *conversation gambit* (a technique for getting someone to have a conversation with you). Elicit suggestions as to why enticing someone into a conversation with you could be advantageous to you in different situations, business-related and personal. Focus students' attention on the quotation from George Bernard Shaw at the top of the page and ask students if they agree with it. What kind of things do most people want to know about other people?

1   Focus students' attention on the picture and ask them where they think this is and what they think the people are doing. Then give them time to read the text thoroughly and think about the questions. When they have discussed the questions in pairs, ask them to report back to the class on their opinions.

Introducing yourself

2 📼 **12.1** Elicit several ideas for ways to start a conversation with a stranger before you play the recording for students to complete the conversations. Stronger students could be asked to try to predict what should go in the gaps before listening.

All the conversations end with the people introducing themselves, but they each start with a slightly different conversation gambit. Ask students to describe what these are (1 asking for information about the conference; 2 commenting on the surroundings; 3 mentioning a problem you're having and asking if the other person has it, too; 4 asking if someone knows anything about the speaker at a conference).

You could ask students to take each of these conversation gambits and suggest another opening line for each.

Ask students whether they think the conversations would have been equally successful if the first speaker in each case had simply walked up to the other person and said 'Hi, I'm …'.

Starting a conversation

3 Read the situation with the class and ask for suggestions as to how Allan might start a conversation.

4 📼 **12.2** When students have completed the conversation and listened to it to check their answers, they could practise it in pairs.

📼 12.1

1
A: Excuse me, **are you here for the ITM conference?**
B: Yes, that's right.
A: Me too. Do you know where to register?
B: I think it's over there.
A: Oh, yes. Right, **I'm Paulo, by the way.**
B: Hello, Paulo, I'm Kate. Let's go and register.

2
C: Phew! Is it me, or is it boiling in here?
D: Yes, they always seem to have the heating on full.
C: **So, it's not your first time.**
D: No, it's my fourth time here.
C: Oh, right, **so you're an old hand.** I'm Boris.
D: David. **Pleased to meet you.**

3
E: Is it my mobile phone, or is there some problem with coverage here?
F: Oh, hang on. No, mine seems to be working okay.
E: Typical, flat batteries and nowhere to charge up.
F: **Can I lend you mine?**
E: **Oh, that's very kind**, but I was expecting a call on this number.
F: I see.
E: **My name's Nadine, by the way. From Xanadu Electronics.**
F: Pleased to meet you. I'm Miko.

4
G: Excuse me, **do you know anything about this speaker?**
H: No, I'm sorry, I don't.
G: **I can't find my programme notes.**
H: Oh, here. **Borrow mine.**

G: Thanks. **By the way, I'm Bill Smart from Silicon Technologies.**
H: Right, **how do you do?** I'm Kazuo Yamada from Lexico.

📼 12.2

A: Excuse me. **Would you mind if I had a quick look at your newspaper?**
B: Er, **no, go ahead.** I've finished with it.
A: There's just something I want to check out.
B: **No problem. Take your time.**
A: Thanks. **By the way, my name's Allan. I'm here on a business trip.**
B: Oh, right.

Introducing yourself

2 🔊 **12.1** You are at a conference and you don't know anybody. What can you say to start a conversation with someone? Listen and complete the four conversations below.

1 A Excuse me, _are you here for_ _____ the ITM conference?

   B Yes, that's right.

   A Me too. _Do you know where to register?_ _____

   B I think it's over there.

   A Oh, yes. Right, I'm Paulo, _by the way._ _____

   B Hello, Paulo, I'm Kate. _Let's go and register._ _____

2 A Phew! _Is it me, or is it boiling in here?_ _____

   B Yes, they always seem to have the heating on full.

   A So, it's not _your first time._ _____

   B No, it's my fourth time here.

   A Oh, right, so _you're an old hand._ _____. I'm Boris.

   B David. _Pleased to meet you._ _____

3 A Is it _my mobile phone_ , or is there some problem with coverage here?

   B Oh, _hang on._ . No, mine seems _to be working_ okay.

   A Typical, flat batteries and nowhere to charge up.

   B _Can I lend you mine?_ _____

   A Oh, _that's very kind_ , but I was expecting a call on this number.

   B I see.

   A _My name's_ Nadine, by the way. From Xanadu Electronics.

   B Pleased to meet you. I'm Miko.

4 A Excuse me, _do you know anything about this speaker?_ _____

   B No, I'm sorry, I don't.

   A _I can't find my programme notes._ _____

   B Oh, here. _Borrow mine._ _____

   A Thanks. By the way, I'm Bill Smart from Silicon Technologies.

   B Right, _how do you do?_ ? I'm Kazuo Yamada from Lexico.

Starting a conversation

3 Allan Vilkas is having a quiet drink in a hotel in Dublin after dinner. The other customer in the bar has a newspaper, but he's not reading it. What do you think Allan says to begin a conversation?

4 🔊 **12.2** Complete the conversation using the phrases in the box. Then listen and check your answers.

> finished with it   your time   if I had a quick look at   here on
> to check out   go ahead   the way

Allan Excuse me, would you mind _if I had a quick look at_ your newspaper?

Stranger Er, no, _go ahead_ . I've _finished with it_ .

Allan There's just something I want _to check out_ .

Stranger No problem. Take _your time_ .

Allan Thanks. By _the way_ , my name's Allan. I'm _here on_ a business trip.

Stranger Oh, right.

5 ▣ 12.3 Now Allan has the newspaper. Giving it back is another excuse to begin a conversation. Which of the following do you think he does?

a mention the political situation   ⓒ say something about sport
b comment on the weather forecast   ⓓ invite the other person for a drink

Listen to find out.

6 In first meetings, people often ask each other some of the following questions. Reorganise the words to make questions. Then match them to the answers 1–10. There are two possible answers for each question.

a you where are from

Where are you from?   ☐1 ☐7

b been have long you how here

How long have you been here?   ☐5 ☐9

c long staying how are you

How long are you staying?   ☐2 ☐3

d think what you Dublin do of

What do you think of Dublin?   ☐4 ☐8

e business here you on are

Are you here on business?   ☐6 ☐10

1 I'm from Turkey.
2 Until Friday.
3 Another four or five days.
4 It seems very nice.
5 I've been here for a couple of days now.

6 Yes. I'm visiting some customers.
7 I come from South Africa.
8 It's a bit cold for me.
9 Since Saturday.
10 Yes. I'm here to buy some machinery.

7 ▣ 12.4 Listen to the conversation. Which of the questions and answers in 6 do the speakers use? Circle them.   a, c, d, e, 4

Conversation topics   **8** The two men in the conversation in 7 talk about football and golf. Sport is a 'safe' topic. What other topics are safe? Which should you avoid? Circle the safe topics.

> cars   religion   politics and the state of the world   personal life
> business   the stock exchange   money and personal finance
> the weather   art   music   local attractions   the opposite sex

Although 'safe' topics vary from culture to culture, the following are usually safe anywhere:
cars   business   the stock exchange
the weather   art   music   local attractions

5 [cassette] **12.3** Read through the instructions with the class and ask students to discuss in pairs which of the gambits they think Allan will use. Then play the recording for them to see if they were right.

6 These are useful questions for students to learn, which they will be able to use in a variety of situations. After students have matched the questions and answers, check the answers by having one student ask the question and another provide the answer so that the class hear the language used in a natural context.

7 [cassette] **12.4** Play the recording. Students listen and circle the questions and answers that they hear. Then check the answers with the class.

Conversation topics

8 Students have now learned several ways to start up a conversation. The focus now turns to what they can talk about once the introductions are over. Ask students to discuss in pairs which topics in the box they think are 'safe' to discuss with people you don't know very well, and which ones they think you should avoid.

[cassette] **12.3**

A: Here's your paper then. Thanks very much.
B: **Don't mention it.**
A: I'm afraid my team didn't win.
B: Sorry?
A: The football results.
B: Oh, I see.
A: **Can I buy you a drink? If you don't have anything else to do, that is.**
B: **I was just about to go, actually,** but … yes, why not, … Al, I think you said your name was.
A: Allan, Allan Vilkas.

[cassette] **12.4**

B: I'm Sean, Sean O'Malley.
A: **Pleased to meet you, Sean. What would you like to drink?**
B: A beer, please.
A: Right. Two beers, please.
C: Right, sir.
B: **So, Allan, where are you from?**
A: Well, I was born in Lithuania, but I've lived in Germany most of my life. Are you from here?
B: **Yes, what do you think of Dublin?**
A: Well, I've only just arrived today and it's my first visit, but it seems very nice. Lots of character.

B: **Are you here on business?**
A: Yes, that's right. I have a meeting tomorrow. I'm a bit nervous about it.
B I'm sure it'll go all right. **How long are you staying?**
A: **Just a couple of days**. I go back on Thursday morning. I was just looking at your paper to see how Bayern Munich did yesterday. **Do you like football?**
B: If it's a good match, but I'm not that keen. **Actually, I prefer golf myself.**
A: **Do you mean you play golf?**
B: That's right.
A: I play myself. What's your handicap?

Saying goodbye

9 ▭ **12.5** Students try to complete the conversation between Allan and Sean before they listen to the recording and check their ideas.

10 The ability to end a conversation is just as important as the ability to start one. There are many reasons for wanting to end a conversation, including dislike of the person you are talking to or simple boredom with the conversation. Whatever the reason, it should be done politely and several gambits are given here which students will find useful.

You may like to ask students whether they think the other person will genuinely believe the excuse that is given for ending the conversation. In most cases, probably they won't, but these are polite and accepted formulae for ending conversations which will not give offence. You might like to point out, however, that saying you've got a call on your mobile and then just turning round to talk to someone more attractive behind you would not be acceptable!

Fluency

11 Give students a few minutes to think about what they are going to say, but don't allow them to write scripts and read them out. You could also point out that the suggested first line *Have you seen this article about …?* cannot simply be followed by repetition of the headline. They will need to rephrase it to say what it is about.

If you're short of time

Omit the *Remote Lounge* text on page 54 and start with the section on introducing yourself.

Preparation for exercise 11 on page 57 could be done at home.

▭ **12.5**

B: Oh, well, Allan, it's getting late. **I have to be off. Thanks for the drink, and good luck with your meeting.**
A: Right, **it was nice talking to you.**
B: **It was nice to meet you too.** Cheerio, then.
A: Bye.

Saying goodbye **9** 🔊 **12.5** Complete the conversation. Then listen and compare your answers.

Sean Oh, well, Allan, it's getting late. I have to _be off_____. Thanks for the
_drink_____, and good luck with your _meeting_____.

Allan Right, it was nice _talking to you___.

Sean It was nice to _meet you too__. Cheerio, then.

Allan Bye.

10 When Sean wants to end the conversation, he says *It's getting late. I have to be off.* Match the parts of the sentences below to make other ways to end a conversation.

a	Excuse me, but I've just ...	**1**	... a call on my mobile. I'll catch you later.
b	I think they're going ...		
c	Excuse me, but I think ...	**2**	... someone is trying to catch my attention.
d	Mm, that's interesting. Excuse me, but, ...	**3**	... do you know where the toilets are?
e	Hang on a minute, but I think I have ...	**4**	... seen someone I have to talk to.
		5	... to start. I'll see you later.
f	Sorry to cut you off, but I arranged ...	**6**	... to meet someone at the bar five minutes ago.

Fluency **11** Work with a partner. Look at the headlines below. Imagine you borrowed your partner's newspaper and you are now giving it back. Start a conversation about one of the headlines. Maintain the conversation as long as possible. Start like this: *Thank you for the newspaper. Have you seen this article about ...?*

- Prime Minister says economic situation 'hopeless'
- Scientists discover link between golf and IQ
- Mobiles banned on public transport
- UK to drive on right
- Dog wins lottery
- Intelligent life discovered on Mars
- Princess Diana alive and living in New Jersey
- US President consults private astrologer

13 Air travel

If God had meant us to fly, he would have given us wings. *Common saying*

Discussion

1   Discuss the following questions with other people in the class.

   a   How often do you fly?

   b   What things can go wrong when you travel by air?

   c   Have you had any bad flying experiences?

   d   For you, which is the best seat – near the front or back, an aisle seat, a window seat or the one in the middle?

2   ▣ 13.1 Listen to the conversation. Which seat does the passenger get? Circle it on the seating plan on the left.

3   Complete the conversation using the words in the box. Listen again and check your answers, if necessary.

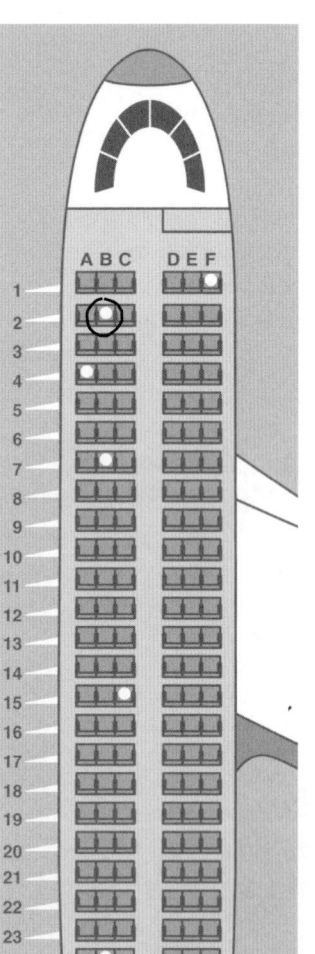

aisle	passport	laptop	allowed	boarding pass	check in	exit
gate	pack	left	available	busy		

Check-in clerk Good morning.

Passenger Hello. Is this where I __check in__ for flight BA 264?

Check-in clerk Yes. Can I see your __passport__, please? Thank you. Did you __pack__ your bags yourself, sir?

Passenger Yes. Excuse me, but apart from my __laptop__ I only have this small bag. Is it okay if I take it on as hand luggage?

Check-in clerk Well, officially, you're only __allowed__ one piece of hand luggage, but it's not a large bag, is it? So, that's all right, I suppose.

Passenger Thanks very much. Could I have an __aisle__ seat, please, near the front? Or a window seat?

Check-in clerk I'm sorry, the flight's quite __busy__. There are no window or aisle seats __left__.

Passenger Oh ... could you show me where the __available__ seats are?

Connecting # 13 Air travel

With increased globalisation, many people now find that they have to travel abroad on business, which means long hours on planes and at airports. This unit looks at flying and gives students useful language for the formalities of checking in for a flight and advice on how to secure the best seat. A reading text examines the recent phenomenon of air rage and looks at strategies airlines are adopting to combat it. Finally, students take part in a negotiation game, in which they gain points by successfully negotiating such things as price, quantity and delivery date of a product.

The grammatical focus is on conditionals with *will*, and the lexical focus is on negotiating and air travel.

In this first section, students begin with a general discussion of flying and their attitudes to it. They then listen and complete a conversation at an airport check-in desk.

Warm-up

Focus students' attention on the quotation at the top of the page. Find out how many students in the class enjoy flying and if there is anyone who absolutely hates it. Encourage them to give their reasons.

Brainstorm as many words as students can think of which are connected with flying and arrange them in a spidergram on the board with *flying* in the middle and different sections for things such as airport words, things in a plane, feelings about flying, things that can go wrong, etc.

Discussion

1   Divide the class into small groups for this discussion. You could appoint a secretary in each group who takes notes and then reports back to the class on what was said. Make sure students give their reasons for their choice of best seat on an aeroplane.

2   **13.1** Focus students' attention on the seating plan and tell them that the first time they listen to the recording, all they have to do is find out which seat the passenger gets. Allow students to compare their answer in pairs or small groups before checking the answer with the class.

3   Focus students' attention on the words in the box and make sure that everyone understands what they mean.

Students should first try to complete the conversation before listening to the recording again. When they have finished, play the recording for them to check their answers.

Ask what the advantage is of only having hand luggage. Do students try to travel light so that they don't have to check-in their luggage? Do they get frustrated when the overhead lockers of the plane are full of everyone else's hand luggage?

13.1

A: Good morning.
B: Hello. **Is this where I check in for flight BA 264?**
A: Yes. **Can I see your passport, please?** Thank you. Did you pack your bags yourself, sir?
B: Yes. Excuse me, but apart from my laptop I only have this small bag. Is it okay if I take it on as hand luggage?

A: Well, officially, you're only allowed one piece of hand luggage, but it's not a large bag, is it? So, that's all right, I suppose.
B: Thanks very much. **Could I have an aisle seat, please**, near the front? Or a window seat?
A: I'm sorry, the flight's quite busy. There are no window or aisle seats left.
B: Oh … **could you show me where the available seats are?**

A: Yes, sir. Here, here and here.
B: Right, I'll take the one up front near the exit on the left.
A: Okay. **Here's your boarding pass.** The flight will be boarding at gate number 23 in 20 minutes. **Have a good flight.**
B: Thanks. Goodbye.
A: Goodbye.

Battle of the armrests

In this section, a text on how to avoid getting the worst seat on the plane is used to practise conditionals with *will*. Students also learn some useful tips on getting a good seat on a plane and making the best of a bad one.

1   Ask a student to read the introduction aloud and then elicit suggestions from the class as to what the strategies for avoiding the worst seat on the plane that it refers to might be.

Conditionals with *will*

2   Go through the example sentences with the class, pointing out that the part of the sentence with *if* is the condition and the part with *will* is the consequence, i.e. what will happen as a result of the condition. This type of conditional is known as a 'first conditional' because there are other types.

Direct students' attention to the Grammar link on page 112 where they will find more information on conditions with *will*, and exercises to practise it.

Look at the conditions and the consequences in the table with the class. Ask three different students to read out the examples next to item a so that students hear them as complete sentences, rather than just seeing them as matched numbers. Then allow students to work in pairs to match the rest of the conditions to the consequences.

When checking the answers, ask students to read out their complete sentences. Other students can challenge if they think a sentence is not logical.

3   ▭ **13.2** Students listen and circle the combinations that the speaker mentions. When you have checked the answers, have a class discussion on whether students agree with the advice.

Discussion

4   Students could write out their lists neatly on posters to be displayed in the classroom. Encourage them to use first conditional sentences where appropriate, i.e. giving the reasons for the advice (or the consequences of not following it).

▭ **13.2**

Book as early as possible – within three weeks of the flight. With an early booking you can choose the seat you want. However, **if you book months in advance, you'll be too early for a seat assignment.**

If you use a travel agent, make sure they have a record of your seating preferences – aisle or window. Tell them you want to sit close to the front. **If you sit at the front, you'll get on and off the plane faster.**

When you receive your ticket and boarding pass or e-ticket confirmation, check the seat assignment. Mistakes happen. **If you have time, cross reference with the airline seating chart.**

If you are unable to confirm a seat, be sure to get to the airport early – at least 45 to 60 minutes before the flight.

If you do have an assignment for your preferred seat, don't check in too late.

Those few minutes reading magazines in the newsstand can translate into hours of discomfort in the air.

Finally, the gate check-in attendant can be your best friend. Ask politely if there is a better seat available. Saying that you are claustrophobic might not hurt, but don't feign an illness or say you're pregnant if you're not. There's no point in feeling guilty the entire flight.

If, in spite of your best efforts, you end up with the middle seat, here are some tips to cope:

If you are late boarding and have your choice of middle seats, go for the one up front near the exit.

Check out the aisle and window passengers. Do they look like they will be self-contained and give you plenty of room? Observe their body language and trust your instincts.

Capture as much personal space as you can right away. Dominate the two armrests. This will force your seatmates to give you more space. Be polite, but establish your territory. After all, they have 'personal space' on either side.

Don't work on the laptop during the flight. A cramped space becomes even more claustrophobic when you bring out the hardware. And don't try to read a newspaper. Stick to small paperbacks.

Although it is important to keep hydrated in the air, don't drink water by the gallon. **If you climb over seatmates repeatedly to get to the bathroom, they'll get annoyed.**

Get up once during the flight to stretch your legs. Even if you don't have to use the restroom. This time away will allow your companions to move around as well and refresh the whole row.

Check-in clerk Yes, sir. Here, here and here.

Passenger Right, I'll take the one up front near the ___exit___ on the left.

Check-in clerk Okay. Here's your ___boarding pass___. The flight will be boarding at ___gate___ number 23 in 20 minutes. Have a good flight.

Passenger Thanks. Goodbye.

Check-in clerk Goodbye.

Battle of the armrests

1 Read the introduction to an article on avoiding a travel problem. What do you think the 'strategies' are?

> ### THE MIDDLE SEAT
>
> It's happened to everyone – even the most experienced business traveller and frequent flier. A last-minute trip, no seat assignment on the aeroplane and the only seat left on a packed flight? You've guessed it – the middle seat. It can make your trip miserable. Here are some strategies to help you avoid the worst seat.

Conditionals with *will* 2 Look at this 'first conditional' sentence:

Conditions	Consequences
If + present	*will* + infinitive
If you book early,	you'll be able to choose your seat.
or You'll be able to choose your seat if you book early.	

Match the conditions to the consequences. Make as many logical combinations as possible.

Conditions		Consequences	
a	if you book months in advance ② 5 6	1	you'll get on and off the plane faster
b	if you sit at the front ①, 4, 6	2	you'll be too early for a seat assignment
c	if you check in late ⑦ 10	3	you'll have to go to the toilet a lot
d	if you're polite to the check-in attendant ⑤ 6	4	you'll be able to stretch your legs
e	if you pretend to be ill or pregnant 1, 3, 5, 6, ⑩	5	you'll sometimes be able to change your seat
f	if you trust your instincts ⑧	6	you'll get more personal space
g	if you dominate the armrests ⑥ 10	7	you'll pay for it with an uncomfortable seat
h	if you use your laptop ⑨ 10	8	you'll choose better seatmates
i	if you drink too much ③ 10	9	you'll feel claustrophobic
j	if you get up during the flight ④, 5	10	you'll feel guilty the entire flight

Grammar link

for more on conditionals with *will* see page 112

3 🔊 13.2 Listen to someone giving advice about getting a good seat. Circle the combinations in 2 which correspond to what the speaker says. Do you agree with the advice?

Discussion 4 Work in groups. Make a list of five *dos* and five *don'ts* for business air travellers.

Air rage

1 Look at the headline from a newspaper article. What word do you think is missing?

RUDE **PASSENGERS GROUNDED**

Now read the article.

IMAGINE you are checking in at Heathrow airport and the check-in clerk
informs you that you don't have a seat on your flight because of overbooking.
Naturally you are upset, but be careful what you say. If you are rude to the
ground staff, you will not be allowed to board your flight. Not if you're flying with
5 British Airways, that is.

The company has introduced new rules prohibiting customers from boarding
flights if they use 'threatening, abusive or insulting words to ground staff or crew'.
The airline claims that last year their staff dealt with over 200 cases of air rage,
including minor disagreements over smoking on board, but also more serious
10 incidents involving violent or drunken behaviour. However, check-in staff believe
that they can prevent these problems if they deal with difficult passengers before
they actually get on the plane.

Owen Highley, a BA lawyer who helped to draw up the new rules, told *The Times*
newspaper in London: 'If we think someone is going to be a disruptive passenger,
15 the most obvious thing to do is to deny them boarding. But there has to
be common sense. We are not going to ban from flight everybody who
gets a bit stroppy.'

A spokeswoman for BA said: 'Some people are understandably
angry when they check in if they have missed a connecting
20 flight because of a delay or some other problem. It is only
if we fear they could become a danger that we will act.'
However, BA will not offer a refund to passengers
who are banned from boarding their planes
unless they have a fully flexible fare,
25 and those involved in the most serious
incidents will get a lifetime ban.
You have been warned!

Discussion 2 Sometimes air travel can be very frustrating. Things can go wrong and people
get angry. Do you think the BA rules are fair? Do you ever get 'a bit stroppy'?

3 Complete the following sentences, which summarise the rules in the article in 1.

a If _customers use threatening, abusive or insulting words_ , they won't
be allowed to get on planes.

b There won't be incidents of air rage during flights if _we deal with difficult_
passengers before they get on the plane.

c We will deny someone boarding if _we think they will be disruptive._

d If a passenger just gets 'a bit stroppy', _we will not ban them_
from getting on the plane.

e If _you are involved in a serious incident_ , BA will ban you for life.

Air rage

In this section, students read about the action one airline is taking about the increasing problem of drunken, violent and abusive passengers. More practice of first conditionals is given by an exercise in which students summarise the rules the airline is introducing. They then look at some common verb and noun collocations.

Warm-up

Focus students' attention on the title of this section, *Air rage*, and ask them what they think it might mean (abusive and violent behaviour by airline passengers). Tell them that a number of expressions using *rage* (which means *anger*) have entered the English language in recent years (and are common in the tabloid press) which describe bad behaviour in certain situations, mainly caused by frustration or people's inability to control their anger. Find out if students know any more of these expressions. Probably the best known is *road rage*, when one driver takes out his or her frustrations and anger on another by driving in a threatening and intimidating manner. In some cases drivers have been forced off the road and physically attacked. Other expressions include *trolley rage* (pushing a supermarket trolley in a way that threatens or injures others) and *rail rage* (abuse of railway staff by passengers fed up with dirty overcrowded trains and delayed and cancelled services). Find out if any of these problems occur in the students' own countries.

1   Students predict what the missing word in the headline could be. The original article had *Rude*, but other possibilities could include *Angry, Violent, Drunken, Abusive*, etc.

Students then read the article. Answer any questions they may have about difficult vocabulary. *Overbooking* is the policy that many airlines have of selling more tickets than there are seats on the plane, in the expectation that not all the passengers will turn up for the flight. If they do, there will not be room for all of them and some will not be allowed to board. *Being a bit stroppy* means showing how cross or frustrated you are by being rude or difficult.

You may like to exploit the text a bit more by asking students to list all the words which refer to passengers' bad behaviour or by giving them a list of words and asking them to find their opposites in the text, e.g. *allowing (prohibiting), polite (insulting), peaceful (violent), sober (drunken), easy (difficult), pleased (angry), trivial (serious)* .

Discussion

2   Elicit students' reactions to the text. Do their sympathies lie with the airline staff or with frustrated passengers, angered by delays, cancellations, bureaucracy and rules which prevent them from smoking? Do they ever become 'a bit stroppy' when they are frustrated? What sorts of things make them frustrated when they are travelling?

3   Remind students of the work they have already done on conditionals with *will*. Ask them to complete the summary of the rules individually and go round making sure that they are making conditional sentences correctly. Allow them to compare their sentences in pairs before checking the answers with the class.

4 The collocations here can all be found in the text on page 60, but encourage students to try to find the wrong verbs and move them to the correct columns first, before they look back at the text. Then ask them to check their answers by going back to the text, finding the collocations and underlining them.

5 Check the answers with the class when students have completed the sentences and before they discuss the questions. Ask them to discuss the questions in small groups and report back to the class on their findings.

Direct students' attention to the Lexis link on page 113 where they will find more on the vocabulary of negotiating and air travel.

The negotiation game

In this section, the focus moves away from air travel to negotiation. Students follow the instructions on the relevant pages to play a game in which they negotiate the price, quantity, delivery time, etc. of a product.

1 🔲 **13.3** Read the situation with the class, then play the recording for the students to hear two people playing the game. Point out the speakers' use of conditionals with *will* (*If I order 100 units, will you give me a price of 5.5 euros,* etc.)

Fluency

2 In pairs, students decide what the product is. Student A is the buyer and Student B is the seller. They turn to their respective pages where they will find the instructions, a chart telling them how many points they will score for each category and a box of useful language. Make sure everyone understands what they have to do.

As students negotiate, go round offering help and encouragement. Make a note of any particularly successful negotiations which can be performed for the class. At the end find out who scored the most points as buyer and who the most as seller.

If you're short of time

Set *Battle of the armrests* exercise 4 for homework.

Ask students to read the article on *Air rage* on page 60 at home.

Set the *Grammar and Lexis links* exercises for homework and check the answers at the beginning of the next class.

🔲 **13.3**

A: If I order 100 units, will you give me a price of 5.5 euros?
B: No, I'm sorry. I can't do that. On 150 units I'll give you a price of six euros.
A: Six euros. And what about payment?
B: Payment is within 60 days.
A: If we pay within 30 days, will you lower the price?
B: I'll go down to 5.5 euros if you order 200 units or more. That's my best offer.
A: Well, what about the guarantee?

4   The verbs in each of the four lists below often accompany the nouns on the right. One verb in each list is wrong. Delete the verb from the wrong list and add it to the correct list.

~~receive~~
miss
book   a flight
board
take
catch
_catch_____

~~tackle~~
introduce   rules
obey
ignore
break
_break_____

claim
~~catch~~   a refund
offer
_receive___

deal with
solve
give   a problem
~~break~~
_tackle____

Lexis link

for more on the vocabulary of negotiating and air travel see page 113

5   Use the verb + noun combinations in 4 to complete the sentences below. Then answer the questions in brackets.

a   You should not _obey___ _rules____ if you don't think they are sensible. (*Do you agree?*)

b   In my job I have to _solve___ a lot of _problems__ every day. (*Is this true for you?*)

c   If I ever need to _book__ a ____ flight___, I always shop around at different travel agents to get the best deal. (*Is this what you do?*)

d   If you buy something that doesn't work, you _claim__ a ____ refund__ or get the shop to change it. (*When was the last time you did this?*)

The negotiation game

1   📼 13.3 You are going to play a game in which you have to negotiate the price, quantity, delivery time, payment terms and guarantee period of a product to gain points. Before you play, listen to two people playing the game as an example.

Fluency   2   Work with a partner. First of all, decide what the product is.

Speaker A you are the buyer. Look at the instructions and chart on page 129.
Speaker B you are the seller. Look at the instructions and chart on page 132.

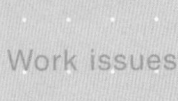

14 Hiring and firing

Sack the lot! *Letter to The Times, September 2nd, 1919 (on overmanning and overspending within government departments)*

1   Look at the headline below. What do you think the article is about?

2   Read the article to see if you are correct. Then answer the questions.

IBIZA PHONE-IN PRIZE WINNER FIRED Nicola Williams, a 31-year-old single mother from Newbridge in South Wales, couldn't believe her luck when she was told she was the winner of a Mediterranean holiday for herself and her six-year-old daughter. The week's break on the sunshine island of Ibiza was the prize in a radio phone-in competition.

5   She told reporter Hefina Rendle on BBC Wales television that she was 'totally over the moon, really excited'. However, only minutes later she was laid off. Nicola, an electronic parts worker, who phoned the radio station from work using her own mobile phone, was unaware that her boss was standing nearby. He asked her to hang up, took her into his office, and told her she was sacked. She was ordered to leave the factory immediately.

10   This was her first job since the birth of her daughter, and she was fired by the same manager who originally hired her.

But the story may have a happy ending. The commercial radio station which ran the competition is now trying to find her another job. A spokesman for the station said that people should be allowed to take part in competitions from work, as they are in general life. He said it was sad

15   that the manager couldn't see the good side and just congratulate Nicola on her good luck.

Skytronics, Nicola's former employer, refused to be interviewed by the BBC, and later issued a statement supporting the action of their manager.

a Do you think the sacking was justified?

b Would this be possible in your company, or in your country?

c What advice would you give to Nicola?

3   Find two more verbs in the article that are similar in meaning to 'sack'. Which verb is more formal than the others?   <u>fired, laid off (this is more formal)</u>

The passive

4   Find sentences in the article that are similar in meaning to the following:

a   They laid her off.   <u>She was laid off.</u>

b   They ordered her to leave the factory immediately.

<u>She was ordered to leave the factory immediately.</u>

5   Compare the two pairs of sentences in 4.

a   Which are active and which are passive?   <u>a and b are active; the</u>
<u>sentences from the article are passive</u>

b   Who is mentioned first in the active sentences?   <u>They (the company)</u>

c   Who is mentioned first in the passive sentences?   <u>She (Nicola)</u>

d   Who is the story about?   <u>Nicola Williams</u>

e   What is the advantage of using the passive sentences?   <u>It puts the</u>
<u>emphasis on Nicola and what happened to her.</u>

f   The agent in the active sentences is 'they'. What happens to it in the passive sentences? Why?   <u>It is omitted. We either already know or are not</u>
<u>interested in the person doing the action.</u>

Work issues # 14 Hiring and firing

In this unit, students look at issues around getting and losing a job. In the first section, they read a newspaper article about a woman who was fired for taking part in a radio competition while she was at work. This article is used to present and practise the passive. Students then read a report giving the manger's viewpoint on the same incident and practise rewriting short texts in the passive.

The next section is about applying for a job and students read extracts from four letters of application. They examine the formality of the language used and write a paragraph introducing their own CV.

In the next section, students look at a CV and a job advert, and listen to an interview. They decide whether or not they think the company appointed the candidate.

In the final section, they talk about wider issues around employment and relationships between workers and employers.

The grammatical focus is on the passive, and the lexical focus is on procedures.

In this first section, students read the story of Nicola Williams who was sacked for taking part in a radio phone-in programme while she was at work. They examine the vocabulary used in the article and look at the use of the passive. They then read the manager's report on the incident which gives an entirely different viewpoint. This text uses the passive in order to sound more formal and objective and students go on to rewrite short texts using the passive. They then discuss the issue of sacking.

Warm-up

Write the words *hire* and *fire* at the top of two columns on the board and ask students what they mean (to give someone a job, and to take a job away from someone). Then ask how many other words they know that mean the same thing as *hire* and *fire* or are connected with them. If they don't know any, you could put this list on the board and ask them to decide which column they should go in: *take someone on, lay off, sack, appoint, downsize, let someone go, terminate someone's employment, recruit.*

1 Encourage students to make predictions based on the headline alone and not to read the article yet.

Establish that a phone-in is a radio programme in which listeners are invited to phone the radio station and give their opinions on air. Sometimes these involve competitions or quizzes in which people can win prizes.

2 Students read the article and see if their predictions in exercise 1 were correct. You could use the questions at the side of the text as the basis for a class discussion of students' reactions to what they have read or ask them to discuss them in pairs or small groups.

3 Ask students to underline the verbs in the text which mean the same as *to sack* and to discuss in pairs which verb is the most formal. Point out that informal words (such as *fired* or *sacked*) are usually used in newspaper headlines because they have more impact.

The passive

4 Again, suggest that students underline the sentences in the article when they find them.

5 Do this exercise with the whole class to make sure that everyone understands.

If your students are unfamiliar with the passive, direct their attention to the Grammar link on page 114 where they will find more information on the form and use of the passive, and practice exercises to help them use the passive form correctly.

6 Students read the manager's report, which shows that there are two sides to every story. Point out the use of the passive to make a text sound more objective and formal in style. Elicit that *subjective* is the opposite of *objective* and implies more emotional involvement with the case. An objective account of something sticks to the facts.

When you have checked the answers, ask whether students have changed their minds about whether they think the sacking was justified as a result of reading the manager's report or not.

7 Ask students what the source of the story about Nicola Williams that they read first was (a newspaper). Elicit that a newspaper is more likely to be sympathetic to Nicola than to the management of her company for a number of reasons: newspapers and their readers like 'hard-luck' stories and stories with happy endings; newspapers like to think they champion the ordinary person against the power of big business.

Ask students if they think that newspapers usually publish all the facts of a case.

Students discuss in pairs or small groups how the details of the incident are different in the two accounts.

8 The instructions here tell students to improve the texts by changing one verb into the passive. When you have checked the answers, ask them why they think this improves the texts (mainly because the most important information is brought to the beginning of a sentence where it is more prominent and has more impact; also because these are formal texts and the passive eliminates the use of the pronouns *they* and *it* which makes the original texts sound more informal).

Discussion

9 Go through the items in the box with the class to make sure everyone understands them. Students then discuss the question in small groups. You could appoint a secretary in each group to take notes and report back to the class on what was said. Emphasise that students can include any ideas of their own.

6 Read the manager's report of the incident in 2. He uses the passive to sound more objective and formal in style. Complete the report using the verbs below in the passive.

| ask give note inform warn give inform |

On two occasions in November Ms Nicola Williams, an employee in the assembly plant, (a) **was warned** that using a mobile phone in work hours was against the company rules. Both these warnings (b) **were given** by another supervisor, and (c) **were noted** in her file. Then, in December, on a further occasion, she (d) **was given** a written warning. Finally, On Friday, 12 January at 10.30 I (e) **was informed** of a problem on the factory floor. When I arrived there, I found a lot of noise and shouting going on. Ms Williams was using her mobile phone to participate in a radio phone-in programme. Apparently she had won a prize. I asked her to put the phone down immediately, and to come in to my office. I decided to terminate her employment, and in the presence of Ms Jones, my deputy, Ms Williams was told that she was being sacked. She became hysterical and abusive, and (f) **was asked** to leave the factory immediately. She (g) **was informed** that her possessions would be forwarded to her by post.

7 In what way are the details about the incident different?

The manager said he gave Nicola verbal and written warnings. There was a lot of noise and disruption. Nicola became hysterical and abusive.

8 Improve these short texts by changing one verb to the passive in each one.

a They have laid off over 35,000 people in the last five years, unemployment is rising, and there are social problems in the region.

35,000 people have been laid off in the last five years, unemployment is rising, and there are social problems in the region.

b The business is a great success. They are hiring new staff and it is expanding fast. The business is a great success. New staff are being hired and it is expanding fast.

c As there was a recession and the number of orders decreased, they closed one of the factories. As there was a recession and the number of orders decreased, one of the factories was closed.

d To improve margins, it is making the new model in Hungary where labour costs are lower. To improve margins, the new model is being made in Hungary where labour costs are lower.

e Ford has several plants in Europe. One of them is in Valencia and it produces the Escort there. Ford has several plants in Europe. One of them is in Valencia and the Escort is produced there.

f They have announced plans for the new industrial estate. It will cover ten hectares and create space for over fifteen business ventures. _____
Plans have been announced for the new industrial estate. It will cover ten hectares and create space for over fifteen business ventures.

Grammar link

for more on the passive
see page 114

Discussion **9** Work in groups. In what situations do you think sacking is justified? Think about the following:

| dishonesty punctuality disrespect to superiors
not meeting objectives or achieving results violence inappropriate dress
industrial action (going on strike) revealing company secrets |

Add your own ideas, if you like.

Applying for a job

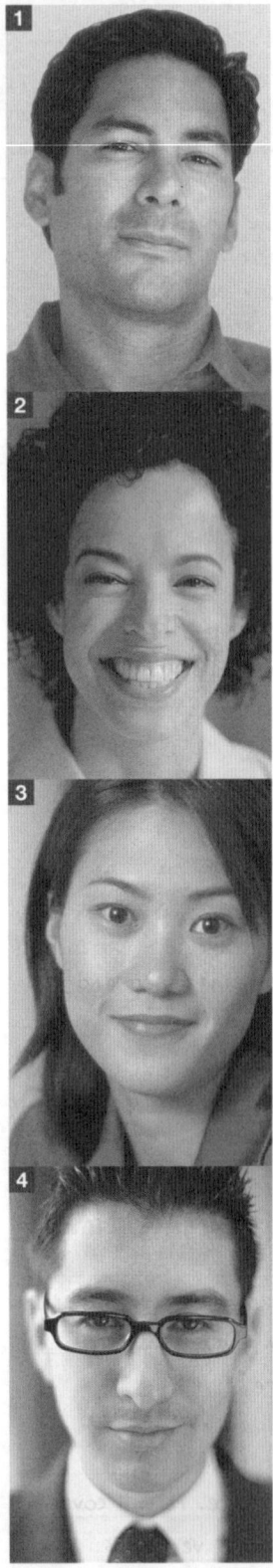

1 📼 14.1 Listen to four people talking about their approach to applying for a job. Take notes and match the people on the left to the summaries below.

 a I'm looking for a chance to develop and demonstrate my true potential. ☐4
 b My qualifications and experience speak for themselves. ☐3
 c I'm so brilliant at whatever I do, they would be lucky to have me working in their company. ☐1
 d There may be people with better qualifications and experience, but no one is more enthusiastic or hard working than me. ☐2

2 Which speaker(s) do you agree with? What approach did you use to get your present job? Does the approach you use depend on the job?

3 Read the following extracts from letters of application. Match them to the summaries in 1.

> **d**
> I am very keen to work for your company because of its excellent ⟵a
> reputation. I do not have the specific qualifications or experience referred to ⟵c
> in your advertisement. However, I am applying because I feel I am able to
> make up for this through hard work and willingness to learn.

> **c**
> If you believe in the pursuit of excellence, then I am interested in joining ⟵b
> your company. I set high standards for myself and expect them from
> others, especially the organisations that I work for. I look forward to an
> opportunity to add to the list of already outstanding achievements, which
> are outlined in my CV.

> **a**
> From my CV, you will see that five years at a chemicals multinational have ⟵h
> given me a solid business background. I am responsible for my
> department's logistical planning, which has developed my organisational ⟵f
> skills. However, I am now looking for opportunities for further development ⟵g
> and responsibility, which my present employer cannot offer.

> **b**
> As a commercially aware and linguistically trained university graduate, I have ⟵d
> a broad range of employment experience at blue-chip companies in both the ⟵
> USA and Europe. I am dynamic and creative, with a strong team spirit and
> leadership qualities. I have a proven record of working with individuals at all ⟵e
> levels through highly developed interpersonal and communication skills.

Reading between the lines

4 Read the extracts in 3 again. There are certain formal phrases people use in letters of application to talk about their qualities and achievements. Underline phrases which mean the following:

 a I'd really like to work for you because you're such a great company.
 b If you think doing things well is important, I'd like to work for you.
 c I don't really have the profile of the ideal candidate.
 d I've worked with many different, important companies.
 e I've shown I can work with all kinds of people and get on with everyone.

Applying for a job

In this section, students listen to people talking about their approach to applying for a job and match them to extracts from their application letters. These are then examined for examples of formal language which is appropriate for such letters. Students are invited to decide what this formal language really means. They then write a paragraph introducing their own CVs.

Warm-up

Find out what the normal procedure is for applying for a job in the students' own countries. They may be interested to know that in the UK, most jobs are advertised in the press. Some of the adverts ask people to contact them to receive an official application form. Others ask for a letter of application and a CV (curriculum vitae), which lists the applicant's personal details, education, qualifications, job experience and interests. In both cases, applicants would write a covering letter, explaining why they are interested in applying for the job and noting any relevant points that they wish to highlight from their CVs or which are not covered in either the CV or the official application form. Application letters are written in formal language.

1   🔲 **14.1** Focus students' attention on the pictures of the four people. Ask them to speculate on what kind of people they are. What adjectives would they use to describe them?

Make sure students have read the summaries before you play the recording so that they know exactly what they are listening for. Then play the recording and ask them to match the people to the summaries. Check the answers with the class.

2   Elicit students' reactions to the people they listened to. Which one(s) do they agree with?

Ask students to discuss in pairs which approach they used to get their present job and whether the approach depends on the job. If your students are not yet employed, ask them to discuss which approach they think would be the most successful. Again, would this depend on the type of job?

3   Establish that these are extracts from letters of application written by the four people featured in exercise 1. Allow students to work in pairs to match them to the summaries. Then check the answers with the class.

Reading between the lines

4   Ask students what they think the expression *reading between the lines* means (working out the motivation that lies behind what the writer has written and what the words *really* mean as opposed to what they *appear* to mean). Find out if there is a similar expression in the students' own language.

In letters of application, people want to make themselves sound as good as they can, without actually lying about their abilities, qualifications and experience. Formal language is often used to give the impression that something is true, without actually giving false information. This will be demonstrated in the next section. Here it is simply used to make the application letter sound more formal and impressive.

Students read the extracts again and find the formal phrases that match sentences a to h.

🔲 **14.1**

Speaker 1
I think that these days you have to really sell yourself. Certainly this is what employers expect in the US. You should show them how great and self-confident you are. Modesty isn't going to get you anywhere and no one is going to mind if you exaggerate a bit and dress things up to sound more impressive. Make the potential employer feel that, although this is the job you always wanted and of course you are the ideal person for it, if they don't snap you up, someone else will. So, they had better hire you before they lose the chance.

Speaker 2
It's not often that qualifications and experience totally match up to an advertised post, so it's preferable to emphasise other qualities like your willingness to learn and the fact that you work hard. In fact, you should be careful not to give the impression you are over-qualified for the job. I think that employers are often more interested in things like loyalty and ability to fit in. A high-flier who knows too much can create a bad working atmosphere and break a team. Personally, I want the employer to think that I am going to be easy to work with and won't create too many waves.

Speaker 3
No one likes a 'big head' but, on the other hand, don't be falsely modest either. Basically, your qualifications and experience tell their own story so you're not going to impress anyone by adding a lot of adjectives like 'excellent' and 'outstanding' to your CV. Usually this will make an experienced recruitment officer suspicious. It doesn't hurt to acknowledge one or two weaknesses either – areas that you would like to improve and you want a chance to develop. Above all, be honest, because if you exaggerate or lie, in the end someone is going to catch you out, and you'll end up looking stupid.

Speaker 4
People's motivations interest employers. If you want to work for a specific company, tell them why, especially if you are changing jobs. Valid reasons would be that you are frustrated by the limitations of your present post, or that you can't fulfil the potential of your background and education. Don't whine, though, and don't blame your current employers: you've learnt a lot with them, but it's time to move on. Tell potential employers that you have a lot to offer, and all you need is an opportunity to show it. If someone gives you a break, they won't be disappointed.

5 This writing exercise could be set for homework. Make sure that students use suitably formal language for their paragraphs.

A job interview

In this section, students look at a job advert and the CV of a woman who applied for it. They then listen to the interview that she had for the job. This reveals how she used formal language to suggest that she was better qualified and more experienced than she really was. Students are asked to complete phrases from the interview and decide whether or not she would have got the job.

1 Go through the advert and the CV with the class and explain anything they don't understand. A *resumé* is the same as a CV and is the preferred word in American English. Ask why they think Sara applied for the job and whether from looking at her CV they think she would be a suitable candidate. They may point out that the job offers an attractive salary and benefits and that Sara's language abilities would match one of the employer's preferences. Don't pre-empt the listening by pointing out at this stage that Sara has no real management or sales experience and that *Management Team Co-ordinator* and *SPC Professional* are vague titles which give no idea of the amount of responsibility she actually had in either of these jobs.

2 ▢ **14.2** Play the recording for students to listen. Find out how many students think the company would have employed her and how many think they wouldn't. Encourage students to give reasons for their opinions.

Answer

> It is unlikely that the company would have employed her as they were looking for an executive with managerial and sales experience and Sara's previous jobs were little more than secretary and personal assistant. Also her confusion at the end of the interview when she is asked to speak Spanish suggests that she has not been totally honest about her language abilities.

3 Play the recording again for students to complete the phrases. Then check the answers with the class.

Direct students' attention to the Lexis link on page 115 where they will find more on the vocabulary of procedures.

4 Have a class discussion on whether they think the interviewer was fair or not. How far do they think job applicants should exaggerate their qualifications and experience in order to secure an interview? The interviewer here had clearly 'read between the lines' of Sara's CV. Do they think she would even have got an interview if she had been clearer and more honest about her work experience?

▢ **14.2**

A: Right, shall we make a start? My name is Philip Rickett. I work in the human resources department and I'm responsible for recruitment.
B: Right, pleased to meet you.
A: Did you find us all right?
B: Yes, the map you sent me was very clear.
A: Good. Now, this is just a preliminary interview to check out some details. If you're successful, you'll go on to a more in-depth interview this afternoon. Is that all right?
B: Yes, I don't have to be back at work until tomorrow morning so as long as I have time to drive back this evening, that's fine.
A: Do your present employers know where you are?
B: No. I asked for a day's unpaid leave for personal reasons. I didn't say why.
A: What don't you like about your current position?
B: Actually, there are a lot of things I do like about it, but no job is perfect. I think I am ready for more responsibility and when I saw your advert, I thought I should apply.

A: I see. Well, Sara, can I ask you a few questions about your CV?
B: Sure.
A: You know this job is a managerial position. Do you, in fact, have any managerial experience? It's not very clear from your CV.
B: Well, in my present job I'm a management team co-ordinator.
A: So, you are the manager of a team?
B: Not exactly. I assist the general manager in running the department.
A: In other words, your role is that of a personal assistant?
B: I think it's a bit more than that …
A: But you personally don't actually have any decision-making power?
B: I suppose not.
A: In your previous position you were an 'SPC professional'. What exactly does that mean? Is Sales Productivity Centre basically a sales department?
B: Yes, we provided backup for twenty salesmen from different sectors of the company.
A: Were you directly involved in sales at all?

B: No, it was more about providing support to help drive sales and increase productivity.
A: I see. So, you were mainly just preparing documentation?
B: Yes, but I would say that it was a position that required a lot of time management skills and prioritising of tasks. It gave me a lot of insight into the sales process.
A: As a department secretary.
B: Not exactly. Okay, some of the work was secretarial but I am applying for your post because I think I am capable of doing far more. I'd like more responsibility and to be able to use my studies and my languages.
A: Yes, your English is obviously excellent and you speak Spanish as well.
B: Yes, it's not bad.
A: Could you tell me about your degree course … in Spanish?
B: I'm sorry? Oh, I beg your pardon … Well, I need a little time to think … Let's see …

f I look after the practical day-to-day aspects of department organisation.

g I want a new job because my company probably won't be able to promote me.

h I have five years of international business experience working for a chemicals company.

5 Use some of the phrases in 3 to write a paragraph introducing your own CV.

A job interview

1 Read the job advert and CV below. Why do you think Sara applied for the job?

Sara Verkade
58, Stoppard Drive, London SW16
Tel: 353 865 344872   E-mail: sara.verkade@gmz.net

Date & place of birth	23.7.78, Maassluis, The Netherlands
Marital status	Single
Nationality	Dutch
Qualifications	September 1996 – July 1999 BComm, Marketing Management, Haagse Hogeschool, The Hague
Employment history	**June 2000 – present** *Management Team Co-ordinator, Helena Rubinstein, L'Oreal* Organising meetings, events and conferences. Analysing sales figures and producing relevant reports and charts. Customer relations and responding to complaints and queries. **June 1999 – June 2000** *SPC Professional, Sales Productivity Centre, IBM* Sales team support. Research, pricing and proposal-writing on million dollar bids.
Languages	Dutch, English, German, Spanish
IT Skills	Proficient user of Microsoft Office suite

2 🔲 14.2 Sara was interviewed for the job. Listen to the interview. Do you think they employed her? *Probably not - she wasn't qualified for the job.*

3 Listen again and complete the phrases below.

a Now, this is just a preliminary interview to __check out some__ details.

b Do your present __employers know where__ you are?

c What don't you __like about your current__ position?

d Well, Sara, can I ask you a __few questions about__ your CV?

e Do you, in fact, have any __managerial__ experience?

f ... an 'SPC professional'. What __exactly does that__ mean?

g Yes, we provided __backup for__ twenty salesmen from different sectors of the company.

h ... it was a position that required a lot of time __management skills__ and prioritising of tasks.

i I'd like more responsibility and to be able to __use my studies__ and my languages.

Lexis link

for more on the vocabulary of procedures see page 115

4 Do you think the interviewer was fair in the interview?

What about the workers?

1 What is happening in the photographs on this page? How do you think these situations relate to employment and staffing?

2 Work with a partner. You will each read an article relating to the employment situation in a country and do three exercises. When you have finished, turn back to this page. Student A see page 127. Student B see page 133.

3 Complete the sentences with words and phrases from the articles in 2. Are the sentences true for you? Discuss them with your partner.

  a An advanced society should pay __unemployment benefits__ to people who can't find work.

  b The average age of my country's __workforce__ is getting younger.

  c Flexible labour laws help to reduce the __unemployment rate__.

  d Using __temporary staff__ causes job insecurity and lower productivity.

  e __Workers' rights__ are more important than the interests of big business.

  f Money and security are the __incentives__ in most people's work.

  g If the __unemployed__ can't find work, they should take any job they are offered.

  h Companies should invest more in training if they need __skilled workers__.

  i It is often hard to predict your __staffing__ needs over a long period.

  j A good salary doesn't necessarily __make up__ for a lack of job security.

4 The noun / verb combinations in the box were in the articles in 2. The verbs were in the passive. Can you remember the sentences? Tell your partner.

> **A** survey / carry out   firms / contact   staff / pay
>   salaries / negotiate   conditions / agree
>
> **B** country / bring   strike / call   offers / put
>   anyone / sack   reforms / defend

Discussion

5 Discuss the following questions in relation to your country.

  a What are the laws about unemployment benefits? Do you think they are fair?

  b What rights do workers have? How do they affect employment?

  c Why do you think there is a shortage of skilled workers? Do you think the use of temporary labour is a good solution to the problem?

  d 'It is increasingly difficult to provide people with jobs for life.' Do you think this is true?

What about the workers?

In this section, the focus turns to wider issues of employment and the relationship between workers and employers. Students look at two pictures and say what is happening in them and how the situations relate to employment. They then read articles about the employment situation in two different countries and work together to complete sentences with vocabulary from the texts. They then reconstruct some sentences in the passive and discuss various issues related to employment in their country.

1 Elicit various opinions on what is happening in the photographs and how the situations pictured relate to employment and staffing.

Possible answers

> Top photo:
>
> People are being trained/retrained as computer operators.
>
> Possible significance: The number of jobs where computer skills are needed is increasing. Traditional manufacturing industries are being replaced by industries where knowledge of computers is more important than manual skills.
>
> Bottom photo:
>
> Striking workers are marching through the streets.
>
> Significance: Workers sometimes strike, usually for better pay and conditions; sometimes they organise marches to demonstrate against company or government policies.

2 First divide the class into pairs and have them decide who is A and who is B. Students will need to stay in these pairs for Exercise 3 as well. The two articles are quite difficult, so allow students plenty of time to read them and to do the exercises accompanying them. In the third part of the exercise, you may need to point out that only five of the definitions relate to the five words in bold in the article. The other five definitions relate to words in the article their partner is reading. Allow plenty of time for the discussion in the fourth part of the exercise as students will need to summarise their articles for their partners.

3 In the same pairs, students work together to complete the sentences. Check the answers with the class before students go on to do the discussion part of the exercise.

4 As Student A tries to reconstruct the sentences, Student B could look at the text on page 127 that Student A read and help by prompting a little if necessary. They then reverse roles with Student B attempting to reconstruct the sentences and Student A prompting where necessary from the text on page 133.

Discussion

5 In monocultural classes, this could be done as a class discussion. Otherwise you could either form groups of students from the same country and ask them to discuss and report back to the class on the situation in their country, or have mixed groups and have each student contribute information on their particular country.

If you're short of time

Omit some of the discussion questions, e.g. exercise 9 on page 63 or *What about the workers?* exercise 5 on page 66.

Ask students to do *What about the workers?* exercise 2 at home and come to class prepared to work on exercise 3 with a partner.

Set the *Grammar and Lexis links* exercises for homework and check the answers at the beginning of the next class.

Work issues 15 Time

The aspects of time examined in this unit include attitudes to time, effective time management, an interesting experiment by one company to do away with time and one writer's advice on how to be a good time waster.

Students learn some important collocations with the word *time*, study some useful techniques for organising their time and then practise talking about plans for the working day.

The grammatical focus is on *going to* versus *will*, and the lexical focus is on working conditions.

In this first section, students discuss some sayings and statistics about time, look at some useful collocations and talk about their working hours.

Warm-up

Write the word *time* on the board and ask students to tell you as many expressions with *time* and sayings about time as they can think of, either in English or in their own language. You might like to start them off with a few English sayings such as *Time flies like an arrow* and *Time waits for no man*.

Focus students' attention on the quotation from John Braine at the top of the page and ask them if they agree with it.

Discussion

1   Ask students to discuss the questions in small groups and report back to the class on their findings. At this point you could ask students to say whether they are *larks* (people who have most of their energy in the morning but tend to get flag as the day goes on) or *owls* (those who are not much good in the morning but are able to stay awake, concentrate and act energetically till late at night). If you do any team activities during this unit, you could use this division to form the teams.

Collocations

2   Students should be able to complete these words fairly easily. When checking the answers, ask students to read the whole collocation aloud so that they get used to hearing the words in combination. You could also ask them to put the collocations into sentences as you check the answers, though they will be using them to complete sentences in the next exercise.

3   When students have completed the sentences, they should discuss in pairs or small groups whether they are true for them or not.

Direct students' attention to the Lexis link on page 117 where they will find more on the vocabulary of working conditions and practice in using common collocations.

Discussion

4   After students have discussed the questions in pairs, ask several pairs to report back to the class on their discussion.

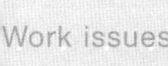 
15 Time

Time, like a loan from the bank, is something you're only given when you possess so much that you don't need it.

John Braine, British novelist

Discussion

1 Discuss the following questions with other people in the class.

> British workers put in the longest hours in Europe. However, they are 25% less productive than the French, and 15% less than the Germans.

  a The Pareto Principle, also known as the 80:20 rule, says that 80% of what we produce derives from 20% of our activity. Does this mean that:

  - we should work just one day a week?
  - almost perfect is good enough?
  - most work time is unproductive?
  - something else?

  b A proverb says that 'An hour in the morning is worth two in the evening.' Do you agree?

  c Read the information in the box. Why do you think this is?

     most work time is unproductive

Collocations

2 Put vowels in the spaces to complete the verbs below.

s p **e** n d
s **a** v **e**
w **a** s t **e** | money
h **a** v **e** | time
i n v **e** s t

Vilfredo Pareto, 1848 – 1923

3 Complete the sentences using words from 2. Are they true for you?

  a At work I **spend** a lot of time on the phone to people and answering e-mails.

  b I plan my day carefully. If you prepare things well, you can **save** a lot of time.

  c I don't **have** much time for myself, but when I do, I like to get some exercise.

> **Lexis link**
>
> for more on the vocabulary of working conditions see page 117

  d Computers are supposed to make you more efficient, but they can also make you **waste** a lot of time.

Discussion

4 Discuss the following questions with a partner.

  a Some people say 'Time is money'. Do you agree?

  b In what ways do you think you waste or save time and money?

  c What are your working hours? If you could choose, how would you organise your working hours?

Time management

1   You are going listen to a talk on time management. The words on the left are from the talk. Match them to the definitions on the right.

a	resource	1	determined
b	assign	2	things which have to be done
c	approach	3	level of importance or urgency
d	ruthless	4	time limits for finishing a job
e	delegated	5	something you need to do a job
f	priority	6	way of doing things
g	tasks	7	given to someone else to do
h	deadlines	8	give

a	5	b	8	c	6	d	1	e	7	f	3	g	2	h	4

2   ▭ 15.1 Listen to the talk and number the speaker's slides in the correct order.

3

TIME MANAGEMENT
ORGANISE
• Blocks of time
• Deadlines
• Time of day

2

TIME MANAGEMENT
PRIORITISE
• Important and/or Urgent

4

TIME MANAGEMENT
ANALSYSE
PRIORITISE
ORGANISE

1

TIME MANAGEMENT
ANALSYSE
• Record
• Reduce
• Delegate

3   Explain the slides in your own words.

4   Now read the presentation and complete it using the words in 1. Listen again and check, if necessary.

TECHNIQUES FOR EFFECTIVE TIME MANAGEMENT

Good morning and welcome. I'm here today to talk about time management. My aim is to share some techniques which will help you to use your time more efficiently.

5   Time is like money, people and equipment. It's a limited (1) _resource_. Time management is about making the best possible use of it. So, what are the basic concepts of time management? Today we're going to look at three fundamental steps.

10 The first step is to analyse how you use your time now.

This requires a methodical (2) _approach_. Break your day into half hour periods. Record what you do in each period.

15 Look at the list. Ask yourself which (3) _tasks_ were really necessary. Cut everything that isn't necessary. Be (4) _ruthless_. Most wasted time is the result of unquestioned activity.

20 Take a look at the necessary tasks. Could someone else do them? Never do work yourself that can be safely (5) _delegated_. Other people may not perform the task as well as you. But without experience they'll never learn.

25 The next step is to prioritise.

Take the tasks which genuinely require your attention and put them in order of (6) _priority_ – which are the most important, which are urgent needs.

30 Lastly, organise your time and your tasks.

Ask yourself 'How much time will I need?' Be realistic because work tends to expand to fill the time available.

Set realistic (7) _deadines_. The right amount of pressure brings speed and high performance, but on the other hand, too much pressure means things can go wrong.

35

When possible, organise your work so as to have large blocks of time for top priority tasks like problem analysis and forward planning. Discover the time of day when you are at your best and (8) _assign_ the most difficult tasks to it.

40

So, analyse, prioritise, organise. Now I'd like to look at what this means in more detail ...

Time management

In this section, students match words relating to time management with their definitions. They then listen to a talk on time management, put the speaker's slides in order and practise explaining them in their own words. They then look at the text of the presentation and complete it with the words they studied previously.

1   Allow students to work in pairs or small groups to match the words with the definitions so that they can help each other. Check the answers with the class.

2   📼 **15.1** Read through the slides with the class and ask students to say what order they think the slides should be in before you play the recording.

Play the recording for students to order the slides. You may need to play the recording a second time.

Then check the answers with the class. The more usual order is to start with the slide that presents the three headings, Analyse, Prioritise and Organise, and then take each of these three topics in turn. This would fit in with the advice often given to presenters to begin by telling the audience what your topic is and give them a map of the points you are going to talk about, then take each point in turn. By doing this, you show the audience what the structure of the talk is and they will be able to follow it more easily.

3   Ask students to work in pairs to produce their explanation of the slides. Go round offering help and encouragement and then ask one or two pairs to give their explanations to the class.

4   Students have already heard the presentation on the recording, so this task should not be too daunting. When checking the answers, ask individual students to read out different paragraphs, supplying the missing words as they go. Play the recording again for them, if necessary.

📼 **15.1**

Good morning and welcome. I'm here today to talk about time management. My aim is to share some techniques which will help you to use your time more efficiently.

Time is like money, people and equipment. It's a limited resource. Time management is about making the best possible use of it. So, what are the basic concepts of time management? Today we're going to look at three fundamental steps.

The first step is to analyse how you use your time now.

This requires a methodical approach. Break your day into half hour periods. Record what you do in each period.

Look at the list. Ask yourself which tasks were really necessary. Cut everything that isn't necessary. Be ruthless. Most wasted time is the result of unquestioned activity.

Take a look at the necessary tasks. Could someone else do them? Never do work yourself that can be safely delegated. Other people may not perform the task as well as you. But without experience they'll never learn.

The next step is to prioritise.

Take the tasks which genuinely require your attention and put them in order of priority – which are the most important, which are urgent needs.

Lastly, organise your time and your tasks.

Ask yourself 'How much time will I need?' Be realistic because work tends to expand to fill the time available.

Set realistic deadlines. The right amount of pressure brings speed and high performance, but on the other hand, too much pressure means things can go wrong.

When possible, organise your work so as to have large blocks of time for top priority tasks like problem analysis and forward planning. Discover the time of day when you are at your best and assign the most difficult tasks to it.

So, analyse, prioritise, organise. Now I'd like to look at what this means in more detail …

Collocations

5 You could do this as a team game (owls against larks, perhaps) with teams racing to complete all the collocations first. Then check the answers with the class.

Discussion

6 Make sure students ask and answer questions to obtain the information to complete the table. Remind them that the percentages should add up to 100%.

They then discuss the differences and any reasons for them. Encourage students to share what they have found with other pairs.

7 When students have completed their texts and checked the answers, focus their attention on the two pictures and ask them which one comes closest to their style of working. Do they think an untidy desk is always an indication of an untidy mind, or is it possible to be a good manager without being very organised? What kind of managers are they?

5 Without looking back at the text, match the words to make seven collocations.

a	assign	*tasks*	approach
b	be	*ruthless*	deadlines
c	delegate	*tasks*	priority
d	limited	*resource*	resource
e	methodical	*approach*	ruthless
f	set	*deadlines*	tasks
g	top	*priority*	tasks

6 How well do you manage your time? Complete the 'You' column with approximate percentages for the time you spend on the different activities. Add other activities, if necessary. Then complete the 'Your partner' column by asking *How much time do you spend on ...?* Then change round.

Activity	You	Your partner
planning & delegating		
meetings		
correspondence		
telephoning		
reading		
dealing with problems		
	100%	**100%**

What differences are there between the way you and your partner manage your time? Why do you think this is?

7 Complete the descriptions of two types of manager using the words in the box. Then look at page 129 to check your answers. Which kind of manager are you?

> meetings   emergency   busy   problems   suppliers   delegates   administration

The busy manager

His life is not planned. Perhaps that is why he is __busy__. His use of time indicates an entirely responsive approach to his job, with more time devoted to __administration__ than customer service. The high level of __emergency__ shows there are serious problems.

The effective manager

She __delegates__ correspondence to subordinates and deals with major issues herself or by telephone. Her __meetings__ are well planned. She is popular with customers and __suppliers__ because she gets to know them well and her reading makes her knowledgeable. She doesn't just discuss __problems__; she solves them.

Just in time

1 Read the article and answer the questions below.

a How did they try life without time? _They took away all the clocks at their HQ and covered computer time displays with tape._

b What was the aim of the experiment? _To see how pressure of time leads to stress and see how a clockless environment would affect productivity and workflow._

c Why do companies use time as a measure of productivity? _Because it is easy to measure._

d Why is the normal working timetable (nine to five) inefficient? _The human biological clock does not respond to it._

e What was the result of the experiment? _Most people carried on as normal. Some liked it, others didn't and found it chaotic and disorientating._

Life without time

How dependent are we on time? Is life without clocks less stressful? One company decided to find out. If you really want to know how dependent you are on time, try removing your watch
5 for a day and count how many times you find yourself looking at your bare wrist. At AOL they decided to take the experiment one step further by taking away all the clocks at their UK headquarters and covering the time displays on computers with tape. Then they
10 told everybody to carry on working as usual.

The idea was to investigate how pressure of time can lead to stress, and to see how a clockless environment would affect productivity and workflow. After all, they say that time is money and it is true that
15 companies use time to control their activities because it is easy to measure. But humans have a biological clock which doesn't necessarily correspond to the standard eight-hour working day. We are more productive in the morning and then our efficiency
20 tends to drop off after lunch. So, if you're feeling hungry, why not have something to eat instead of waiting for the lunch break? Or, if you've finished your work, don't hang on until it's time to clock off, just go home. (Yes, but what if it's time to go home
25 and you haven't finished your work? asks the boss!)

So, what happens when we rely on our internal body clock instead of artificial deadlines? According to one worker, 'Most people carried on as normal although some took advantage of the opportunity to
30 have an early lunch.' Another said 'This is ideal. It makes sense to be able to work when you need to and leave the office when you don't.' On the other hand, one secretary found the experience 'disorientating. We have a fixed routine and it's
35 difficult to change habits.'

However, one office manager was in no doubt: 'Thank goodness we are going to bring the clocks back tomorrow. Make no mistake, a clockless office leads to chaos. Some people may be less stressed
40 without clocks, but you need to know where people are and when, and meetings, for example, can last forever if you don't have a time limit.'

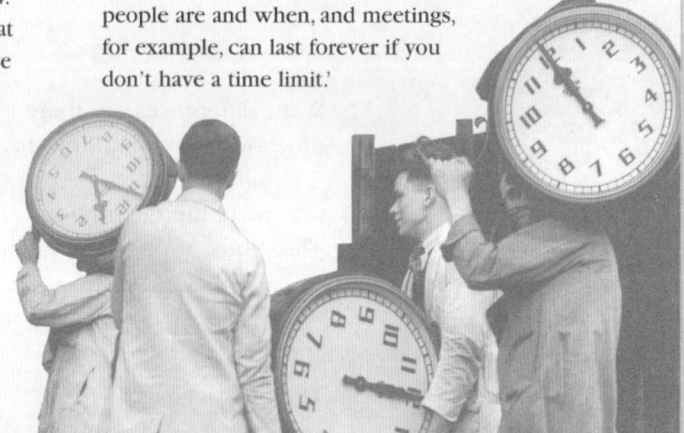

2 Discuss the following questions.

a What do you think of this experiment? Is it useful, interesting, or a waste of time?

b How aware do you need to be of time in your job?

c Could you work without a watch or clocks?

d Do you have lunch etc. at the same time every day?

Vocabulary **3** Find words and phrases in the article which mean the same as the following:

a continue _carry on_

b fall quickly _drop off_

Just in time

1 Encourage students to read the questions first and to predict what the text will be about. This will make it easier for them the first time they read it.

After students have read the article and answered the questions, allow them to compare their answers in pairs before checking with the class.

2 These questions are designed to elicit students' reactions to what they have read. You could also exploit the text further by dividing the class into teams and having them write more comprehension questions for the other team to answer.

Vocabulary

3 This could be done as a race with the first pair of students to find all the words and phrases raising their hands. They then read out their list to the class so they can all check their answers.

4   Check the answers with the class before going on to the discussion question in exercise 5.

5   When students discuss the sentences, make sure they give reasons for their opinions.

Going to

6   Do this exercise with the whole class, making sure everyone is clear about the use of *going to* to talk about future plans and intentions. There is more information in the Grammar link on page 116 if students need more exposure to the structure before moving on.

7   Encourage students to give as much detail as possible and to make plans for their entire day.

Going to & will

8   🔲 **15.2** Make sure students have completed all the gaps before you play the recording. You could also ask students to read the conversations in pairs.

9   Ask students to work in pairs to look at the conversations and make their choices. Refer them back to the work they did on the use of *will* for unplanned decisions in Unit 6.

Direct students' attention to the Grammar link on page 116 where they will find more information about the uses of *going to* and *will*, and practice activities to reinforce the difference between the two structures.

🔲 **15.2**

Conversation 1
A: Where are you going?
B: Well, I've finished everything I had to do so **I'm going to leave early**.
A: What about the sales predictions for next month?
B: Oh, I'd forgotten about that. **I'll start on them tomorrow** first thing. I've arranged to meet someone at five.

Conversation 2
C: Have you planned Mr Logan's visit? What about lunch tomorrow?
D: **I'm going to take him to** *The Redwing*.
C: I seem to remember he's a vegetarian.
D: Is he? In that case **I'll phone to check** they have a vegetarian menu.

Conversation 3
E: Is everything confirmed for your trip to San Sebastian?

F: Yes, the plane goes to Bilbao. **I'm going to take the train from there**.
E: No, don't do that – it takes forever. The bus is much faster.
F: Is it? Well, **I'll take the bus**, then.

c result in _lead to_

d wait _hang on_

e quantify _measure_

4 Use the words and phrases in 3 to complete the following sentences.

a Time management methods _lead_ to unnecessary stress.

b In some businesses it is difficult to _measure_ efficiency.

c When you have to make a decision, it's best to _hang on_ until the last minute.

d If you _carry on_ in the same job for a long time, you lose interest.

e The amount of activity in an office _drops off_ on a Friday afternoon.

5 Which of the sentences in 4 do you agree with?

Going to **6** Look at this sentence from the article on page 70 and answer the questions.

*Thank goodness we **are going to** bring the clocks back tomorrow.*

a Does the sentence refer to the past, present or future? _future_

b Which of the following is closest in meaning to 'we **are going to** bring the clocks back'?

- We would like to bring the clocks back ...
- <u>We are intending to bring the clocks back ...</u>
- We have to bring the clocks back ...

7 Plan how you are going to spend your next working day. Then explain your plans to your partner like this.

*At 9.00, when I arrive at work, **I'm going to** check my e-mail. Then ...*

Going to & Will **8** 🔲 15.2 Complete the following conversations using the verb in brackets with either *going to* or *will*. Then listen and check your answers.

Conversation 1

A Where are you going?

B Well, I've finished everything I had to do so I (a) _'m going to leave_ (leave) early.

A What about the sales predictions for next month?

B Oh, I'd forgotten about that. I (b) _'ll start_ (start) on them tomorrow first thing. I've arranged to meet someone at five.

Conversation 2

C Have you planned Mr Logan's visit? What about lunch tomorrow?

D I (c) _'m going to take_ (take) him to *The Redwing*.

C I seem to remember he's a vegetarian.

D Is he? In that case I (d) _'ll phone_ (phone) to check they have a vegetarian menu.

Conversation 3

E Is everything confirmed for your trip to San Sebastian?

F Yes, the plane goes to Bilbao. I (e) _'m going to take_ (take) the train from there.

E No, don't do that – it takes forever. The bus is much faster.

F Is it? Well, I (f) _'ll take_ (take) the bus, then.

9 Read the conversations again and look at how *will* and *going to* are used. Underline the correct option in the following sentences.

You can use *will* or *going to* to talk about decisions and plans:

a <u>*Will*</u> / *Going to* shows that you are making a decision now.

b *Will* / <u>*Going to*</u> shows that you made the decision earlier.

Grammar link

for more on *going to* and *will* see page 116

10 Work with a partner. Have similar conversations as in 8 using the prompts below and following this pattern:

A Say what you are **going to** do. *I'm going to walk to the station.*
B Mention a problem with the plan. *But it's raining.*
A React with an alternative plan using **will**. *Oh, in that case, I'll take a taxi.*

Plan	Problem	Alternative
walk to the station	it's raining	?
attend Japanese classes	you're too busy – you'll miss classes	?
buy a bargain computer	it's an old model – it'll be obsolete very soon	?
give up smoking	you'll get fat	?
get an easier job	you'll earn less money	?
take a taxi to the airport	the taxi drivers are on strike	?
take up roller skating	it's dangerous – there are lots of accidents	?

Wasting time

Collocations **1** Match the words to make four common collocations.

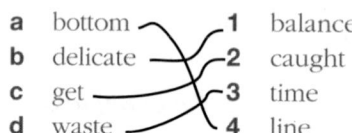

a bottom   1 balance
b delicate   2 caught
c get   3 time
d waste   4 line

2 Use the collocations in 1 to complete the article.

3 Here are the headings from the rest of the article. What tips do you think the author gives under each heading?

- Be sloppy
- The computer
- The Internet
- Office conversations
- Meetings

4 Look at page 125 to see what the author recommends.

WASTING TIME
AT WORK

Lots of people are so afraid of getting caught, they never (a) __waste time__ at work. They work the entire eight hours. They are right to be afraid. There is a (b) __delicate balance__ between not doing any work and doing too much. The (c) __bottom line__ is you must get your work done. If you start wasting hours at a time, you'll (d) __get caught__. To be an effective time waster, you have to find small ways to eat up time. Remember, you can't waste the company's time if you don't work for the company. However, with a little effort no one will ever know how little you do.

5 Complete the sentences below with words from the text on page 125 that mean the same as the words in brackets.

a 'Your papers are __a mess__.' 'Yes, but I know where everything is so don't touch anything.' (untidy)

b Before making an important call you should __set aside__ time to prepare it. (reserve)

c I only use the Internet to get specific information. I don't have time to __surf__ the web. (move around from link to link with no particular aim)

d My job requires a lot of __research__ so I need a good Internet connection. (information searching)

e People who always __nod__ and agree with everything are no use at all. (move head up and down)

6 Work with a partner. What other ways of wasting time can you think of?

10 Go through the example with the class so that everyone understands what they have to do. You might like to highlight the different ways that the speakers in exercise 8 introduced the problems (*What about …? I seem to remember … No, don't … .*), so that they don't just follow the example and use But … .

As pairs have their conversations, go round and note any particularly successful ones which could be performed for the class later. Encourage pairs who finish early to think up their own situations and problems.

Wasting time

In this section, students read a humorous text in which the writer recommends ways of wasting time at work without getting caught. The text is used for more practice of useful collocations and office vocabulary.

Collocations

1 Students match the collocations. When checking the answers, encourage them to use the collocations in sentences of their own so that they hear them in a context.

2 When checking the answers, ask different students to read out sections of the text, supplying the missing words as they go.

Elicit students' reactions to the text. Do they think it is funny or shocking? Do they ever waste time at work? Why and how?

3 You could ask students to work in small groups, to choose one or two of the headings and to write out short texts giving their tips for time wasting. Read them out or display them in the classroom for the others to read and enjoy.

4 Students read the author's tips on page 125. Were any of them the same as their recommendations? Have they ever done any of these things?

5 Students find words in the text on page 125 to complete the gaps. When checking answers, ask students read out the completed sentences. Then elicit their reactions to the sentences.

6 In pairs, students discuss other ways of wasting time. If they are uncomfortable about confessing their own time wasting activities, they could talk about those that they have observed other people employing.

If you're short of time

There is quite a lot of discussion in this unit, so you could cut some of the discussion questions or reduce the time allowed.

Time management exercise 4 and exercise 7, and *Just in time* exercise 1 could be set for homework.

Set the *Grammar and Lexis links* exercises for homework and check the answers at the beginning of the next class.

Conversation skills 16 Getting things done

This unit is about persuading other people to do things for you – and reacting to similar requests from others. It begins by introducing language for asking for favours, and looks at ways of saying no tactfully and recognising the difference between requests, persuasion and threats.

In the second section, students study two conversations, one in which a passenger secures an upgrade when he checks in for a flight and the other in which a hotel guest makes an unsuccessful complaint about his room.

In this first section, students listen to and practise short dialogues asking people to do something for them and asking people to allow them to do something. They then learn how to refuse a request tactfully and practise conversations in which they say no without giving offence. Finally, they re-order a conversation and identify requests, persuasion and threats used to try to persuade someone to do something she doesn't want to do.

Warm-up

Brainstorm all the kinds of favours students need to ask other people for during their working lives. Try to organise them on the board so that there are two sections: things you ask other people to do for you (make some photocopies for you, etc.) and things you ask other people to allow you to do (borrow their car, etc.) Encourage students to say how they try to persuade other people to grant them favours.

Focus students' attention on the quotation from Harry S Truman at the top of the page and ask for reactions.

Asking favours

1 📼 **16.1** Allow students to work in pairs to complete the extracts. Make sure they have completed all the gaps before you play the recording for them to listen and check. See if any pairs had other suggestions for ways to complete the gaps that make sense in the context.

2 Students could begin by practising the two extracts in exercise 1 before they move on to making their own conversations.

Go through the prompts in the table with them first to make sure that they understand everything. As they act out their conversations, go round and make a note of any particularly interesting ones that can be performed for the class later.

Saying 'no'

3 📼 **16.2** Ask students how many of the requests in exercise 2 they would agree to. How many would they refuse and why?

Go through the instructions and the questions with the class before playing the recording. Then elicit the answers to the questions.

Ask students for their reactions to Richard's attitude. Would his response be acceptable in their country? What adjectives can they use to describe him? Would they respond to the request in the same way? Try to find out which of their possessions students are happy to lend to other people and which are not. Is it always a question of value or are there other factors at work, e.g. sentimental attachment, dislike of other people handling personal possessions, etc.?

📼 **16.1**
Conversation 1
A: Oh, look outside!
B: What's up?
A: I've got to go to the Post Office to pick something up and it's raining. **Could you lend me your umbrella?**
B: Of course. **As long as you don't lose it**.
A: Oh, right. Don't worry, I won't.

Conversation 2
C: Gert, I have a meeting with an agent this afternoon, and they're decorating my office.

D: Lucky you.
C: The thing is that I need somewhere quiet where we won't be interrupted. **Could I use your office?**
D: All right, **as long as it's free by four**. I've got a meeting myself.
C: Don't worry, it won't take that long.

📼 **16.2**
A: Richard, I wonder if I could ask you a favour?
B: Depends what it is.
A: I've got to go over to the warehouse to do something, and I haven't got my car. **Would you lend me yours?**

B: No way!
A: What?
B: I never lend my car! In any case, where's your car?
A: It's in the garage. Eh, I had a little accident.
B: And you expect me to trust you with mine?
A: It's just a minor scratch. **Oh, don't worry. I'll think of something else**.

16 Getting things done

The president spends most of his time kissing people on the cheek in order to get them to do what they ought to do without gettting kissed.

Harry S Truman (1884–1972), US statesman

Asking favours

1 ▭ 16.1 Complete the extracts from two conversations below which take place in an office. Then listen and compare your answers.

Extract 1

A I 've got to _____ go to the Post Office to pick something up and it's __raining_____ . _Could you_____ lend me your umbrella?

B Of course. As long as _you don't lose it_ .

Extract 2

A The thing is that I need _somewhere quiet_ where we won't be interrupted. _Could I_____ use your office?

B All right, as long as _it's free by four_ . I've got a meeting myself.

What's the difference between *Could I ...?* and *Could you ...?* _The first is asking_ _if you can do something; the second is asking someone to do something for you._

2 Work with a partner. Act out conversations using the prompts below. Use the conversations in 1 as a model.

Problem	Request	As long as ...
phone home / mobile batteries flat	use / your mobile	just a short call
send an e-mail / computer not working	use / computer	not take too long
be at airport at five / taxi services not answering	give / lift	get back before six
post a letter / can't leave the office	post it on your way home	have it ready by five o'clock
translate this letter / no dictionary	borrow yours	get it back by this afternoon
take notes / no pen	lend me one	give it back later
make copies / photocopier not working	take / photocopy shop	answer the phone while I'm out

Saying 'no'

3 ▭ 16.2 It is important to say 'no' to a request tactfully. Otherwise you can create problems for the future. Listen to the conversation and answer the questions.

a What favour does the speaker ask Richard? _to borrow his car_

b How does Richard react? _He refuses strongly/rudely._

c How do you feel about lending things to people?

4 Use the phrases in the box to complete the conversation so that it sounds more polite.

> I'd take my own, of course, but it's being repaired.   Nothing serious, I hope.
> What's the problem?   Well, actually, I'm not very keen on the idea.
> It's just that I don't feel happy about other people driving my car.
> Oh, all right. Not to worry.

A   Richard, I wonder if I could ask you a favour?

B   <u>What's the problem?</u>

A   I've got to go over to the warehouse to do something, and I haven't got my car. Would you lend me yours?

B   <u>Well, actually I'm not very keen on the idea.</u>

A   <u>Oh, all right. Not to worry.</u>

B   <u>It's just that I don't feel happy about other people driving my car.</u>

A   <u>I'd take my own of course, but it's being repaired.</u>

B   <u>Nothing serious I hope.</u>

A   It's just a minor scratch. Oh, don't worry. I'll think of something else.

Requests, persuasion and threats

5 ▭ 16.3 Put the conversation in the correct order. Then listen and check your answer.

Jeff

[11] **a**   ... but on the other hand, if you do it, I'll see it as a personal favour.

[3] **b**   I know, but you can take the time later on.

[5] **c**   No, there isn't. Look, I know it's inconvenient, but I can't think of any other solution.

[1] **d**   Sandra, we need someone to answer the phone from 2.00 til 4.00 while Julia is off sick. Could you do it?

[13] **e**   Yes, in principle, yes. But you never know. Your contract is up for renewal next month. Enough said?

[9] **f**   No, it isn't, and obviously I can't force you to do it, but ...

[7] **g**   Not really. It creates such a bad impression. Listen, I'd do it myself but I've got to be somewhere else.

Sandra

[2] **h**   From 2.00 to 4.00? It's not my hours.

[6] **i**   Well, can't we just put the answer phone on for a couple of hours?

[14] **j**   Yeah, enough said.

[4] **k**   It's not the time. I'll have to get someone to pick the kids up from school. Isn't there anyone else?

[12] **l**   I see. I don't really have much choice, do I? I hope it's just this time ...

[10] **m**   But?

[8] **n**   I'm sure you would, but it's not my problem, is it?

6   Identify phrases in 5 for the following:

a   a request <u>... we need someone to answer the phone from 2.00 to 4.00 ... Could you do it?</u>

b   a suggestion <u>Can't we just put the answer phone on for a couple of hours?</u>

c   emotional blackmail <u>... if you do it, I'll see it as a personal favour.</u>

d   a threat <u>Your contract is up for renewal next month. Enough said?</u>

4 Establish that Richard's reaction in the conversation in exercise 3 was rather abrupt and rude and that it is possible to say no but still be polite. Give students a few minutes to construct a conversation which is more polite.

Check the answers by having a pair of students perform the conversation for the class. Elicit what make this conversation more polite than the one they heard in exercise 3 (less direct language and more hesitancy – *Well, actually … It's just that …*, giving a reason for reluctance to agree to a favour, expressing interest in and sympathy for the other person's problem).

Requests, persuasion and threats

5 📼 **16.3** Elicit the meaning of the three words in the subheading (request = asking someone to do something for you; persuasion = talking someone into doing something for you; threat = telling someone that unless they do something for you, you will do something bad to them).

Students put the conversation in order and compare their answers in pairs before listening to the recording.

6 Students identify the different features in the text in exercise 5. Check the answers with the class and elicit the difference between a *threat* (telling someone that there will be bad consequences for them if they don't do as they're told) and *emotional blackmail* (playing on someone's sympathies by linking the request with your personal relationship). Ask whether students think threats and emotional blackmail are ever acceptable to persuade someone to do something. Does the context (office life or personal life) affect their opinion?

📼 **16.3**

A: Sandra, **we need someone to answer the phone from 2.00 til 4.00 while Julia is off sick**. Could you do it?
B: From 2.00 to 4.00? It's not my hours.
A: I know, but you can take the time later on.
B: It's not the time. I'll have to get someone to pick the kids up from school. Isn't there anyone else?
A: No, there isn't. **Look, I know it's inconvenient, but I can't think of any other solution**.

B: Well, can't we just put the answer phone on for a couple of hours?
A: Not really. It creates such a bad impression. Listen, I'd do it myself but I've got to be somewhere else.
B: I'm sure you would, but it's not my problem, is it?
A: No, it isn't, and **obviously I can't force you to do it, but …**
B: But?
A: … but on the other hand, **if you do it, I'll see it as a personal favour**.

B: I see. I don't really have much choice, do I? I hope it's just this time …
A: Yes, in principle, yes. But you never know. Your contract is up for renewal next month. Enough said?
B: Yeah, enough said.

Upgrade

In this section, students study two conversations in which people try to get their own way. In the first, an airline passenger successfully negotiates an upgrade to business class by being charming to the check-in clerk. In the second, a hotel guest tries to get a better room by complaining to the receptionist, but his manner is rude and aggressive and he doesn't succeed.

Warm-up

Ask students to say what kind of customer they think they are. Do they try to get what they want by gentle persuasion or do they think that the best way to get what you want is to make as much noise as possible and complain if anything is not 100% right? Encourage them to tell the class of any experience they have of getting or not getting what they wanted.

1 ▭ **16.4**

Conversation 1

Make sure students have read the questions before you play the recording so that they know exactly what information they are listening for. Play the recording and allow students to read the script as they listen. Then elicit the answers from the class.

Encourage students to talk about their own experiences of air travel. Have they ever got an upgrade? What do they think is the best way to get one, e.g. should you dress smartly, try to chat up the check-in clerk, etc.?

Conversation 2

Again, make sure students have read the questions before you play the recording. When you have checked the answers to the questions, elicit the differences between the two conversations (the man in the second is rather rude and aggressive and he is not successful in getting what he wants). Ask students if they think the outcomes in the two conversations are representative of real life. Do quiet, polite and charming people usually get what they want? Is rudeness and aggression always unsuccessful?

2 In pairs, students act out conversation 2, this time making the guest polite. If they want to introduce more variety, the student playing the guest could use one of the suggestions made in answer to question d to change the reason why the room is unsuitable. Emphasise that the student playing the receptionist should listen carefully to the guest and decide what to do, based on their impression of the guest and their feelings towards him or her. As they act out their conversations, go round and make a note of any particularly successful ones which could be performed for the class afterwards.

Ask students how they feel when they are confronted by rude and aggressive people. Do they feel more inclined to give them what they want (to get them out of the way as quickly as possible) or do they resist them because they are irritated by their attitude?

If you're short of time

Students could do exercise 5 on page 74 for homework.

▭ **16.4**

Conversation 1
A: Good afternoon, sir.
B: Hello. I'm on flight IB 603. **I was wondering if there's any chance of an upgrade to business class**.
A: Well, I don't know. It depends how crowded the flight is.
B: Yes, **I quite understand, but I'd really appreciate it if you could have a look**. I don't mind paying the extra. It's just that I've had a really hard day and **it'd be really nice to have a bit more space and comfort**.
A: Just a minute, sir.
B: **I'm sorry to put you to any trouble**.

A: No, that's okay. Oh, yes, there's lots of space in business class. I think we can do it.
B: Oh, fantastic. How much is that?
A: That's all right, sir. Don't worry.
B: **Oh, thank you ever so much**.
A: You're welcome. Have a good flight.

Conversation 2
A: Good evening, sir.
B: Look, I'm not at all happy with the room you've given me. It's on the wrong side of the hotel. It faces on to the road and it's far too noisy.
A: I'm sorry, sir. No one has ever said anything before.
B: I can't believe that. Are you going to change it?

A: I don't think I can, sir. We're a bit full tonight.
B: Look, I'm really tired, and the last thing I want to do is argue about my room. If you don't change it, I'll tell my company not to use this hotel again.
A: I'm sorry. There's no other room available.
B: Oh, come on.
A: There's nothing I can do.
B: What about some sort of discount, then?
A: I'm afraid I'm not authorised to offer a discount on your room.
B: So, I have to pay the full price for a noisy room. Brilliant!
A: Sir, if you want, I can call you a taxi …

Upgrade

1   🎞 16.4

Conversation 1   A passenger is checking in for a flight. Listen to the conversation and answer the questions.

A   Good afternoon, sir.

B   Hello. I'm on flight IB 603. <u>I was wondering if there's any chance</u> of an upgrade to business class.

A   Well, I don't know. It depends how crowded the flight is.

B   Yes, <u>I quite understand</u>, but <u>I'd really appreciate it if you could</u> have a look. I don't mind paying the extra. It's just that I've had a really hard day and <u>it'd be really nice</u> to have a bit more space and comfort.

A   Just a minute, sir.

B   <u>I'm sorry to put you to any trouble.</u>

A   No, that's okay. Oh, yes, there's lots of space in business class. I think we can do it.

B   Oh, fantastic. How much is that?

A   That's all right, sir. Don't worry.

B   Oh, <u>thank you ever so much.</u>

A   You're welcome. Have a good flight.

a   What is an upgrade? _a seat in a higher class than the ticket is for_

b   Do you think the passenger really expects to pay for the upgrade? _no_

c   Is the passenger polite? _yes_

d   Does he get what he wants? _yes_

e   Underline the phrases in the conversation which the passenger uses to sound polite.

Conversation 2   A guest is checking in to a hotel. Listen to the conversation and answer the questions.

A   Good evening, sir.

B   Look, I'm not at all happy with the room you've given me. It's on the wrong side of the hotel. It faces on to the road and it's far too noisy.

A   I'm sorry, sir. No one has ever said anything before.

B   I can't believe that. Are you going to change it?

A   I don't think I can, sir. We're a bit full tonight.

B   Look, I'm really tired, and the last thing I want to do is argue about my room. If you don't change it, I'll tell my company not to use this hotel again.

A   I'm sorry. There's no other room available.

B   Oh, come on.

A   There's nothing I can do.

B   What about some sort of discount, then?

A   I'm afraid I'm not authorised to offer a discount on your room.

B   So, I have to pay the full price for a noisy room. Brilliant!

A   Sir, if you want, I can call you a taxi ...

a   Do you think the guest's request is reasonable? _yes_

b   Is the guest polite? _no_

c   Does he get what he wants? _no_

d   What other reasons can you think of for wanting to change your room?

2   Work with a partner. Act out conversation 2. This time the guest is polite. Use the phrases you underlined in conversation 1. If you are the receptionist, decide what to do.

17 Office gossip

No one gossips about other people's secret virtues. *Bertrand Russell, British philosopher*

1 🔊 17.1 Listen to the conversation and answer the questions.

a Why has Trixy been out of the office?

She has had a few days' holiday

b What is the news which she hasn't heard?

The company is restructuring and some staff will lose their jobs.

c Is Prescott their boss or a colleague?

their boss

d Why are they worried?

They may lose their jobs.

e Why don't they think that Maureen will be worried?

She's having an affair with Prescott.

f The expression 'There's no smoke without fire' means that when people gossip about something, there's usually some truth in what they say. Do you have an equivalent saying in your language? Do you think it's true?

Reported speech

2 Look at this sentence from the conversation in 1.
... he said that we were overstaffed.
The original statement was 'You are overstaffed.'

Listen to the conversation again and complete the reported statements.

a You will have to let some people go.

This consultant chap _told him they would_ *have to let some people go.*

b How many people does it involve?

Prescott _asked him how many people_ *it involved.*

c It depends on individual performance and attitude.

He _said it depended_ *on individual performance and attitude.*

d I often see them coming out of *The Green Man* together.

I'm not saying who, but someone _told me he often sees_ *them in* The Green Man *together.*

Grammar link

for more on reported speech see page 118

e Will you stay behind to work on something with me?

The other day he _asked her if she would_ *stay behind to work on something together.*

Say and *tell*

3 Which of the sentences below needs *said* and which one needs *told*?

a He _said_ we were overstaffed.

b He _told_ me we were overstaffed.

What is the main difference between *say* and *tell*? _We use say + something and tell + somebody + something_

Question words

4 What words are missing from the following sentences?

a 'Where are you going?' He asked me _where_ I was going.

b 'When are you going?' He asked me _when_ I was going.

Work issues 17 Office gossip

This unit uses the topic of office gossip and small talk at work to practise reported speech. Students also look at the wider implications of office gossip and discuss whether it is harmful or productive. A text about an attempt to ban gossiping at work leads to a roleplay in which a management consultant tries to persuade a client to abandon a strict policy aimed at discouraging gossip at the coffee machine.

The grammatical focus is on reported speech, and the lexical focus is on relationships at work.

In this first section, students listen to and discuss some office gossip. They then examine the language used and explore how we report speech and how we use *say* and *tell*. They do further work on question words and tenses in reported speech and then complete conversations and report them.

Warm-up

Focus students' attention on the quotation from Bertrand Russell at the top of the page. Point out that *secret virtues* is not a common collocation, it is the opposite of a common collocation which is being used here for effect. Ask students to speculate on what the original common collocation might be (*secret vices*) or, at least what it might mean, i.e. the things that people do gossip about, which are normally a person's bad points rather than their good points. Then brainstorm the sorts of things people gossip about at the office and make a list on the board. Encourage students to say when and where they think most gossip in the office is exchanged (coffee machine, dining room, toilets, etc.).

1 **17.1** Make sure students have read the questions before you play the recording so that they know exactly what information they are listening for. Ask a couple of students to speculate on what the conversation will be about. Then play the recording and check the answers. You could make the final question a class discussion. Play the recording a second time, if necessary.

Reported speech

2 Go through the example sentences with the class. Elicit what has happened in the change from direct speech to reported speech (the tense of the verb has shifted back from Present Simple to Past Simple and the pronoun has changed from *you* to *we*).

Establish that the first sentence in each pair (a–e) is what the person actually said and the second sentence is the reported speech. With stronger students, ask them to try to complete the reported speech before they listen to the recording again.

When you have checked the answers, ask students to identify and underline the parts of the sentences which have changed when they are reported.

Direct students' attention to the Grammar link on page 118 where they will find more information on direct and reported speech and how words change from one form to the other. There is also a further transformation exercise to practise reporting what people have said.

Say and tell

3 Ask students to work in pairs to decide which sentence needs *said* and which *told*. Check the answers with the class and elicit the difference between them. Ask students to produce one or two example sentences of their own using *say* and *tell*.

Question words

4 Students complete sentences a, b and c. Elicit when we use the word *if* in reporting questions. Ask students for one or two more examples of their own.

You could divide the class into two teams and have them take turns to say a question for the other team to report. Each team gets a point for every correctly reported question. To make this more challenging, ensure that the questions are a mixture of questions with question words and yes/no questions.

17.1

A: Hi Quin. How's it going?
B: Trixy! Where have you been?
A: I had a few days' holiday owing to me.
B: Go anywhere interesting?
A: I wish! No, I went up north to stay with my parents.
B: So, you haven't heard the news.
A: What news?
B: About the 'restructuring'.
A: What restructuring?
B: They want to reorganise marketing and sales.
A: No! Really? Is it official?
B: No, but somebody overheard Prescott talking to one of the management consultants.

A: What did he say?
B: Apparently **he said that we were overstaffed in some areas.**
A: Never!
B: Yes, **this consultant chap told him they would have to let some people go.**
A: But that's awful.
B: Yes, **Prescott asked him how many people it involved.**
A: And what did he say?
B: **He said it depended on individual performance and attitude.**
A: Does that include Maureen?
B: What do you mean?
A: Well, you know what they say about her and Prescott.
B: Go on …

A: I'm not saying who, but **someone told me he often sees them in *The Green Man* together.**
B: That little pub on the Oxford Road?
A: That's right.
B: Well I never! The other day **he asked her if she would stay behind to work on something together.** I heard him.
A: There you are, then. There's no smoke without fire.
B: Listen, don't tell anyone I told you.
A: Now, come on, Quin, you know me better than that.
B: Back to work, then.
A: Right. Catch you later.
B: Bye.

Tenses

5   Remind students of the tense shift they saw in exercise 2 and ask them to complete sentences a and b. Then check the answers with the class and elicit answers to questions c and d.

6   ▭ **17.2** Emphasise that students can complete the gaps in the four conversations with any words that make sense in the context. Allow them to compare their answers in pairs. Then play the recording for them to listen and compare their version with the recording.

▭ **17.2**

Conversation 1

A: Jeff, have you finished last month's production figures?

B: No, Jane, I'm sorry. Can I give them to you this afternoon?

A: It's no good being sorry. There's always some excuse. If they're not on my desk by 4 o'clock, I'll have to speak to Mr Bradley.

B: Yes, Jane. I'll start straight away.

Conversation 2

C: David, have you got a minute? There's something I want to discuss with you … in my office.

D: What's it about?

C: Oh, well, we're missing a laptop computer from the store.

D: What has that got to do with me?

C: Well, you are the only other person with a key to the store and …

Conversation 3

E: Marie, the figures you need are ready.

F: Thanks, Pedro. Is everything okay?

E: Yes, no problems. Would you like to look at them with me?

F: Yes, but I'm a bit busy this afternoon.

E: Me too. Er, do you know that new café they've just opened? It's nice and quiet. We can go through them there after work.

F: Oh, I suppose so, but I won't be able to stay for long.

E: Great. See you there at about six, then?

F: Yes, all right. See you there.

Conversation 4

G: Hi, Monica.

H: Oh, hello Jim. How are things going?

G: Great. In fact, you can be the first to congratulate me.

H: Yes, you look very pleased with yourself. What's up?

G: I'm the new head of the eastern sales team.

H: Oh, really? What salary are you on now, then?

G: Sixty grand a year.

H: I can't believe it. Sixty thousand!

G: And they're giving me a new company car.

H: Oh really? Congratulations, then. The drinks are on you. See you later.

G: Yes. Bye.

c 'Are you going?' He asked me __if__ I was going.

When reporting questions, when do you use the word *if*? __when reporting__ __yes/no questions__

Tenses **5** Complete the sentences below.

a 'I'm busy.' He said he __was__ busy.

b 'I'll start straight away.' He said he __would start__ straight away.

c What changes do you make to the Present Simple in reported speech?

__In reported speech it changes to the Past Simple.__

d What changes do you make to *will* in reported speech?

__It changes to 'would'.__

6 🔊 17.2 Look at the conversations below. Complete them with words and phrases which make sense. Then listen and compare your answers.

Conversation 1

A Jeff, __have you finished__ last month's production figures?

B No, Jane, I'm __sorry__. Can I give them to you this afternoon?

A It's no good being sorry. There's always some __excuse__. If they're not on my desk by 4 o'clock, I'll have to __speak to__ Mr Bradley.

B Yes, Jane. I'll start __straight away__.

Conversation 2

C David, have you got __a minute__? There's something I want to __discuss__ with you ... in my office.

D What's it about?

C Oh, well, we're missing a laptop __computer__ from the store.

D What has that got to do with me?

C Well, you are the only other person with a __key__ to the store and ...

Conversation 3

E Marie, the figures you need are __ready__.

F Thanks, Pedro. Is everything __okay__?

E Yes, no problems. Would you like to __look at__ them with me?

F Yes, but I'm a bit __busy__ this afternoon.

E Me too. Er, do __you know__ that new café they've just opened? It's nice and __quiet__. We can go through them there after __work__.

F Oh, I __suppose__ so, but I won't be able to stay for long.

E Great. __See you__ there at about six, then?

F Yes, all right. See you there.

Conversation 4

G   Hi, Monica.

H   Oh, hello, Jim. __How are__ things going?

G   Great. In fact, you can be the first to congratulate me.

H   Yes, you look very __pleased__ with yourself. What's up?

G   I'm the new __head__ of the eastern sales team.

H   Oh, really? What salary are you on now, then?

G   __Sixty grand__ a year.

H   I can't believe it. Sixty thousand!

G   And they're giving me a new __company car__.

H   Oh, really? Congratulations, then. The __drinks__ are on you. See you later.

G   Yes. Bye.

Lexis link

for more on the vocabulary of relationships at work see page 119

7   You are at the coffee machine having a gossip with a colleague. You have overheard the conversations in 6. Use the frameworks in the box to tell your partner what you heard. It is not necessary to report everything.

> I heard ... talking to ...   ... said that ...   ... told ... that ...   ... asked ...

Gossip

1   Read the following news article.

   a   What is the new law? __Public employees who spread rumours or gossip about colleagues will lose their jobs.__

   b   Do you think it's a good idea? Why/why not?

> ## City Council gags workers
>
> Municipal employees in the Brazilian city of Cascavel have been banned from gossiping during working hours. Under a new law approved by the city council, public employees who spread rumours or gossip about their colleagues face the sack. The city says civil servants have the right to work in a professional environment and claim the new law will promote integrity in public offices.

2   Find words and phrases in the text which mean the following:

   a   ordered not to do something __banned from__

   b   pass on information which is not official and may not be true
       __spread rumours or gossip__

   c   be in a position where you can be dismissed __face the sack__

Discussion   3   Discuss the following with other people in the class.

   a   How do you define gossip?
   b   Is it always a bad thing?
   c   Is it possible to ban it?
   d   Does your company have a policy on gossip? Have you ever heard of a company that does?

7 Students work in pairs and take turns to report the conversations they heard in exercise 6. As students practise their conversations, go round offering help and encouragement and make a note of any particularly good conversations which could be performed to the class.

Direct students' attention to the Lexis link on page 119 where they will find more vocabulary on the subject of office relationships. There is also a crossword puzzle on the same topic.

Gossip

In this section, students begin by reading a newspaper cutting about a new law against gossiping introduced by a Brazilian city council. They discuss the law and look at some of the vocabulary used in the text. They then discuss the subject of gossip and talk about policies in their own companies. Next they read a selection of e-mails on the subject of gossip and complete sentences to give their own point of view. Then they listen to a radio interview about gossip and discuss statements about it. Finally, they do a roleplay in which a management consultant tries to persuade a client to relax a strict policy banning gossip at work.

1 Give students a few minutes to read the article and discuss it in pairs. Then ask them to answer the questions.

Have a class vote on whether the ban on gossiping is a good idea or a bad one. Would students like to introduce a ban on gossiping in their English classes?

2 Students should scan the text quickly to find the matching words. Then check the answers and ask students to use the new words in sentences of their own.

Discussion

3 Divide the class into small groups and appoint a secretary in each one to take notes of the discussion and report back to the class.

4   Go through the table headings with the class before they
    read the e-mails. Then ask them to read the texts and
    classify them according to the headings.

    Allow students to compare their notes in pairs before
    checking the answers with the class. Elicit which, if any,
    of the e-mails they agree with.

5   Ensure that students understand that they should
    complete the sentences with their own ideas, not find the
    phrases in the texts and copy out the words that were
    used there. Ask them to compare their completed
    sentences in pairs or small groups and see how much
    consensus there is. Then have a class feedback session.

4 The e-mails below were sent to a website for office workers. Read them and classify them in the table. Then compare your answers with a partner.

Gossip is good	Mixed feelings	Gossip is bad
A, B, D, H	E, G	C, F

A A friendly and chatty work environment makes employees happy. This results in a better level of work from employees, which means the company makes more money. Any employer who bans office gossip will lose money by making the workforce less productive.
James Pittman, England

B In my place of work gossip is the only way of finding anything out about the company strategy. The management refuse to talk to most of the staff.
Janet Jones, Wales

C There's nothing worse than gossip – and it's mostly propagated by women who have nothing better to do than YAP YAP YAP.
Luke McCarthy, Australia

D Gossip isn't a bad thing. Is there another way to learn about office politics? I see it as a healthy activity and part of working in an office.
Nicole Martin, France

E Gossip is what someone, somewhere, doesn't want you to know. A delicious pastime – unless you are the one being gossiped about. And certainly not a sackable offence.
Pieter Groot, Netherlands

F Having started a new job a year ago, I made an effort never to engage in gossip. If I'm in a group where gossip starts, I find a reason to leave the area. It can be very damaging to your career and general workplace relations.
Sanjay Patel, India

G Isn't freedom of speech a basic human right? However, there's a fine line between harmless and hurtful remarks. I think it's best left to individuals to decide which is which.
Claudia Weber, Germany

H Some of my biggest insights into problems at work have occurred while chatting by the coffee machine. Having a (brief) chat about totally unrelated matters, although not directly productive, can actually improve productivity by breaking up the day a little.
John Mason, Scotland

5 The phrases below are from the e-mails above. Complete the sentences with your own words and ideas.

a In my place of work _____

b Any employer who _____ will

_____

c There's nothing worse than _____

d _____ isn't a bad thing.

e I make an effort never to _____

f A _____ work environment makes employees

_____

6 You are going to listen to an interview about office gossip from a radio programme. The words and phrases on the left are from the interview. Match them to the definitions on the right.

a drive for efficiency   1 talking informally
b scrapped   2 mobile refreshments service
c human resources   3 effort to get more work done
d encouraged   4 seen as positive
e chatting   5 not continued with
f tea trolley   6 organisation and management of company staff

a	3	b	5	c	6	d	4	e	1	f	2

7 Before you listen, decide if you agree with the following statements.

a Companies who provide an opportunity for their workers to socialise are making a mistake.

b People have less time to talk to each other and socialise than before.

c The differences between a good job and a bad job are the social aspects.

d Employees are more productive when they are happy.

e When employees share information and knowledge, the company benefits.

f Companies should take measures to encourage gossip.

8   17.3 Listen to the interview to see if the speaker agrees with you.

The speaker disagrees with 7a and agrees with 7b, c, d, e and f.

Roleplay   9 Work with a partner and perform the following roleplay about office policy on coffee breaks and gossiping. Speaker A read the instructions below. Speaker B look at the instructions on page 133.

Speaker A

You are one of the management consultants who prepared the study mentioned in the interview in 8. In a client's company you see the notice below next to the coffee machine. Try to persuade the client to change the policy.

COMPANY NOTICE

Employees may take up to three coffee breaks per day.
Maximum time at coffee machine: four minutes.
All 'gossip' or discussion of non-work related matters is prohibited.

Writing   10 Complete the memo below.

From: Personnel Manager
To: Managing Director   *(example answer)*

With regard to the company policy on coffee breaks, *I have seen the notice next to the coffee machine, and I am concerned about it.*

In my opinion, *we should reconsider the policy and remove the notice.*

According to a report by the Industrial Society, *efficiency drives that remove opportunities for people to chat are counter-productive.*

In the report the author says that *happy employees are productive employees.*

It is a question of balance, but *preventing gossip does not lead to efficiency.*

In conclusion, *I think we should change our policy.*

6 Students work individually to match the words and definitions and then compare their answers in pairs. When checking the answers, you could ask them to use each word in a sentence.

7 You could ask people to raise their hands if they agree with each statement. Alternatively, have all the students stand up, read out the statements one by one and ask students who agree with each one to remain standing and those who disagree to sit down. Make a note of the majority view on each one.

8 🔲 **17.3** Play the recording and ask students to listen for whether the speaker agrees with the statements in exercise 7 or not.

Roleplay

9 Students work in pairs to do the roleplay. Give them plenty of time to prepare what they are going to say, but discourage them from writing out a script. When they do their roleplays, go round offering help and encouragement. At the end, find out how many of the managers were convinced by the consultant's arguments and persuaded to change their policy.

Writing

10 The memo is easiest to complete if the personnel manager believes the policy should be changed. However, you could give students the option of backing the policy in spite of the evidence from the Industrial Society's report.

If you're short of time

Set *Gossip* exercises 4, 5 and 10 for homework.

Set the *Grammar and Lexis links* exercises for homework and check the answers at the beginning of the next class.

🔲 **17.3**

A: In this week's *Business Today*, we talk to Karina Schmidt. Karina is the author of a report by the Industrial Society which looks at workplace relations, and how they've changed over the years. Karina, first of all, welcome to the programme.

B: Thank you, it's a pleasure to be here.

A: In your report, you say that many companies nowadays have abandoned some useful institutions which allowed for social interaction.

B: Yes, these days there's less opportunity to gossip and socialise. For example, often the tea trolley has been scrapped, and having a chat in the tea break was an important part of the working day. The drink after work at the pub around the corner is another example.

A: And why do you think these things have disappeared?

B: I think it's all part of the revolution in human resources. Some of these traditions have become unfashionable. Talking about things not connected to work is now seen as bad and as wasting time. There are even theories about removing chairs from meeting rooms, so that the meetings are more efficient and finish quickly.

A: And are we more efficient now, then?

B: Well, that's a good question, but in any case, something has been lost from the workplace which is very important. And perhaps in the long term, with these drives for efficiency, companies are making false economies.

A: In what way?

B: The difference between a good job and a bad job are the human, emotional elements. In other words, happy employees are productive employees. People enjoy the social aspects of work, the personal interaction with colleagues, the friendships …

A: And the gossip!

B: And the gossip. Yes, in some ways gossip is the glue that holds the organisation together. Providing communal space such as coffee areas or lunch rooms allows employees to share information and build relationships that benefit both the company and the employees.

A: Are you saying that gossip should be encouraged?

B: Not exactly, it's obviously a question of balance. All gossip and chatting doesn't make for an efficient company, but neither does no gossip or chat. All I'm saying is that I think companies would do well to remember this when trying to improve efficiency and bring down costs.

A: Karina, I'm afraid that's all we've got time for. Thank you very much for talking to us. It's been very interesting.

B: Thank you for inviting me.

A: That's all for now from *Business Today*. So, until next week, goodbye.

Connecting 18 E-commerce

With the rapid growth of the Internet in recent years, e-commerce has become more than an interesting option for many companies, and experience in it is an increasing requirement for those seeking jobs in sales. This unit looks at the factors which are involved in persuading someone to buy something, the efficacy and morality of targeting teenagers in Internet marketing and the future of e-commerce.

The grammatical focus is on *will* for future predictions, and the lexical focus is on shopping and the Internet.

In this first section, the topic of e-commerce is introduced by looking at people's reasons for buying things and the factors which affect their decisions. Students discuss their own attitudes to shopping and listen to an extract from a radio programme on marketing which looks at the advantages and problems of targeting teenagers in Internet marketing. Students complete notes and then a report on the subject. They then examine some of the language used in the discussion to compare and contrast different points of view.

Warm-up

Find out what students' attitudes to selling things are. Do they think you have to be a certain kind of person to enjoy selling things or to be successful at it? Focus their attention on the quotation from Robert Louis Stevenson at the top of the page. Do they agree with him that everyone lives by selling something? What experience do they have of selling things or being sold things by other people?

1 Allow students to work in pairs or small groups to discuss and complete the sentences. Make sure they have made firm decisions before they check with the sentences on page 125. Then have a class feedback session to find out if they agree or not.

Discussion

2 Students should discuss the questions in pairs and be prepared to report back to the class on what they said. Ask anyone who has bought something on the Internet to tell the class about it. Did they have any problems in doing it? Were they happy with the item when it arrived? Did the experience encourage them to buy again from the Internet or did it put them off? What are the advantages and disadvantages of buying things in this way?

18 E-commerce

Everyone lives by selling something. *Robert Louis Stevenson*

1   Complete the sentences using the phrases in the box. Then compare them with those on page 125. Do you agree?

> you're interested in quality   who cares?   you're interested in price
> you're interested in quality and price

a   When you buy something for yourself with your own money,
    <u>you're interested in quality and price</u>

b   When you buy something for someone else with your own money,
    <u>you're interested in price</u>

c   When you buy something for yourself with someone else's money,
    <u>you're interested in quality</u>

d   When you buy something for someone else with someone else's money,
    <u>who cares?</u>

Discussion   2   Work with a partner. Ask each other the following questions.

a   When was the last time you bought something for:
   • yourself?
   • somebody else?
   • a customer or client?
   • your company?

b   What did you buy?

c   What factors influenced your decisions?

d   What kind of shopping do you like/dislike?

e   Have you ever bought anything on the Internet?

focus group noun [C] a small group of people who are interviewed together and give their opinions about particular subjects, usually to help a company or political party make decisions

from *Macmillan English Dictionary*

3 You are going to listen to a focus group discussion from the radio programme *Marketing Today*. The topic is marketing to teenagers on the Internet. Before you listen, look at the headings on the notepad below. What do you think the participants will say about the different topics?

Teenagers and Internet marketing

Opportunities
Attitude to technology and the Internet:
<u>comfortable with it and positive about it</u>
Financial responsibilities and spending power:
<u>no financial responsibilities - so money to spend</u>

Problems
Differences between teenage age groups:
<u>11-18 too big a group - big differences between different ages</u>
Main uses teenagers make of the Internet:
<u>chatting and sending e-mails</u>
Main problem teenagers have when they buy online:
<u>They don't have credit cards and don't want to ask parents for money.</u>
Morality of marketing to teenagers:
<u>They make irrational, emotional purchases - is it right?</u>

Possible solution - 'Splash Plastic'
What is it?
<u>magnetic swipe card</u>
How it works:
<u>can be topped up with cash at stores and used to buy online</u>
What products teenagers can buy with it:
<u>only those suitable for under 18-year-olds</u>

4 **18.1** Listen to the focus group discussion between the host and four marketing experts. Complete the notes in 3.

5 You are preparing a report on using the Internet to market to teenagers. Use your notes in 3 to complete the introduction to the report.

TEENAGERS AND THE INTERNET

TEENAGERS are an opportunity for companies marketing over the Internet for two reasons. Firstly, their attitude to new technology is generally <u>positive</u>. Secondly, unlike adults, they have no <u>financial responsibilities</u>.

However, marketing to this age group presents special problems. One problem is age. The average age
5 of the heaviest users is <u>13</u>, but they want to buy things aimed at <u>18-year-olds</u>. Another is that they don't want to ask <u>their parents for money</u>. As a result, they tend to use the Internet for communication, but <u>not shopping</u>. One possible solution is the Splash Plastic magnetic swipe card. Kids can top it up with cash at selected stores, and then use it to <u>buy online</u>. This avoids problems with the parents because <u>they can only buy products suitable for children</u>.
10 However, for some people there is also a <u>moral problem</u> in marketing to teenagers who will buy things in an impulsive and irresponsible way.

In conclusion, in spite of the problems, for e-commerce to be a success in the future, we have to take advantage of the fact that <u>they want to buy online</u>.

6 Listen again and complete the sentences. There is a space for each missing word. Contractions count as one word.

3 Focus students' attention on the definition for *focus group* before they do the exercise. Go through the headings with the class and elicit their ideas on what the speakers might say about each topic.

4 🔲 **18.1** Play the recording for students to complete the notes in exercise 3. You may need to play it more than once or pause it at certain points to allow students time to write their notes. Then check the answers with the class.

5 This exercise could be done for homework. Check the answers with the class.

6 The sentences are all from the recording. You could ask students to try to complete them before you play it again. Then check the answers with the class.

🔲 **18.1**

A: There are nearly seven million teenagers in the UK. According to their parents, they wear too much make-up, treat the house like a hotel and run up huge phone bills. **At the same time**, for e-commerce teenagers are a dream because they're so comfortable with the Internet and positive about new technology. And without the financial responsibilities of adults, they generally have money to spend. The sites targeted at these teenagers offer them chat, competitions and e-mail access, as well as things to buy. Lucy, you're the marketing manager of one of these teen sites – Wicked Colours. **How do you see** the future of e-commerce in this market?

B: **I think the main problem is** age. Some sites try to target an age group that's too wide. As a result, they don't satisfy anyone. Some target from 11 to 18-year-olds. But an 11-year-old is nothing like an 18-year-old. We aim our site at younger teenagers. The site is designed for them. The average age would be 13 but we go as young as 11. It's this group that spends the most time at the computer. The 16 to 18-years-olds are interested in other things

like going out to clubs. **Would you agree**, Nick?

C: **Yes, and the other problem is that** all 13-year-olds want to be 18-year-olds. If you look at the magazines aimed at young teenage girls, most of them have disappeared. The younger kids like to read adult magazines like *Marie Claire* and *Vogue*.

A: Okay, **the right audience is one thing, but getting them to buy directly from your site is another**. Most of these sites sell online, but teenagers don't want to ask their parents for their Visa card. Nick?

C: **That's right, and** that's why, in my opinion, the teenager market has no future. Apart from the fact that teenagers don't have credit cards, they use the Internet differently from adults. They see it mainly as a means of communication. They will spend hours chatting and sending e-mails – but not shopping. So, you can make some money from advertising, but not much from direct sales. **I think Brian will back me up on that**.

D: **Actually, I don't agree**, Nick. Lee is right, they don't want to ask their parents for money every time they want to buy

something, but if you free them from that parental control, teenagers will buy online. So, what we do is give them their own magnetic swipe card called *Splash Plastic*. They can use their allowance to top the card up with cash at a number of stores around the country. Then when they're at home, they can use the card to buy online, but only in sites that *Splash Plastic* has authorised as suitable, and only products suitable for under 18-year-olds. In other words, they can't buy X-rated videos. That keeps the parents happy.

A: But even if these new payment methods work, isn't there a moral problem? Teenagers make irrational, emotional purchases. So, is it right to market to them so heavily in the first place? Lucy?

B: **Well, that's a good question**, but rightly or wrongly, the current generation of teenagers will have an important influence on the future of e-commerce. It's clear that they want to buy online, and if we don't take advantage of that, someone else will.

7 📼 **18.2** Read the example sentence to the class or play that part of the recording again so that students hear the correct intonation. The stress is on the words in bold which establish that a comparison is being made between two things.

Students then make similar sentences with the prompts. When checking the answers, ask students to read the sentences aloud, using the correct intonation.

Then play the recording for students to listen and compare their answers.

📼 **18.2**

a The right qualifications for a job **are one thing**, but having experience **is another**.
b A high turnover **is one thing**, but making good profits **is another**.
c Having a good idea **is one thing**, but putting it into practice **is another**.
d High productivity **is one thing**, but improving staff motivation **is another**.
e Creating a good product **is one thing**, but selling it **is another**.

a According to their parents, teenagers wear too much make-up, treat the house like a hotel and run up huge phone bills. _At_ _the_ _same_ _time_, for e-commerce teenagers are a dream.

b Lucy, you're the marketing manager of one of these teen sites – Wicked Colours. _How_ _do_ _you_ _see_ the future of e-commerce in this market?

c _I_ _think_ _the_ _main_ _problem_ is age. Some sites try to target an age group that's too wide.

d Yes, _and_ _the_ _other_ _problem_ _is_ _that_ all 13-year-olds want to be 18-year-olds.

e _That's_ _right_, and that's why, in my opinion, the teenager market has no future.

f I think Brian will _back_ _me_ _up_ _on_ _that_ .

g Actually, _I_ _don't_ _agree_, Nick.

h Well, _that's_ _a_ _good_ _question_, but rightly or wrongly, the current generation of teenagers will have an important influence on the future of e-commerce.

7 Look at this phrase from the discussion.

The right audience **is one thing, but** *getting them to buy directly from your site* **is another**.

Make similar sentences using the following prompts.

a the right qualifications / have experience

The right qualifications for a job are one thing, but having experience is another.

b a high turnover / make good profits

A high turnover is one thing, but making good profits is another.

c have a good idea / put into practice

Having a good idea is one thing, but putting it into practice is another.

d high productivity / improve staff motivation

High productivity is one thing, but improving staff motivation is another.

e create a good product / sell it

Creating a good product is one thing, but selling it is another.

18.2 Now listen and compare your answers.

8 Make three examples relating to your job using the same structure as in 7.

9 Discuss the following questions.

    a What makes teenagers want to buy things?

    b What products do they buy?

    c How do you sell them things?

    d In your opinion, is it ethical to target teenage consumers as a market? Should there be government limitations? If so, what should they be?

10 Work in groups of three. You all work for a marketing company. Market studies have shown that retired people spend a significant amount of their free time surfing the Internet. You have formed a focus group to explore the possibility of marketing to the over-sixties using the Internet. Make notes about what you are going to say. Use some of the expressions in 6 and 7 in your discussion.

Speaker A You think this is a fantastic idea. Think of arguments to support it.

Speaker B You think this is a ridiculous idea. Think of arguments against it.

Speaker C You are the focus group leader. You are not sure about this idea. Lead the discussion, listen to the others and ask questions.

The future of e-commerce

1 The words and phrases a–h are from an article on the future of e-commerce. Match them to the explanations 1–8.

    a to comparison shop

    b catalogue shopping

    c voice recognition

    d a keyboard

    e a range of options

    f historical preferences

    g to virtually shop

    h to try on

    1 to compare the products offered by different suppliers

    2 the thing you use to type text into a computer

    3 to see if clothes fit you and suit you

    4 to buy things online

    5 information based on past customer choices

    6 a system where customers buy by post

    7 a number of different choices

    8 a system where a computer understands spoken instructions

a	1	b	6	c	8	d	2	e	7	f	5	g	4	h	3

2 Match the headings below to the paragraphs in the article on page 85. There is one heading you don't need. Write the correct heading number in each box.

    1 What consumers really want

    2 'Real' e-commerce

    3 Consumers want more than just convenience

    4 Why e-commerce isn't working

    5 The virtual shopping assistant

    6 Goodbye to the keyboard

8   Give students time to make three sentences with the structure which relate to their jobs and go round the class eliciting examples.

Discussion

9   Students can discuss these questions in pairs or small groups. Then have a class feedback session to find out how much consensus there is with regard to question d.

Roleplay

10   Students could decide which roles they are going to take and do their preparation for the roleplay at home. If you do this in class, they will need sufficient time to prepare properly. In either case, allow them to make brief notes of what they are going to say, but don't allow them to write out scripts. In their roleplays, they should listen and respond to what the other members of the focus group say as well as contributing their own opinions.

The future of e-commerce

In this section, students look at some useful vocabulary for talking about e-commerce and then match headings to the paragraphs of a text about how it will develop in the future. They then complete statements with the words they have studied and discuss how far they agree with each one.

Warm-up

Ask students to work in pairs and to produce a list of the number of different ways that you can buy something. You could set a time limit of two minutes and then declare the pair with the longest list the winners. Ask them to read their list to the class and the other students to add any other ideas that they had. If you have time, you could put the final list on the board and ask students to number the ideas according to how much they either like or dislike these ways of shopping.

Vocabulary

1   Working on these words will give students a head-start when they read the long text on page 85. When checking the answers, encourage them to say if they have any experience of any of these things.

2   Go through the headings with the class before they read the article. Students then read the text and match the headings. Allow them to compare their answers in pairs before checking with the class. Elicit reactions to the text. Would students prefer to shop for clothes in the ways outlined in the text, or would they prefer to go into a shop and actually try the garment on?

You might like to exploit this text further by asking students to write comprehension questions on it for other students to answer. You could also read it aloud, stopping at certain points and inviting students to provide the next word or phrase.

SHOPPING
FROM HOME

3 **What forms of e-commerce will dominate the next millennium?** What is it
that the consumer really wants and will pay for? For a while, companies
believed that consumers wanted convenience more than the best price.
Catalogue shopping works on this principle, but it makes up only two per
5   cent of the economy.

1 **Consumers really want things to be simple, easy and fast.** They want to be
entertained when they shop. They want to comparison shop. They want the
best service. They want great prices. The Internet and e-commerce can
provide all of this.

10 **5** **High definition graphics and video will be part of the everyday online
shopping experience.** People will be able to virtually shop and interact with
their friends without leaving home. Artificial intelligence will put a virtual
shop assistant at the service of every online shopper. She will suggest
colours, sizes and other features that match the shopper's preferences. These
15   will be stored on the company's computers.

6 **The biggest obstacle to the Net is the keyboard.** Voice recognition will
make it obsolete. The consumer will access the network from anywhere –
from home, the car, or perhaps even from a pair of glasses.

2 **The consumer will say, 'I'd like to buy a red sweater today, something in
20   the $25 to $30 range.'** The network will take that request, along with any
other historical preferences the consumer has – such as size, style and fabric.
It will assemble a range of options at different prices from a variety of
stores. All in the consumer's exact size. Then the consumer will be able to
virtually try on the different sweaters using a 3D model of herself stored in
25   the computer. And that is real e-commerce.

(heading 4 is not used)

3 Complete the sentences below with the vocabulary items in 1. Each sentence expresses an opinion. Do you agree?

a They should completely redesign the computer <u>keyboard</u>. It's uncomfortable and badly organised.

b I would never buy a suit online. I love going to shops and having the opportunity <u>to try on</u> clothes and feel the quality of the material.

c <u>Catalogue shopping</u> may be popular in the USA but nobody buys things that way in my country.

d I don't like the idea of <u>voice recognition</u>. I feel silly talking to a machine and it probably wouldn't understand me well.

e I never have time <u>to comparison shop</u>. If I see something I like, I usually buy it on impulse.

f I think I will always prefer to go to a high street clothes store than <u>to virtually shop</u>.

g I like shopping in big shopping centres because they offer <u>a range of options</u> that small shops can't compete with.

h I object to the way some websites leave 'cookies' on your computer which record your <u>historical preferences</u> from previous visits.

Lexis link

for more on the vocabulary of shopping and the Internet see page 121

Making predictions

1 Look at this sentence from the article on page 85.

*The consumer **will access** the network from anywhere.*

This is a prediction. You express predictions about the future using ***will***. Underline other predictions in the article.

Grammar link

for more on *will* for future predictions see page 120

2 Do you agree with the predictions in the article? Discuss them like this:

A **I think** DVD **will replace** the cinema.
B Do you? I don't. / Me too.
A **I don't think** the keyboard **will become** obsolete.
B Don't you? I do. / Me neither.

3 What other predictions can you make about the Internet? For example:

*In ten years all banking **will be** online.*

Discussion   **4** Tick Y (yes) or N (no) against the predictions in the chart so that they are true for you. Then discuss them with a partner. For example:

A Do you think you'll change your job in the next five years?
B Yes, I do. I don't really like what I do now. How about you?
A No, I don't think I will. Things are going well and I like my job.

	next year	Y	N	in five years	Y	N	in the next ten years	Y	N
my life	I'll change jobs.	☐	☐	I'll leave and start my own company.	☐	☐	I'll make a million and retire.	☐	☐
my company	Our main competitor will go bankrupt.	☐	☐	Everybody will work at home most of the time.	☐	☐	Most employees will be replaced by computers.	☐	☐
the world	There will be an economic boom.	☐	☐	The USA will have a black president.	☐	☐	There'll be a world government.	☐	☐

3   Refer students back to the vocabulary items they studied in exercise 1. They should use these to complete the sentences. Allow students to compare their sentences in pairs before checking answers with the class

Draw students' attention to the Lexis link on page 121 where they will find more vocabulary on shopping and the Internet.

Making predictions

In this section, students practise using *will* to make predictions about the future. Students look at the predictions made in the article they read in the previous section and discuss and make their own predictions both about e-commerce and their own working situation.

1   Go through the example with the class and ask students to underline the predictions in the article on page 85.

2   Ask a pair of students to read the example dialogue. Students practise it in pairs and then go on to make their own dialogues about the other predictions in the article on page 85. Go round offering help and encouragement.

3   In this freer exercise, students are invited to make their own predictions about the future of the Internet. Give them time to think about this, then elicit suggestions and write them on the board. Make sure that students use *will* correctly in their predictions.

Direct students' attention to the Grammar link on page 120 where they will find more information on *will* for future predictions.

Discussion

4   Students work individually to decide whether the predictions are true for them or whether or not they think they will come true. They then discuss them in pairs.

Go through the example dialogue with them. They can use this as a model for talking about the other items in the table. Fast finishers can make other suggestions for predictions and discuss them in pairs.

If you're short of time

Set exercise 5 on page 82 and the preparation for the roleplay in exercise 10 on page 84 for homework.

Set *The future of e-commerce* exercise 2 for homework.

Set the *Grammar and Lexis links* exercises for homework and check the answers at the beginning of the next class.

Work issues # 19 Working from home

This unit explores the issues around working from home, something which has been made more possible in recent years because of advances in computer technology and changing attitudes to working styles.

Students begin by looking at a news item about a company which is trying to persuade more of its employees to work from home and have a discussion on whether they themselves would want to do this.

Next the focus turns to teleworking and students look at two case studies. They listen to interviews with the people and complete a chart about their work. Then they discuss the advantages and disadvantages for them of working from home. This leads into a text on the advantages and disadvantages of home working and students examine some of the vocabulary used in this text. Finally, they take part in a roleplay between the manager of a company who wants to introduce a system of working at home and a union representative who is against it.

The grammatical focus is on conditionals with future reference, and the lexical focus is on teleworking.

In this first section, students are introduced to conditionals with future reference through the discussion of a news item about a company that wants to introduce a system of working from home and how the students would feel if they worked for this company.

Warm-up

Find out how common working from home is in the students' country and in their particular industry. If any of them have experience of working from home, ask them to tell the others about it. Is it easy for them to get down to work or do they find it distracting to be in their home environment? Do their partners or children interfere in their work in any way? Do they think they get more done at home or in the office?

1   Students read the news item and discuss the questions in pairs. The news item presents the situation from the company's point of view and lists some of the perceived advantages of having employees work from home. You could ask students to come up with a list of possible disadvantages for the employer and for the employees themselves.

Conditionals (future reference)

2   Remind students of the work they did on conditionals with *will* in Unit 13. Then focus their attention on question c in exercise 1. Ask students to identify the verb forms used in the *if* clause (Past Simple) and in the other clause (*would*). Establish that the question is about an imaginary situation in the future.

Students then complete the three sentences. Go round checking that they are using the forms correctly.

3   Students find the other example of the structure in the article in exercise 1. There is more about conditionals with future reference, sometimes called second conditionals, in the Grammar link on page 122.

4   When students have completed the company manager's conditional chain, they could create one of their own. You could also have a team game in which one member of a team forms a sentence, e.g. *If I won a lot of money, I'd buy a car*. A member of the other team then has to make the next sentence in the chain, e.g. *If I bought a car, I'd drive to Paris next weekend*. A member of the first team makes a sentence beginning, e.g. *If I drove to Paris next weekend, I'd ...*, and so on. Teams score a point for each correct sentence.

Check the answers by going round the class with each student adding the next sentence in the chain.

Possible answer

If I left my job, I'd spend more time at home. If I spent more time at home, I'd be more relaxed. If I were more relaxed, I'd have time to think. If I had time to think, I'd come up with a really great business idea. If I came up with a really great business idea, I'd set up a company. If I set up a company, it would be an enormous success. If it were/was an enormous success, I'd have a lot of responsibilities. If I had a lot of responsibilities, I'd have to work harder than I want to. If I had to work harder than I wanted to, I would be completely stressed out again.

19 Working from home

Mid pleasures and palaces though we may roam,
Be it ever so humble, there's no place like home;
Home, home, sweet, sweet home!
There's no place like home! There's no place like home!

John Howard Payne, US actor and dramatist

1   Read the news item below and discuss the questions with a partner.

GO HOME AND WORK

A major international telecommunications company wants to persuade 10,000 of its employees to work from home. They believe that if the staff used computers, fax machines, mobile phones and the Internet, they would maintain the same levels of productivity as when they work in the office. In their talks with the unions, the company argues that amongst other advantages, the plan will make it possible to:

*   close down office buildings and save on expensive city centre rents
*   demonstrate the effectiveness of its telecommunications equipment
*   reduce investment in new offices and office improvements
*   improve the quality of life for workers
*   help preserve the environment by reducing home to office travel

a   What do you think of the company's arguments in favour of the plan?

b   What is the most important reason for the proposal?

c   How would you feel about the plan if you worked for this company?

**Conditionals
(future reference)**

2   Look at question c in 1 again. Answer it using the words below.

If I worked for this company, _____

I'd be happy if _____
.

I wouldn't be happy if _____

3   You use *if* + past + *would/could* to talk about hypothetical or imagined situations. Underline another example of this structure in the news item in 1.

4   A company manager is sitting in his office dreaming about how he could change his life. Put his ideas into a chain of conditionals to recreate his dream like this:

If I left my job, I'd spend more time at home.   If I spent more time at home, ...

> have time to think   come up with a really great business idea
> have a lot of responsibilities   be completely stressed out again
> set up a company   be more relaxed
> have to work harder than I want to   be an enormous success

5 In what circumstances would you ...

- work from home?
- stop working altogether?
- change jobs?
- refuse a promotion?
- ask for a pay rise?
- accept a cut in pay?

For example: *I'd work from home if my company offered us the opportunity.*

Grammar link

for more on conditionals (future reference) see page 122

teleworker /ˈteliˌwɜːkə/ noun [C] someone who works at home on a computer and communicates with their office or customers by telephone, fax, or email

from Macmillan English Dictionary

Teleworking

1 [cassette] 19.1 Listen to two interviews with people who telework. Which speaker:

a has children? _2_

b lives in the country? _1_

c doesn't have fixed hours? _1_

d gets up later than before? _2_

e wears her slippers to work? _2_

f is self employed? _1_

g works for a company? _2_

2 Listen again and complete the chart.

	Speaker 1	Speaker 2
Country	UK	USA
What did she do before?	conference organiser	hotel concierge
What does she do now?	virtual assistant	virtual hotel concierge
What are the advantages of her new work?	can live in the country travel time	no long drive to work; easier family life
What are the advantages for her employers/clients?	They only use her when they need her; better qualified person for same money; flexible hours	If she left, it would be difficult to replace her. Guests are happy.

Discussion 3 Which of the speakers is making a better use of technology, in your opinion? What would the main advantages and disadvantages of working from home be for you?

4 Read the advantages and disadvantages of working from home in the magazine article on page 89. Put each in the correct category in the chart below. The first one has been done for you.

Does working at home really work?	Advantages	Disadvantages
The workplace	13	10
The working day	12	8
Commuting	5	3
Technology	11	15
Efficiency	2	9
Costs	7	6
Motivation	16	14
Family	4	1

5 Ask students to discuss these questions, using the conditional structure. Go round and check that they are using the conditional correctly. Check the answers by asking several students to say their sentences to the class.

Direct students' attention to the Grammar link on page 122 where they will find more information on conditionals with future reference and practice exercises to help them use the structures correctly.

Teleworking

In this section, students listen to two interviews with people who telework. Their circumstances are quite different. Students match items to the speakers and then complete a chart about their jobs. They then discuss the advantages and disadvantages that working from home would have for them personally before moving on to a text that lists some of the good and bad points of teleworking. They look at some of the vocabulary in the text and use it to complete sentences. Finally, they do a roleplay in which one person argues in favour of working at home and the other against.

Warm-up

Ask students if they think there are any jobs that can be done totally from home. Are there any in which they think it would be impossible to do any part of the job at home? Start them off with a few suggestions, e.g. firefighter, brain surgeon, secretary, journalist, and ask them in each case to justify which category they would put each into.

1 🔘 **19.1** Focus students' attention on the definition for *teleworker* before they do the exercise. Make sure students have read the questions before you play the recording so that they know exactly what information they are listening for. Then play the recording and see if they can match the items to the speakers. Play it again, if necessary for them to check their answers.

Elicit students' opinions on what they have heard and whether they were surprised that either job could be done from home.

2 Go through the chart before you play the recording again. With stronger students, you could ask them to fill in as much as possible from what they remember from the first listening. Then play the recording and allow students to compare their answers in pairs or small groups before checking with the class.

Have a class discussion of the last two questions.

Discussion

3 Students discuss the questions in pairs. Encourage them to give details of their situations and full reasons for their opinions. In a class feedback session, make a list on the board of the various advantages and disadvantages that are suggested.

4 Give students plenty of time to read the text. Make sure they understand that they have to identify the correct category for each point and whether it is an advantage or a disadvantage in order to complete the chart. Allow students to compare answers in pairs or small groups before checking the answers with the class.

🔘 **19.1**

Interview 1

A: The Internet and other new technologies have changed the way we work and the titles of our jobs. For example, instead of the secretary, meet Jill Spencer, a 'virtual assistant'. Jill, what exactly is a virtual assistant?

B: Virtual assistants, or VAs, work from home. We offer services to businesses which don't have sufficient work to justify employing someone full-time.

A: Why did you decide to be a virtual assistant?

B: I retired from my job as a conference organiser, but I wanted to earn some extra money. I became a VA because it meant I didn't have to leave my country home down here in Cornwall.

A: Yes, it's a lovely place – I can understand why you didn't want to move away. So, how did you start?

B: I had a lot of contacts from my previous work. I began by providing things like bookkeeping but now I offer a range of services for clients all over the UK.

A: It's going well, then.

B: Yes, I wasn't looking to earn a fantastic amount of money. The biggest advantage is that you can do as little or as much as you want. If it's a lovely sunny day, I can sit out in the garden and do the work in the evening.

A: What do you need to get started?

B: The basic tools are a computer with an Internet connection, a fax machine and a mobile phone. Anyone with basic office skills could do the job. Apart from that it depends on the kind of services you're going to offer and what the clients want.

A: And what's in it for the companies?

B: Companies get a huge amount out of it because they only use a virtual assistant when they need one. Also, they can perhaps get someone with a higher professional level than they could get if they had to pay someone full-time. There's also no problem of office hours. A businessman can be out of the office all day, but his assistant is still available in the evening if he needs to discuss things. I think it could make a big difference to everyone's lifestyle.

Interview 2

A: Anna, what exactly do you do?

B: I'm a concierge at the Westin Hotel in Santa Clara, California.

A: What was life like before you became a teleworker?

B: I had to get up at three in the morning so I could shower and dress, take my kids to my mother's, and set off to work by 4.30.

A: 4.30!

B: Yes, there was a lot of traffic. On a good day I got there by 6.30. That gave me half an hour to relax before starting my shift at seven o'clock.

A: It sounds awful.

B: Yes, I was getting up in the dark and getting home in the dark. I never saw my husband or children. I liked my job but my life was a nightmare.

A: And what is life like now?

B: Oh, I feel like the luckiest person alive. I now get up at 5.30. My mother still looks after the children but I don't have the 80-mile drive to work along Highway 101. We've set up my workplace in one of the bedrooms. I sit down in front of a camera, pin on a microphone and I'm ready for business.

A: How does it work at the hotel?

B: Guests still go up to the concierge desk, but instead of me in person, they see me on a giant TV screen. They can only see my head and shoulders, so I can wear my slippers while I work.

A: What do your employers think about it?

B: Oh, they're happy because they can't afford to lose me. In the hotel industry we don't have the high salaries of Cisco, Palm or Sun Micro, so there's a high turnover of staff. With unemployment around here so low it's hard to replace workers. It cost them $50,000 but they thought it was worth a try.

A: And the guests?

B: They're happy. Apart from anything else they don't have to leave a tip!

5 Students can check their answers to exercise 4 on page 125.

Vocabulary

6 Students will find the vocabulary focused on here useful when they come to talk about work and working situations. Students should scan the text quickly to find the matching words. Then check the answers with the class.

WORKING AT HOME
THE ADVANTAGES AND DISADVANTAGES

What do people _really_ think about working from home? We interviewed a cross section of people from different industries about their experiences of teleworking. As you will see, there was quite a wide variety of opinions.

1 'There is no getting away from the family. When you work in an office you get a chance to escape and meet new people.'

2 'I think us home workers get more done in a shorter time. There are no phone calls or colleagues to slow you down.'

3 'Without the journeys to and from the office you don't get a chance to relax and prepare your mind before you work, or to wind down before you get home. I miss the separation between home and leisure time.'

4 'You _do_ get to see more of your children. The problem is, though, that you're supposed to be WORKING.'

5 'You don't have to sit in traffic jams or walk to work in the rain. Or listen to people talking loudly on their mobiles on the train.'

6 'I think financially you miss out on perks like subsidised refreshments or travel.'

7 'Life is definitely cheaper for the employee. You save on things like transport and smart clothes. It's also cheaper to have lunch at home.'

8 'It's a bit dangerous for workaholics. You can easily find your working time creeping into your leisure time.'

9 'Sharing ideas and problems with your colleagues can make you more productive in some jobs. And the gossip can be really inspiring!'

10 'Space can be a problem. Rooms can become an unpleasant mix of home and office.'

11 'You don't have to work with those obsolete office computers and the company intranet which always seems to be down.'

12 'The flexibility is great. You can work at five in the morning or on a Sunday afternoon.'

13 'I like the freedom. You can open the window, play music and generally make yourself comfortable.'

14 'It can be difficult to get down to work. You have to be very self-disciplined.'

15 'If you have a technical problem, you're on your own. There's no IT expert to call on.'

16 'No boss cracking the whip!'

5 Look at the chart on page 125 and check your answers.

Vocabulary 6 Find words and phrases in the text which mean the same as:

a relax _wind down_

b queues of cars and lorries unable to move forward _traffic jams_

c benefits not included in your salary _perks_

d people who can't stop working _workaholics_

e out of date and no longer useful _obsolete_

f informal exchange of news and information _gossip_

g start _get down to_

h trying to make people work harder _cracking the whip_

7 Complete the sentences with the words and phrases from 6.

a As I have to travel so much I miss out on all the office ___gossip___.

b When I get home, I like to ___wind down___ by listening to some classical music with a glass of wine.

c My boss is a complete ___workaholic___. She just doesn't know how to relax and turn off.

d It's better to have a higher salary than ___perks___ like a company car or free meals.

e The problem with buying a computer is that in a couple of years it's ___obsolete___.

f I find it difficult to ___get down to___ the accounts and usually leave them until the last minute.

g I leave home very early to avoid getting caught in ___traffic jams___ on the way to work.

h ___Cracking the whip___ is part of any manager's job.

Lexis link

for more on the vocabulary of teleworking see page 123

8 Are the sentences in 7 true for you? If not, change them so that they are.

Roleplay **9** Work with a partner and perform the following roleplay about the advantages of working at home or in the office. Use the phrases in the box to help you.

Speaker A You are a manager in your company. You are negotiating with the unions to introduce the policies mentioned in the news item on page 87. Convince your partner of the advantages of working at home.

Speaker B You are a union representative in speaker A's company. The management wants to introduce working from home but you are against it. Convince your partner of the advantages of office work.

> If people worked from home, ...   Most people find / would find that ...
> From the worker's / company's point of view, it would mean ...
> At the moment, people have to ...   There'd be all sorts of problems if ...
> I agree with that, but ...   That's not necessarily true, because if ...

7 Students use the words from the previous exercise to complete the sentences. Check the answers by having them read out the completed sentences so that they hear the words in context.

8 Students can discuss in pairs whether or not the sentences in exercise 7 are true for them. They should then change the ones which are not true to make them true.

Direct students' attention to the Lexis link on page 123 where they will find more on the vocabulary of teleworking.

Roleplay

9 This is quite a difficult roleplay, so students will need time to prepare what they are going to say. They may like to do this at home. Remind them that various opinions have been expressed throughout the unit, so they can go back over it and have a look for ideas. Allow them to make brief notes, but discourage them from writing a script of what they are going to say. Draw their attention also to the useful vocabulary in the box at the bottom of the exercise and to the Lexis link on page 123.

As the students perform their roleplays, go round offering help and encouragement. At the end, find out who 'won' the argument in each pair.

If you're short of time

Set *Teleworking* exercise 4 and exercise 7 for homework. The preparation for the roleplay in exercise 9 could also be done at home.

Set the *Grammar and Lexis links* exercises for homework and check the answers at the beginning of the next class.

Conversation skills 20 Working lunch

In this unit, students learn some useful language for conversing with business colleagues over lunch. The conversation moves from ordering food and recommending local specialities to establishing who does what in a company and finally getting down to business, where cultural expectations play an important role.

In this first section, students listen to two businessmen having a working lunch in Japan. They answer questions and put lines of the dialogue in order. They then study some practical expressions for describing different dishes and how they are prepared.

Warm-up

Find out how often students have business lunches either with colleagues from the same company or business contacts from outside. Ask them to list the kinds of things they talk about over lunch and the kinds of places they would take guests for lunch. Elicit any amusing stories or incidents they know which are connected to business lunches.

1   🔲 **20.1** Make sure students have read the situation and the questions before you play the recording so that they know exactly what information they are listening for. Establish that it is most likely that Satoshi Tanaka is the host and Neil Klein the guest as the restaurant is in Japan. Play the recording for students to answer the questions. Then check the answers with the class.

2   Allow students to work in pairs to number the dialogue in the correct order. Encourage them to take one role each and read it aloud to check that it sounds right. Then play the recording again for them to check their answers.

Ask students what they do when they are a guest and someone recommends something to eat which they know they will not like or can't eat. Does Neil handle the situation politely?

🔲 **20.1**

A: **This looks like a very nice place**, Satoshi.

B: Yes, **I thought you would like it**.

A: Yes, **I really like the decor**. Er, **could you order for both of us**, Satoshi?

B: Of course. **I think we could have some miso soup to start with**. They do it very well here.

A: Okay. **Sounds good**.

B: And then **I think you should try some** *unagi*.

A: What's that?

B: It's eel – grilled and served on a bed of rice. It's delicious.

A: Hm, I'm sure it is. Actually, **do you think I could have a steak?**

B: Well, **I'm afraid they don't serve steak here**.

A: **I'll try the** *unagi*, **then**.

B: Fine. **Would you like some sake, or would you prefer some beer?**

A: No, no, **let's have some sake**.

B: Right. **Sake it is, then**.

20 Working lunch

Vegetables are interesting but lack a sense of purpose when unaccompanied by a good cut of meat. *Fran Lebowitz*

1   20.1 Neil Klein and Satoshi Tanaka are having a working lunch at a restaurant in Japan. Listen to their conversation and answer the questions.

    a   Why does Neil like the restaurant? <u>He likes the decor.</u>

    b   Who orders the food? <u>Satoshi does.</u>

    c   What does Neil want to eat? <u>steak</u>

    d   What does Neil decide to eat? <u>unagi (grilled eel)</u>

2   Put the lines of the conversation in 1 in order. Then listen again and check.

    Neil Klein

    [1]   This looks like a very nice place, Satoshi.

    [11]   I'll try the *unagi*, then.

    [5]   Okay. Sounds good.

    [7]   What's that?

    [3]   Yes, I really like the decor. Er, could you order for both of us, Satoshi?

    [9]   Hm, I'm sure it is. Actually, do you think I could have a steak?

    [13]   No, no, let's have some sake.

    Satoshi Tanaka

    [6]   And then I think you should try some *unagi*.

    [8]   It's eel – grilled and served on a bed of rice. It's delicious.

    [2]   Yes, I thought you would like it.

    [10]   Well, I'm afraid they don't serve steak here.

    [12]   Fine. Would you like some sake, or would you prefer some beer?

    [4]   Of course. I think we could have some miso soup to start with. They do it very well here.

    [14]   Right. Sake it is, then.

3 **a** Make a list of some of the typical dishes which restaurants serve in your area, using the local name.

b Imagine you are entertaining a visitor. Sometimes you can translate the names of dishes, but you may also have to explain how they are cooked. Act out a conversation with a partner and explain what each dish consists of. Use the phrases on the right to help you.

	a type of	fish
		meat
		vegetable
		pie
	a	rice dish
		pasta dish
It's	made with	eggs
	made from	fruit
	served with	vegetables
		a salad
		potatoes
		a sauce
	cooked	with garlic
		with spices
		with herbs
		in olive oil

Who does what?

1 20.2 Complete the second part of Neil and Satoshi's conversation with the phrases in the box. Then listen and check your answers.

> job title   report to   responsible for

Satoshi Neil, I met Jeff Segram earlier this year. What exactly is his _job title_ ?

Neil He's the Managing Director.

Satoshi Do you mean the CEO?

Neil Yes, that's what the Americans say. He's the person on the board who is _responsible for_ the day to day running of the company.

Satoshi And what about you?

Neil I'm the Product Development Director. I'm on the board as well, but I _report to_ Jeff.

Satoshi Right, I see.

2 Find phrases in the conversation in 1 which are similar in meaning to the following:

a is in charge of _is responsible for_

b Jeff is my boss. _I report to Jeff_

c What does he do? _What exactly is his job title?_

3 Act out conversations like the one in exercise 1 using the prompts below. Use your own ideas, if you like.

Who you met	Job title	Responsibilities	Your job title	Who you report to
John Atherstone	Chairman/President	long-term strategy and planning	Managing Director	John Atherstone
Sisi Albright	Director of Marketing/ Vice-President Marketing	marketing policy and the worldwide sales force	Head of Asian Sales Department	Sisi Albright

3 If students come from a variety of countries, encourage them to work with a partner from a different country. This will give more authenticity to their explanations of their local specialities. In monocultural classes, ask students to discuss in pairs which dishes foreign visitors are unlikely to have heard of.

Students take turns to be the host and the guest and explain their dishes. Focus students' attention on the useful language section at the side.

Elicit any stories students have about ordering foreign food or entertaining foreign guests.

Who does what?

In this section, students look at typical language for establishing who does what in a company, i.e. giving people's job titles and explaining the company structure. This is important information for business contacts who will need to know who the decision makers are in the company and who they should go to for different things. Students listen to the second part of the conversation in the restaurant and complete the gaps in the tapescript. They then act out similar conversations and use information from their own companies to practise talking about jobs and responsibilities.

Warm-up

If students come from the same company, ask them to draw a diagram showing their company hierarchy on the board, with the CEO at the top and the various executives underneath with lines showing who reports to whom. If students are from various companies, you could ask them to come to class with a diagram of their company structure to explain to a partner or to the class.

1 ▭ **20.2** Students should try to complete the conversation before they listen. Check that they understand the meaning of the phrases in the box by asking several students to say what their job titles are, who they report to and what they are responsible for.

Check the answers with the class and then play the recording for them to check.

2 Students match the three expressions with phrases in the conversation. Check the answers with the class.

3 Encourage students to use their own information as well as the prompts in the box. They can use the conversation in exercise 1 as a model but change any details they like. Go round offering help and encouragement.

▭ **20.2**

B: Neil, I met Jeff Segram earlier this year. **What exactly is his job title?**
A: He's the Managing Director.
B: **Do you mean the CEO?**

A: Yes, that's what the Americans say. **He's the person on the board who is responsible for the day to day running of the company**.
B: And what about you?

A: I'm the Product Development Director. I'm on the board as well, but **I report to Jeff**.
B: Right, I see.

4 In pairs, students follow the instructions. When they have finished, encourage them to compare notes with other pairs or groups.

Down to business

In this section, students learn about the outcome of Neil Klein's business lunch in Japan as he reports back to his boss. They then hear his conversation with Satoshi and decide what he did wrong. A short text on doing business in Japan raises issues about the cultural implications of different business attitudes. Students replace the original conversation between Neil and Satoshi with one in which he follows the advice in the text. They then discuss their experiences of doing business in different cultures.

Warm-up

Focus students' attention on the picture at the bottom of the page. Ask them to choose some adjectives to describe the man. Do they think they would enjoy doing business with him? Would he be typical of business people in their country?

1 20.3 Make sure students have read the questions before you play the recording so that they know exactly what information they are listening for. Then play the recording. Ask students to discuss their answers to the questions in pairs or small groups before checking with the class. Ask them to speculate about what went wrong.

2 20.4 Play the recording and elicit various ideas on what Neil did wrong.

3 Go through the text with the class and explain anything they don't understand. Ask if the ideas in the text confirm what they thought in exercise 2. If your students have experience of doing business in Japan, ask them if their experience matches the text.

4 Students may need time to prepare their conversations and they may find it useful to refer to the tapescript on page 143, though they should make notes rather than write out a script for their new conversation. Tell them that they can invent any extra information that they need. When they act out their conversations, go round and take a note of any particularly successful conversations which can be performed for the class.

5 This could be done as a class discussion with students swapping information and experiences.

If you're short of time

Students could order the conversation in exercise 2 on page 91 at home and the description of local dishes in exercise 3 on page 92 could be set for homework and checked in the next class.

Preparation for the conversation in *Down to business* exercise 4 could be done at home.

20.3

C: So, any news from Tokyo, Neil?
A: No, I'm afraid not, Jeff. It looks like they're not interested.
C: **How did it go with Mr Tanaka?**
A: Oh, he was really nice. He took me to a great restaurant. Actually, everything went okay until we got down to business.
C: **What happened?**
A: I don't know. I thought the sale was a sure thing, but he seemed to lose interest. I don't know what I did wrong.

20.4

A: Mm, **that was delicious**.
B: **I'm glad you enjoyed it**. So, Neil, tell me about this digital control software. Why do you think we should be interested?
A: Because it's easily the best program for the job on the market.
B: The system we use at the moment works okay. Why should we change?
A: It's a question of costs. It could save you up to 30%. If you look at the competition, there's just no comparison.
B: Can you give me some information about your sales?
A: Er … about two million dollars worth worldwide.
B: Could I see the documentation?
A: Well, I'm afraid that's confidential, but listen, if we can make a deal today, I can offer you an even better discount.

4 Work with a partner.
   a List five job titles in your company, or in other companies.
   b Do you know the equivalent job titles in English?
   c Explain what each person does.

Down to business

1 ▶ 20.3 Listen to Neil Klein talking to Jeff Segram when he returned to head office, and answer the questions.

   a Was the trip a success? _NO_
   b What do you think happened when they got down to business?

2 ▶ 20.4 Now listen to the conversation between Neil and Satoshi. What do you think Neil did wrong?

   too aggressive, criticised the competition, refused to give figures/information

3 Read the information on the right about doing business in Japan. Does this confirm your ideas in 2?

4 Act out the conversation between Neil and Satoshi, but this time Neil should follow the advice in the text.

5 Do you have any similar experience of doing business with different cultures? What other differences in the way of doing business do you know about?

The
Hard Sell

A hard sell is often seen as offensive in Japan. Japanese business people may think that you are trying to
5 convince them because your product is no good. It is better to use a low-key sales pitch and give them objective information. Japanese are not
10 accustomed to aggressive American techniques that use a persuasive 'winning' argument. If you are not completely honest about your
15 product, your credibility will be damaged and what you say will lose influence. Don't say that yours is 'the best on the market'. It is better to say,
20 'We sold two million units last year. As you know, our closest competitor sold less than a million.' At the same time, be careful not to criticise
25 competing products. In fact, the Japanese will respect you if you mention the assets of the competition.

Present Simple

Affirmative	
I you we they	**work**
he she it	**works**

Negative	
I you we they	**don't work**
he she it	**doesn't work**

Interrogative		
do **don't**	I you we they	**work?**
does **doesn't**	he she it	**work?**

You use the Present Simple to talk about

* routine actions and habits.
  *I **go** to work by bus.*
  *He **works** late on Tuesdays.*

* ongoing situations we see as stable.
  *We **live** in London.*
  *They **employ** over 250 people.*

Present Continuous

Affirmative	
I'm (am)	
you're (are) we're (are) they're (are)	**working**
he's (is) she's (is) it's (is)	

Negative	
I'm not	
you aren't we aren't they aren't	**working**
he isn't she isn't it isn't	

Interrogative		
am **aren't**	I	
are **aren't**	you we they	**working?**
is **isn't**	he she it	

You use the Present Continuous to talk about

* activities happening at the moment of speaking.
  *He's **wearing** a grey suit, a white shirt and a blue tie.*
  *Don't interrupt me, please. I'm **trying** to concentrate.*
  *'What **are** you **doing**?' 'I'm **preparing** this month's sales figures.'*

* activities or situations you see as temporary.
  *We're **using** this office until the new one is ready.*
  *I'm **working** from home for a few days so don't phone me at the office.*

* situations which are changing.
  *The economic situation **is getting** better.*
  *Our company share price **is** steadily **improving**.*

You often use the Present Continuous with time expressions *at the moment, this week/month/year* etc.

*We **are having** a lot of problems with our suppliers **at the moment**.*

*I'm **doing** a course **this month**, but it's not very interesting.*

Practice 1 Complete the sentences using the verbs in the box in the correct form – Present Simple or Present Continuous. Use each verb twice.

work	get	sell	do	think	live

a Normally I am in the office in the afternoon but this month I **'m doing** a course.

b In the winter the reps **sell** more than in the summer.

c Our most important market is the Far East. We **do** business with several companies there.

d Our new product line **is selling** very well this year.

e Our boss **works** very long hours.

f He **'s thinking** of changing his job because he's not very happy.

g 'What's your address?' 'I **'m living** in a hotel until we find a nice flat.'

h In June the weather **gets** hot there so take some cool clothes.

i He **thinks** his job is really interesting.

j It **'s getting** hotter. We need to get some air conditioning for this office.

k At present we **'re working** on new products and services for the future.

l During the week he **lives** in his city flat and at the weekend he goes to the country.

Practice 2 Write questions about the information which is missing.

a The company makes money by ...
How does the company make money?

b Our business is expanding because ...
Why is your business expanding?

c They are setting up a business in ...
Where are they setting up a business?

d We are looking for $ ...
How much money are you looking for?

e He has previous experience in the ... business.
What kind of business does he have previous experience in?

f Their competitive advantage is ...
What is their competitive advantage?

g My company employs ... people.
How many people does your company employ?

h The manager of the company is ...
Who is the manager of the company?

i They are talking to ... about further investment.
Who are they talking to about further investment?

Lexis: Business & the Internet

Running a business Complete the sentences using the words in the box.

> average   worth   campaigns   costs
> experience   Internet   investment   turnover
> employs   margin   website

a The company _employs_ over 2,000 workers in Europe, located in four different factories.

b Our running _costs_ include rent, electricity and equipment hire, as well as salaries.

c Direct mail _campaigns_ can sometimes be very effective, but it depends on the product.

d Our company _website_ provides information about our services and products, but we don't sell anything online.

e We need more _investment_ to finance our marketing plan, so we are talking to venture capitalists in the USA.

f The _average_ of 4, 6, 8 and 10 is 7.

g He has an MBA but does he have any previous _experience_ in this kind of business?

h For the company to survive, our _turnover_ needs to grow by 20% this year.

i In my opinion, the BBC has one of the best websites on the _Internet_.

j They make a profit of $4.20 on each book they sell, which represents a _margin_ of 60%.

k The business is _worth_ over $30m.

The Internet & computers Complete the crossword.

Across
2 We are designing a new _____ at the moment.
3 Please add our site to your _____ of favourites.
5 If you give me your address, I can send you an _____.
7 A _____ with no cable is much more comfortable to use.
9 It's like the Internet but the pages are only accessible inside the company.
10 We pay them to include a _____ to our website on their page.
11 How much do you pay for your Internet _____ per month?
14 Our system is infected by a _____.
16 I don't have much time to _____ the Internet at work.

Down
1 I'll send you the document as an e-mail _____.
4 Don't get so close to the _____. It's bad for your eyes.
6 You can _____ music and pictures from our site.
8 Nowadays I buy all my CDs and books _____.
12 _____ here for further information.
13 I'm looking for a web_____ with information about share prices.
15 In order to _____ the web in comfort you need a good computer.

Answers on page 124

2 Women in business

Expressing frequency

To say how often something happens you use:

- Adverbs of frequency

  always   usually   often   sometimes   not often
  hardly ever   never

  The adverb comes *before* the main verb:

I You We They He She	(don't/doesn't) **usually** (don't/doesn't) **often** **sometimes** **never**	drive(s) to work. go(es) out for lunch.

but *after* the verb 'to be'.

I	am		
You We They He She	are is	(not) **usually** (not) **often** **sometimes** **never**	late. tired.

- Frequency expressions

  every day/week
  once/twice/three times a day/week/month/year   etc.

  These expressions come at the beginning or end of
  the sentence.

I You We They He She	have (has) a break go(es) on holiday	**every day.**	
		once twice three times four times	a day. a week. a month. a year.

Every day			
Once Twice Three times Four times	a day a week a month a year	I you we they he she	have (has) a break. go(es) on holiday.

Practice 1 Reorganise the words and phrases to make
correct sentences.

a abroad   times   I   a   year   travel   four

  I travel abroad four times a year.

b a   on   department   meeting   we   always   have
  Monday   morning

  We always have a department meeting on
  Monday morning.

c often   he   to   Germany   doesn't   go

  He doesn't often go to Germany.

d manager   the   department   usually   leaves   on
  Friday   early

  The department manager usually leaves early
  on Friday.

e I   use   the   car   never   can't   because   drive   I

  I never use the car because I can't drive.

f has   the   office   canteen   she   always   lunch   in

  She always has lunch in the office canteen.

g often   they   for   work   aren't   late

  They aren't often late for work.

h always   Microsoft   is   the   news   in

  Microsoft is always in the news.

i my   every   I   change   mobile   year

  I change my mobile every year.

j ever   do   you   have   parties   office?

  Do you ever have office parties?

k often   to   how   gym   you   the   do   go?

  How often do you go to the gym?

l you   your   do   use   much   laptop?

  Do you use your laptop much?

Practice 2 Rewrite the question using question words
what, who, when etc.

a Do you go to work by car? On foot?

  How do you go to work?

b Do you use the phone a lot? Ever?

  How much do you use the phone?

c Do you get to work at 8.30? 9.00?

  When do you get to work?

d Does he do the housework because he likes it?
  Because he has to?

  Why does he do the housework?

e Does he play squash every day? Every week?

  How often does he play squash?

f Does she go to work with her husband? A friend?

  Who does she go to work with?

g Do you spend the morning making plans? Having
  meetings?

  How do you spend the morning?

Photocopiable

h Do you work 35 hours a week? Forty hours a week?

How many hours a week do you work?

i Does it take you 20 minutes to read the newspaper? Half an hour?

How long does it take you to read the newspaper?

j Do you work so hard because it's fun? Because you need the money?

Why do you work so hard?

Lexis: Work & routines

1 Match the parts of the sentences below.
  a Professor Axt thinks that lazing ...
  b Doing as little as possible is better ...
  c Lying about is the key ...
  d Take a midday break instead ...
  e He's in favour ...
  f Try to take ...
  g We only have a limited ...
  h If you get up early, you are likely to ...

  1 ... around is good for you.
  2 ... of playing squash or going for a run.
  3 ... amount of energy.
  4 ... it easy this weekend.
  5 ... than going to the gym.
  6 ... to a long life.
  7 ... of moderate exercise like walking.
  8 ... feel stressed for the rest of the day.

a	b	c	d	e	f	g	h
1	5	6	2	7	4	3	8

2 Write in the missing pairs of words below.

> developing + sales   engineer + degree
> ratio + to   experience + qualifications
> charge + hiring   productive + day
> marketing + women   get + off

  a We only _get_ half an hour _off_ for lunch.

  b You should get some practical _experience_ as well as _qualifications_.

  c She's in _charge_ of _hiring_ and firing.

  d Why do _marketing_ departments have more _women_ than men?

  e If you want to be an _engineer_, you'll need a _degree_.

  f The _ratio_ of men to women is two _to_ one in my job.

g Nobody can be _productive_ sixteen hours a _day_.

h She's involved in _developing_ new _sales_ strategies.

Do as an auxiliary Complete the conversation using *do, does, don't* or *doesn't*.

A (a) _Do_ you do a lot of exercise?

B Yes, I suppose I (b) _do_. Why do you ask?

A Well, it's better if you (c) _don't_, according to a German scientist.

B What (d) _does_ he say about it?

A He (e) _doesn't_ say that exercise is bad for you exactly, but that if you do too much, you use up all your energy.

B That (f) _doesn't_ make sense. Sport is good for you and makes you feel better.

A Yes, but according to him people who run marathons and play squash (g) _don't_ usually live to an old age.

B Well, I (h) _don't_ believe it. He probably just (i) _doesn't_ like sport.

Jobs Reorganise the letters to form words related to jobs. Then complete the sentences using the words.

> soipoint   driteer   litte   texecuvie   nacharim
> contacaunt   nagream   denistrep

a She's the chief _executive_ officer.

b He's the _chairman_ of the board.

c He doesn't work, he's _retired_.

d The CEO is the top _position_ in the company.

e Her job _title_ is 'vice president'.

f It's hard to explain what I do, but I guess I'm a sort of _manager_.

g The financial director of the company is a qualified _accountant_.

h The job title '_president_' sounds more important than 'chairman'.

3 Telephone talk

Indirect questions

Direct questions	Indirect questions	Differences
Where **are you** from?	Can you tell me where **you are** from?	• Word order
How **is she**?	how **she is**?	• No *do* or *does*
Where **are we** meeting?	Can you remember where **we're** meeting?	• *if* in Yes/No questions
Where **do you live**?	Could you tell me where **you live**?	
How much money **does he earn**?	how much money **he earns**?	
Does he like football?	Do you know **if he likes** football	
Has he got my address?	**if he has got** my address?	

Practice 1 Reorganise the words to make indirect questions or statements.

a tell if got my me could you she message
Could you tell me if she got my message?

b know be back will do when he you
Do you know when he will be back?

c do long know takes you how it
Do you know how long it takes?

d remember the what bus time can leaves you
Can you remember what time the bus leaves?

e this know do what word you means
Do you know what this word means?

f know think he wants what you to do
What do you think he wants to know?

g idea the is time I've no what
I've no idea what the time is.

Practice 2 Change the direct questions into indirect questions.

a What time does the meeting begin?
Do you know what time the meeting begins?

b How much is the hotel?
Could you tell me how much the hotel is?

c Why is he angry?
Do you know why he is angry?

d Is there a restaurant car on the train?
Can you tell me if there is a restaurant car on the train?

e Where can I park the car?
Can you tell me where I can park the car?

f Is the office near the town centre?
Can you remember if the office is near the town centre?

Lexis: On the telephone

Numbers Write the full form of the numbers and figures.

a 321 three hundred and twenty-one

b 69% sixty-nine percent

c 3,428 three thousand, four hundred and twenty-eight

d 6.392 six point three nine two

e £3m three million pounds

f $9.39 nine dollars and thirty-nine cents

g 24,678,902 twenty-four million, six hundred and seventy-eight thousand, nine hundred and two

Telephone phrases

1 Put the conversation below in the correct order.

[1] Hello, ADH Graphics.

[6] Yes, please. Could you ask him to phone John Clarkson from Bellstone & Smith? He has the phone number.

[3] Just one moment ... I'm sorry, there's no answer.

[7] Yes, of course. Could I just check your name? John Clark from Bellstone & Smith.

[10] Thank you. Goodbye.

[4] Oh, dear. I'm phoning for some information. It's quite urgent. Do you know where I can contact him?

[2] Oh, good morning. Could I speak to Peter White, please?

[5] No, sorry, I'm afraid I don't. Can I take a message?

[8] No, it's Clarkson. He knows what it's about.

[9] Oh, sorry, Mr Clarkson. I'll tell him as soon as he's available.

Photocopiable

2 Complete the conversation using the words and phrases in the box.

> Could I speak to   hold   put me through
> Can I take a message?   call me   bad line
> This is   engaged   You're through
> dialled the wrong number

A Sales Department. Can I help you?

B Oh! I must have

(a) __dialled the wrong number__. Can you

(b) __put me through__ to Customer

Services, please?

A I'm sorry, it's a (c) __bad line__.

Did you say Customer Services?

B Yes, that's right.

A Just one moment. I'm sorry, but the line is

(d) __engaged__. Do you want to

(e) __hold__?

B All right.

A (f) __You're through__ now.

B Hello. (g) __Could I speak to__ the

department manager, please?

C I'm afraid he's not in the office this morning.

(h) __Can I take a message?__?

B Yes, please. (i) __This is__ George

Smith. Could you ask him to

(j) __call me__?

C Yes, of course. Goodbye.

B Bye.

3 Match the parts of the sentences below.

a Tell her it's Mr Jenkins. I'm returning ...

b Typical! I got cut ...

c I hate it when they put you ...

d I keep getting an engaged ...

e Could you say ...

f Can you read that ...

1 ... on hold, and then forget about you.

2 ... back to me, just to check?

3 ... tone. Maybe his phone is off the hook.

4 ... her call this morning.

5 ... that again, please? I didn't understand.

6 ... off in the middle of the call.

a	b	c	d	e	f
4	6	1	3	5	2

4 Match the words to their definitions.

8	**a** telephone directory		3	**g** wrong number
4	**b** engaged		2	**h** switchboard
1	**c** dialling tone		5	**i** extension number
6	**d** reverse charge call		7	**j** cell phone
10	**e** national call		9	**k** directory enquiries
12	**f** off-peak call		11	**l** operator

1 A continuous sound that means you can dial the number you want.

2 The equipment which distributes calls to the different departments and offices in a company.

3 A phone number you dial by mistake.

4 Busy – someone is using the line you want.

5 The number of each different phone in a company.

6 A call which is paid for by the person you are calling.

7 Also called a mobile phone.

8 A book with a list of telephone numbers.

9 A service you phone if you want to find a number.

10 A call to a different part of the country.

11 A person who helps you make a call.

12 A call made in the evening or at the weekend which has a lower charge.

5 Rewrite the following conversation to make it sound more polite.

Galaxy Computers Galaxy Computers. What do you want?

a __Galaxy Computers. Can I help you?__

Michael Jones I want to speak to Harris.

b __I'd like to speak to Mr Harris, please.__

Galaxy Computers Who are you?

c __May I ask who is calling?__

Michael Jones Jones. ABC Industries.

d __This is Michael Jones from ABC Industries.__

Galaxy Computers Who? What's your name again?

e __I'm sorry. Could you repeat that, please?__

Michael Jones Michael Jones.

Galaxy Computers He's speaking to someone on his line. Want to wait?

f __Mr Harris's line is engaged at the moment.__
__Would you like to hold?__

Michael Jones No. Tell him I called, right?

g __No. Could you please tell him I called?__

Galaxy Computers No problem. Bye.

h __Certainly, Mr Jones. Goodbye.__

5 Company histories

Past Simple

Affirmative		Negative	
I you he she it we they	**worked**	I you he she it we they	**didn't work**

Interrogative		
did **didn't**	I you he she it we they	**work**?

Formation: regular verbs

infinitive
- *work – work**ed***

infinitive ending in *e*
- *like – like**d***

infinitive ending in consonant + *y*
- *hurry – hurr**ied***

one syllable verbs ending in one vowel + one consonant
- *stop – stop**ped***
  (except verbs ending in *w* or *y*)
- *play – play**ed**, show – show**ed***

two syllable verbs with the stress on the second syllable
- *prefER – prefer**red**, admIT – admit**ted***

two syllable words with the stress on the first syllable
- *VISit – visit**ed**, ENter – enter**ed***

Formation: irregular verbs

Many of the most common verbs are irregular.
*go – **went**, come – **came***

You use the Past Simple to express finished actions, events or situations.
*We **moved** to a new office last year.**
*Before I got married I **lived** in Lisbon.*
*In my first job, I **travelled** a lot.*

*You often use the Past Simple with expressions describing completed periods of time: *three weeks ago, last year, on Tuesday, in March, at Christmas,* etc.

Time expressions

To say *when* things happen in the past, you use:
- *in* + month / year – *in March, in 1987*
- *on* + day / date – *on Monday, on 5th December*

- *at* + time / special periods – *at 5.00, at Christmas*
- length of time + *ago* – *five minutes ago, a week ago*
- *when* + past situation / action – *when I was younger, when he arrived*

Practice 1 Write the Past Simple of the verbs below.

work <u>worked</u>   marry <u>married</u>
stop <u>stopped</u>   plan <u>planned</u>
live <u>lived</u>   reach <u>reached</u>
start <u>started</u>   arrive <u>arrived</u>
use <u>used</u>   fit <u>fitted</u>
travel <u>travelled</u>   visit <u>visited</u>
drop <u>dropped</u>   call <u>called</u>
carry <u>carried</u>   increase <u>increased</u>
tip <u>tipped</u>   like <u>liked</u>

Practice 2 The twelve verbs below are some of the most common in English. They are all irregular. Write the Past Simple of each.

tell <u>told</u>   make <u>made</u>
say <u>said</u>   do <u>did</u>
get <u>got</u>   go <u>went</u>
give <u>gave</u>   come <u>came</u>
take <u>took</u>   write <u>wrote</u>
put <u>put</u>   have <u>had</u>

Practice 3 Complete the sentences with one of the words in the box or put 'X' when no word is necessary.

ago   in   for   at   when   on

a John started working here <u>at</u> Christmas and he spoke to me for the first time ten minutes <u>ago</u>.

b I travelled a lot <u>X</u> last year.

c <u>On</u> Monday I had a meeting with Mr Leblanc.

d I sent them the fax <u>on</u> Monday.

e <u>When</u> I lived in London, I usually went away <u>for</u> the weekend.

f The delegation from Geneva arrived <u>at</u> three o'clock.

g I worked for IBM <u>for</u> three years.

h We had a really interesting business trip to Turkey <u>in</u> March.

i I had a meeting <u>at</u> 9.30 <u>in</u> the evening and eventually got to my hotel <u>at</u> two <u>in</u> the morning.

j When I woke up __X__ yesterday morning, I didn't know where I was.

k Did Mr Heinkers phone __when__ I was out?

Practice 4 The following facts are incorrect. Make the sentences negative. Then give the correct information.

a Bill Gates founded Oracle.

<u>Bill Gates didn't found Oracle, he founded Microsoft.</u>

b On October 4 1929 the Wall Street Crash started a worldwide economic boom.

<u>The Wall Street Crash didn't start an economic boom, it started an economic depression.</u>

c On March 25 1957 six European states signed the Treaty of Madrid, creating the EEC.

<u>The six European states didn't sign the Treaty of Madrid, they signed the Treaty of Rome.</u>

d On January 1 1999 eleven member states of the European Union adopted the pound as a common currency.

<u>The member states didn't adopt the pound as a common currency, they adopted the euro.</u>

e Henry Ford manufactured the first mass produced electronic components.

<u>Ford didn't manufacture the first mass produced electronic components, he manufactured cars.</u>

f In 2001 Napster had legal problems over people downloading books.

<u>Napster didn't have problems over people downloading books, they had problems over people downloading music.</u>

Answers on page 127

Practice 5 Write questions about the missing information.

a I went to ____ on my last business trip.

<u>Where did you go on your last business trip?</u>

b He set up the company in ____.

<u>When did he set up the company?</u>

c They started selling ____ last year.

<u>What did they start selling last year?</u>

d At first the product sold well because ____.

<u>Why did the product sell well at first?</u>

e They made a profit by ____.

<u>How did they make a profit?</u>

f He worked for ICI for ____ years.

<u>How many years did he work for ICI?</u>

g I spoke to ____ at the conference.

<u>Who did you speak to at the conference?</u>

h ____ invented the mobile phone.

<u>Who invented the mobile phone?</u>

i ____ people work in the Lille factory.

<u>How many people work in the Lille factory?</u>

j I travelled from Munich to Berlin by ____.

<u>How did you travel from Munich to Berlin?</u>

Practice 6 Complete the article using the verbs in the box in the Past Simple.

| be   convert   develop   begin   be   grow   become |

Like many other aspects of the computer age, *Yahoo!* started as an idea, (1) __grew__ into a hobby and then (2) __became__ a full-time passion. The two developers of *Yahoo!*, David Filo and Jerry Yang, (3) __were__ Ph.D. students in electrical engineering at Stanford University when they (4) __began__ working on *Yahoo!* in April 1994. At first it (5) __was__ a way to keep track of their personal interests on the Internet. Later they (6) __converted__ their personal lists into a database designed to serve the needs of any user. They (7) __developed__ software to help them locate, identify and edit material stored on the Internet. Today, *Yahoo!* contains organised information on tens of thousands of computers linked to the Web.

Lexis: Business verbs

Complete the sentences below with an appropriate verb.

a His ambition is to __become__ the president of the company.

b The company plans to __launch__ a new product line.

c To make money companies need to __expand__ quickly.

d A lot of dot.coms don't really __produce__ anything.

e The present president didn't __found__ the company, his father did.

f When did Nintendo __establish__ its subsidiary in the USA?

g Our objective is to __achieve__ sales of $30 million this year.

h We want to __negotiate__ a new deal with our suppliers.

i The fastest way for the company to grow is to __buy__ smaller companies.

j Consultancies __provide__ services for other businesses.

k How much did your turnover __increase__ last year?

Answers on page 127

6 Correspondence

Will for unplanned decisions

You use *will* + infinitive to show you are making an on-the-spot or new decision.

Practice 1 When would you say the following sentences? Match the decisions a–g to the situations 1–7.

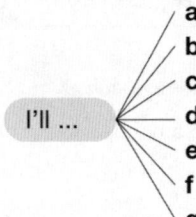

a open the door for you.
b take a taxi.
c catch an earlier train.
I'll ... **d** lend it to you, if you like.
e have a look on the Internet.
f speak to the boss about it.
g have another look at the figures.

a	b	c	d	e	f	g
5	3	2	7	4	6	1

1 A customer asks if you can give him a better discount.
2 Your boss asks you if you can start work before the usual time.
3 A colleague reminds you about a meeting with a client on the other side of town in ten minutes.
4 Someone asks you where you can get a new battery for a laptop computer.
5 A colleague is carrying a lot of files and documents and has both hands occupied.
6 Your wife/husband asks if you can take a day off work.
7 A colleague admires a new CD you are listening to.

Practice 2 What would you say in these situations? Reply using the word in brackets.

a Someone offers you something to drink. You can have tea or coffee. (coffee)
  I'll have a coffee, please.

b You are ordering a meal in a restaurant. You can have either soup or salad for a starter. (salad)
  I'll have salad.

c You go out with some friends. You decide to pay for the drinks. (pay)
  I'll pay for the drinks.

d A colleague who you like is having problems with a new computer program you are familiar with. (help)
  I'll help you, if you like.

e Someone reminds you that you are taking a flight at 10.30. It is now 9.15. (taxi).
  I'll take a taxi.

f A colleague has heard on the radio that the buses are on strike and can't get home. You have your car. (lift).
  I'll give you a lift, if you like.

Lexis: Business communication

Prepositions Match the parts of the sentences below.

a There is a message ...
b There is a mistake ...
c I asked him to phone ...
d I sent you an e-mail ...
e We confirmed the date of the meeting ...
f I will send you the packet ...
g I'd like to apologise ...
h We are giving top priority ...

1 ... in writing last week.
2 ... in the letter you sent me.
3 ... to your order form.
4 ... about this problem last week.
5 ... back this afternoon.
6 ... for what happened.
7 ... by courier this afternoon.
8 ... from Dave Cartwright for you.

a	b	c	d	e	f	g	h
8	2	5	4	1	7	4	3

Photocopiable   In Company Pre-intermediate Teacher's Book © Macmillan Publishers Limited 2003

Crossword Complete the crossword. All the words are from unit 6.

Across

1 The _____ date for this order is June 26th. (when the order is supposed to arrive with the customer)
6 We'd like a _____ reply. ('quick' or 'fast')
8 People see e-mails as an _____ way of communicating. (the opposite of 'formal')
9 I'm sorry, I can't read his _____. (He wrote it with a pen.)
10 Machine used to send documents by telephone. (not a modem)
13 We hope to do more _____ with them in the future. (buy or sell things or services)
15 I need to look at the _____ again. (the noun of 'correspond')
19 To make sure something is correct.
21 Sometimes it's difficult to make a _____. (the noun of 'decide')
22 Could I leave a _____, please? (what you leave when someone is not there)
24 I'm really _____ he hasn't phoned me. (irritated)
28 'Thank you.' 'You're _____.'
29 Could I take _____ the details? (the opposite of 'up')
30 Could you _____ that you have received this e-mail? (the verb of 'confirmation')

Down

2 Please do it _____. (at once)
3 The opposite of 'cheap'.
4 The name written at the bottom of a document.
5 Could you confirm the _____ in writing, please? (bits of information)
7 A service which picks up and delivers documents. (like UPS)
11 I'd like to _____ for the mistake. (say sorry)
12 I'm still waiting for a _____ from John to my letter.
14 Nowadays I use it for all my research and for sending e-mails.
16 I'm very _____ about this. (the adjective of 'worry')
17 I'm _____ about the order. (calling)
18 Error.
20 'Hello, is _____ John?' 'Yes, speaking.'
23 Bad writing _____ cost companies a lot of money. (abilities)
25 I want to place an _____ for 300 units.
26 Can you _____ it to me by e-mail?
27 How much will it _____ us to send it?

Answers on page 128

Writing e-mails The following e-mails have arrived but there is a problem. There is no punctuation or capital letters. Correct the e-mails so that they make sense.

a dear mr gonzalez thank you for contacting lexington technical support unfortunately I do not understand the nature of the problem you are having or in fact even the product you are using can you please write back with as much information as you can about what product you are using what you are trying to do what problem you are having etc best regards kamal bouaissi technical support engineer

b dear richard tennant thank you for registering your lexington product your new customer number is 55563500 when calling technical support (925-253-3050) or lexington customer service (800-225-4880) please have your customer number ready we recommend writing your customer number in your lexington manual keeping it with our phone numbers and filing this e-mail for future reference thank you for your interest in lexington if there is anything we can do for you please let us know we will be happy to help you regards lexington customer service

7 Making comparisons

Comparatives & superlatives

Adjective type	Adjective	Comparative	Superlative
1 syllable	rich	rich**er**	**the** rich**est**
	cheap	cheap**er**	**the** cheap**est**
1 syllable with 1 vowel + consonant	hot	hot**ter**	**the** hot**test**
	big	big**ger**	**the** big**gest**
2 syllables ending in -y	early	earl**ier**	**the** earl**iest**
	heavy	heav**ier**	**the** heav**iest**
2 syllables or more	economical	**more** economical	**the most** economical
	interesting	**more** interesting	**the most** interesting

You can often use the comparative form of adjectives with *than* to compare people, places and things.
- *Life is **easier than** in the past.*
- *The company is **more profitable than** its competitors.*

You can use *much, a lot, a bit* and *a little* to show if the differences are big or small.
- *Mexico City is **a lot** bigger than Rome*
- *London is **much** more expensive than Madrid.*

You can also use *not as ... as* to show differences.
- *Travelling by train is **not as expensive as** by plane.*

You use the article *the* with the superlative form of the adjective.
- *Taking important decisions is **the hardest** part of management.*
- ***The most useful** aspect of the Internet is communication.*

You can use *second, third* etc. with superlatives.
- *Locally we are the **second** largest provider of Internet services.*

You can also use *less ... than* and *the least* to show differences.
- *Life in the past was **less** comfortable **than** it is now.*
- *His company is **the least** profitable on the stock exchange.*

Practice 1 Rewrite the sentences using the opposite of the adjective.

a The Internet is faster than the post.
The post is slower than the Internet.

b Hotels are more expensive than motels.
Motels are cheaper than hotels.

c English is easier to learn than Chinese.
Chinese is more difficult to learn than English.

d Trains are more comfortable than buses.
Buses are more uncomfortable than trains.

e People think that marketing is more interesting than accounting.
People think that accounting is more boring than marketing.

f Flying is safer than driving.
Driving is more dangerous than flying.

g Small meetings are more efficient than large ones.
Large meetings are more efficient than small ones.

h This job is better paid than my last one.
My last job was worse paid than this one.

i The economic situation is worse than it was four years ago.
Four years ago the economic situation was better than it is now.

Practice 2 *As* or *than*? Complete the sentences.

a The job isn't as interesting as I hoped.
b The journey was more expensive than I expected.
c This office has more space than the old one.
d I'm feeling more tired than yesterday.
e Fords aren't as good as Audis.

Practice 3 Complete the second sentence so that it means the same as the first sentence.

a It's easier to build hotels in the US than in Europe.
It's not as difficult to build hotels in the US as it is in Europe.

Photocopiable In Company Pre-intermediate Teacher's Book © Macmillan Publishers Limited 2003

b The Maserati GT is more powerful than the Chevrolet.

The Chevrolet isn't <u>as powerful as the Maserati.</u>

c The Chevrolet isn't as expensive as the Maserati.

The Maserati is <u>more expensive than the Chevrolet.</u>

d Profitability is more important than turnover.

Turnover isn't <u>isn't as important as profitability.</u>

e Sales aren't as good as last year.

Sales are <u>worse than last year.</u>

f This computer is faster than the old one.

The old computer wasn't as <u>fast as this one.</u>

g It isn't as hot as yesterday.
Yesterday <u>was hotter than today.</u>

Practice 4 Who are the richest people in the world today? Look at the table below and complete the sentences. Has the situation changed since the information was published?

The 10 richest people in the world

1 Robson Walton
Country USA
Business Retailing (Wal-Mart)
Wealth in 2002 £73bn
Wealth in 2001 £45.3bn

2 Bill Gates
Country USA
Business Software (Microsoft)
Wealth in 2002 £37.5bn
Wealth in 2001 £37.5bn

3 Warren Buffett
Country USA
Business Investments
Wealth in 2002 £24.8bn
Wealth in 2001 £17.3bn

4 Forrest Mars Jr
Country USA
Business Confectionery
Wealth in 2002 £19.2bn
Wealth in 2001 £14bn

5 Karl & Theo Albrecht
Country Germany
Business Supermarkets
Wealth in 2002 £19bn
Wealth in 2001 £13.3bn

6 = Paul Allen
Country USA
Business Software (Microsoft)
Wealth in 2002 £17.8bn
Wealth in 2001 £17bn

6 = King Fahd
Country Saudi Arabia
Business Oil
Wealth in 2002 £17.8bn
Wealth in 2001 £17.3bn

8 Larry Ellison
Country USA
Business Computers (Oracle)
Wealth in 2002 £16.7bn
Wealth in 2001 £29bn

9 Barbara Cox Anthony & Anne Cox Chambers
Country USA
Business Media
Wealth in 2002 £14.3bn
Wealth in 2001 £13.3bn

10 Prince Alwaleed
Country Saudi Arabia
Business Investments
Wealth in 2002 £14.2bn
Wealth in 2001 £13.3bn

Adapted from *The 50 Richest in the World*, Forbes Magazine

In 2002 ...

a Robson Walton was the <u>richest</u> person in the world.

b King Fahd wasn't <u>as rich</u> as Warren Buffett.

c Robson Walton was <u>richer than</u> Bill Gates.

d Warren Buffett was one of the <u>richest</u> people in the world.

e Bill Gates was <u>as rich as</u> before.

f Larry Ellison was <u>not as rich</u> as in 2001.

g Paul Allen was <u>as rich as</u> King Fahd.

h Most of the people in this list were <u>richer than</u> in 2001.

Lexis: Hotel services

1 Number the lines of the dialogue in the correct order.
Receptionist

[3] Yes, sir. What would you like?

[1] Room service. Katherine speaking. Can I help you?

[5] Well, I'll have to ask in the kitchen to see if they have any *foie gras*. Would you like it with some toast?

[11] You're welcome, sir. Goodbye.

[7] Yes. Dry, medium or sweet?

[9] Right, sir. It will be with you in a few minutes.

Guest

[2] Hello, Katherine. This is room 208 here. I'm feeling a bit hungry. I'd like to order a snack.

[10] Thank you, Katherine.

[8] Oh, as dry as possible, please, and nicely chilled.

[4] Oh, I don't know. Perhaps a little *foie gras*?

[6] Yes, please. And I'd also like some champagne.

2 Complete the sentences using the correct form of the words in brackets.

a Some international hotel chains have a <u>worldwide</u> database with information about their guests' preferences. (world)

b If you call room service, they will <u>deliver</u> meals to your room. (delivery)

c We can't afford to <u>employ</u> any more staff. (employer)

d A lot of our revenue comes from food and drink but our rooms are more <u>profitable</u>. (profit)

e Hotel guests from the USA <u>prefer</u> a standard room layout. (preference)

f You can <u>convert</u> old buildings into hotels but there is a limit to what you can do. (conversion)

g We have to meet our customers' <u>expectations</u>. (expect)

h Multinational companies often expand by taking over smaller <u>operations</u>. (operate)

9 Spirit of enterprise

Present Perfect

Affirmative

I You We They	've (have)	finished the report.
He She	's (has)	

Negative

I You We They	haven't	finished the report.
He She	hasn't	

Interrogative

Have Has	I you we they	finished the report?
Has Hasn't	he she	

Short answers

Have you seen John?
Yes, I have. / No, I haven't.
Has Jane sent the letter?
Yes, she has. / No, she hasn't.

The past participle of regular verbs is the same as the Past Simple, but with many common irregular verbs it is different:

- *go – went – gone*
- *come – came – come*
- *eat – ate – eaten*

The tense you use to talk about past events depends on how you see them.

If you see actions and situations as part of a sequence of finished past events and situations (e.g. stages in your life, events in history, events in a narrative, etc.) you use the **Past Simple**.

- *I studied economics at university.*
- *His first wife was Argentinean.*
- *Her last job was with an engineering firm.*
- *Bill Gates founded Microsoft with a friend.*
- *Some people made a lot of money in the war.*
- *Suddenly he stopped talking and left the room.*

If past actions or situations are not related to other past events or time periods (they simply happened before now), you use the **Present Perfect**. Often it is because you are referring to recent events, or to contrast a present situation with the past.

- *I've had a fantastic idea!*
- *We've developed a new product for our range.*
- *Our turnover has grown by 10%.*
- *The photocopier has broken down.*

There is one important exception:

- *What did you say?* not ~~*What have you said?*~~

Practice 1 Write the past participles of the verbs below.

see	_seen_	write	_written_
buy	_bought_	break	_broken_
sell	_sold_	set	_set_
do	_done_	read	_read_
find	_found_	fall	_fallen_
come	_come_	rise	_risen_
put	_put_	meet	_met_
take	_taken_	think	_thought_

Practice 2 Reorganise the words to make sentences in the Present Perfect.

a lost glasses I have my
I have lost my glasses.

b gone by 3% prices have up
Prices have gone up by 3%.

c has stable economic remained growth
Economic growth has remained stable.

d prices last years have in fallen five the
Prices have fallen in the last five years.

e has 2,000 workers sacked Molinex
Molinex has sacked 2,000 workers.

f company has the Mr Rodriguez left
Mr Rodriguez has left the company.

g not a John week I have for seen
I have not seen John for a week.

Practice 3 Write a sentence using the verbs in the box and the Present Perfect for the situations below.

> give ~~stop~~ move be lose arrive
> change break

a Half an hour ago it was raining and now it isn't.
It's stopped raining.

b The photocopier doesn't work. Half an hour ago it did.
The photocopier has broken down.

c Ten minutes ago you called for a taxi. It's now outside the office.
The taxi _has arrived._

d Last year your company was based on a site outside town. Now its offices are located in the centre of town.

The company has moved into the centre of town.

e You can't find your notes for a presentation.

I've lost my _____ notes.

f You're giving a presentation. You did the same presentation last week and the week before.

This is the third time _I've given this_ _presentation._

g Philip Windish works for a company. A week ago he worked for a different company.

He's changed companies.

h A friend comments that nowadays he never sees you.

I've been _____ very busy lately.

Practice 4 Match the questions to the answers.

a Where is my pen?
b Why are you looking so pleased with yourself?
c How is the new product line doing?
d Why are you looking for a new car?
e What's our share price today?
f Why are you looking so tired?
g Where's Jeremy?

1 It's gone up by four cents.
2 I've achieved my sales target for this month.
3 Because I've sold my old one.
4 It's been a really long day.
5 It's been very successful so far.
6 He's gone to Sydney for the week.
7 I don't know. I haven't seen it.

a	b	c	d	e	f	g
7	2	5	3	1	4	6

Practice 5 Complete the text with the verbs in the box, using either the Past Simple or the Present Perfect.

reach	create	acquire	commence	add
increase	go	install	turn	launch

The Inditex group consists of almost a hundred companies dealing with textile design, production and distribution. Its unique management techniques and its successes (a) _have turned_ Inditex into one of the world's largest fashion groups.

Over the years the group (b) _has added_ other chains to the original Zara, each covering a different market sector. In 1991 the group (c) _created_ Pull & Bear, and in 1995 (d) _acquired_ 100% of

Massimo Dutti. Bershka (e) _commenced_ its activity in 1998, followed by the acquisition of Stradivarius in 1999. More recently, Inditex (f) _launched_ Oysho, a chain specialising in fashionable lingerie and underwear.

In the last four years the number of shops in the group (g) _has reached_ a figure of over a thousand, and the group now has operations in 39 countries worldwide. In the same period, sales (h) _have increased_ by 27% and net profits by 31%. In May 2001 the group was floated on the Madrid stock exchange and its share price (i) _has gone_ from strength to strength.

Despite its size, the group still controls its activities from Arteixo, a village in the north west of Spain, where this year it (j) _installed_ its headquarters in a new building.

Answers on page 129

Lexis: Word building

Complete the table below with the appropriate form.

verb	noun	adjective
acquire	acquisition	acquired
reject	_rejection_	rejected
grow	_growth_	growing
succeed	success	_successful_
benefit	_benefit_	beneficial
innovate	_innovation_	_innovative_
flex	_flexibility_	flexible
operate	operation	operating
profit	_profit_	profitable
increase	increase	_increasing_
fall	fall	fallen/falling
install	_installation_	installed

10 Stressed to the limit

Have to

I You We They	have to don't have to	
		work at night.
He She	has to doesn't have to	
Do Does	I/you/we/they he/she	**have to** work at night?

Should

I You He/She We They	should shouldn't	do the job for free.

You use *has to/have to* to show that it is necessary to do something.
- *Everyone **has to** pay taxes.*
- *We all **have to** use the same computer programs.*

When you want to show that it isn't necessary to do something, you can use *doesn't have to/don't have to*.
- *He **doesn't have to** travel much in his job.*
- *We **don't have to** dress formally for work.*

You use *should* or *shouldn't* to show that it is a good or bad idea to do something.
- *You **should** use the Internet for getting new ideas.*
- *You **shouldn't** work so hard if you want to live to an old age.*

Practice 1 Complete the sentences in an appropriate way. Use *has to, have to, doesn't have to* or *don't have to* and the verbs in the box.

get up	make	come	show	wear
finish	work	sign	get	do	go

a All visitors to the factory _have to sign_ a register.

b Our company has a 'casual Friday' policy which means you _don't have to wear_ formal clothes in the office on Fridays.

c 'Why are you working so late?' 'Because I _have to finish_ this report for tomorrow.'

d To get to work on time he _has to get up_ at 5.30 a.m.

e Every Monday morning we _have to go_ to a departmental meeting.

f I like holidays because you _don't have to do_ anything.

g If you want to see Mr Smith you _have to make_ an appointment. He's a very busy man.

h You _don't have to come_ if you don't want to. We can do it without you.

i You _(don't) have to get_ a visa if you travel to certain countries.

j When you cross an international border you usually _have to show_ your passport.

k He's so rich he _doesn't have to work_, but he still does. He's a workaholic.

Practice 2 Reorganise the words to make questions.

a finish this do have I today to
Do I have to finish this today?

b dress do have work for to you formally
Do you have to dress formally for work?

c year abroad how to go many you times a do have
How many times a year do you have to go abroad?

d complete when have order we the to do
When do we have to complete the order?

e do English go this have year classes we to to
Do we have to go to English classes this year?

f your have drive do in you job to much
Do you have to drive much in your job?

Practice 3 Give appropriate advice using *should* or *shouldn't* and the verbs in the box.

set up	leave	go	work	have	spend
~~go~~					

a I can't get a job because I don't speak any foreign languages.
You should go to English classes.

b I don't know how to use this new accountancy program.
You should go on a course.

c I keep getting these headaches.

You shouldn't spend _____ so much time staring at figures.

d My plane is at 2.30.

You should leave _____ or you'll miss it.

e I have this constant pain in my chest.

You should have _____ a check-up.

f My family is complaining they never see me.

You shouldn't work _____ so late.

g I don't like working for someone else.

You should set up _____ your own business.

Practice 4 Complete the sentences using a form of *have to* or *should* (affirmative or negative). Sometimes there are two possible answers.

a The doctor says I _should/have to_ take things easy.

b You _shouldn't_ spend so much time in front of a computer – it's bad for your eyes.

c Managers _should/have to_ be good communicators.

d You _shouldn't_ just give people orders, you _should_ motivate them to do a good job.

e I _have to_ do this job even if it is stressful – I need the money.

f I'm going home now because I _have to_ get up early tomorrow to catch my plane.

g If you need travel information, you _should_ look it up on the Internet.

h You _shouldn't_ speak to the boss like that.

i If you want to know more about the company, you _should_ visit them.

j You _don't have to_ come with me. I can do the presentation on my own.

Lexis: Stress at work

1 Complete the sentences with the correct form of the word in brackets.

a An air traffic controller has a very _stressful_ job. (stress)

b A _telephonist_ has to answer the phone all day. (telephone)

c His work involves a lot of different _responsibilities_. (responsible)

d Our boss is always shouting at us. I don't find it very _motivating_. (motivate)

e Too much stress is bad for the workers, and it's also bad for the _employer_. (employ)

f Stress-related _illness_ is the cause of half of lost working days. (ill)

g It's a problem of _communication_ – we never know what's happening in the company. (communicate)

h Nobody knows how to use the new machine – we need urgent _training_. (train)

i Employees shouldn't work under _unnecessary_ pressure. (necessary)

j You should _recognise_ your mistakes and correct them. (recognition)

k One of the benefits of reducing stress is better _relationships_ with clients and colleagues. (relate)

l Workers need to rest and recuperate their _creative_ energies. (create)

m The experts say that bad _management_ is the main cause of stress. (manage)

n Policies such as _performance_-related pay demotivate a work force. (perform)

2 Complete the second sentence so that it means the same as the first.

a Does your work cause you stress?
Do you find your work _stressful_?

b My boss makes life difficult.
My boss doesn't make life _easy_.

c My husband isn't very helpful.
My husband doesn't _help much_.

d At times I get nervous.
At times I get a bit on _edge_.

e 75% of visits to the doctor are because of stress.
75% of visits to the doctor are the _result_ of stress.

f People don't think that teaching is a difficult job. Everyone thinks that teaching is an _easy job_.

g I hope things improve for you.
I hope things get _better_ for you.

h Worrying about things doesn't help you.
There's _no point_ in worrying about things.

i I don't work for anyone. I'm self-employed.
I work for _myself_.

11 Top jobs

Present Perfect – the unfinished past

You use the Present Perfect to say when present situations began. For example:

Past Simple: *I started working here 25 years ago.*
Present Simple: *I work here now.*
Present Perfect: *I've worked here for 25 years.*
NOT ~~I am working here for 25 years.~~ *

Past Simple: *I met John for the first time in 1985.*
Present Simple: *I still know him.*
Present Perfect: *I've known John since 1985.*
NOT ~~I know John since 1985.~~ *

* In many languages, you use a present tense to express this idea so these are very common mistakes. In English you can only use the Present Perfect.

To say when the action began you use *since* or *for*. You use *since* with a point in time and *for* with a period of time.

since	for
8 o'clock	2 years
1975	a month
August	a few minutes
last week	half an hour
I was born	ages
he arrived	hundreds of years

*Things have been better **since** we changed offices.*
*He has lived here **for** ten years.*
NOT ... ~~since ten years ago.~~

You can also use *for* with the Past Simple. Compare these sentences:

Present Perfect: *I've lived in Manchester **for** three years / **since** 1998.* (I still live in Manchester.)
Past Simple: *I lived in Manchester **for** three years / **from** 1995 **to** 1998.* (Now I live somewhere else.)

Practice 1 Complete the sentences with *since* or *for*.

a Mr Bianchi has been out of the office <u>since</u> last Thursday.

b We haven't had a holiday <u>since</u> the summer.

c They have been friends <u>since</u> they were at university together.

d He's had his own business <u>for</u> a few years now.

e I haven't seen you <u>for</u> a while. How are things going?

f I've known Pete <u>since</u> we met at a trade fair nearly ten years ago.

g They've had that old car <u>for</u> years.

h Mr Gonzalez has been here <u>since</u> 9.30. He's waiting for you in reception.

i <u>Since</u> his wife had a baby, he's spent more time at home.

j He's waited for this promotion <u>for</u> months.

Practice 2 Write questions with *How long ...?* and the Present Perfect.

a you / work / here
<u>How long have you worked here?</u>

b he / know / about this problem
<u>How long has he known about this problem?</u>

c she / be / a director of the company
<u>How long has she been a director of the company?</u>

d you / want / change jobs
<u>How long have you wanted to change jobs?</u>

e they / have / their website
<u>How long have they had their website?</u>

f he / be / interested / in working for us
<u>How long has he been interested in working for us?</u>

g he / have / a company car
<u>How long has he had a company car?</u>

h she / be / responsible for that account
<u>How long has she been responsible for that account?</u>

Practice 3 Rewrite the following sentences using the Present Perfect.

a He works here – he started work in January.
<u>He's worked here since January.</u>

b He lives in Paris – he was born there.
<u>He's lived in Paris since he was born.</u>

c He's a computer programmer – he became a programmer when he left university.
<u>He's been a computer programmer since he left university.</u>

d They make furniture – they started making furniture over a hundred years ago.
<u>They've made furniture for over a hundred years.</u>

e She owns a business – she set it up five years ago.
<u>She's owned a business for five years.</u>

f They lead the market – they became market leaders in 1998. <u>They've led the market since 1998.</u>

Practice 4 Rewrite the following sentences using the Present Perfect.

a I met him at university.

I've known him since university.

b Mr Jones arrived here hours ago.

Mr Jones has been here for hours.

c When did you buy your car?

How long have you had your car?

d I got this job in January.

I've had this job since January.

e They told me about the problem yesterday.

I've known about the problem since yesterday.

f They got divorced two years ago.

They've been divorced for two years.

Practice 5 Read the biographical details of James Brown. Then use the prompts to write sentences using either the Present Perfect or the Past Simple and *for, since,* or *from ... to.*

James Brown

1974 started smoking

1976 went to university to study engineering

1979 graduated with a degree in engineering

1980 got a job with Rolls Royce as an aeronautical engineer

1981 became interested in boats

1982 got married

1983 bought his first yacht

1985 got a job with P & W in Canada and moved to Montreal

1991 moved back to the UK and went to work at the P & W factory in Manchester

1993 gave up smoking

1996 moved to a new job in the P & W offices in Portsmouth

a be / an aeronautical engineer

He's been an aeronautical engineer since 1980.

b smoke

He smoked from 1974 to 1993.

c study engineering / university

He studied engineering at university from 1976 to 1979.

d be / interested / boats

He's been interested in boats since 1981.

e be / married

He's been married since 1982.

f work / Rolls Royce

He worked for Rolls Royce for five years.

g have / yacht

He's had a yacht since 1983.

h live / Canada

He lived in Canada for six years.

i live / the UK

He's lived in the UK since 1991.

j have / job / Portsmouth

He's had a job in Portsmouth since 1996.

k work / for P & W

He's worked for P & W since 1985.

l not smoke

He hasn't smoked since 1993.

Lexis: Company news

Match the parts of the sentences.

a Dan Colman graduated from York University in 1980 with ...

b He and some student friends founded ...

c In 1998 they moved ...

d At the beginning it was a small firm which produced components ...

e The company quickly expanded and set ...

f Recently, it has launched ...

g The engineers responsible ...

h It has also entered the ...

i Dan Colman has held ...

j The company has recently celebrated ...

1 ... for other manufacturers.

2 ... mobile phone market.

3 ... the top position since it was founded.

4 ... a degree in electronic engineering.

5 ... a range of computer accessories, which is doing very well.

6 ... its twentieth anniversary.

7 ... up new divisions.

8 ... its headquarters to Milton Keynes.

9 ... for this success have become directors of the company.

10 ... the company ALTS in 1982.

a	b	c	d	e	f	g	h	i	j
4	10	8	1	7	5	9	2	3	6

13 Air travel

Conditionals with *will*

If + Present, *will/won't* + infinitive
- If I **have** time, I'**ll finish** the figures this afternoon.
- If they **don't offer** me more money, I **won't accept** the job.

Will/won't + infinitive + *if* + Present
- He **won't wait** if you **arrive** late.
- I'**ll phone** you if I my mobile **works** there.

You can use conditionals with *will* to talk about future events which depend on other things happening.

Practice 1 Match the parts of the sentences.

a If you don't leave now, ...
b You'll be late ...
c If I get a promotion, ...
d I'll buy a better car ...
e If people are rude to BA ground staff, ...
f If we make a good offer, ...
g I'll take longer to get to the airport ...
h I'll put on weight ...
i If you don't have any plans for tonight, ...
j They'll get more work done ...

1 ... they won't be able to get on the plane.
2 ... if I go to so many business lunches.
3 ... you'll miss your flight.
4 ... if you don't keep interrupting them.
5 ... if you don't call a taxi now.
6 ... if we coincide with the rush hour.
7 ... I'll earn more money.
8 ... if they increase my salary.
9 ... will you have dinner with me?
10 ... we'll get the contract.

a	b	c	d	e	f	g	h	i	j
3	5	7	8	1	10	6	2	9	4

Practice 2 Complete the sentences using one of the verbs below in the correct tense.

phone	find	lose	pay	improve	be
need	adopt	have	tell		

a If I see John, I _'ll tell_ him what you said.
b If anyone _needs_ to contact me, tell them I'll be back at four.
c We _'ll be_ able to get the 10.14 train if we hurry.

d If you _find_ my keys, will you let me know?
e Your English _will improve_ if you spend some time in the USA.
f I _'ll phone_ you if there's any news.
g If we _pay_ within 30 days, will you drop the price?
h If BA's policy on rude passengers is a success, other airlines _will adopt_ it.
i If he checks in late, he _'ll lose_ his seat assignment.
j You _'ll have_ to hurry if you want to catch you flight.

Practice 3 Write a sentence using the conditional with *will* based on each piece of advice.

a You should confirm your booking or you won't get a good seat.
   If you confirm your booking, you'll get a good seat.

b You should pretend you're not interested in buying from them or they won't drop the price.
   If you pretend you're not interested in buying from them, they'll drop the price.

c You should apologise to the boss or you will have problems.
   If you apologise to the boss, you won't have problems.

d You shouldn't drink too much on the flight or you'll have to keep going to the toilet.
   If you don't drink too much on the flight, you won't have to keep going to the toilet.

e You should leave for the airport now or you'll miss your flight.
   If you leave for the airport now, you won't miss your flight.

f You shouldn't 'get stroppy' with the ground staff or they won't let you on the plane.
   If you 'get stroppy' with the ground staff, they won't let you on the plane.

g You should study something practical or you won't get a job.
   If you study something practical, you'll get a job.

h You shouldn't work so hard as you do or you'll get ill.

  If you work as hard as you do, you'll get ill.

  _____

i You should take the client out to lunch or you won't get his business.

  If you take the client out to lunch, you'll get his business.

Lexis: Negotiating & air travel

Negotiation Complete the dialogue with the words in the box.

10%	price	accept	do	business
up	deal	deliver	discount	payment
order	more			

A Okay, we want to do (a) _business_ with you, but we need to talk about the (b) _price_ .

B Well, the catalogue price is $30.25.

A I know, but we're talking about a big (c) _order_ here. If we order 100 units, for example, what (d) _discount_ will you give me?

B If you order (e) _more_ than 100 units, I'll give you a discount of (f) _10%_ .

A 10%. And for 150 units?

B For 150 units, I'll go (g) _up_ to 12%.

A 12%. That sounds good. What about (h) _payment_ ?

B Payment is within 60 days.

A Er, if you let us pay within 90 days, I'll (i) _accept_ a lower discount ... say 10% on 150 units.

B So, you're saying that if I offer a discount of 10% on the catalogue price for an order of 150 units, with payment within 90 days, we'll have a (j) _deal_ ?

A Yes, we'll have a deal ... if you can (k) _deliver_ in two weeks.

B All right, then. I think we can (l) _do_ that. It's a deal!

Air travel

1 Imagine you are flying from Europe to the USA. Number the following events in a logical order.

- [1] **a** Book your flight over the Internet or by phoning the airline.
- [3] **b** Check in at least 45 minutes before your flight.
- [4] **c** Go through the metal detector and wait for your flight to be announced.
- [6] **d** Fasten your seat belt and take off.
- [5] **e** Show your boarding pass at the boarding gate and get on the plane.
- [2] **f** Check the details of your reservation and seat assignment.
- [7] **g** Dominate the armrests!
- [10] **h** Go through customs.
- [11] **i** Take a taxi to your hotel.
- [8] **j** Land at JFK airport and get off the plane.
- [9] **k** Go through passport control and pick up luggage in baggage reclaim.

2 Match the parts of the sentences.

- **a** You should ask for the seat you want when you book ...
- **b** It's important to tackle ...
- **c** There was a traffic jam and I missed ...
- **d** The flight was overbooked so they offered me ...
- **e** If he gets stroppy, don't pay ...
- **f** I don't think the new BA rules will solve ...

- **1** ... your flight
- **2** ... my flight.
- **3** ... the problem of air rage.
- **4** ... any attention to him.
- **5** ... problems before they get too big.
- **6** ... a refund or a later flight.

a	b	c	d	e	f
1	5	2	6	4	3

14 Hiring and firing

The passive

The object in active sentences becomes the subject in passive sentences.

Active
Someone services the machine every year.
They have closed down five factories.
They decorated the offices last year.
They've closed the old factory.
They are encouraging her to apply for the job.
They don't clean the office on Friday.

Passive (to be + past participle)
The machine is serviced every year.
Five factories have been closed down.
The offices were decorated last year.
The old factory has been closed.
She is being encouraged to apply for the job.
The office isn't cleaned on Friday.

You often use the passive to put the important information at the beginning of a sentence. The passive can be more impersonal than the active. For this reason, you can use it in formal documents such as reports.

You can use *by* to emphasise who or what performed an action.
- *The book was written by Peter Hudson.*
- *The equipment is damaged by prolonged exposure to sunlight.*

Practice 1 Reorganise the words to make correct sentences.

a June was at the contract the signed end of
The contract was signed at the end of June.

b sacked slowly Sheila was working too for
Sheila was sacked for working too slowly.

c damaged fire the the in was office
The office was damaged in the fire.

d workers accident injured were the in some
Some workers were injured in the accident.

e measures announced the have new been
The new measures have been announced.

f staff employed new no year this be will
No new staff will be employed this year.

g redesigned corporate is image being our
Our corporate image is being redesigned.

h salaries increased year have this been our
Our salaries have been increased this year.

Practice 2 Rewrite the sentences in the passive.

a They have cancelled the order.
The order has been cancelled.

b They haven't finished the new building.
The new building hasn't been finished.

c Someone told him about the meeting.
He's been told about the meeting.

d Someone stole the plans for the new engine.
The plans for the new engine have been stolen.

e Someone will pick you up at the airport.
You'll be picked up at the airport.

f They didn't ask him if he wanted the job.
He wasn't asked if he wanted the job.

g Did anyone tell you about what happened at the meeting? Were you told about what happened at the meeting?

h They hold a sales conference every year.
A sales conference is held every year.

i Something delayed his flight.
His flight was delayed.

j They are answering the complaints in writing.
Complaints are being answered in writing.

Practice 3 Answer the questions using a sentence in the passive and *by*.

a Who was the inventor of the light bulb?
The light bulb was invented by Thomas Edison.

b What currency was the replacement for the peseta, franc and lira in 2002?
The peseta, franc and lira were replaced by the euro.

c How many countries form the United Kingdom?
It is formed by four countries: England, Scotland, Wales and Northern Ireland.

d Who is the author of this book?
This book was written by Simon Clarke.

e Who is the owner of this book?
The book is owned by (me).

f What type of heating have you got in your office – oil, gas or electric?
My office is heated by …

Photocopiable

g Who was the director of the film *Some Like it Hot?*
The film 'Some Like it Hot' was directed by Billy Wilder.

h Which company was the original manufacturer of the PC? The PC was originally manufactured by IBM.

Answers at foot of page

Lexis: Procedures

1 Match the parts of the sentences.

a She was employed ...
b The incident was reported ...
c John was consulted ...
d The staff have been informed ...
e She was sacked ...
f The conditions were agreed ...
g He didn't accept the offers which were put ...
h The worker was injured ...
i The flight was delayed ...
j The passive is used ...

1 ... on a temporary basis.
2 ... about the decision.
3 ... for writing reports.
4 ... for stealing office stationery.
5 ... to him by the employment office.
6 ... by the bad weather.
7 ... to the supervisor.
8 ... at a company wide level.
9 ... of the new working hours.
10 ... by an explosion in the chemical plant.

a	b	c	d	e	f	g	h	i	j
1	7	2	9	4	8	5	10	6	3

2 Combine one word from box A with one word from box B to complete each sentence below.

A	**B**
electronics	application
written	secrets
job	position
company	rights
workers'	needs
job	security
previous	workers
skilled	warning
temporary	staff
unemployment	benefits
staffing	industry

a For young people job security is not usually as important as a good salary.

b We gave the employee a written warning for arriving late to work two days running.

c In the summer there is more work so we have to take on more people to meet our staffing needs.

d He was accused of revealing company secrets to a competitor.

e A hundred years ago workers' rights didn't exist because there were no unions.

f You always have to include a CV in your job application.

g Education is important because industry needs a supply of skilled workers.

h Was your previous position a full-time post?

i In many countries there are no unemployment benefits for people who have no work.

j At Christmas, shops take on temporary staff because it's a busy time of year.

k The electronics industry is an important sector of the local economy.

3 Reorganise the letters to form words to complete the sentences.

kasc	veritwine	kemart	girinf
dali fof	revbal	nowd	

a Two hundred workers at the factory have been laid off because of the bad financial situation.

b This mobile phone is the smallest on the market.

c I asked her to put the phone down and come into my office.

d They can't sack you without giving you at least two warnings in writing.

e Firing someone is one of the most difficult things a manager has to do.

f The first thing you have to do is give the employee a verbal warning.

g How did your interview go, then? Do you think you got the job?

Going to vs will

be + *going to* + infinitive

I	am 'm not	
You We They	are aren't	**going to** apply for the job.
He She	is isn't	

Are(n't)	you they we	
Is(n't)	he she	**going to** phone later?

You can use *going to* to talk about intentions and decisions you have made about the future before the moment of speaking.

- *We're going to open a new office in Berlin.*
- *I'm going to ask for an application form for the new post.*

Going to or will?

You use *will* to show you are making a decision at the moment of speaking.

A   *Could I speak to Mr Gomez, please?*
B   *I'm afraid he's out at the moment. Can I take a message?*
A   *No thanks, **I'll phone** later.*

Practice 1 Write sentences using *going to* and the word prompts.

a   this evening / meet / friends / a drink.
This evening I'm going to meet some friends for a drink.

b   they / employ / more staff / deal with the new order
They're going to employ more staff to deal with the new order.

c   you / meet / me / airport?
Are you going to meet me at the airport?

d   what / you / say / at / meeting?
What are you going to say at the meeting?

e   next year / I / study / German
Next year I'm going to study German.

f   he / look for / new job
He's going to look for a new job.

g   she / not / accept / our offer
She isn't going to accept our offer.

h   we / take / train / bus?
Are we going to take the train or the bus?

Practice 2 Complete the responses with the verb in brackets using either *going to* or *will*.

a   We've run out of toner for the photocopier.
Have we? I 'll order (order) some more.

b   What are your plans for the weekend?
We 're going to visit (visit) some friends in the country. Do you want to come?

c   Did you remember to book the hotel?
No, I forgot! I 'll phone them (phone) now. I hope they still have some room.

d   You should consult George about the production problems.
I've already mentioned it to him. We 're going to discuss (discuss) it this afternoon.

e   Have you seen their offices? They're miles from anywhere in this really old building.
Yes, I know. But they 're going to move (move) to a new place next year.

f   I'm dying for a cup of coffee.
All right, I 'll make (make) one now. Do you take sugar?

g   Why are you working so hard?
Because I 'm going to leave (leave) on time today, for a change, and I want to finish this before I go.

h   I have to go to the airport and my car won't start.
Don't worry. I 'll lend (lend) you mine.

Practice 3 Complete the conversation using the words in the box.

| start | information | time | do | urgent |
| easier | strategy | someone | learn | |

A What are you doing?

B I'm putting this customer (a) __information__ into the database.

A Why don't you get (b) __someone__ else in your team to do it?

B Well, it's (c) __easier__ if I just do it myself.

A Yes, but if you do it yourself, they'll never (d) __learn__.

B Yes, you're probably right. I'll (e) __do__ that next time.

A Anyway, have you finished the marketing (f) __strategy__ for the new product launch?

B No, I'm going to (g) __start__ that this afternoon.

A Oh, come on! It's really (h) __urgent__. We're all waiting for it.

B I know, but I haven't had (i) __time__.

Lexis: Working conditions

1 Combine one word from box A with one word from box B to complete each sentence below.

A	**B**
realistic	planning
eight-hour	deadline
long	forecasts
sales	line
forward	hours
bottom	day

a Monday is too soon for us: next Friday is a more __realistic deadline__.

b The traditional __eight-hour day__ does not suit our natural daily rhythm.

c According to our __sales forecasts__ we are going to sell over 20% more next year.

d In any business the __bottom line__ is that you have to make enough money to survive.

e You should give priority to important tasks such as __forward planning__ and problem analysis.

f In the UK, people work __long hours__ but their productivity is not as high as in France or Germany.

2 Complete the sentences using the correct form of the words in brackets.

a Most people __perform__ better in the morning. (performance)

b A psychologist is going to __observe__ the staff to see how they work. (observation)

c Time management __specialists__ will not be impressed by the results of the experiment. (specialise)

d We are not so __productive__ after a good lunch. (production)

e They __intend__ to reduce the working week to 35 hours in some countries. (intention)

f Have you __decided__ what to do about the situation? (decision)

g The __discussion__ went on for hours and the meeting ended very late. (discuss)

"You're always so busy, Carter. You come to work early, you leave late. What are you up to?"

Reported speech

Say & tell

You can use *say* or *tell* to report what someone said.

say + something

• He **says** (that) he is happy in his new job.

tell + somebody + something

• He **tells** everyone (that) he is the company boss.

Tense

If you use the past forms *said* or *told*, you have to change the verbs in the original.

Present → past

• I **like** working on my own. → He said he **liked** working on his own.

Will → *would*:

• I**'ll** help you. → He said he **would** help me.

Pronouns

I → he/she
me → him/her
my → his/her
your → my

• I speak to **your** secretary every day. →
He told me **he** spoke to **my** secretary every day.

Adverbs of time & place

now → then/at that moment
today → that day
here → there
tomorrow → the next day/the following day
yesterday → the day before/the previous day

• I'll see you **here tomorrow**. → He said he would see me **there the next day**.

Most of these changes are logical and natural and often similar in other languages. They depend on the differences in time, place and people between the original conversation and the reported conversation.

Asked

For reported questions you can use *asked* + *what/when*/etc.

• What do you want? →
He **asked** me **what** I wanted.

or *asked* + *if* for reporting yes/no questions.

• Is it official? →
He **asked** me **if** it was official.

Practice 1 Complete the second sentence to report the first one.

a I'm really enjoying my job at the moment.

She says <u>she's really enjoying her job at the moment.</u>

b It's too late to cancel the meeting.

I said <u>it was too late to cancel the meeting.</u>

c We are having a lot of problems with the production department today.

He told me <u>they were having a lot of problems with the production department that day.</u>

d What time is Mr Keegan going to arrive?

He asked <u>what time Mr Keegan was going to arrive.</u>

e We should buy a new computer system.

He keeps telling me <u>we should buy a new computer system.</u>

f Is Mr Marchain available?

She asked <u>if Mr Marchain was available.</u>

g The fixed costs include the office rent and equipment hire.

She said <u>that the fixed costs included the office rent and equipment hire.</u>

h Where do you work now?

They asked me <u>where I worked now.</u>

i I'll meet you at the airport at eight o'clock.

She said <u>she would meet me at the airport at eight o'clock.</u>

j I want to see you about the arrangements for tomorrow.

He told me <u>he wanted to see me about the arrangements for the next day.</u>

k Does the office open on Saturdays?

He asked me <u>if the office opened on Saturdays.</u>

l When will the documents be ready?

She asked <u>when the documents would be ready.</u>

m I'm the best salesman in the company.

He keeps saying <u>that he's the best salesman in the company.</u>

n Can I make a phone call?

He asked if <u>he could make a phone call.</u>

o What do you think of the new website?

He asked me <u>what I thought of the new website.</u>

Practice 2 Complete the sentences with *say/said*, *tell/told*, or *ask/asked*.

a Why didn't you __tell__ me you weren't happy with your job?

b What will people __say__ if we try to ban office gossip?

c Did he __ask__ what time you had to be there?

d The boss always __says__ that I should keep my desk more organised.

e He __told__ me he was having second thoughts about applying for the job.

f Will you __ask__ him if he's going to come?

g I can't read the small print on this. What does it __say__?

h Every time I visit them they __ask__ me how you are.

i I'll __tell__ you if you promise not to __say__ anything to anybody else.

Lexis: Relationships at work

1 Combine one word from box A with one word from box B to complete each sentence below.

A	B
coffee	consultant
company	room
human	policy
meeting	resources
management	machine

a People have the best ideas in conversations around the __coffee machine__.

b The company has hired a __management consultant__ to give advice on improving internal communications.

c What do you think about this idea of removing the chairs from the __meeting room__ so we don't spend so long talking about things?

d What is the __company policy__ on taking coffee or tea breaks?

e Nowadays people say __human resources__ instead of 'personnel'.

2 Complete the puzzle using the clues below. Sometimes the first letter has been given.

1 Having communal areas benefits relations in the w___.

2 We are having a ___ for efficiency. (You also ___ a car.)

3 What this unit is about.

4 Let's make an ___ not to waste time.

5 It's not a good idea to ___ rumours.

6 Have you heard the ___?

7 There's no ___ without fire.

8 We have banned smoking in the o___.

9 They don't a___ of people taking long tea breaks.

10 Let's go to the pub for a ___ on Friday night.

11 We should encourage employees to ___ their ideas.

12 What has happened to the tea ___?

1	w	o	r	k	P	l	a	c	e
		2	d	R	i	v	e	
		3	g	O	s	s	i	p
	4	e	f	F	o	r	t	
5	s	p	r	E	a	d		
6	n	e	w	S				
		7	S	m	o	k	e	
8	o	f	f	I	c	e		
9	a	p	p	r	O	v	e	
10	d	r	i	N	k			
11	s	h	A	r	e			
12	t	r	o	L	l	e	y	

"The whole company is being relocated but nobody will tell me where to."

18 E-commerce

Will for future predictions

<table>
<tr><td colspan="2">Affirmative</td></tr>
<tr><td>I
you
he
she
it
we
they</td><td>will
('ll)   work</td></tr>
</table>

<table>
<tr><td colspan="2">Negative</td></tr>
<tr><td>I
you
he
she
it
we
they</td><td>will not
(won't)   work</td></tr>
</table>

<table>
<tr><td colspan="2">Interrogative</td></tr>
<tr><td>will
won't</td><td>I
you
he
she
it
we
they   work?</td></tr>
</table>

You can use *will* + infinitive to express predictions or beliefs about the future.

- *This year the economy **will grow** by 3%.*
- *I'm sure we **will finish** the order on time.*

The negative of *will* is *won't*.

- *I'm sorry, but things **won't get** any better.*
- *No, there **won't be** a recession.*

Put *will* before the subject to make questions.

- **Will** people **use** *the Internet for most of their shopping in the future?*
- **Will** *the economy **recover** by next year?*

You often introduce predictions with *I think* ...

- *I think the DVD **will replace** the CD.*
- *I think the meeting **will end** on time.*

Avoid saying *I think ... won't ...*
Use *I don't think ... will ...*

- *I don't think the keyboard **will become** obsolete.*
  (*NOT ~~I think the keyboard won't become obsolete~~.*)
- *I don't think the meeting **will end** on time.*
  (*NOT ~~I think the meeting won't end on time~~.*)

Practice 1 Join the sentence beginnings with the endings using *will* + the verbs in the box.

have	~~continue~~	take	get	affect	be	go	retire	arrive

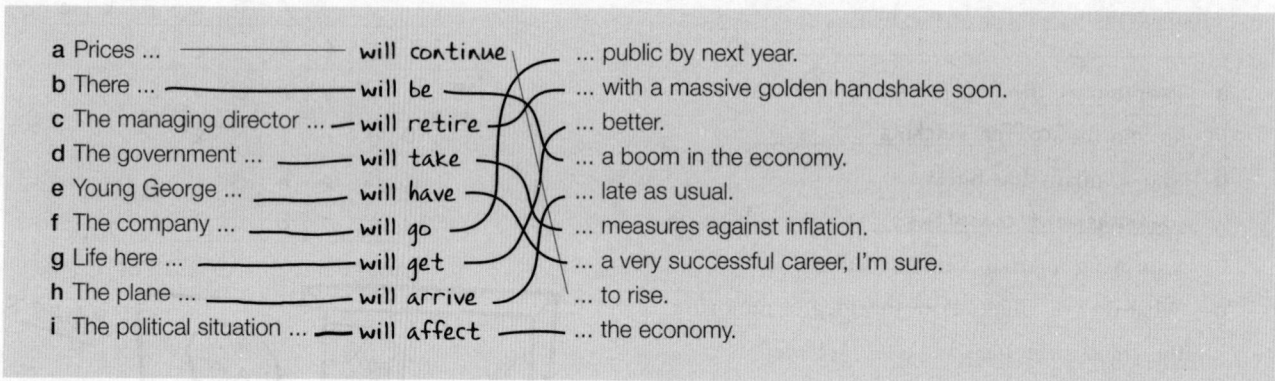

a Prices ... ———— will continue ... public by next year.
b There ... ———— will be ... with a massive golden handshake soon.
c The managing director ... — will retire ... better.
d The government ... ———— will take ... a boom in the economy.
e Young George ... ———— will have ... late as usual.
f The company ... ———— will go ... measures against inflation.
g Life here ... ———— will get ... a very successful career, I'm sure.
h The plane ... ———— will arrive ... to rise.
i The political situation ... — will affect ———— the economy.

Practice 2 Reorganise the words to make correct sentences.

a any new you system won't with have problems the
<u>You won't have any problems with the new system.</u>

b information think the Internet I you'll on find the
<u>I think you'll find the information on the Internet.</u>

c Berlin you'll good have time think I a in
<u>I think you'll have a good time in Berlin.</u>

d Juan Montes think see you'll there don't I
<u>I don't think you'll see Juan Montes there.</u>

e think do write report time you'll the you to have?
<u>Do you think you'll have time to write the report?</u>

f time you what arrive will?
<u>What time will you arrive?</u>

g long how us it will get there take to?
<u>How long will it take us to get there?</u>

h we'll shopping I to think go time any don't have
<u>I don't think we'll have any time to go shopping.</u>

(Photocopiable)

i make think money I he'll lot a of

I think he'll make a lot of money.

j want people see buy will always to
products they before them most

Most people will always want to see products
before they buy them.

Practice 3 Make questions with *do you think ...
will ...?* and then write answers that are true for you.

a What time / get home tonight?

What time do you think you'll get home
tonight? About 7.30.

b What / have / dinner?

What time do you think you'll have dinner?

c Where / go / next holiday?

Where do you think you'll go for your next
holiday?

d change / jobs / next five years?

Do you think you'll change jobs in the next five
years?

e lose / weight / this month?

Do you think you'll lose any weight this
month?

f How long / take / do this exercise?

How long do you think you'll take to do this
exercise?

g ever have / own business?

Do you think you'll ever have your own
business?

h ever drive / Ferrari?

Do you think you'll ever drive a Ferrari?

i work as hard / five years from now?

Do you think you'll work as hard five years
from now?

Lexis: Shopping & the Internet

Collocations Match each verb on the left to the item
on the right that it collocates with. Then use the phrases
to complete the sentences.

compare	a bill
influence	the conversation
listen to	a network
run up	prices
try on	the decision
access	a sweater

a I like to _compare prices_ before I buy
anything expensive.

b His children have _run up a bill_ of
over $300 by surfing on the Internet all day long.

c When she asked to _try on a sweater_,
they told her they didn't have one in her size.

d To _access a network_ you have to
obtain a user name and a password from the
administrator.

e Did you _listen to the conversation_ in the
canteen yesterday?

f What factors do you think will most
influence the decision on salaries?

Buying online Complete the anecdote using the
words in the box.

crashed   website   message   security   came
e-mail   complain   online   reply   button
charge   pay   download   clicked

Why I will never buy anything on the Internet again

Ask most people how shopping will be in the future
and inevitably they will mention the Internet. Well, the
other day I had a bad enough experience shopping
(a) _online_ to put me off for life. I heard about a
book you could download from a (b) _website_
before it was published and sold in bookshops. As it
was by an author I adore, I decided to investigate.

I found the page and read the information. They
charged sixty euros for the (c) _download_. Not a
massive amount but you had to use a credit card. I
completed the form with the endless details requested,
including my (d) _e-mail_ address. Finally I entered
my credit card number, because they solemnly promised
that there was no (e) _security_ risk. When the
payment was authorised – it took about a minute – a
new screen appeared with a (f) _button_ which said
'download now'. I (g) _clicked_ on the button but
nothing happened so I clicked again. Then a
(h) _message_ came up saying 'Download suspended
due to network overload. Please try again later.'

Finally the system (i) _crashed_ and I had to turn
off the computer. When I reconnected, the same forms
as before (j) _came_ up but I didn't want to risk
paying again, so I wrote an e-mail to the company
explaining the problem. I never got a (k) _reply_.

I assumed that as I never got the book I wouldn't
have to (l) _pay_, but when I got my credit card
statement at the end of the month I saw the
(m) _charge_ for sixty euros was there. It was too
late to do anything and there was no one to
(n) _complain_ to. Okay, so it was only sixty euros – no
big deal – but the question I ask myself is this: why risk
buying online when it amounts to what is basically an
act of faith? In any case, it will be a long time before I
try buying something over the Internet again.

19 Working from home

Conditionals (future reference)

You can use *if* + past + *would/could* to talk about hypothetical or imagined situations in the future. This is often called the 'second conditional'. Look at these examples:

Condition	Consequence
*If I **knew** the answer,*	*I'd **tell** you.*
*If we **got** the order,*	*we'd **have** years of work.*

Compare these two sentences:

* *If the factory **shuts**, over 200 people **will lose** their jobs.*
  (The speaker thinks the situation is likely to happen in the future.)
* *If the factory **shut**, over 200 people **would lose** their jobs.*
  (The speaker thinks the situation is unlikely or improbable in the future.)

Practice 1 Match the parts of the following conditional sentences.

a   If we worked from home, ...
b   If I spent less time travelling, ...
c   The company would save money ...
d   People would need good computers ...
e   Our quality of life would improve ...
f   If I never saw my colleagues, ...
g   There'd be problems with this plan ...

1   ... I'd have more time with my family.
2   ... if the staff didn't agree with it.
3   ... if they had to work from home.
4   ... if we didn't have to commute.
5   ... I'd miss the personal contact.
6   ... we'd spend less time travelling.
7   ... if it invested in home working.

a	b	c	d	e	f	g
6	1	7	3	4	5	2

Practice 2 David and Sarah are a couple who live in London with their two young children. Read their conversation and complete it using the verb in brackets in the appropriate tense.

Sarah Why don't we move out of the city into the country? I'm fed up with living here. It's so stressful.

David If we (a) __lived__ (live) in the country, it
(b) __would take__ (take) about ten minutes for you to get bored with it.

Sarah No it wouldn't. We (c) __could get__ (get) a nice big house – somewhere with a garden. The kids
(d) __could go__ (go) to a little village school, and we
(e) __could forget__ (forget) about all the street violence, traffic and pollution.

David But they (f) __like__ (like) living in the city, and they (g) __'d miss__ (miss) their friends. Also, if we (h) __moved__ (move) into the country, we (i) __'d spend__ (spend) all our time in the car travelling in and out to work.

Sarah Not necessarily. If you (j) __asked__ (ask) your company, they (k) __'d let__ (let) you work from home some of the time, and mine would to.

David I don't think so. I (l) __have__ (have) to be in contact with people in my job. Anyway, if I
(m) __were__ (be) in the house all day, I
(n) __would go__ (go) crazy.

Sarah Don't be so negative. If you (o) __spent__ (spend) more time at home, we (p) __'d see__ (see) more of you, and we could do more things like going for walks and playing tennis. You (q) __'d have__ (have) a better quality of life.

David I'm sorry. I just don't think you're being realistic. It (r) __'s__ (be) a dream.

Sarah If you (s) __were__ (be) less selfish, you'd at least think about it.

David Okay, I promise I (t) __'ll give__ (give) it some thought if that's what you want.

Practice 3 Write conditional sentences using the prompts.

a   He doesn't work hard so he isn't very successful.
   __If he worked harder, he'd be more successful.__

b   You don't have enough experience so we can't give you the job. __If you had more experience, we could give you the job.__

c   He can't drive so he has to take taxis all the time.
   __If he could drive, he wouldn't have to take taxis all the time.__

d   I don't have the information so I can't help you.
   __If I had the information, I'd be able to help you.__

e I don't like sport so I don't go to the gym.
If I liked sport, I'd go to the gym.

f He works long hours because he enjoys his job.
If he didn't enjoy his job, he wouldn't work long hours.

g She only does the job because she hasn't got any choice. _If she had any choice, she wouldn't do the job._

h My car is in the garage so I can't take you to the airport. _If my car wasn't in the garage, I could take you to the airport._

i Things take him a long time because he isn't very organised. _If he was more organised, things wouldn't take him as long._

j He drives an expensive car because he can afford it. _If he couldn't afford it, he wouldn't drive an expensive car._

Practice 4 Give advice by completing the sentences.

(example answers)

a If you got up earlier, _you wouldn't be late to work so often._

b If you did a computer course, _you could get a better job._

c You would make a better impression _if you dressed more formally._

d If you had a mobile phone, _I could contact you more easily._

e You wouldn't be so stressed _if you didn't work so hard._

f If you used the Internet, _you could find the information more quickly._

g You'd do better at the interview _if you weren't so nervous._

h If you didn't complain all the time, _people would be more willing to help you._

Practice 5 Reorganise the words to form questions.

a job do what would you if choose you could
What job would you do if you could choose?

b live you abroad you where if would to had go
If you had to live abroad, where would you go?

c treat people boss how you would were if you the
How would you treat people if you were the boss?

d didn't language study would what you English you if learn
If you didn't study English, what language would you learn?

e would earn how a you the wasn't living salary if important
How would you earn a living if the salary wasn't important?

Lexis: Teleworking

The text below is an extract from an article about teleworking. Complete it using the words in the box.

> desk   home   flexibility   office   local
> commute

'The key word for the future is (a) _flexibility_. We're not suddenly going to see massive numbers of people working from (b) _home_ instead of going into the (c) _office_. We'll see a much more hybrid existence where some of the time people are in the office, maybe at a shared (d) _desk_, and some of the time at home. And there are of course 'telecentres' – serviced offices which provide an intermediate stage where people can find a (e) _local_ office instead of having to (f) _commute_ into a town or city centre.'

Additional material

1 Selling your company

Jon Day's verdict on Moonpig (p6, ex7)

There are two types of Internet business models that I like – ones that solve an existing problem, such as Tesco.com, which delivers bulky grocery items to my door, and those that could not exist without the Internet, such as the eBay auction site. Moonpig has elements of both. It offers a convenient way to select greetings cards without going to a shop and allows the cards to be customised, a possibility the Internet opens up.

While investigating Moonpig I ordered a few cards and found the service to be user-friendly and the personalisation of cards a unique selling point. My biggest concern is their estimated cost of converting offline customers to online customers. To reach their target of 750,000 customers would cost almost £10 million.

My score: 7.5/10

Answers: Lexis link (p95, crossword)

Across		Down	
2	website	**1**	attachment
3	list	**4**	screen
5	e-mail	**6**	download
7	mouse	**8**	online
9	intranet	**12**	click
10	link	**13**	site
11	connection	**15**	surf
14	virus		
16	browse		

2 Women in business

Statistics (p10, ex2)

Women in the workplace

46.5% of US labour force

49.5% of middle management positions

12.5% of senior managers

11.7% of board directors

4.1% of top earners

2 Fortune 500 CEOs

3 Telephone talk

Customer frustration (p17, ex2)

The five main frustrations customers experience in dealing with telephone staff are:
- taking too long to answer
- being put on hold and forgotten
- being transferred and having to repeat their enquiry
- being answered by voicemail and other machines
- not having calls returned

Indirect questions (p18, ex2)

A InterAir / help?
B Yes, please / like / information / flight / Munich
A Yes / know / flight number?
B The flight number? / sure / know / leaves Munich / 1730
A yes / IA 345
B Yes / tell / time / gets in?
A arrival / 1910
B 1910 / know / delay?
A No / flight / on time
B Right / thank / much
A welcome / goodbye

4 Networking

Answers (p21, ex4)

a Who do you work for?
b Where is your company based?
c Where are you staying?
d Do you speak (*German*)?
e Who is (*Alex*) talking to?
f What do you do? / What's your job?
g Have you got any children? / Do you have any children?
h Where are you from? / Where do you come from?
i Are you married?
j Do you play golf?
k Do you know (*Adriana Bellini*)?

15 Time

Wasting time (p72, ex4)

Be sloppy

A good hour or two can be gained every few weeks if you keep your desk in a mess. Friday afternoons and Monday mornings are perfect times to set aside for cleaning up your work area. (28 minutes to an hour once a week)

The computer

Load your computer with unnecessary programs that make your machine run more slowly. While you're waiting for the PC to process information, sit back and relax. If the boss questions you, just say, 'Damn computers.' He'll laugh and agree with you. (roughly 42 minutes a day)

The Internet

Be very careful misusing the company PC to surf the Net for personal enjoyment. Your boss knows the Internet is a big waste of time and is watching for people who are doing web searches for MP3s and games. The best way is to use it for all research. If you need a phone number for a client across town, use the Internet to find it. Most people just reach for a phone book, which is faster than using the Internet. (roughly 9 to 33 minutes a day.)

Office conversations

Enter business conversations around the office that are taking place in the open. You don't have to be a part of the conversation very much. The important thing is to be there physically. Just listen and nod your head when appropriate. (23 minutes to 1.3 hours)

Meetings

Go to every meeting you can get into. You'd be surprised at how many people miss the opportunity to waste time by avoiding meetings. Once you're in a meeting, it's all about planning your weekend, or thinking about the football game you watched the night before. (According to Office Studies International the average meeting takes 42 minutes and meetings happen every 5 hours. Count on 2–3 meetings a week).
Adapted from 'Wasting time at work' by Galen Black

18 E-commerce

Sentences for comparison (p81, ex1)

a   When you buy something for yourself with your own money, you're interested in quality and price.
b   When you buy something for someone else with your own money, you're interested in price.
c   When you buy something for yourself with someone else's money, you're interested in quality.
d   When you buy something for someone else with someone else's money, who cares?

19 Working from home

Teleworking (p89, ex5)

Does working at home really work?	Advantages	Disadvantages
The workplace	13	10
The working day	12	8
Commuting	5	3
Technology	11	15
Efficiency	2	9
Costs	7	6
Motivation	16	14
Family	4	1

6 Correspondence

Dialogue (p32, ex6)

A: S-A-G, can I help you?

B: Yes, this is Elena Moretti from Stern Hydraulics. Could I speak to John Bird, please?

A: Oh, hello, Elena. I'm afraid John isn't here at the moment. Can I take a message?

B: Yes, he sent me an order confirmation – the reference is DH010601 – but the delivery date is wrong.

A: Oh, dear. Can you give me the details?

B: Yes, it says July the 7th, but the agreed delivery date was June the 22nd. It's really important.

A: I see. Well, I'll tell him as soon as he comes in.

B: Thank you. I'm not at all happy about this. A lot depends on this order.

A: Right, Elena, leave it with me. I'm terribly sorry about this.

B: No, it's not your fault. Just ask John to phone me.

A: All right, then. Bye for now.

B: Goodbye.

2 Women in business

Fluency (p12, ex7)

Speaker A

Your partner has the missing information. Complete the chart by asking questions like the ones in exercise 6 on page 12.

Name	Janice	Della
Job title		Director of Retail Sales
Type of company		chain of clothing stores
Working hours		45
Responsibilities		Leading a team of 25. Accounts and stock control. Maintaining inventory in stores.
Weekend/Late evening work		One evening and one weekend day a week. Sometimes 'on call' with a pager in case of emergencies.
Most enjoys		Satisfying internal clients. People she works with.
Travel		Not often. Trips to different stores. 3 trade fairs a year.
Holidays		2 weeks. 3 weeks after 5 years' service.
Ratio of women to men in position/field		60% male, 40% female

3 Telephone talk

Roleplay (p19, ex2)

Speaker A

Situation 1

You work as the Publications Officer in the marketing department of Miki-chan Fashion Accessories. You are currently producing your new company brochure. This is a 32-page, full colour brochure on high quality paper. You need 30,000 copies. Phone ADH Graphics for an estimate. The only problem is that the brochure needs to be ready in ten days. Can they do it?

Situation 2

You work for ADH Graphics. A potential client phones you. Listen to what the customer wants and complete the phone contact form below with the necessary information.

Phone Contact Form ADH Graphics

Date:
Call initiated by:
Call handler:

Client:

Address:

Contact:

Position:

Tel:

E-mail:

Nature of business:

Purpose of call:

Comments:

Action required:
By whom:
Date and time:

---

5 Company histories

Answers: Grammar link (p101, Practice 4)

a Bill Gates didn't found Oracle, he founded Microsoft.

b The Wall Street Crash didn't start a worldwide economic boom, it started an economic depression.

c The six European states didn't sign the Treaty of Madrid, they signed the Treaty of Rome.

d The eleven member states of the European Union didn't adopt the pound as a common currency, they adopted the euro.

e Henry Ford didn't manufacture the first mass produced electronic components, he manufactured cars.

f Napster didn't have problems over people downloading books, it had problems over music.

Answers: Lexis link (p101, Business verbs)

a	become	**e**	found	**i**	buy
b	launch	**f**	establish	**j**	provide
c	expand	**g**	achieve	**k**	increase
d	produce	**h**	negotiate		

---

14 Hiring and firing

What about the workers? (p66, ex2)

Student A

1 Read the article, then answer the questions.

2 Find and underline in the article five examples of the passive. (examples of the passive underlined)

3 Match the five words and phrases in **bold** in the article to five of the definitions below. Ask your partner which words match the other five definitions.

- compensate for _make up for_
- percentage of working population without jobs _____
- employees with training and abilities to do technical tasks _skilled workers_
- people who are unemployed for a long time _____
- what employees can legally expect from their employers _____
- motivating factors _____
- money paid to people who don't have jobs _____
- all the people who work in a country or for a company _workforce_
- the number of employees a company requires to do its work _staffing needs_
- workers who have contracts limited to a period of time _temporary staff_

4 Which country do you think the article is about? Could it be your country? Why? Why not? Explain your reasons to your partner.

Skills shortage linked to job insecurity

According to a survey which was carried out by the Confederation of Industry, almost two thirds of the country's companies are experiencing a shortage of **skilled workers**. It is a problem
5 which particularly affects the electronics industry.

The companies claimed that they provided training for their **workforce**, but that this on its own was not sufficient to cover their **staffing**
10 **needs**.

In an attempt to **make up for** this lack of skilled workers, nearly half of the 670 firms which were contacted said that they had increased their use of **temporary staff**, and over a
15 quarter intended to do the same in the next year.

According to a spokesman for the Confederation, a result of this skills shortage is an increase in feelings of job insecurity among a third of employees. 'It is increasingly difficult to
20 provide people with jobs for life,' he said.

Although over 60% of firms said staff were paid based on their skills and level of competence, the Confederation noted that while salaries at management level were frequently
25 negotiated individually, conditions for clerical and manual workers were usually agreed at a company-wide level.

6 Correspondence

Answers: Lexis link (p103, crossword)

Across		Down	
1	delivery	2	immediately
6	prompt	3	expensive
8	informal	4	signature
9	handwriting	5	details
10	fax	7	courier
13	business	11	apologise
15	correspondence	12	reply
19	check	14	Internet
21	decision	16	worried
22	message	17	phoning
24	annoyed	18	mistake
28	welcome	20	that
29	down	23	skills
30	confirm	25	order
		26	send
		27	cost

7 Making comparisons

Answers: Road test (p35, ex1)

- The Chevrolet has a **bigger** motor **than** the Maserati.
- The Maserati is **more powerful than** the Chevrolet.
- The Maserati is **faster than** the Chevrolet.
- The Chevrolet is **more economical** (to run) **than** the Maserati.
- The Chevrolet is **longer than** the Maserati.
- The Chevrolet is **wider than** the Maserati.
- The Maserati is **higher than** the Chevrolet.
- The Chevrolet has a **bigger** boot **than** the Maserati.
- The Maserati has a **bigger** fuel tank **than** the Chevrolet.
- The Maserati is **heavier than** the Chevrolet.
- The Maserati/Chevrolet is/looks **better than** the Chevrolet/Maserati. (*your own opinion*)
- The Maserati/Chevrolet is/looks **more attractive than** the Chevrolet/Maserati. (*your own opinion*)
- The Maserati/Chevrolet is/looks **more stylish than** the Chevrolet/Maserati. (*your own opinion*)
- The Maserati/Chevrolet is/looks **sexier than** the Chevrolet/Maserati. (*your own opinion*)

Room service (p37, ex3)

Speaker A

Phone room service to make requests for:

- a bottle of Glenfiddich whisky
- someone to fix the minibar
- someone to explain how the TV pay channels work
- someone to sew on a button
- an extra set of clean towels
- (*your own request*)

9 Spirit of enterprise

The worm man (p41, ex7)

THE WORM MAN

Picture the scene. You go to your bank manager and ask him for money to develop a great business idea – a worm farm. Not surprisingly, the bank manager finds it difficult
5 to keep a straight face. But this isn't an imaginary tale. It's the true story of a business success ...

Let's begin at the beginning. Four years ago, Simon Taylor acquired some land on his
10 family's farm. The river Trent was very near, so at first he thought about fish farming. He rejected the idea. 'The initial investment required was very high, and I'm not the world's biggest risk-taker.'
15 So, he opted for a worm farm. The start-up costs were low, and Simon began by growing worms and packing them for fishermen into pots ranging in size from 25g to several kilos.

Traditionally, worms eat organic waste in
20 soil, but Simon feeds them salad waste from supermarkets and restaurants. Demand for the worms has grown, so he is looking at the possibilities of using different types of worm food, including toxic waste from the paper
25 industry. When the worms digest the waste, it breaks down into less harmful elements which can be recycled, rather than buried in expensive waste dumps.

'Worms can do things that greatly benefit
30 our environment,' says Simon. This year, the Newark entrepreneur has produced over ten tons of worms, but expects to double production to some twenty tons next year. 'UK fishermen use some 250 tons of worms every
35 year, so there is a healthy demand for a variety of worms already. But we're also looking at using worms in other areas.'

Adapted from *The Worm Man* by Lee Stokes

9 Spirit of enterprise
Answers: Grammar link (p107, Practice 5)

The Inditex group consists of almost a hundred companies dealing with textile design, production and distribution. Its unique management techniques and its successes (a) **have turned** Inditex into one of the world's largest fashion groups.

Over the years the group (b) **has added** other chains to the original Zara, each covering a different market sector. In 1991 the group (c) **created** Pull & Bear, and in 1995 (d) **acquired** 100% of Massimo Dutti. Bershka (e) **commenced** its activity in 1998, followed by the acquisition of Stradivarius in 1999. More recently, Inditex (f) **launched** Oysho, a chain specialised in fashionable lingerie and underwear.

In the last four years the number of shops in the group (g) **has reached** a figure of over a thousand, and the group now has operations in 39 countries worldwide. In the same period, sales (h) **have increased** by 27% and net profits by 31%. In May 2001 the group was floated on the Madrid stock exchange and its share price (i) **has gone** from strength to strength.

Despite its size, the group still controls its activities from Arteixo, a village in the north west of Spain, where this year it (j) **installed** its headquarters in a new building.

10 Stressed to the limit
The ten most stressful jobs (p44, ex4)

Measured by level of 21 specific job demands, in the USA the ten most stressful jobs are:

1 Inner-city high school teacher
2 Police officer
3 Miner
4 Air traffic controller
5 Hospital doctor
6 Stockbroker
7 Journalist
8 Customer complaint worker
9 Waiter
10 Secretary

13 Air travel
The negotiation game (p61, ex2)

Speaker A: Buyer

Negotiate with your partner to get the best deal possible. You get points for each category of the deal – price, quantity, delivery time, and so on. For example, if you agree on a price of 6 euros, you get 2 points, or 3 points if the price is 5.5. Add your points for each category to get your score. To be a successful negotiator you have to get at least ten points.

Points	1	2	3	
Price	6.5	6	5.5	€
Quantity	200	150	100	units
Delivery	3	2	1	weeks
Payment	30	60	90	days
Guarantee	6	12	18	months

Useful language

Let's talk about (*price*).
That's my best offer.
Okay, I can go with that.
It's a deal!

I can't go any higher/lower.
I can't do that.
Can you help me on this?

15 Time
Time management (p69, ex7)

The busy manager

His life is not planned. Perhaps that is why he is **busy**. His use of time indicates an entirely responsive approach to his job, with more time devoted to **administration** than customer service. The high level of **emergency** shows there are serious problems.

The effective manager

She **delegates** correspondence to subordinates and deals with major issues herself or by telephone. Her **meetings** are well planned. She is popular with customers and **suppliers** because she gets to know them well and her reading makes her knowledgeable. She doesn't just discuss **problems**; she solves them.

2 Women in business

Fluency (p12, ex7)

Speaker B

Your partner has the missing information. Complete the chart by asking questions like the ones in exercise 6 on page 12.

Name	Janice	Della
Job title	Production Manager	
Type of company	software company	
Working hours	Normally 40-50 hours but can be up to 75.	
Responsibilities	Managing website. Liasing with international offices.	
Weekend/Late evening work	Not in her present position.	
Most enjoys	Doing something that makes a real difference to the company.	
Travel	Occasional trips to other offices.	
Holidays	3 weeks	
Ratio of women to men in position/field	Half the department are women but only two have technical skills.	

---

3 Telephone talk

Roleplay (p19, ex2)

Speaker B

Situation 1

You work for ADH Graphics. A potential client phones you. Listen to what the customer wants and complete the phone contact form below with the necessary information.

Situation 2

You work as the Marketing Manager in the marketing department of a clothes manufacturer, Lewis & Co. You are looking for someone to print some labels for your new range of jeans. The labels have to be printed on quality card in two colours. They also have to be cut to the shape of the company logo. You want 10,000 labels. Phone ADH Graphics for an estimate.

Phone Contact Form ADH Graphics

Purpose of call:

Date:
Call initiated by:
Call handler:

Client:

Address:

Contact: Comments:

Position:

Tel:

E-mail: Action required:
                                            By whom:
Nature of business: Date and time:

6 Correspondence

Problems	Solutions
I've got a headache.	I'll get you an aspirin.
I can't understand these figures.	I'll explain them to you.
My computer keeps crashing.	I'll call the IT technician.
We didn't get your fax.	I'll send it to you again.
This report has lots of errors in it.	I'll go through it and correct them.
I can't remember his phone number.	I'll look it up for you.
I need to speak to you urgently.	I'll phone you this afternoon.
I haven't booked my flight to Berlin.	I'll reserve the tickets for you this morning.
The printer is not working properly.	I'll change the ink cartridge.
I don't know how to use this program.	I'll show you how it works.
I need three copies of this proposal.	I'll print them out for you.
I don't know anything about this company.	I'll look for information on the Internet.
Our e-mail system isn't working.	I'll fax the details to you instead.
I can't get an answer from the taxi service.	I'll take you to the airport.

7 Making comparisons

World leaders (p36, ex1)

Speaker B

Look at the tables below. Your partner has the missing information. Ask questions to complete the tables.
For example, *Which is **the second biggest** hotel chain / car manufacturer in the world?*
Where is it based? How many rooms does it have / cars does it sell?

The six biggest hotel chains ranked by number of rooms	Company		Country	Number of rooms
	1	Cendant Corporation	USA	542,630
	2	Bass Hotels & Resorts	UK	471,680
	3	Marriott International	USA	355,900
	4	Accor	France	354,652
	5	Choice Hotels	USA	338,254
	6	Best Western	USA	313,247

Top six car manufacturers in the world ranked by sales	Company		Country	Sales (in millions)
	1	General Motors	USA	6.60
	2	Ford Group	USA	4.83
	3	VW Group	Germany	4.00
	4	Toyota	Japan	3.87
	5	Daimler Chrysler	Germany	2.83
	6	Fiat Group	Italy	2.61

6 Correspondence

On-the-spot decisions (p30, ex5)

Speaker B

Speaker A will begin by telling you a problem. Offer a solution from the table. Say *Don't worry, I'll ...*
Then tell Speaker A about a problem from the table. Begin *I've got a problem ...* Speaker A will offer a solution.

For example: **A** I've got a problem, the battery in my mobile's flat. **B** Don't worry, I'll lend you mine.

Problems	Solutions
I can't understand these figures.	... look it up for you.
My computer keeps crashing.	... look for information on the Internet.
I need to speak to you urgently.	... reserve the tickets for you this morning.
The printer is not working properly.	... send it to you again.
I don't know how to use this program.	... get you an aspirin.
Our e-mail system isn't working.	... go through it and correct them.
I can't get an answer from the taxi service.	... print them out for you.

Answers on page 131

Fluency (page 32, ex8)

Speaker B

You are John Bird. You understand why Elena Moretti is angry. Her company is one of your best customers. Your production department let you down. They promised to meet the delivery date but there was a transport strike and some components didn't arrive. Apologise as much as you can for what happened and invent excuses for everything. Offer to pay for a holiday weekend in London for Elena, but don't make any promises you can't keep.

---

13 Air travel

The negotiation game (p61, ex2)

Speaker B: Seller

Negotiate with your partner to get the best deal possible. You get points for each category of the deal – price, quantity, delivery time, and so on. For example, if you agree on a price of 6 euros, you get 2 points, or 3 points if the price is 6.5. Add your points for each category to get your score. To be a successful negotiator you have to get at least ten points.

Points	1	2	3	
Price	5.5	6	6.5	€
Quantity	100	150	200	units
Delivery	1	2	3	weeks
Payment	90	60	30	days
Guarantee	18	12	6	months

Useful language

Let's talk about (*price*).   I can't go any higher/lower.
That's my best offer.   I can't do that.
Okay, I can go with that.   Can you help me on this?
It's a deal!

3 Telephone talk

Could you tell me ...? (p19, ex4)

Speaker B

You were just about to send this e-mail to a colleague, when they ring you. Answer their questions.

To:
From:
Subject: Annual sales meeting
You're on flight BA 44362 at 1955 on the 21st December from London Heathrow terminal 2. You'll be met by a taxi which will take you to the factory to meet Mr Fuentes. It's about 40 kilometres from the airport. You've got one hour with Mr Fuentes. Then you leave to get to the hotel for the meeting. You'll need to go across country. Avis have either a Range Rover 3.6 or Jeep Grand Cherokee, whichever you prefer. An armed guide will accompany you. Don't forget that you'll need to carry your passport and international driving licence at all times.
The hotel is The Lodge. It's in the middle of the forest, twenty miles from the nearest town, and has 5 stars. All the rooms (including the meeting room) have been booked for the whole week.
All the best,

9 Spirit of enterprise

Change (p42, ex4)

Speaker B
Look at the information in the table. Work with your partner to complete the missing information and find out how Inditex has changed over the last four years.

Inditex	four years ago	now
Shops worldwide	748	
Shops in Spain	489	
Shops in rest of world	259	
Countries where the group operates	21	
Chains in group	Zara, Pull & Bear, Massimo Dutti	
Net revenues	€1,615 million	
Net profits	€153 million	
Headquarters	Arteixo, La Coruña, Spain	

14 Hiring and firing

What about the workers? (p66, ex2)

Student B
1 Read the article, then answer the questions.
2 Find and underline in the article five examples of the passive.
3 Match the five words and phrases in **bold** in the article to five of the definitions below. Ask your partner which words match the other five definitions.
- compensate for _____
- percentage of working population without jobs unemployment rate
- employees with training and abilities to do technical tasks _____
- people who are unemployed for a long time long-term unemployed
- what employees can legally expect from their employers workers' rights
- motivating factors incentives
- money paid to people who don't have jobs unemployment benefits
- all the people who work in a country or for a company _____
- the number of employees a company requires to do its work _____
- workers who have contracts limited to a period of time _____

4 Which country do you think the article is about? Could it be your country? Why? Why not? Explain your reasons to your partner.

17 Office gossip

Gossip (p80, ex9)

Speaker B
You are the personnel manager of the company with the notice below about coffee breaks. You think a lot of time is wasted by people chatting and gossiping when they are supposed to be working. You are under pressure from the Managing Director to improve the efficiency of the company. Also, recently there have been a lot of rumours about staff cutbacks. Most of them are false but some are true, and this is creating a lot of problems.

COMPANY NOTICE

Employees may take up to three coffee breaks per day.

Maximum time at coffee machine: four minutes.

All 'gossip' or discussion of non-work related matters is prohibited.

Unions general strike threat

The whole of the country will be brought to a halt if plans for a general strike go ahead. The threatened strike has been called by the unions in reaction to the government's attempts to cut **unemployment benefits**. With the
5 proposed changes unemployed workers will have to take one of the first three 'acceptable' job offers which are put to them, if the place of work is within 30 km of their homes. If they refuse, they will lose their benefits. Also, anyone who is sacked from their job but appealing
10 against the decision will lose their salary entitlement during the period of the appeal.

The two main unions, each with over a million members each, say that the reforms are a direct attack on **workers' rights**. They say the changes will be especially
15 negative for those who lose their jobs, and the **long-term unemployed**. They also claim that the new law will make it easier and cheaper for companies to lay off staff, and will lead to increased job insecurity.

With an 11.3% **unemployment rate**, the highest in
20 the European Union, the reforms have been defended by the government, which says they are necessary in order to be competitive and provide an open and flexible labour market. It says the measures will help solve the problem of unemployment by increasing the **incentives**
25 for people to find jobs. Although its relations with the labour movement have been generally good for the last six years, trade union officials say that this time the government has gone too far.

Contents: Resource materials

134

Worksheet & author	Timing	Aim	Task
11a Nannies Mark Powell	45 minutes	To practise interviewing and negotiating skills	To read an article about high-earning nannies, then roleplay a series of short job interviews between nannies and prospective employers
11b Top boss? Jon Hird	30 minutes	To promote discussion about the qualities needed to be a good boss	To complete a questionnaire about attitudes to being a good boss
12 Start it up! Nicholas Sheard	40 minutes	To practise expressions used for starting up conversations	To categorise expressions used for starting up conversations and use them in roleplays
13a How was your trip? Paul Emmerson	35 minutes	To practise vocabulary relating to business trips, and learn phrases with the word *trip*	To talk about a business trip
13b Negotiating a deal Nicholas Sheard	40 minutes	To practise the language of negotiating	To roleplay a negotiation between a company finance director and an airline company to reduce the cost of air travel
14a Unfair dismissal? Simon Clarke	30 minutes	To practise reading for detail and to revise language related to the theme of sacking and labour laws	To read two jumbled newspaper articles, put them in order and then discuss the labour laws issues raised in the articles
14b Tricky decision Simon Clarke	30 minutes	To promote discussion on the theme of making somebody redundant	To discuss which of three secretaries should be made redundant, then write an e-mail explaining the reasons why
15 Plenty of time Nicholas Sheard	35 minutes	To practise idiomatic expressions relating to time	To complete sentences with idiomatic expressions relating to time and use them to talk about students' own experiences
16 Things to do Paul Dummett	40 minutes	To practise making requests and saying yes and no politely	To roleplay making last minute preparations for a business trip
17a Say something! Paul Dummett	30 minutes	To learn the difference between *say, tell, speak, talk* and *discuss*, and some common expressions with *say, tell, speak, talk* and *give*	To complete gapped sentences and questions with *say, tell, talk, speak* or *give*, then discuss questions with a partner
17b But you said ...! Jeremy Taylor & Jon Wright	30 minutes	To practise reported speech	To roleplay a conversation between a builder and a dissatisfied client
18a How wrong can you be? Jon Hird	30 minutes	To practise *will* for prediction	To complete famous predictions with *will* and an appropriate verb and match them to who said them
18b A–Z race Gina Cuciniello	40 minutes	To revise grammar from *In Company Pre-intermediate* Student's Book	To play a timed team game identifying and correcting grammar mistakes in 26 sentences
19 What if ...? Jon Hird	30 minutes	To practise conditionals with future reference by discussing hypothetical situations about work	To work in small groups taking it in turns to ask conditional questions from prompts for hypothetical or imaginary situations and then discuss the answers
20 That's not right! Mark Powell	30 minutes	To practise describing food and drink	To choose the correct sentence in a pair to produce a three-stage business lunch conversation

1a 60-second pitch

Overview

Students read a definition of a 60-second pitch, then order the transcript of a 60-second pitch by matching common word partnerships and collocations. Then using the transcript as a model, they make a 60-second pitch about a business idea.

Preparation

One copy of the worksheet for each student.

Procedure

1   Hand out copies of the worksheet. Introduce the topic of a 60-second pitch by reading the definition in exercise 1 with the class. Explain that it is similar to the elevator pitch on page 4 of the Student's Book but that it is used to describe quickly a business idea you have, rather than promote your company to a potential client.

2   Write *customer loyalty scheme* on the board and make sure everybody understands what it means. Brainstorm arguments which could be included in a 60-second pitch about this type of scheme, e.g. repeat business, new customers if attractive benefits, etc.

3   Individually or in pairs, students put the two sections of the pitch in exercise 2 in order. Monitor, helping with vocabulary as necessary.

4   Check the sequence by asking students to read the pitch aloud in the correct order. Explain the meaning of any unfamiliar collocations or word partnerships. Then focus students' attention on the discourse markers used in the pitch (*First, Second, Third, Finally*) to introduce each new argument.

5   In exercise 3, students prepare and make a 60-second pitch on one of the topics. Monitor, helping with vocabulary as necessary. (You may like to have students work in pairs during this preparation stage, and then divide students into new pairs to make the pitch.)

Answers

1 d   2 b   3 h   4 f   5 c   6 a   7 g   8 i   9 e   10 n   11 r
12 j   13 o   14 l   15 q   16 m   17 p   18 k

1b Answering machine

Overview

Students review how to say a variety of numbers, then take turns to read out answering machine messages for their partner to take notes on the main points (dates, times, flight numbers, telephone numbers, e-mail addresses, etc.).

Preparation

One copy of the worksheet for each pair of students. Cut the worksheet into two.

Procedure

1   Review saying numbers, dates, telephone numbers, product reference numbers, letters of the alphabet and times with the class, e.g.

2,363	two thousand, three hundred and sixty-three
7.4	seven point four
1 March 1999	the first of March, nineteen ninety-nine
23 June 2003	the twenty-third of June, two thousand and three

020 7491 6692	(tel number) oh two oh, seven four nine one, double six nine two
DZK345	D-Z-K, 3-4-5
5:15	five fifteen (or a quarter past five)
8:45	eight forty-five (or a quarter to nine)

2   Teach/Review the symbols used in e-mail addresses, e.g.

@	at
.	dot
/	forward slash
-	hyphen
_	underscore
com	pronounced /kɒm/
uk	pronounced U-K

3   Divide the class into pairs and give each student one half of the worksheet. Explain that students are answering machines and they are going to 'play' their messages for their partner to note down the important information, e.g. dates, times, phone numbers, etc. Tell students not to show each other their messages. Give students time to prepare to read their messages and to check any unfamiliar vocabulary.

4   Students take turns to read their messages for their partner to take notes. Monitor, helping with pronunciation as necessary. Students can 'play' their messages as often as they like, but they cannot ask their 'answering machine' any questions or stop him/her while the message is playing.

5   Give students time at the end to compare their notes with the original message. Did they write down all the important information?

2a Ideal company

Overview

Students discuss the importance of different criteria for an ideal company and write sentences using adverbs of frequency to describe an ideal boss.

Preparation

One copy of the worksheet for each student.

Procedure

1   Write *My ideal company* and *My ideal boss* on the board. Brainstorm suggestions for each category with the class. Encourage students to describe the best company and/or boss they have ever worked for.

2   Divide the class into pairs and give each student a copy of the worksheet. Look at the criteria in exercise 1 with the class and explain any unfamiliar vocabulary. Working in pairs, give students five minutes to discuss the items and to choose the five most and five least important. Monitor, helping with vocabulary if necessary. Have a short feedback session. Can the class as a whole agree on the five most and least important?

3   Read through the prompts in exercise 2 with the class and explain any unfamiliar vocabulary. Ask students to make sentences from the prompts which are true for them using the adverbs of frequency in the box. Then they compare their sentences with a partner.

4   Have a feedback session. Ask students to share their ideas with the class.

2b Working style

Overview

Students read 30 statements about attitudes to work and tick the ones they agree with. Then they look at an analysis section to find out which type of working style they have: team worker, finisher, supporter or leader.

Preparation

One copy of the worksheet for each student with the analysis section folded over.

Procedure

1   Introduce the topic of different working styles by writing *team worker, finisher, supporter* and *leader* on the board. Briefly discuss what each of these mean. (See the analysis section in the worksheet but don't go into too much detail at this stage.) Ask students to tell you which of the four working styles they think they have, and to explain why.

2   Hand out copies of the worksheet. Ask students to read the statements and tick the ones they agree with. Set a time limit of ten minutes so that students do the activity quickly and don't ponder over each statement. Monitor, helping with vocabulary as necessary.

3   Ask students to unfold the analysis section and check to see if they have scored mainly As, Bs, Cs or Ds. Then tell them to read the analysis text to find out what kind of working style they have.

4   Have a class feedback session. Ask students if they agree with their analysis.

3a Could you tell me …?

Overview

Students play a board game in which they ask and answer direct and indirect questions. When they answer a question, the aim is to speak for 30–60 seconds without pausing or repeating themselves.

Preparation

One copy of the worksheet for each group of two to four students. Each group will need a die and each student a counter.

Procedure

1   Elicit/Remind students of the grammar of indirect questions, and of why and when we use them. (If necessary, direct them to the Grammar link on page 98 of the Student's Book.)

2   Divide the class into groups of two to four students and give each group a copy of the worksheet and a die. Students can use pieces of paper with their names written on as counters.

3   On the throw of a die, students take turns to move around the board. On landing on a square, the student to the player's left asks him/her a question beginning with the prompt on the square. The player answers the question, talking for approximately 30–60 seconds.
    - If the player doesn't talk for long enough or speaks with too many pauses, he/she goes back to the nearest 'too busy to play' square and starts from that square next turn.
    - If the student who asks the question uses the wrong form, he/she moves back to the nearest 'too busy to play' square.

- If a student lands on a 'too busy to play' square, he/she misses a turn.

The winner is the first student to reach the finish. Monitor, helping with vocabulary as necessary.

3b Telephone trouble

Overview

Students prioritise eight phone messages and then roleplay returning the most important messages. The language of telephoning is practised.

Preparation

One copy of the worksheet for each student.

Procedure

1   Divide the class into pairs and give each student a copy of the worksheet. Read the eight phone messages with the class and explain any unfamiliar vocabulary.

2   In pairs, students discuss the messages and prioritise them according to the order in which they would return them. Monitor the activity, helping with vocabulary as necessary. Encourage students to explain their reasons.

3   Have a class feedback session. Ask *Which calls represent business opportunities? Which calls would you ask someone else to do for you?*

4   Students, in their pairs, prepare and then act out the three telephone calls they decided were the most important to return. Monitor, helping with vocabulary as necessary.

4 Did you, really?

Overview

Students practise keeping a conversation going by asking five follow-up questions to an initial question and reacting with interest to each response.

Preparation

One copy of the worksheet for each pair of students.

Procedure

1   Write *What did you do yesterday evening?* on the board and ask individual students to answer the question. Write one answer on the board, e.g. *I went to the cinema.*

2   Explain that students are going to practise keeping a conversation going. Elicit five follow-up questions from students, helping with vocabulary and question formation as necessary, e.g. *Who did you go with? What did you see?* etc.

3   Point out to students that they also need to show interest when responding to the answers to their questions otherwise they may sound as if they are 'grilling' the other person. Brainstorm some useful phrases, e.g. *Really?, Did you?, That's interesting, That's funny, Wow, That's sounds great/fantastic/amazing*, etc.

4   Divide the class into pairs and give each pair a copy of the worksheet. Students practise the example conversation, then take turns to start and keep a conversation going using one of the questions on the worksheet and asking five follow-up questions. Monitor, helping and correcting as necessary.

5   Have a class feedback session. Ask students to report to the class any interesting information they discovered about each other.

5 The rise and fall of Enron

Overview

Students read a jumbled text about the history of Enron and put it in order using discourse markers as a guide. They then discuss the causes of the company's downfall.

Preparation

One copy of the worksheet for each student.

Procedure

1   Introduce the topic by asking students to tell you what they know about the company, Enron. Help with vocabulary and check/pre-teach: *to be appointed, to launch, to invest, to acquire, to merge, to expand, to diversify, to lie, to go bankrupt, to be sacked, to resign, trading, share price, regulator.*

2   Divide the class into pairs and give each student a copy of the worksheet. In pairs, students put the events in exercise 1 in order. Tell students to first read through the sentences and decide if they relate to the initial successful stage of the company or if they relate to the collapse of the company. This will make ordering the sentences less daunting as they will be dealing with smaller chunks of the text. Monitor, helping with vocabulary as necessary.

3   Check the sequence by asking students to read the history of Enron aloud in the correct order.

4   Look at exercise 2 with the class and explain any unfamiliar vocabulary. In pairs or small groups, students discuss the question. Monitor, helping as necessary.

5   Have a class feedback session.

Answers

1 D   2 A   3 F   4 K   5 H   6 C   7 L   8 G   9 I   10 J
11 B   12 M   13 E

6 Get it write!

Overview

Students identify and correct common grammar and spelling mistakes in a job application letter. This provides practice in accuracy but also provides a model for a job application letter in English.

Preparation

One copy of the worksheet for each student.

Procedure

1   Ask students if they always read over something they have written in English, e.g. an e-mail, letter, etc. before they send it. Have a brief class discussion about the types of errors students make when they write in English.

2   Divide the class into pairs and give each student a copy of the worksheet. Explain that students are going to find and correct three grammar mistakes and two spelling mistakes in each paragraph of the job application letter. Tell them the types of grammar mistakes to look out for, e.g. tenses, prepositions, single/plural forms, relative pronouns, verb forms, etc.

3   Students find and correct the mistakes. Monitor, helping as necessary.

4   Check the answers with the class.

Answers

Paragraph 1: reply **to, which was** in today's
(advertisement, Services)

Paragraph 2: graduate**d**, **have** four years', compan**ies**
(experience, **G**reat Britain)

Paragraph 3: responsible **for**, Last year I **implemented**, for
deal**ing** (system, complaints)

Paragraph 4: would like **to**, interest**ed**, opportunity **to**
(professional, opportunity)

Paragraph 5: you**r** reference, to **come**, to **make**
(enclose, necessary)

7 Away day

Overview

Students choose a venue for a company away day. The language of comparatives and superlatives is practised.

Preparation

One copy of the worksheet for each student.

Procedure

1   Introduce the topic of an away day by reading out the opening paragraph of the worksheet to the class. Make sure everybody understands. Then ask students to think of other reasons why a boss would want to send his/her staff on a day out like this, e.g. for staff to get to know each other better, to improve relations between departments, as a reward for hard work, etc.

2   Divide the class into pairs and give each student a copy of the worksheet. Read the rest of the instructions, the speech bubble text and the adverts for the four away-day venues with the class. Explain any unfamiliar vocabulary.

3   Ask students, in their pairs, to compare the venues, e.g. *The food and wine course is closer to London than the health spa. The wine tasting sounds more interesting than the opera. The adventure farm is the most exciting*, etc. They then try to choose the away day which they think would best suit everybody in the company. Monitor, helping with vocabulary as necessary. Encourage students to use the comparative and superlative forms when discussing the different venues.

4   Have a class feedback session. Ask pairs to tell the class the venue they have chosen and to explain why.

8 Storytelling

Overview

Students read and order a gapped story, completing the gaps with linking words, then build up an anecdote from prompts using past tenses, linking words and *did* for emphasis.

Preparation

One copy of the worksheet for each student.

Procedure

1   You might like to start off by recounting a humorous short anecdote to your students, based on your own experience. Then hand out copies of the worksheet and go through the five stages of a story with the class, referring them back to the stages of your story.

2   Pre-teach the following vocabulary: *improvise, notes, speech, power cut, clap, translator.* Then give students, working in pairs, five minutes to read the story and put the five sections in the correct order according to the five stages. Tell them not to worry about the gaps in the text at this stage. Monitor, helping with vocabulary as necessary. Then check the answers with the class.

3 Ask students to find an example of *did* for emphasis in the story. Then briefly revise how this structure is used. (If necessary, refer students to page 39 of the Student's Book.)

4 Look at the linking words and phrases in exercise 2 with the class, eliciting contexts in which the phrases could be used. Ask students, in their pairs, to fill in the gaps in the text. Tell them to work through the story in order, i.e. starting with paragraph D rather than gap 1. Then check the answers with the class.

5 In their pairs, students choose five of the prompts in exercise 3 and create their own anecdote using the five stages. Monitor, helping with ideas and vocabulary as necessary. Encourage students to use *did* for emphasis at least once in their anecdote, as well as linking words.

6 Combine pairs of students to take turns to tell their story. Invite several pairs to tell their story to the class.

Answers

Exercise 1
1 D 2 C 3 E 4 A 5 B

Exercise 2
1 In the end 2 but 3 When 4 later 5 Just then
6 Because of this 7 However 8 but soon 9 So
10 and then eventually

9a The idea is easy …

Overview

Students act out a meeting between a bank manager and an entrepreneur who is asking for a bank loan to develop and market a new invention. Finance vocabulary and the use of the Past Simple and Present Perfect is revised and practised.

Preparation

One copy of the worksheet for each pair of students. Cut the worksheet into two.

Procedure

1 Ask students to imagine that they have just invented one of the major global brands, e.g. Coca-Cola. Brainstorm how they would persuade a bank to lend them the money to launch the product. During this discussion, pre-teach the following vocabulary which students will need for the worksheet: *launch a product, lend, borrow, owe, pay back a loan, personal investment, entrepreneur, sales channel (e.g. wholesale, mail order), sales forecast, patent*.

2 Divide the class into pairs and give each student one half of the worksheet. Explain that Students A are entrepreneurs and they have a meeting with their bank manager, Students B, to try to secure a loan for their latest invention, a 'Button Fixer'. Give students time to read their instructions, check any unfamiliar vocabulary and prepare for the meeting.

3 In their pairs, students act out the meeting. Monitor, helping with vocabulary as necessary and making sure students use the Past Simple and Present Perfect tenses correctly.

4 Have a class feedback session. Ask Students A how effective they were at persuading the bank manager to lend them the money. Ask Students B how much money, if any, they agreed to lend.

9b Making money

Overview

Students work in pairs and take turns to play the part of Mr/Ms Money, a financial advisor, giving advice to different clients. Money verbs and financial vocabulary is practised.

Preparation

One copy of the worksheet for each student.

Procedure

1 Introduce the topic of money by asking students if they have ever had any advice from a financial advisor. Ask if the advice turned out to be good or bad. Have a brief class discussion.

2 Explain that students are going to be financial advisors and give advice to a variety of clients. Divide the class into pairs and give each student a copy of the worksheet. Give students time to read the different situations and to check any unfamiliar vocabulary. Make sure students understand the meaning of the money verbs in bold. (Explain that *afford* is usually used with *can/could*, e.g. *They bought the flat because they couldn't afford the house*.)

3 Quickly brainstorm some language the students might find useful when they come to play the role of Mr/Ms Money, e.g. *It's a good idea to …, Have you thought about …, I'd recommend …,* etc.

4 Ask students, in their pairs, to choose two of the situations on the worksheet and to prepare to act them out. Students should take the part of Mr/Ms Money in one roleplay and the client in the other.

5 When everybody is ready, students act out the conversations. Monitor the roleplays, helping with vocabulary as necessary.

10a Time to relax

Overview

Students complete a crossword using vocabulary connected with stress in the workplace.

Preparation

One copy of the worksheet for each student.

Procedure

1 Divide the class into pairs and give each student a copy of the worksheet.

2 In their pairs, students read the clues and complete the crossword. Monitor, helping with vocabulary as necessary.

3 Check the answers with the class.

Answers

Across
3 user 5 relocated 7 disorder 9 exercise
10 pressure 11 deadline 12 economic 14 town
17 repetitive 18 linked 20 morale 21 thirteen
22 complained

Down
2 chief executive 4 severe 5 reduce 6 decisions
8 relax 9 expectations 13 creative 14 turnover
15 workaholic 16 promoted 19 degree

10b Velvet revolution

Overview

Students read an e-mail from someone who has recently been elected leader of a developing country. In the e-mail, he asks for advice on how to rebuild the country. In groups, students discuss and prioritise the problems facing him, then write an e-mail giving him advice.

Preparation

One copy of the worksheet for each student.

Procedure

1   Explain that you went to university with a man called Harold, who has just become leader of a large developing country after a velvet revolution (one in which no blood is shed). He has e-mailed you for advice on the best way to rebuild the country.

2   Hand out copies of the worksheet and read the instructions and the e-mail with the class. Explain any unfamiliar vocabulary.

3   Divide the class into small groups and ask them to prioritise the problems facing Harold and his country. During the discussions, try to keep a low profile, though monitoring, helping as necessary.

4   Have a class feedback session. Ask each group to tell you their order. There are no 'correct' answers, as long as students can justify their answers.

5   Divide the groups into pairs and ask students to write the e-mail to Harold in exercise 2. Monitor, helping with vocabulary. (This could be set for homework.)

11a Nannies

Overview

Students read an article about the huge sums of money nannies can now earn in Silicon Valley, and the fabulous perks they sometimes also get. They then roleplay a series of short job interviews. The language of exchanging personal information is revised and basic interviewing and negotiating skills are introduced.

Preparation

One copy of the worksheet for each student.

Procedure

1   Hand out copies of the worksheet. Look at the dictionary definition and discussion questions in exercise 1 with the class.

2   In pairs, ask students to read the article in exercise 2 and underline anything they find surprising. Go over any unfamiliar vocabulary at the end. Explain the meaning of the last sentence of the article by telling the students that the full expression is *the hand that rocks the cradle is the hand that rules the world*, and that it refers to the power of those who bring up children over their future lives. Then have a class feedback session for students' reactions to the article.

3   Set up the roleplay. With larger classes, get nannies and employers to prepare in groups. With small groups, it may be better if the teacher plays a number of different nannies and students decide which one they prefer. Make sure the CVs are very short – they're only intended to get students talking at the beginning. Monitor this preparation stage, helping with vocabulary as necessary.

4   During the roleplay, keep the interviews short by signalling every few minutes for students to form new pairs. Allow students to pair up with the same person again if they want to resume negotiations.

5   At the end, ask the nannies to write down their first (and perhaps second) choice of employer. Employers should likewise write down their first (and second) choice of nanny. Everyone reads out their choices and employment contracts are offered.

11b Top boss?

Overview

Students complete a questionnaire about their attitudes to being a boss, and find out if they would make good bosses. Then they discuss the qualities necessary to be a good boss.

Preparation

One copy of the worksheet for each student with the analysis section folded over.

Procedure

1   Hand out copies of the worksheet and ask students to complete the questionnaire in exercise 1. You might like to point out that *them* has been used in the questionnaire rather than specifying he or she.

2   Divide the class into pairs and ask them to compare their answers, giving reasons for their choices. Monitor, helping with vocabulary as necessary.

3   Ask students to unfold the analysis section and work out their score, then read the analysis and discuss with their partner how accurate they think the analysis is.

4   Ask students, in their pairs, to discuss the qualities needed to be a good boss in exercise 3. You might like to write the following on the board to prompt them: *good administrative skills, good communication skills, competitiveness, consistency, decisiveness, dynamism, good education and qualifications, energy, experience, fairness, friendliness, imagination, loyalty, risk-taking, sense of humour, smart appearance, even temperament.*

5   Have a class feedback session.

12 Start it up!

Overview

Students categorise expressions for starting up conversations into appropriate and inappropriate opening gambits. They think about situations in which they could use the appropriate ones and then practise using them in a series of roleplays.

Preparation

One copy of the worksheet for each student.

Procedure

1   Ask students if they find it difficult to think of the right thing to say when starting up a conversation in English.

2   Hand out copies of the worksheet. Students discuss the questions in exercise 1 in pairs.

3   Look at the statements and questions in exercise 2 with the class and explain any unfamiliar vocabulary. Ask students to identify inappropriate ones (1, 7, 8, 11, 13, 19). Model pronunciation of the appropriate ones and elicit situations in which they could be used.

4 Elicit possible reactions to the statements and questions in exercise 2, e.g. *Yes, of course. Go ahead. Thank you very much! No, I don't mind at all. In fact, I think I'll join you*, etc.

5 In pairs, students roleplay short conversations for the situations in exercise 3. Encourage students to react and to show interest in what their partner says, e.g. *What about you? How interesting! I see. Yes, it is, isn't it? No, I don't. Do you? I didn't know that. Have you?* etc. Monitor, helping with vocabulary as necessary.

13a How was your trip?

Overview

Students look at some statements made by business travellers, all containing phrases with the word *trip*, then match phrases of opposite meaning before they go on to interview each other about business trips they have made.

Preparation

One copy of the worksheet for each student.

Procedure

1 Introduce the topic of business trips by asking students about trips they go on for their company. Ask a few students to give examples of trips they have made which were either a success or a disaster for whatever reason, e.g. the meetings themselves, the flight, the hotel, etc.

2 Divide the class into pairs and give each student a copy of the worksheet. Explain that the speech bubbles contain examples of phrases using the word *trip*. Ask students to look at the speech bubbles and try to work out the meaning of the phrases in bold from the context.

3 Look at the first pair of opposites given as an example with the class. Ask students to find the other pairs. Then check the answers with the class. Explain any unfamiliar vocabulary. Ask individual students to read out the speech bubbles to check pronunciation.

4 Look at exercise 2 with the class and brainstorm any vocabulary students may need for this activity. Then students think about a trip and make notes. When everybody is ready, students take turns to interview each other. Set a time limit of five minutes for each interview. Monitor, helping as necessary.

5 Have a class feedback session. Ask students to report back to the class anything interesting from the interviews.

Answers

1 and 6, 2 and 7, 3 and 10, 4 and 9, 5 and 11, 8 and 12

13b Negotiating a deal

Overview

Students discuss the basic principles of negotiating. Then they read a negotiation situation between a Finance Director who wants to reduce the cost of air travel for his company and a representative from an airline company. Students match useful phrases to different stages of the negotiation situation and then roleplay the negotiation.

Preparation

One copy of the worksheet for each student.

Procedure

1 Introduce the topic by asking students to tell you the basic principles of negotiating, e.g. saying what you want, listening to the first offer, rejecting the first offer, listening to the second offer, discussing the second offer, reaching a compromise.

2 Divide the class into pairs and give each student a copy of the worksheet. Read the negotiation situation with the class and explain any unfamiliar vocabulary.

3 Give students a few minutes to read their role which outlines their stages of the negotiation. Monitor, helping with vocabulary if necessary.

4 Ask students to match the phrases in the Useful phrases box with a particular stage in their negotiation and to prepare for the negotiation. Monitor, helping with the phrases as well as additional language the students might need.

5 Students act out the negotiation. Encourage them to use and expand on the phrases in the box.

Answers

a B4, B5   b A3   c B6   d A1   e A3, A4   f A7
g B3, B4, B5   h A2   i B3   j A6

14a Unfair dismissal?

Overview

Students read two jumbled newspaper articles and put them in order. This provides revision and consolidation of language related to the theme of sacking, and features of discourse and collocations. They then discuss the labour laws issues raised in the articles.

Preparation

One copy of the worksheet for each student.

Procedure

1 Hand out copies of the worksheet and explain the meaning of the worksheet title. Ask students what they could or would do if they had been unfairly dismissed.

2 Individually or in pairs, students separate out the two newspaper articles and put the sections in order. Monitor, helping as necessary. Then check the answers with the class and explain any unfamiliar vocabulary.

3 Ask students, in pairs, to answer the questions in exercise 2. Then check the answers with the class.

4 In pairs or small groups, ask students to discuss the questions in exercise 3, then report back to the class anything interesting from their discussions.

Answers

Exercise 1
Worker sacked over Bermuda shorts loses case
1 A   2 I   3 F   4 C   5 E

Man 'sacked for working too hard' wins his job back
1 B   2 G   3 H   4 D   5 J

Exercise 2
a He thought it was against his civil rights.
b No.
c He disobeyed their instructions.
d No.

14b Tricky decision

Overview

Students discuss which of three secretaries should be made redundant and write an e-mail explaining their reasons.

Preparation

One copy of the worksheet for each student.

Procedure

1 Introduce the topic of having to make redundancies because of recession by asking students to brainstorm which factors they would consider when deciding who in a company should be made redundant, e.g. length of service, professional competence, legal complications, financial costs, etc.

2 Divide the class into pairs and give each student a copy of the worksheet. Read through the notes in exercise 1 with the class. Explain any unfamiliar vocabulary.

3 Remind students of useful phrases for discussion, e.g. *In my opinion ..., I (don't) agree ..., That's true, but ...*, etc. and practise them if necessary.

4 In pairs, students discuss the three candidates and decide which one to make redundant. Monitor, helping with vocabulary as necessary.

5 Have a class feedback session where students explain their choices.

6 Students write an e-mail in exercise 2 to their manager explaining their choice. Monitor, helping with vocabulary as necessary.

15 Plenty of time

Overview

Students learn idiomatic expressions relating to time and then practise using them to talk about their own experience.

Preparation

One copy of the worksheet for each student. Cut the worksheet into two. Each pair will need a die and each student a counter.

Procedure

1 Explain that students are going to look at some idiomatic phrases relating to time. Hand out copies of the top part of the worksheet and ask students, in pairs or small groups, to complete the phrases in exercise 1. When they have finished, check the answers and the meaning of each phrase.

2 Divide the class into pairs. Hand out the bottom part of the worksheet and give each pair a die. Students can use pieces of paper with their names written on as counters. Tell students to take turns to throw the die to move around the board. They should think of something from their own experience to describe the situation they land on. Monitor, helping with vocabulary as necessary.

3 In pairs or small groups, students discuss the questions in exercise 3. Monitor, helping with vocabulary as necessary.

Answers

b make up for   c no   d great   e on   f playing
g passed   h take   i flew by   j make   k after
l ran out

16 Things to do

Overview

Students speak to different people in order to get things done in preparation for a foreign business trip or a trade exhibition. Students practise making requests, insisting and persuading, and saying yes and no politely.

Preparation

One copy of the worksheet for each pair of students. Cut the worksheet into three.

Procedure

1 Divide the class into pairs and explain that Student A is going on a business trip to give a sales presentation in Paris tomorrow, and Student B is going to man a stand for a holiday company at a trade fair. Ask students to think about the kind of preparations each will have to make. Have a brief class discussion.

2 Give pairs the first section of the worksheet with the useful language and quickly revise making requests.

3 Hand out the worksheets and ask students to read the instructions and look at their list of things to do. Ask them to think about how they are going to make each request, e.g. whether they need to ask politely or be firm, etc. Answer any questions they have about the items on their list and explain any unfamiliar vocabulary.

4 Explain to students that they are going to respond to each of their partner's requests, and that they will have to adopt different roles, e.g. a colleague, a sales assistant, etc. Ask students to look at their roles and the notes they have for responding to the request. Answer any questions they have about the items on their roles and explain any unfamiliar vocabulary.

5 When everybody is ready, students act out their situations. Student A makes all his/her requests, then Student B makes all his/her requests. Monitor the roleplays, helping with vocabulary as necessary.

17a Say something!

Overview

Students learn the difference between *say, tell, speak, talk* and *discuss*, and some common expressions with *say, tell, talk, speak* and *give*. They practise the verbs by completing sentences and questions and then use the questions to talk about their own experiences.

Preparation

One copy of the worksheet for each student.

Procedure

1 Write *Can you say me the time?* and *He told that it was a very good idea* on the board. Ask the students to tell you what is wrong with each of these sentences (see notes in answer key).

2 Divide the class into pairs and give each student a copy of the worksheet. Ask students to choose the correct verb in sentences a–f in exercise 1. Then check the answers with the class and have a class discussion about the verbs (see notes in answer key). Students then complete sentences g–l. Check the answers with the class.

3 Focus students' attention on the expressions with the verbs in the speech bubbles in exercise 2. Explain any unfamiliar vocabulary.

4 Ask students to fold back the worksheet so that they cannot see the phrases at the top and then, in pairs, complete exercise 3. Students then discuss the questions. Monitor, helping with vocabulary as necessary.

5 Check the answers with the class.

Answers

Exercise 1

a told   b said   c talked   d discussed   e speak/talk
f speak/talk   g said   h spoke/talked   i discuss
j speak/talk   k told   l talking

Say and *tell* are basically the same in meaning, but grammatically they are different. *Tell* must be followed by a person as a direct object: to tell *someone* something. *Say* does not have a direct object: to say something (*to* someone), e.g. *He told me that I should wait* (or *He told me to wait*). *He said that I should wait* (or *He said to me that I should wait*).

Talk about and *discuss* are basically the same in meaning, but *discuss* does not need *about* or any preposition after it.

Speak and *talk* are basically the same in meaning and grammatically – to speak or talk to someone about something is also the same.

Exercise 3

a give   b speak   c told   d telling   e say   f talk   g speak

17b But you said …!

Overview

Students read a telephone conversation between a client and a building contractor discussing some building work. The work didn't go to plan and students read about each person's grievances. They then roleplay the conversation where the client phones the contractor to complain about the work. Reported speech is practised.

Preparation

One copy of the worksheet for each student with exercise 2 folded over and the rolecards for students A and B removed.

Procedure

1 Introduce the topic by recounting a time when you contracted someone to do work for you and had been disappointed with the result, e.g. work at your office or home, etc. Invite students to share their own experiences.

2 Explain that students are going to read a phone conversation between the head of a modelling agency and a builder. Divide the class into pairs and give each student a copy of the worksheet with exercise 2 folded over. Read through the dialogue with the class and explain any unfamiliar vocabulary. Then ask students, in their pairs, to practise reading the dialogue aloud.

3 Ask students what they think of the situation. Do they think the work will go well? Why / Why not? Then explain that things did in fact go badly wrong. Both Ms Jones and Mr Owen are not happy.

4 Ask students to fold back exercise 2 and read the instructions. Then give each student in a pair a rolecard. Ask students to read their rolecard to find out why their character is not happy. (Make sure students realise that Ms Jones and Mr Owen have probably had subsequent phone conversations, so some of the information here will be new to what they read in the initial conversation.)

5 Tell pairs of students to prepare to roleplay the conversation when Ms Jones phones Mr Owen to complain. (You might like to have groups of students playing each role sitting together during the preparation stage.) Monitor, helping with vocabulary as necessary and encouraging students to use reported speech.

6 When everybody is ready, students roleplay the conversation using the example lines of the conversation at the bottom of the worksheet to start. Monitor, helping as necessary.

18a How wrong can you be?

Overview

Students complete famous predictions with *will* and an appropriate verb, then match the predictions to the people who made them.

Preparation

One copy of the worksheet for each student.

Procedure

1 Hand out copies of the worksheet. Individually or in pairs, ask students to complete the predictions in exercise 1 using *will* and the verbs in the box. Monitor, helping with vocabulary as necessary. Then check the answers with the class and explain any unfamiliar vocabulary.

2 Ask students to match the predictions with the people who made them in exercise 2. Monitor, helping with vocabulary as necessary.

3 Check the answers with the class and explain any unfamiliar vocabulary. Ask students if they know of any similar predictions.

Answers

Exercise 1

2 will (never) go   3 won't be able, will (soon) get
5 will (never) work   7 will be used   8 will (ever) be
10 will prove   11 will (never) be   13 will (forever) be
14 will (never) reach

Exercise 2

1 g   2 c   3 j   4 d   5 m   6 b   7 f   8 k   9 e
10 l   11 h   12 n   13 a   14 i

18b A–Z race

Overview

Students play a timed team game identifying and correcting grammar mistakes in 26 sentences.

Preparation

One copy of the worksheet for each group of two to four students.

Procedure

1 Divide the class into teams of an equal number of two to four students.

2 Give each group a copy of the worksheet face down. Explain that they have ten minutes to find and correct the sentences with grammar mistakes. The mistakes cover all the grammar they have seen so far in the Student's Book. Make sure they realise that some of the sentences are correct.

3 When the time is up, tell students to put down their pens and swap their worksheet with another group for marking.

4 Using the board, go through the sentences, correcting the mistakes with the class. Students award one point for each sentence accurately corrected (or identified as being correct) on the worksheet they are marking.

5 The team with the most points wins. Direct students to the Grammar links at the back of the Student's Book for grammar points they still find difficult.

Answers

A   I usually go to work by car.
B   The climate is getting warmer because of global warming.
C   My boss often stays in luxury hotels.
D   Could you tell me where the meeting room is?
E   correct
F   This Internet search engine was developed without the use of advertising.
G   Could you tell me where you live?
H   Food served in British restaurants isn't as bad as you think.
I   correct
J   correct
K   Have you heard the news? Our competitor has gone bankrupt!
L   correct
M   I'll take that call if you like.
N   I don't have to back up my work. My computer automatically does it for me.
O   I'm absolutely exhausted. I've been at my desk since eight o'clock this morning.
P   No, really Carlo. I'll pay for the drinks. I insist!
Q   What are you doing after the conference, Anna?
R   The Marketing Manager told us that we should promote it on the Internet.
S   Who did you visit when you went to Turkey?
T   correct
U   If we don't leave now, we'll be late for the Managing Director's presentation.
V   I'm not going to buy any more shares until the market improves.
W   His company is the most profitable in this sector.
X   Shall I order a taxi for you?
Y   She tells everyone she's the manager when she's really only the assistant.
Z   correct

19 What if ...?

Overview

Students work in small groups, taking turns to ask conditional questions for hypothetical or imaginary situations from question prompts for the rest of the group to answer and discuss.

Preparation

One copy of the worksheet for each group of two to four students. Cut the worksheet into cards.

Procedure

1 Elicit/Remind students of the grammar and the use of conditionals for hypothetical situations (second conditional). Direct them to the Grammar link on page 122 of the Student's Book, if necessary.

2 Divide the class into groups of two to four students and give each group a set of cards face down on the table.

3 Explain that students are going to take turns to pick up a card and ask a question using the prompt on the card, e.g. *If you were the boss of your company, what's the first thing you would do? If you could wear whatever you wanted to work, what would you wear? If you could change one thing about your office, what would it be?* Each question is asked to the whole group with the questioner acting as chairperson, encouraging discussion and making sure that everybody contributes. When the question has been exhausted, another student takes a card and the process is repeated. Monitor, helping with vocabulary as necessary.

4 When all the cards have been used, ask students to report to the class anything interesting from their discussions.

5 As a follow up, ask students to write sentences using the prompts, e.g. *If I were boss of my company, the first thing I'd do is give myself a pay rise.*

20 That's not right!

Overview

Students work in pairs to produce a three-part conversation they might have during a business lunch. The language of describing food and drink is revised.

Preparation

One copy of the worksheet for each student.

Procedure

1 Divide the class into pairs and give each student a copy of the worksheet. Read the instructions with the class and make sure everyone understands what they have to do.

2 Students read out the pairs of sentences to each other one by one and score through the one they think is wrong each time.

3 Check the answers with the class.

4 Students act out all three stages of the conversation by reading the correct sentences. Students A read the odd numbered sentences, and Students B read the even numbered sentences.

Answers

1 B   2 A   3 B   4 B   5 A   6 B   7 A   8 A   9 B
10 A   11 B   12 B   13 A   14 A   15 A   16 B
17 B   18 A   19 B   20 A   21 A

1a 60-second pitch   Jeremy Taylor & Jon Wright

1 Read the definition of a *60-second pitch*.

> Imagine that you have a business idea and you've been trying for weeks
> to set up a meeting with the CEO to discuss it. One day, as you walk into the
> cafeteria at work to get your morning coffee, there he is, standing by the
> coffee machine. This is your chance to tell him your idea. But you haven't
> got much time. You've got to make a '60-second pitch' – a description of
> your idea which is easy for anybody to understand and doesn't take longer
> than 60 seconds to say. That's time for about 150–225 words.

2 Put the lines (a–i and j–r) of this 60-second pitch about introducing a customer loyalty
scheme in the correct order. The first one in each section has been done for you.

a ☐ competitors. Second, we can attract new customers by offering

b ☐ introduce a customer loyalty scheme. First, it's a very simple and

c ☐ quantities. It will also discourage many customers from going to our

d ☐ *1* There are a number of reasons why I think it would be a good idea to

e ☐ of-mouth recommendations from our existing customers.

f ☐ our products, and it should mean they buy more often and in larger

g ☐ attractive benefits such as discounts, exclusive offers and guaranteed price

h ☐ effective way of encouraging our existing customers to continue to buy

i ☐ matching. In turn, this will bring in more customers through word-

j ☐ with their loyalty card, details of the purchase can be stored

k ☐ business which is essential for the long term success of our company.

l ☐ habits and this information will help us to target them more

m ☐ offers or information about products which we already know will

n ☐ *10* Third, if we use a loyalty card system, we can carry out detailed market

o ☐ electronically. From this we can build up a profile of their buying

p ☐ interest them. Finally, if we have loyal customers, we will have repeat

q ☐ effectively in the future. We can also send them news of special

r ☐ research on our customers. Every time a customer buys something

3 Choose one of the topics below and make a 60-second pitch to your CEO (your partner).

- How your company could cut costs
- Setting up a new branch of the company
- Introducing a new product or service
- Changing the company name/logo
- Increasing the research and development budget
- The need to recruit more staff
- Having TV advertising to promote the company
- Introducing a company newsletter for customers

1b Answering machine

Paul Emmerson

Student A

Work with a partner. Take turns to be a human answering machine and read out your messages for your partner to listen to and take notes. Then compare your notes with the original message.

Hi, this is Peter/Paula Howard. I wanted to speak to you about my flight arrangements for next Friday. I can catch a flight that arrives at either 8:15 or 10:40. Can you let me know which one suits you best? Oh, and don't worry about meeting me at the airport – I'll catch a taxi to your offices. One thing though, I couldn't read the address on your fax. Are you number 520 or 528? You can get back to me by e-mail if you prefer; my address is howard@amer-trade.com. That's all. See you on Friday. Goodbye.

Hello, this is Sam/Sarah Taylor here. I'm just calling about your order CJ650. There's a bit of a problem, I'm afraid. You ordered 8,450 items, but we can only supply 6,325 from stock. We'll send them today. The other 2,125 will be ready to ship in the next day or so, and you should receive them around 10 November. I hope that's okay with you. Get back to me if there's a problem. My work number is 020 5360 1854 or you can get me on my mobile which is 09976 425749. Bye.

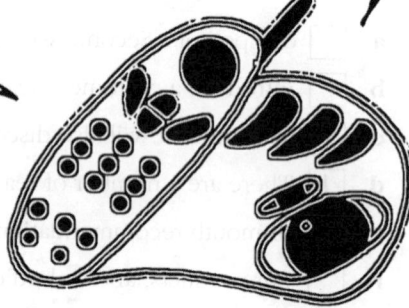

Student B

Work with a partner. Take turns to be a human answering machine and read out your messages for your partner to listen to and take notes. Then compare your notes with the original message.

Hi, this is Nigel/Nigella Compton calling from Australia. It's about that article your magazine is doing on our company. You asked for some details, and I have them here. We were founded in 1986, in Sydney, and then moved to Melbourne in 1994. We have around 170 employees in Australia, and our turnover last year was $7.8 million. If you have any other questions, you can e-mail me; the address is info@media_direct.co.au. Thanks. Goodbye.

Hello, (other student's name) Sorry to call you at home on a Sunday but it's urgent. There's a problem at the office and I can't go to Madrid tomorrow to make that presentation. I'm afraid you'll have go in my place. The flight leaves at 7:30 from Terminal 2 and it's flight YH7406. Ricardo will meet you at the airport in Madrid and take you to Amica Trading. I think there will be about 14 or 15 people in the audience. I've e-mailed you my presentation notes to your home computer. Sorry about this – I know it's short notice. You can ring me at home tonight if you have any questions; the number is 060 9488 6003. Thanks. See you when you get back.

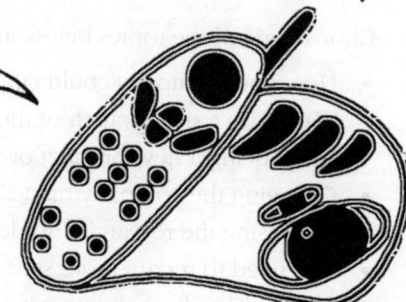

2a Ideal company

Nicholas Sheard

1 Work with a partner. Look at the criteria for an ideal company and choose the five most important and the five least important.

My ideal company:
- has a female CEO
- gives six months' paid maternity leave and one month paid paternity leave
- has a crèche facility
- has a good quality canteen
- gives equal pay to women and men
- gives employees a laptop computer and mobile phone for business and personal use
- has opportunities for promotion and personal development
- awards bonuses and gives fringe benefits to employees
- provides at least six weeks' training a year
- has an annual staff party
- has a generous company pension scheme
- allows women with three children to retire at 55
- has a gym and sports facilities
- pays one month extra salary to employees who have a new baby or who get married

2 Make sentences about your ideal boss from the prompts below using the adverbs of frequency in the box. Then compare your sentences with a partner.

My ideal boss:
- reads my e-mails
- lets me make personal calls at work
- takes me out to dinner
- has regular update meetings with me
- sends me on trips
- calls me by my first name
- phones me at home to discuss work
- leaves me to get on with my work
- chats about his/her family and other non work-related topics
- brings me coffee
- sets regular deadlines and targets
- lets me leave work early
- says thank you
- praises me
- gives me lots of responsibility
- lets me work from home

always	usually	often	sometimes	not often	hardly ever	never
every day	every week	twice a year	once a month			

2b Working style

Gina Cuciniello

Have you ever thought about your working style? Are you a team worker, a finisher, a supporter or a leader? This questionnaire will help you to find out.

1 Read the 30 statements and tick the ones you agree with. You only have ten minutes so do not spend time thinking deeply about each statement. There are no 'right' or 'wrong' answers, so be honest!

1 ☐ I usually meet up with my colleagues socially.

2 ☐ I often find it difficult to advise people on what to do about their problems.

3 ☐ Workplace crèches are a good idea.

4 ☐ I can never remember staff birthdays.

5 ☐ I am an extrovert most of the time.

6 ☐ My boss is hardly ever interested in my opinion.

7 ☐ I am just paid to get results.

8 ☐ I often feel that people do their jobs better than me.

9 ☐ I wish I was somebody else from time to time.

10 ☐ I would only work for an employer who treated men and women equally.

11 ☐ I have always recognised my strengths.

12 ☐ I frequently work overtime and I don't mind doing this.

13 ☐ I can usually help people with their personal problems.

14 ☐ I usually know all the office gossip.

15 ☐ I don't find jokes about minority groups funny.

16 ☐ I think that problems at home can sometimes become problems at work.

17 ☐ I recognise my faults.

18 ☐ I hardly ever take part in gossiping during work hours.

19 ☐ I don't often enjoy doing nothing.

20 ☐ When people criticise me, I sometimes get depressed.

21 ☐ I usually get on well with my colleagues.

22 ☐ I always enjoy meeting new people.

23 ☐ I often take work home with me.

24 ☐ I daydream a lot.

25 ☐ I like working with computers.

26 ☐ I always enjoy job interviews.

27 ☐ My colleagues usually enjoy my company.

28 ☐ Promotion should always be based on length of service in a company.

29 ☐ Taking important decisions hardly ever worries me.

30 ☐ The job will still be there tomorrow.

fold

2 Work out your score. Circle the answers you ticked, then add up how many As, Bs, Cs and Ds you have. Now read the analysis below. Do you agree with it?

1 A	11 D	21 D
2 A	12 B	22 D
3 A	13 B	23 B
4 B	14 A	24 C
5 D	15 A	25 B
6 C	16 A	26 D
7 B	17 C	27 D
8 C	18 B	28 C
9 C	19 B	29 D
10 A	20 C	30 A

Mostly A's: You are a Team Worker
Your relationship with your colleagues is important to you and many may also be friends. You are good at working with others to solve problems. You are a good listener. You understand others' points of view and have a lot of respect for people. You are usually a popular member of the team.

Mostly B's: You are a Finisher
You are always very task-centred and committed to getting the job done. You identify strongly with your organisation and often hide your true feelings. Sometimes your colleagues find you a little difficult to get to know.

Mostly C's: You are a Supporter
You usually think of others in a more positive light than yourself. You occasionally lack confidence and depend too much on other people. However, as you put others' needs before your own, you are often highly valued in an organisation.

Mostly D's: You are a Leader
You are usually confident and clear about what you want and how to get it. You show a lot of respect for others. Good listening skills come naturally to you as you frequently like to understand others' opinions before making a decision.

3a Could you tell me ...?

Jon Hird

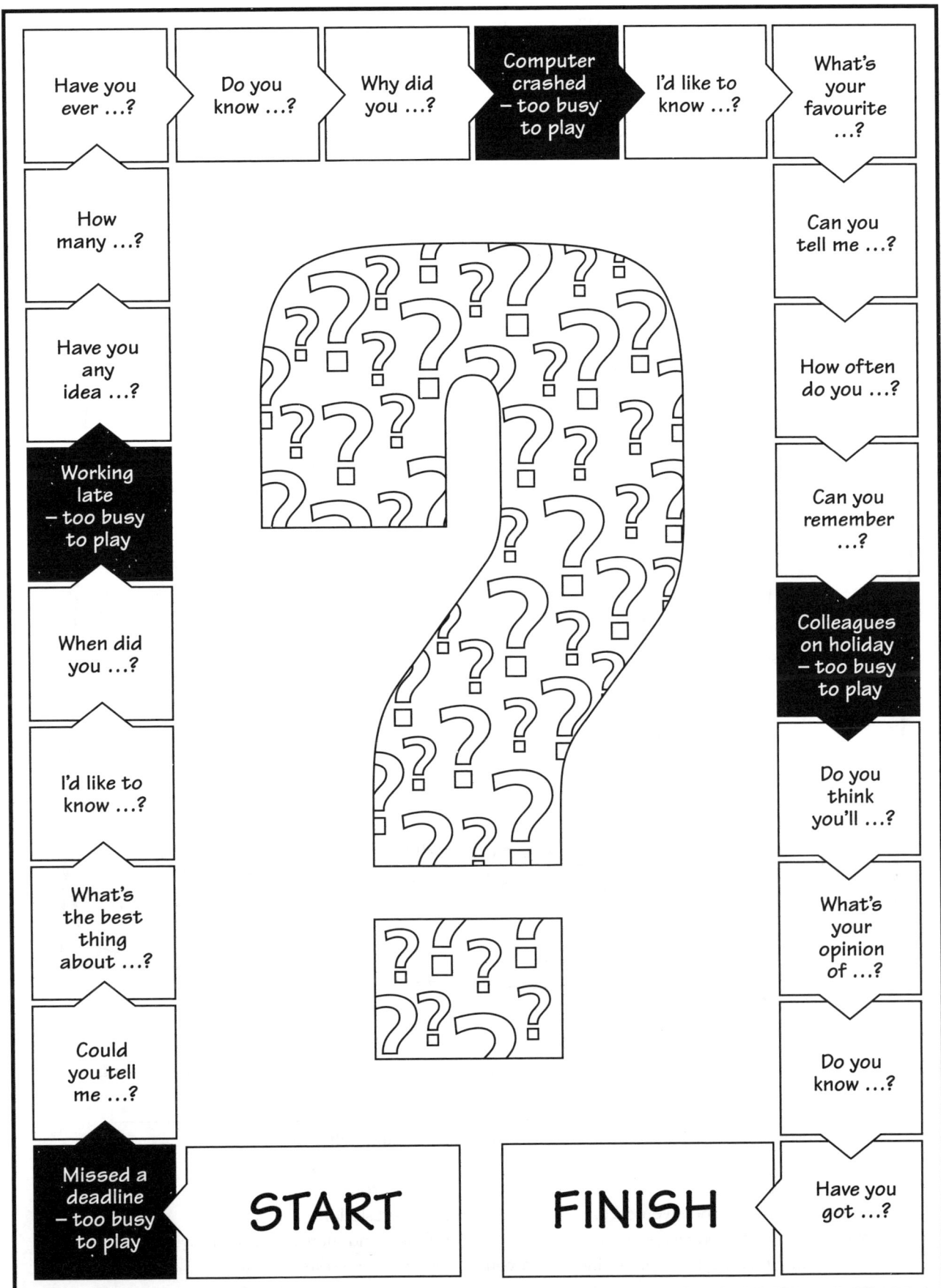

3b Telephone trouble

Jeremy Taylor & Jon Wright

1 You are the manager of a rapidly growing company. When you returned to the office after a recent conference, eight messages had been left for you. Which should you return first? Put the calls in order of importance.

while you were out ...

1   Larry Jaudal of CML Distribution – said it was nice to meet you at the conference. Has some questions about pricing and commission. Please contact him asap.

2   Bill called – he's ill and won't be able to do Friday's presentation about our Internet strategies to MCP Ltd. Wants you to call MCP to explain and arrange new dates.

3   Problem with the staff party for Jane's retirement – the restaurant we wanted is booked for that night. Call Josy Turner (manager of Coco's) to re-arrange.

4   Pat Partridge of ALT Design and Print – there's a problem with the visuals for our new brochure. Too many and too small. Please call to discuss which pictures you want to keep in.

5   Jan Hoover CFI – not happy with our recent work. Is asking for a discount or might use another company in future.

6   Pete Landsdown from World of Work Ltd – will be 2 days late with our order. Has delivery problems.

7   Margot Buno of IST in Munich is interested in co-operating with us on a new venture. Can she visit when she's in England next week?

8   Your mother called.

2 Roleplay your three most important phone calls from exercise 1 with your partner. Use the following expressions.

Could I speak to ..., please?	How can I help?
I'm returning your call.	I got your message.
I'm phoning to/about ...	I'm very sorry ...
I apologise for the inconvenience.	I'm interested in ...
We need to ... as soon as possible.	I understand there's a problem with ...
I'm looking forward to doing business with you.	One possible solution is to ...

4 Did you, really?

Paul Dummett

Work with a partner. Look at the example conversation. Then take turns to start a conversation using one of the questions 1–10 below. Keep your conversation going each time by asking five follow-up questions.

A Really? Does he lecture at Oxford?

B No, he works for Warwick University.

A Oh, what subject does he teach?

B He teaches Business administration.

A That's interesting. Was he in business before?

B Yes, he was a consultant with KPMG.

A Was he? Why did he change?

B It was very stressful. He wanted something quieter.

A And does he like teaching?

B Yes, he loves it.

1 Where do you work?

2 Do you work in an open-plan office?

3 How many people work in your department?

4 Where did you last go on a business trip?

5 Have you ever been to America?

6 How is work going at the moment?

7 What do you do when you're not working?

8 Do you like the cinema?

9 What's happening in your company these days?

10 What are you going to do at the weekend?

5 The rise and fall of Enron

Paul Dummett

1 Work with a partner. Put the events in Enron's history into the correct order. The first one has been done for you.

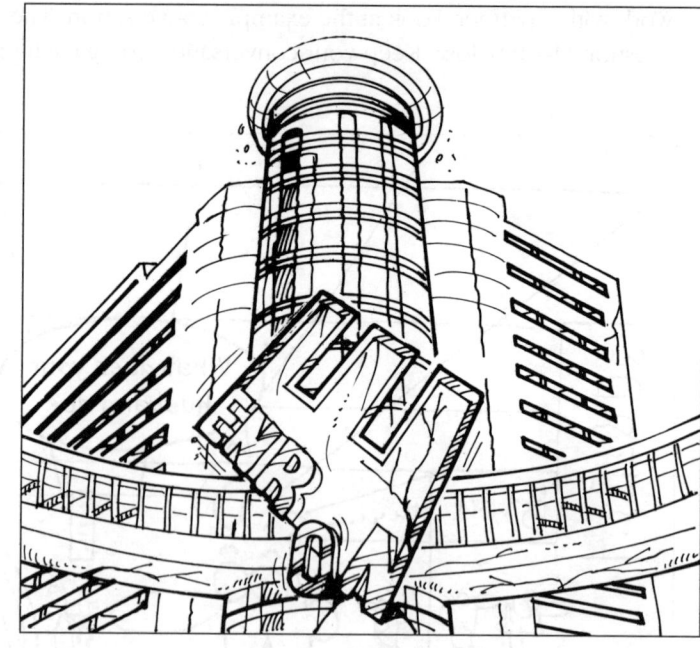

A ☐ Ken Lay, boss of Houston Natural Gas, was immediately appointed CEO of the newly-formed company.

B ☐ When it didn't receive answers, the regulator launched a formal investigation into Enron's investments. As a result, Enron's Chief Financial Officer resigned.

C ☐ During the 1990s, Enron continued to expand and diversify at an incredible rate. It invested $2 billion in a power plant in India, bought a water company in the UK and acquired an electricity company in Portland, Oregon.

D ☐ 1 ☐ Enron was founded in 1985 when two gas companies, Houston Natural Gas and InterNorth, merged to create the first national natural gas pipe network.

E ☐ Finally, the company was declared bankrupt, but the directors had already sold their shares and walked away with the profits.

F ☐ Three years after its creation, Enron opened its first offices abroad as part of a strategy to take advantage of newly-privatised markets.

G ☐ By the end of 2000, annual revenues had reached $100 billion, making Enron the sixth-largest energy company in the world. Most of this was from trading activities.

H ☐ However, Enron was not satisfied with revenue just from gas trading, so it also moved into electricity trading, establishing a trading centre in London. This became the company's most profitable activity.

I ☐ The first evidence of false accounting came in the first few months of 2001 when Enron admitted it had lost $570 million. Its share price fell, causing a cash and credit crisis.

J ☐ In July, the regulator started asking Enron to give more details about its financial performance.

K ☐ At the same time as opening offices overseas, Enron began trading natural gas in North America.

L ☐ By the turn of the century, a highly competitive work culture had developed. Each year 15% of Enron's employees were sacked and replaced with younger, ambitious graduates.

M ☐ The investigation found that the company and its accountants had lied to its shareholders and employees about $2 billion of debt.

2 Discuss with your partner what you think was the main reason for Enron's failure.

- It grew too quickly.
- Its trading business was based on trust, not on capital assets.
- It was not open about its accounts.
- It diversified too much.
- Its directors were only interested in profits for themselves.
- It exploited the deregulation of energy markets and made existing companies jealous.

6 Get it write!

Jeremy Taylor & Jon Wright

Look at the job application letter. In each paragraph, there are three grammar
mistakes and two spelling mistakes. Circle the mistakes and correct them.

Via Garibaldi
18 – 10122 Turin
Italy

Sarah Becket
Personnel Department
International Data Ltd
89 Bridge Road
London
SE1 5BG

16 August

Dear Ms Becket

to   *advertisement*

In reply (of) your (advertisment) who were in today's edition of *The Times*, I am writing to apply
for the position of Customer Servises Manager in your company.

I graduate from Milan University in 1998, and I has four years' expeirince of working in
customer services in company in Italy and great Britain.

I am currently working in the Customer Services department of a large IT company in Turin. I
am responsible of the day-to-day running of the department and I manage a team of three
staff. Last year I have implemented a new systeme for deal with customer complains which
has been extremely successful.

I would like develop my proffesional skills and take on more managerial responsibilities. I am
also interesting in working in London because it will give me the oportunity for improve my
English.

I inclose a copy of my cv for you reference. I would be happy to coming for an interview at
any time but I would need a week's notice to made any nesessary travel arrangements.

Yours sincerely

Marco Brucato

Marco Brucato

7 Away day

Gina Cuciniello

The Managing Director of your company has recently read that fun at work is linked to higher productivity, so he's decided to send all the staff in the London office on an *away day* – a day out to encourage team spirit – and increase productivity!

You and your partner have been asked to choose a venue for the day. You have talked to some members of staff from different departments about what they would like to do. Look at their comments below and the newspaper cuttings and decide which venue would suit most people in the company. You have a budget of €150 per person.

> A relaxing day out would be wonderful with just a little gentle exercise and lots of good food. Can we go somewhere near the office? Oh, and no silly games, please!

James, 45, Accounts

> Can we please do something cultural? What about trying new foods? We want to have fun and spend time relaxing and chatting.

Mandy, 30, Administration

> No boring discussion groups with the old guys in accounts, please! We want lots of fun activities that we've never done before!

Tom, 23, Marketing

SPA HEALTH DAY

Why not reward your hard working staff with a little pampering? Space Health Club offers a variety of corporate days to refresh and relax your staff.

Your package includes:
- unlimited use of the impressive 25m swimming pool with sauna and steam rooms
- supervised workout in the gymnasium
- complete relaxation programme
- yoga and pilates classes

A buffet lunch is included, with complimentary soft drinks and fruit throughout the day.

Prices start from €120 per person.

50 miles from London, off M40 motorway

ADVENTURE FARM DAY

A thrilling package for excitement seekers. An away day that your staff will never forget!

- Go-kart racing
- Bungee jumping
- Rock-climbing
- Clay pigeon shooting

No previous experience is necessary for any of the activities – all of the instructors are trained to coach complete beginners.

A delicious barbecue lunch is served at the farm.

Prices start from €130 per person.

25 miles from London

Food and Wine Courses at Champers

Champers offers its corporate guests the relaxed informality of a private home, but with the facilities, standards of service and cuisine of a quality hotel.

You can relax in the elegant drawing room with log fire and listen to wine experts give informative talks about our extensive cellar of new and old world wines, all of which are available for tasting.

The dining room has excellent views across the valley and guests are served wonderful food cooked by top class French chefs.

Prices start from €135 per person including champagne before dinner.

25 miles from London

Take your staff on an evening out to the Covent Garden Opera House
Turandot!

An unforgettable musical experience in the centre of London.

Enjoy an excellent Italian meal before the show.

Performances start at 8.00 pm. Programmes and interval drinks are included.

Prices start from €145 per person. Discounts for large groups.

8 Storytelling

Nicholas Sheard

1 Stories or anecdotes are usually told in five stages.

1 Introduction   2 Background   3 Problem   4 Resolution   5 Comment

Put the story below in the correct order by matching each paragraph to one of the stages above.

A Beijing surprise

A ☐ (1)_____ somebody lit some candles and put them around the room, (2)_____ I still couldn't see my notes very well. The speech was a complete disaster. You can imagine my surprise when the Chinese businessmen started to smile and clapped loudly when I finished the talk. I sat down and started to eat my meal. (3)_____ I asked the translator sitting next to me why everyone had clapped so enthusiastically, she replied, 'None of the people here speaks English. I'll translate your speech for them (4)_____.'

B ☐ Since then I've never prepared any of my speeches. They seem to work better when I improvise. I did give the translator my notes though!

C ☐ I was in Beijing as part of a trade delegation and our company was one of several asked to give a speech. I had spent a long time preparing my speech and had written about five pages of notes. I suppose there were about thirty people in the room listening to me and I was quite nervous.

D ☐ Have I ever told you about the time I was asked to give a speech to some Chinese businessmen?

E ☐ I started to speak. (5)_____ there was a power cut and all the lights in the room went out. (6)_____ I couldn't see my notes very well at all. (7)_____, I continued speaking, (8)_____ I realised that I had started with page three and couldn't find page four or five. (9)_____ I just improvised (10)_____ I found page one.

---

2 Complete the story in 1 with the linking words and phrases in the box.

in the end	just then	however	when	because of this
and then eventually	but soon	So	but	later

3 Work with a partner. Look at the prompts below. Choose five and use them to create your own story. Tell your story in the five stages described in 1 and include some of the words and phrases in 2. When you are ready, tell your story to another pair.

a secretary	an office party	a car crash	an airport	a text message	the CEO
a bottle of champagne	a business trip	a broken lift	a hotel bridal suite	
a stolen laptop	a strange taxi ride	€60,000	an e-mail	a meal in a restaurant

9a The idea is easy ...

**Paul Dummett &
Nicholas Sheard**

Student A   Entrepreneur/Inventor

You are a self-employed engineer and design consultant. You have advised various companies on the design and production of new products. You have always been good at repairing and building things, and in your workshop at home you have built several new gadgets. Last year you developed a 'Drinking Fountain for Pets' but a loan to develop this product was refused by the bank.

Your latest invention is a 'Button Fixer'. Buttons fall off at the worst possible times, but with 'Button Fixer' you never need to worry again. 'Button Fixer' is a small device which attaches a button with a single push. It's small, portable and very easy to use.

You have already patented this product. Now you would like to negotiate a loan from a bank to develop, manufacture and market it. Here are some details to help you:

Amount of loan	€30,000
Personal Investment	€10,000
Date of Product launch	1 year from today
Production costs (per unit)	€3
All other operating costs (per unit)	€4
Selling price	€15
Sales channel	Mail order (advertising in fashion magazines)
Yearly sales forecast	5,000 units

Student B   Bank Manager

You are a bank manager and you have a meeting with an entrepreneur/inventor who you are meeting for the first time. Last year he/she approached one of your colleagues for a loan to develop a 'Drinking Fountain for Pets'. Your colleague refused the loan because there was not enough market research to support the idea.

First, you need to know more about the entrepreneur's history and personal situation. Then you need to know more about this new idea – what the product is and what the market for it is.

Make sure that you get the following details:

Amount of loan	
Personal Investment	
Date of Product launch	
Production costs (per unit)	
All other operating costs (per unit)	
Selling price	
Sales channel	
Yearly sales forecast	

When you have this information decide what to do – lend the money, not lend the money, get more information.

9b Making money

Nicholas Sheard

Work with a partner. Check that you understand the meaning of the money verbs in bold. Then take turns to play the role of Mr/Ms Money and give financial advice to your client.

1 Buying a property

Client	**Mr/Ms Money**
You **earn** €35,000 a year. Last year your uncle died and you **inherited** €12,000. You have made €8,000 from share investments in the last two years. However, you **owe** €4,000 to a friend and recently **lost** €2,500 at a casino. You are now thinking of **selling** your shares and **spending** all your money and savings on a property in London. You would like to know what price of property you can **afford** and how much you can **borrow** from a bank.	A bank will **lend** three and a half times a person's salary to help him/her **buy** a property. A deposit of 5% of the value of the property is usually required by the bank. You believe that property prices in London are very high at the moment and that it's not the best time to buy. You do, however, think that the stock market is a good place to invest money just now.

2 Retirement and your pension

Client	**Mr/Ms Money**
You are 62 years old and due to retire in three years. You are rather disappointed because your pension is not worth as much as you had anticipated. When you retire you want to be able to **afford** to go on a three-month holiday as well as buy a retirement home in the country. Over the last few years, you have **saved** €10,000 which you could **withdraw** with three months' notice. Your mother is 94 and lives in a house which you own.	Your client's priority is obviously to get enough money to live on when he/she retires. Interest rates are very low at the moment, so you might recommend that he/she **invests** his/her savings in the stock market instead of putting the savings into a building society. Remind him/her, however, that the investment could go down as well as up. You could also (diplomatically!) suggest that when the client's mother dies, he/she could use the money from the sale of the house to buy a retirement home.

3 Ethical investments

Client	**Mr/Ms Money**
You are interested in the idea of ethical investments but you are worried that the returns on your money might be lower than if you **invested** in companies which were not concerned about the issue of Third World exploitation, oppressive regimes, animal testing, etc.	Reassure your client that over the last few years many ethical investments have performed much better than non-ethical investments. Talk to your client about his/her criterion for ethical investments, e.g. Is he/she happy to invest in companies producing alcohol – what about tobacco? What is his/her view on drugs being tested on animals? Is there a particular area which interests him/her – environmental, human rights, etc.? Then explain that you will research companies which match his/her beliefs and arrange another meeting to discuss them in more detail.

4 Setting up a business

Client	**Mr/Ms Money**
You are 23 years old. You need to raise €30,000 to **spend** on setting up a new business – an Internet café in the city centre. You have various options. You could **borrow** the money from a bank, and **pay** it **back** over a period of five, ten or fifteen years. Alternatively, you could ask your friends and family to **lend** it to you. As a last resort you could **bet** or **gamble** some money and hope to **win** enough to start the business!	A bank loan is certainly a good way for your client to raise the money he/she needs. Suggest that your client writes a business plan and presents it to the bank. You'd recommend a ten-year repayment period.

10a Time to relax

Jeremy Taylor & Jon Wright

If you have a stressful job, you need to relax. A great way to relax is to do a crossword!
Look at the clues below and complete the crossword. The first one has been done as an example.

Across

3   Manuals which are easy for people to understand are called u___-friendly.

5   We used to have an office in central London but last year we r___ to Inverness in Scotland. The rent is much cheaper and the air quality is a hundred times better.

7   It is a good idea to keep things tidy as d___ can lead to chaos!

9   You should do some e___ at least twice a week. A healthy body = a healthy mind!

10 Some job advertisements ask: Are you good at working under p___?

11 When you have an important d___ to meet, your stress levels go up.

12 We decided to close the office in Bristol because it didn't make e___ sense to pay all that rent for a staff of two people.

14 Living in a t___ or city is much more stressful than living in the country.

17 Robots can now do some of the boring, r___ jobs that people did 50 years ago.

18 Doctors say that stress is l___ to many different illnesses.

20 If m___ is low in your company, productivity will be low.

21 Many people think that the number t___ is unlucky.

22 The company were worried that introducing shift work would be unpopular, but so far nobody has c___ .

Down

1   A low-fat diet and a low-stress lifestyle are two good ways of reducing your chances of getting h**eart** d**isease**.

2   CEO stands for C___ E___ Officer.

4   Some people think that sacking a person for being persistently late is too s___ a punishment.

5   If you don't r___ your workers' stress levels, their productivity will soon go down.

6   Do you think directors should make important d___ by themselves, or should they spend hours discussing them with the members of the board?

8   Many managers work so hard during the week that they find it difficult to r___ at weekends.

9   She had high e___ when she joined the company but after a few months, she felt unchallenged and started to look for a new job.

13 C___ people such as writers, sometimes suffer from writer's block when they are unable to write anything.

14 If your company has a high t___ of staff, it is a sign that your working conditions are not satisfactory.

15 My brother has his own business. He works fourteen hours a day, seven days a week. He's a w___ !

16 After twelve years of hard work, my sister finally got p___ to senior sales manager.

19 People who go to university and get a d___ often get paid a lot more money than people who go to work straight from school.

10b Velvet revolution

Jeremy Taylor & Jon Wright

1 There has been a velvet revolution in a developing country. The new leader of the country is your teacher's old university friend, Harold. Harold has sent an e-mail asking for advice about the development of his country. Read the e-mail. Which is the most important problem that Harold has to deal with? Which is the least urgent? Work in groups and put the problems in order of importance. Do you think there are any other problems which Harold should deal with?

Hello, my old friend!

I hope things are going well for you. As you know, my father was the old leader of my country. After the old government lost power, the United Nations wanted to find a good person to lead the country. Can you believe it, they chose me! I had a nice business selling shoes to Europe, but now I'm the leader of a huge country with a lot of responsibilities! I can't sleep at night because of the stress of my new job. I really hope you can help. Here are some details of the situation in my country. Which do you think I should look at first? second? etc. I know they are all important but I need to prioritise!

Thank you for any advice you can give. You must come and visit us one day.

Harold

- Primary schools: Only 75% of children receive primary education.
- Universities: There is only one university. Some students are sent to other countries.
- Police force: The former government's police force was badly equipped, badly paid and famous for its corruption.
- Taxation system: There is currently no taxation system. The government gets its money from sales of oil and natural gas.
- Trading links: Currently, only oil and gas are exported. Large amounts of food are imported every year. Should I make trading links with other countries?
- Environmental protection: The last government did nothing for the environment. There are no more lions in the country and the oil fields are polluting the rivers near the coast.
- Hospitals: Malaria is a big problem in some areas.
- Overseas investment: Should I encourage investment from multi-national companies? The only foreign companies in the country are the oil companies and a soft drinks manufacturer.
- Or should I discourage overseas investment? That way I can help local businesses grow without competition.
- Safe drinking water: Only half the population have running water. Diseases like cholera are common and many children die in their first year.

2 Work with a partner. Write an e-mail to Harold telling him which three problems he should deal with first, and why.

11a Nannies

Mark Powell

1 Read the dictionary definition and answer the questions.

a What kind of people hire nannies in your country? Would you hire one?

b Is it possible to be a male nanny?

c Put the following jobs in order of status: lawyer, business consultant, software entrepreneur, nanny, venture capitalist, college teacher.

d Roughly how much money do you think nannies earn a year? Are there any perks of the job?

> **nanny** /ˈnæni/ noun [C] **1** a woman whose job is to look after someone else's children. A nanny usually lives with the family she works for.
>
> *Macmillan English Dictionary*

2 Read the article. Underline anything you find surprising.

Mary Poppins' Portfolio

Annabel Callaghan is what's known as a 'status nanny'. The 49-year-old has a bachelor's degree in English, a master's degree in child development and 20 years of teaching experience.

So in Silicon Valley, Callaghan has no trouble dictating her price. She had two couples bidding for her two years ago. One couple, the husband, a venture capitalist, and the wife, a college teacher, offered $48,000, a membership in a health club and first-class travel around the world, to give Callaghan time away from the kiddies.

Good, but not good enough. She went to the other couple, the wife, a software entrepreneur, and the husband, a lawyer; they offered the traditional Silicon Valley currency – stock options. Today, Callaghan is a proud shareholder in a promising web-software maker.

Silicon Valley's working rich have driven nanny salaries up by 25% in the last year, to an average of $18 per hour. Accomplished nannies can get $80,000 a year in salary, paid health care and pension plus lavish perks. Few will work longer than a 40-hour week, forcing many couples to hire a second nanny.

Nannies have the luxury to be picky about their employers. 'I won't work for people who work at Microsoft or Intel,' says Mary Perkins, an 18-year pro. 'There are those nannies who'll just go to the highest bidder,' says Anne Morrissey, a business consultant and the mother of a 13-month-old boy. She believes her nanny feels as if she's part of the family, but to be safe, she's considered offering the caregiver stock in some software enterprises she advises.

The hand that rocks the cradle rules Silicon Valley.

Extract from 'Mary Poppins' Portfolio' by Julia Pitta. Reprinted by permission of FORBES Global © 2003 Forbes Global Inc.

3 Work in two groups: status nannies and Silicon Valley employers. Read your instructions.

STATUS NANNIES

- Produce a brief CV to give to your prospective employers. Include your age, nationality, qualifications, interests and experience.
- Decide what you want in advance: salary, pension plan, health care, stock options, etc. Also decide what perks you would like: holidays, use of a car, membership of gym, golf or tennis club, etc.
- Decide how many hours a week you are prepared to work.
- Make at least one totally unreasonable demand just to see if you can get it, but be prepared to have it rejected.
- Think of one thing that makes you different from all other nannies, e.g. a special talent, a foreign language you speak, etc.
- When you are ready, spend a few minutes with each employer, answering questions about yourself and asking questions about the job.
- **Keep going from one employer to the next to get the best deal you can, but make sure you get a job!**

SILICON VALLEY EMPLOYERS

- Produce a short profile of your child(ren): age, sex, special needs, interests, etc. How many hours a week do you need a nanny for?
- Decide who would be your ideal nanny: age, sex, personality, qualifications, interests, experience, etc.
- Decide how much you are prepared to pay and what other benefits you can offer: health and pension plans, stock options, foreign travel, etc.
- Make at least one totally unreasonable demand just to see if you can get it, but be prepared to have it rejected.
- Think of one fantastic perk you can offer to the right person.
- When you are ready, spend a few minutes interviewing each nanny and describing what you're offering.
- **Keep going from one nanny to the next to get the best deal you can, but make sure you get a nanny!**

11b Top boss?

Jon Hird

1   Do you have what it takes to be a top boss? Complete the questionnaire and find out. Choose the option (a, b or c) you most agree with.

1 As the boss, do you believe that …
  a you can arrive and leave work at any time?
  b you should work the same hours as everybody else?
  c you should be the first to arrive and the last to leave?

2 If you see someone with a problem, do you …
  a watch to see if they can resolve the problem?
  b resolve the problem for them?
  c give hints or tips on resolving the problem?

3 After an argument with someone, do you …
  a apologise, admitting you were both at fault?
  b wait for them to apologise – you're the boss?
  c wait until the employee cools down and then try to resolve the situation?

4 An employee is clearly being distracted at work with personal problems. Do you …
  a tell them to keep their home issues out of the office?
  b talk to their closest co-workers to see if there is anything you or the company can do to help?
  c offer to spend extra time with them on a personal level to discuss the problems?

5 When you take on a new employee, do you …
  a meet with them at least once a week for their first two months to make sure everything is OK?
  b aim to learn their name within a week or so?
  c take them out to lunch and give them an overview of the company?

6 One of your employees requests a day off with little advance notice. Do you …
  a allow it as a personal favour?
  b tell them it's impossible and remind them of company policy?
  c allow the day off if there's a good reason, but ask for more notice next time?

7 An assistant is late in submitting a report for the second time this week. Do you …
  a tell them you are more upset about the lack of communication than the uncompleted work?
  b tell them to have it ready by the end of the day?
  c arrange for them to be transferred to another department?

8 When faced with a difficult problem, do you …
  a try your best to solve the problem?
  b seek help and advice from others?
  c pass the problem on to someone else?

9 There is a party for a junior member of staff who is leaving. Do you …
  a shake their hand at the end of their last day and wish them luck?
  b spend the evening with the group and pay for the drinks?
  c make an appearance at the party but don't stay too long?

10 What is the main driving force in your life?
  a being liked and respected
  b principles and ethics
  c fame and money

-------- fold --- fold ----------

2   Work out your score. Then read the analysis. Do you agree with it?

1	a 3	b 2	c 1
2	a 3	b 1	c 2
3	a 1	b 3	c 2
4	a 3	b 2	c 1
5	a 2	b 3	c 1
6	a 1	b 3	c 2
7	a 1	b 2	c 3
8	a 2	b 1	c 3
9	a 3	b 1	c 2
10	a 1	b 2	c 3

Over 25 points: Dictators don't last long. You should think about changing your approach. You may be in danger of abusing your position. You need to learn to feel comfortable with a certain level of familiarity with your employees. If not, you will be seen as uncaring.

15 to 25 points: You lead by example and tend to deal with problems on a case-by-case basis. Your approach is similar to that of a schoolteacher or coach – you are both leader and nurturer. You should continue striving to find the right balance of keeping employees happy, motivated and focused. You are a top boss in the making.

Under 15 points: You probably feel uncomfortable telling others what to do. You need to realise that to gain your employees' respect you will sometimes have to be firm and make unpopular decisions. One of the biggest dilemmas for a boss is balancing being friendly and carrying out your duties as the decision-maker. It's a task which requires great skill.

3   Work with a partner. What do you think are the most important qualities of a good boss? Make a list.

12 Start it up!

Nicholas Sheard

1 Work with a partner. Discuss the questions.

a When did you last start up a conversation with a stranger? What was the first thing you said to him/her?

b In what kind of situations do you start up conversations with strangers? In what kind of situations do you never start up conversations with strangers?

2 Look at the following statements and questions. Can you identify any which are inappropriate for starting up a conversation? Think of situations in which you could use the other ones.

1 I don't think much of your laptop!
2 Have you been here before?
3 Do you have the time on you?
4 Could I have a look at your newspaper?
5 Are you here for the conference?
6 How are you enjoying the book?
7 Hello. You look like you could do with a drink!
8 Have you got a tattoo?
9 Did you hear about what happened to …?
10 Have you seen this article about …?
11 Are you single?
12 I like your bag. Where did you get it?
13 I've been watching you for the last ten minutes.
14 Are you going to the trade fair, too?
15 Could I possibly borrow / use / take a look at / see …?
16 This is the first time I've been stuck in a lift. What about you?
17 Excuse me, could you tell me where …?
18 Do you mind if I smoke in here?
19 You look like you earn a lot. / How much do you earn?
20 What do you think of the conference?

3 Work with a partner. Take turns to start up a conversation in each of the following situations.

You are at a conference. You are in the bar and one of the keynote speakers walks in. You were very interested in the talk he/she just gave. Start a conversation with him/her.

You have a meeting with a potential client where you are going to present your company's products to him/her for the first time. You are sitting outside his/her office waiting to be introduced. A secretary has brought you a cup of coffee. Start a conversation with him/her.

You are on a long-haul flight to Brazil. You have been upgraded to first class. The person next to you is reading a book which you have recently read. Start a conversation with him/her.

You are in a hotel restaurant. You are eating breakfast alone. Someone joins you at your table. He/She is also alone. Start a conversation with him/her.

You are sitting in your hotel lobby. You are waiting for a taxi to take you to a trade fair. You notice that a person sitting near you is reading some information about the same trade fair. Start a conversation with him/her.

You are visiting a foreign subsidiary on business. You are in the lift when it breaks down. One other person is in the lift. Start a conversation with him/her.

13a How was your trip?

Paul Emmerson

1 Read these extracts from interviews with people about their business trips. Then look at the words in bold in each extract and find six pairs of opposite phrases. The first one has been done as an example.

1	6										

1 The **trip was a complete disaster.** Everything went wrong – my plane was delayed on the way out and then my meeting was cancelled because the supplier was ill.

2 I don't go abroad often, just **an occasional trip** to Head Office in Frankfurt.

3 I've **arranged my trip** to Milan for the first week in April. I'm really excited – it's my first trip for the company and my first time to Italy.

4 The **trip out** took three hours, and I didn't have to get a taxi from the airport because the supplier was waiting for me to drive me to his offices.

5 I had to **cut short my trip** – there was a crisis back at the office. The clients were very understanding and have agreed to meet me next month instead.

6 The **trip was a great success**. I made a lot of useful contacts. My boss was very pleased when he read my report.

7 I make **frequent trips** to our supplier in Poland. We do a lot of business with them and it means that I earn lots of air miles to use on flights for my family.

8 It was a **one-way trip** – from Paris I went to visit another supplier in Brussels instead of coming straight back to the office.

9 The **trip back** took much longer than I expected – the flight was delayed because of bad weather. My husband came to meet me at the airport but he had to wait for two hours before my plane landed.

10 I've **cancelled my trip** to Madrid – I'm too busy dealing with things here at the office. We're going to reschedule for next spring when things are calmer.

11 I decided **to extend my trip** – I needed more time to visit all our customers.

12 It was just a quick **round trip** – there and back in a day. But it was very tiring. I left early in the morning and got back late at night.

2 You are going to talk about a business trip. Think of a recent trip you have made and write notes to answer each question below.

- Where and when did you go?
- Why did you go?
- How did you go? Did anything interesting happen during the journey?
- Who did you meet?
- What happened during the trip?
- What happened later, as a result of your trip?
- Have you learned anything from the experience?

When you have prepared your notes, work with a partner and interview each other.

13b Negotiating a deal　　Nicholas Sheard

Work with a partner. Read the negotiation situation and your role below, Student A or B. Match the useful phrases in the box to some of the stages (1–7) in your role for the negotiation. (Some phrases can be used in several stages.) Then act out the negotiation. The circles round the numbers in the negotiation stages signal who speaks first each time.

Negotiation situation

The Financial Director of a pharmaceutical company wants to reduce the cost of the company's annual air travel. The company spends approximately €900,000 a year on 1,000 return flights to the USA, an average cost of €900 for each business class ticket. The Financial Director has arranged a meeting with a representative from FlyHigh Atlantic, a leading airline, to try to cut costs by 15–20%. At present, the company flies with a number of different airlines, but the company would agree to work with only one or two if this target could be achieved.

Student A

You are Mr/Ms Riley, the Financial Director. Below are your stages in the negotiation.

(1) Mr/Ms Harris from FlyHigh Atlantic has arrived in your office. Greet him/her. Offer him/her a drink. Have a quick chat before you start the negotiation.

(2) Briefly explain to Mr/Ms Harris what you want to achieve from the negotiation.

(3) Tell Mr/Ms Harris you could offer them a large part of your business if FlyHigh Atlantic can reduce their prices by 20%. Then listen to and reject his/her first offer.

4　Listen to and then reject Mr/Ms Harris second offer.

5　Listen to and then express interest in his/her third offer.

6　Listen to Mr/Ms Harris summarise what he/she could offer. Then say you will need some time to think about his/her offer.

(7) Thank Mr/Ms Harris for coming and say goodbye.

Student B

You are Mr/Ms Harris from FlyHigh Atlantic. Below are your stages in the negotiation.

1　Arrive at Mr/Ms Riley's office. Greet him/her. Have a quick chat before you start the negotiation.

2　Listen to Mr/Ms Riley explain why he/she has asked you here today.

3　Let Mr/Ms Riley start the negotiation. Offer a reduction of 12.5% if the company can guarantee 1,000 flights a year.

(4) Say that you can increase this to 15% if the company agrees to pay for the tickets at the time of purchase.

(5) Say that business class seats get booked up very quickly. Some customers agree to fly economy when business class seats are full. There is less legroom, but you still get business class service. You could offer a further 5% if they are prepared to be flexible at busy times.

(6) Summarise what you could offer.

7　Listen to Mr/Ms Riley and then thank him/her for inviting you and say goodbye.

Useful phrases

a	B4, B5	We would be willing to increase this to … if you agreed to …
b		If you can reduce your prices by …, we would be able to …
c		To sum up, …
d		Can I offer you anything to drink?
e		I'm afraid that would be difficult to accept.
f		Thanks for your time today. I'll be in touch again next week.
g		Would this be acceptable to you?
h		Let me give you a brief outline of what we're looking for.
i		We would be happy to offer you a discount of … if you can guarantee …
j		I'll have to get back to you on that.

14a Unfair dismissal?

Simon Clarke

1 Look at the headings from two newspaper articles. Then organise the sections below to re-construct the two articles about sackings which lead to legal problems.

Worker sacked over Bermuda shorts loses case

1	2	3	4	5
A				

Man 'sacked for working too hard' wins his job back

1	2	3	4	5
B				

A A French man who was sacked for wearing Bermuda shorts at work has lost a case for unfair dismissal. Cedric Monribot was

F technician argued that under French law his sacking was 'abusive and challenging to individual liberty'. However, an employment

B A man who claimed he was sacked for working too hard has won his job back. The Australian Industrial Relations Commission ruled Geoffrey Scott's dismissal was harsh

G and unreasonable. Union leaders had claimed he was sacked from the *Centrelink* agency for helping out colleagues and clients when the office was busy. The 34-year-old was sacked

C tribunal found there were no grounds to his case because he had not suffered any legitimate form of discrimination. He told

H from the company's Wollongong office in December for continually disobeying instructions not to help his fellow workers. The commission ruled that he was unfairly

D treated. Mr Scott said he was relieved by the outcome of the case and that he expected to return to work in the next fortnight. *Centrelink* national manager Hank Jongen said that his company

I sacked from a company called Sagem for refusing to wear trousers at work despite several warnings. The 29-year-old

E a local radio station that he would appeal against the ruling announced by Tribunal President Catherine Leverbe.

J was disappointed the court had failed to support their decision to dismiss a worker for disobeying instructions.

2 Work with a partner. Answer the questions.

   a Why did Cedric Monribot say his sacking was unfair?
   b Did the employment tribunal agree?
   c What argument did *Centrelink* use for sacking Geoffrey Scott?
   d Did the Industrial Relations Commission agree?

3 Discuss the questions in pairs or small groups.

   a Do you know of any similar cases?
   b In your country, what happens when somebody thinks they have been unfairly dismissed?

14b Tricky decision

Simon Clarke

1 You and your partner work in the Human Resources department of a medium-sized engineering company. There is a recession and orders have decreased. You have been instructed to cut costs in the Administration Department by making one secretary redundant. You have been looking at three possible candidates and have made notes about each of them. Look at your notes and decide which secretary should go.

Mary Henderson
- been with the company for ten years
- high salary due to length of service and increments for experience
- generally efficient and competent but doesn't seem interested in learning new skills
- attitude problem? has made negative comments about company and management
- respected by colleagues but not particularly liked
- poor absence record. Four weeks' sick leave last year
- high redundancy compensation costs due to length of service

Nora Jameson
- been with the company for two years
- still on basic starting salary
- is the niece of one of the company's directors. Problems with uncle if she goes?
- has only basic qualifications
- does job adequately but unlikely to be promoted
- very willing but takes longer than average to complete tasks. Stays after hours to finish jobs when necessary
- very shy. Doesn't mix much with other workers
- minimal redundancy compensation costs

Anita Smith
- been with the company for six months. Still on trial period - no redundancy costs
- very competent and reliable. Great with modern office technology
- bright and attractive with lots of personal charm. Popular with colleagues
- doesn't always respect office dress code. Has piercing in tongue!
- great potential for future development and would be an asset for the company
- will easily find another job - perhaps with the competition!
- low salary but has asked for pay rise - ambitious

---

2 Write an e-mail to your manager explaining your decision. Use the words in the box.

> firstly secondly finally but although

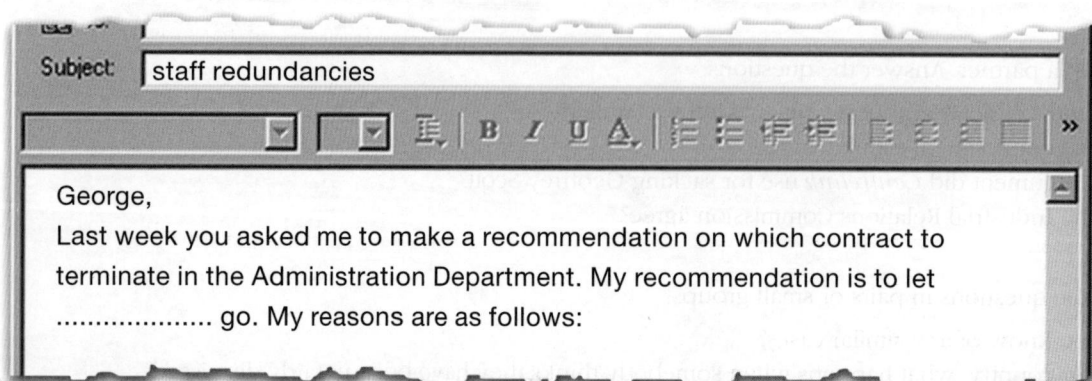

Subject: staff redundancies

George,

Last week you asked me to make a recommendation on which contract to terminate in the Administration Department. My recommendation is to let .... go. My reasons are as follows:

15 Plenty of time

Nicholas Sheard

1 Complete the expressions about time with the words in the box.

after	flew by	~~good~~	great	make	make up for
no	on	passed	playing	ran out	take

a I arrived in __good__ **time** for my presentation because I wanted to check my equipment.
b We were very late so we drove quickly to _____ **lost time**.
c I read the report **in** _____ **time** at all. It was only half a page long.
d We **had a** _____ **time** at the office party last month.
e I must be _____ **time** for the meeting. It's very important.
f He doesn't want to make a decision. He's just _____ **for time**.
g Our train was delayed so we _____ **the time** chatting and playing cards.
h There's no hurry, _____ **your time**.
i It was a wonderful holiday. The **time** _____ .
j It's difficult to _____ **time** for lunch when we have tight deadlines to meet.
k I rebooted my computer **time** _____ **time**, but it still kept crashing.
l She wanted to do more research before the meeting, but she _____ **of time**.

2 Work with a partner. Throw a die to move around the board and describe the situation you land on each time.

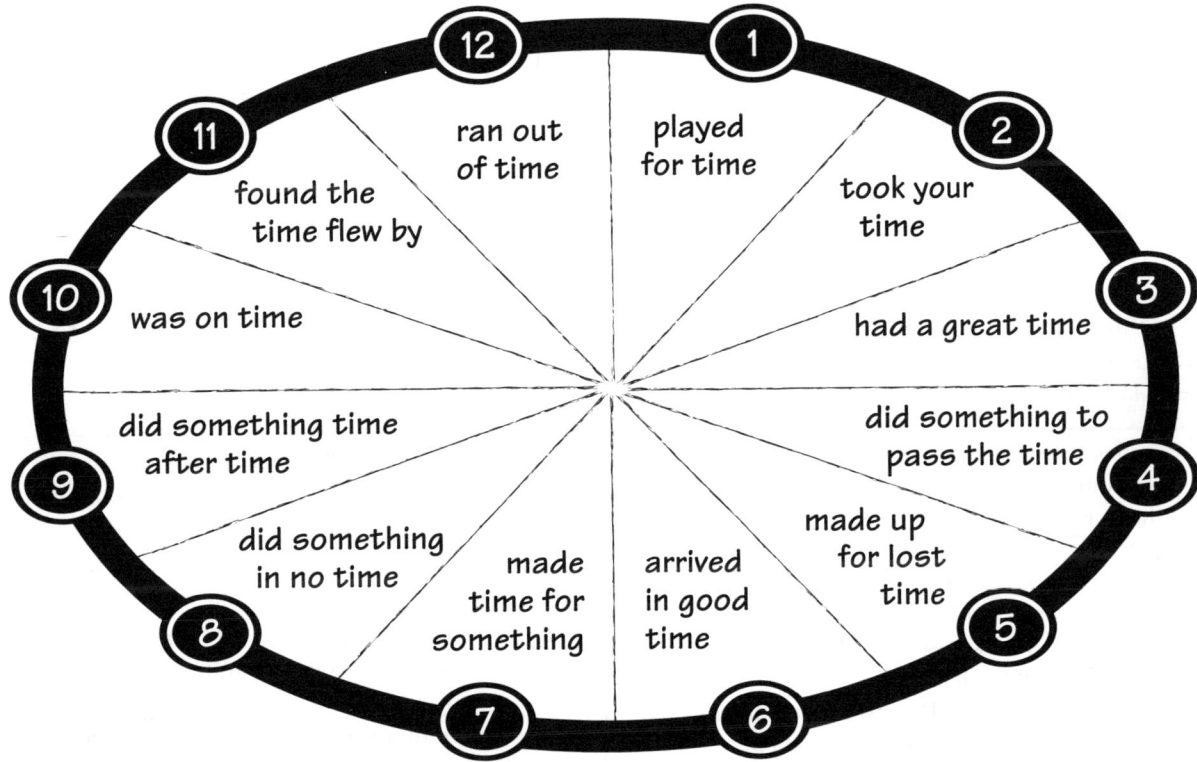

3 Discuss the questions with a partner.

a Are you good at time management?
b Do you usually arrive in good time for meetings and appointments with people?
c Are you normally aware of roughly what time it is?
d How often do you look at your watch at work? at home? on holiday?
e Is it difficult for you to make time for your family and friends during the working week?

16 Things to do

Paul Dummett

Useful language

Requests	Responding
I wonder if you can/could help me. (formal)	Of course. / Sure. / I hope so.
Can you help me?	That's no problem. As long as you …
Can you do me favour? (informal)	I'm afraid I can't help you there.
I'd like (you) to …	That might be difficult.
I need you to …	OK. I'll see what I can do.

Student A

You are going on a business trip tomorrow to Paris for two days. Below is a list of the things you have to do, and people you have to speak to before you leave. Your partner is going to take the role of each person you speak to and deal with all your requests and needs. Look at the Useful language box and decide how you are going to make each request.

Things to do

1   Borrow a map of Paris from Jane.

2   Phone Eurostar to book a flexible return ticket (London – Paris).

3   Ask the IT Services Department to update your laptop with the latest version of PowerPoint (for tomorrow's sales presentation).

4   Tell Jack to forward only urgent e-mails to Paris. (Last time he forwarded everything.)

5   Ask Tom to recommend a good restaurant in the centre of Paris.

Your partner is attending a trade fair tomorrow and he/she also has a list of things to do. Look at your role card and prepare to deal with his/her requests. Use the Useful language box to help you.

Your roles for Student B's requests
a)   Exhibition assistant: You only have one copy of the exhibitor list left. You can lend it to him/her but you need it back.
b)   Exhibition organiser: It's too late to change a stand and you don't have any free near the entrance. As a last resort, you can offer one in the middle of the hall.
c)   Exhibition assistant: The exhibitor can make his/her own photocopies – 10 cents per copy.
d)   Sales Manager: Is it really necessary to have two people on the stand? You will try to find someone; if not, you will come yourself.
e)   Dry cleaner's: A suit takes 24 hours to clean. You could deliver it tomorrow lunchtime for a fee.

When you are ready, act out the conversations with your partner working through your 'Things to do' lists.

Student B

You are at a foreign holidays trade fair to represent your company on its stand. You've arrived a day early and there are a few problems. Below is a list of the things you have to do and people you have to speak to. Your partner is going to take the role of each person you speak to and deal with all your requests and needs. Look at the Useful language box and decide how you are going to make each request.

Things to do

a)   Get list of other exhibitors.

b)   Change stand. You were promised one near the entrance, not at the back of the hall.

c)   Make 500 photocopies of promotional leaflet.

d)   Ring Sales Manager at the office to ask him/her to send someone to help on Saturday (the busiest day).

e)   Take suit to the dry cleaner's. (Needs to be back today.)

Your partner is going on a business trip tomorrow and he/she has a list of things to do. Look at your role card and prepare to deal with his/her requests. Use the Useful language box to help you.

Your roles for Student A's requests
1   Jane, a colleague: You have an out-of-date map of Paris (1994).
2   Eurostar sales assistant: A flexible return ticket costs €310. A fixed return ticket is €220.
3   IT Services Department: Only your boss can authorise upgrades on laptops. He's away until next week.
4   Jack, junior salesman: Ask what he/she means by 'urgent' e-mails. Get examples.
5   Tom, a colleague: You visited a restaurant called Bistro des Dames last year, but you can't remember the address.

When you are ready, act out the conversations with your partner working through your 'Things to do' lists.

17a Say something!

Paul Dummett

1 Do you know the difference between *say, tell, talk, speak* and *discuss*? Circle the best verb to complete each sentence. Sometimes both verbs are possible.

a He (said/told) me that he couldn't attend the meeting.
b He (said/told) that he was sorry for his mistake.
c We (talked/discussed) about the situation in Japan.
d We (talked/discussed) the new marketing plan.
e Did she (speak/talk) to you about the reorganisation plans?
f Did she (speak/talk) about the cost of the project?

When you have checked your answers, work with a partner and discuss the meanings and grammatical rules for the verbs. Then complete these sentences with the correct form of *say, tell, speak, talk* or *discuss*.

g Where is she? She _____ she would be here half an hour ago.
h I phoned your office and _____ to your assistant.
i Do you have a free moment to _____ the Zurich deal?
j I'll _____ for about half an hour and then answer your questions.
k I _____ him that he would have to wait for an answer.
l I'm sorry, I don't understand. What are you _____ about?

2 Work with a partner. Look at the following expressions and check their meaning.

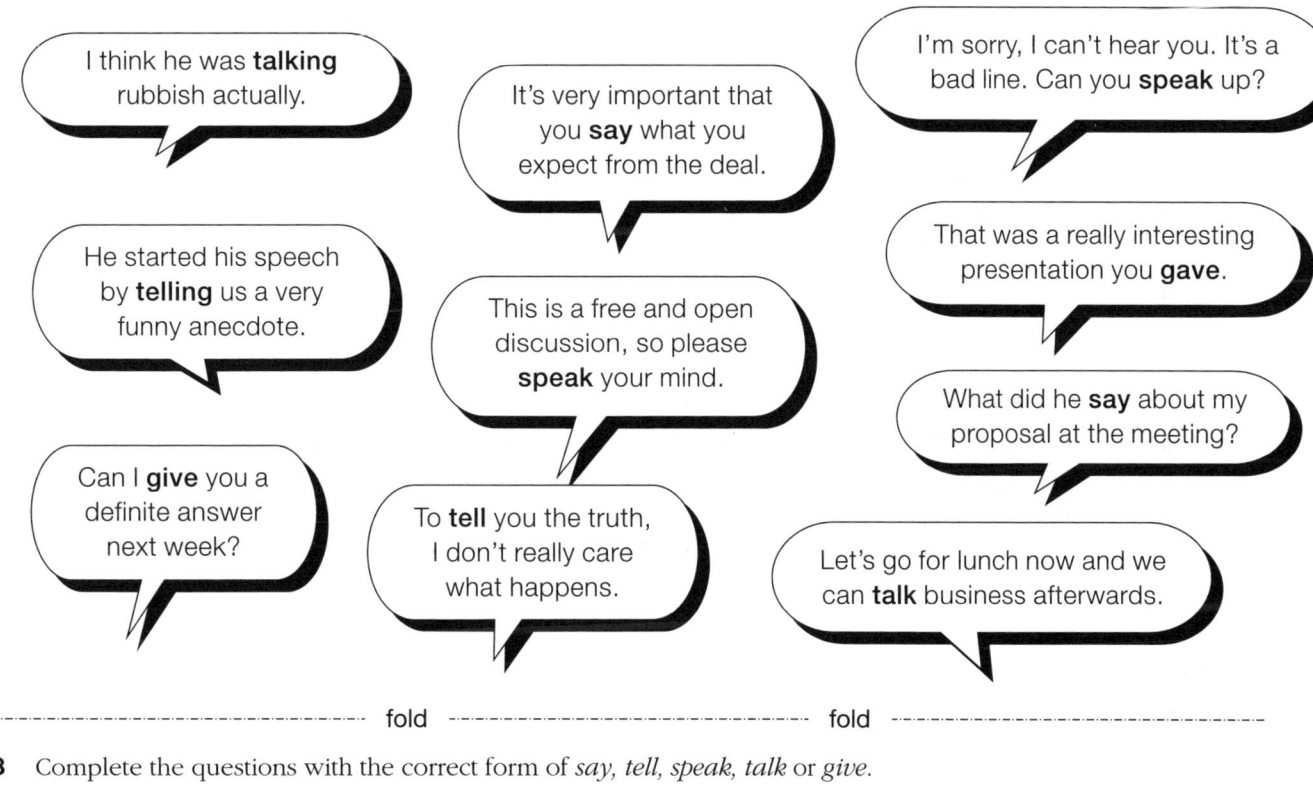

I think he was **talking** rubbish actually.

It's very important that you **say** what you expect from the deal.

I'm sorry, I can't hear you. It's a bad line. Can you **speak** up?

He started his speech by **telling** us a very funny anecdote.

This is a free and open discussion, so please **speak** your mind.

That was a really interesting presentation you **gave**.

Can I **give** you a definite answer next week?

To **tell** you the truth, I don't really care what happens.

What did he **say** about my proposal at the meeting?

Let's go for lunch now and we can **talk** business afterwards.

---- fold ---------------------------------- fold ----------------

3 Complete the questions with the correct form of *say, tell, speak, talk* or *give*. Then discuss the questions with your partner.

a Do you get nervous when you have to _____ a speech in public?
b How many languages do you _____?
c Have you ever _____ a lie to get a job?
d Are you good at _____ jokes?
e Do you find it difficult to _____ 'no' to people when they ask for help?
f Do you prefer to _____ business on the phone or face-to-face?
g Are you the kind of person who likes to _____ your mind?

17b But you said ...! Jeremy Taylor & Jon Wright

1 Last week Karen Jones, who owns a modelling agency, called Paul Owen, a builder, to do some building work for her. Read their conversation with a partner.

Mr Owen	Paul Owen Building Services. How can I help you?
Ms Jones	Good morning. My name is Karen Jones. We're looking for a builder to do some work on an old factory here in Bristol. We're putting on a fashion show and we want to use it as the venue.
Mr Owen	What kind of work do you need done?
Ms Jones	Oh, don't worry, there isn't much to do. We just need someone to tidy up the place a bit, paint the walls white, build an office and a catwalk. That's about all.
Mr Owen	That sounds fine. When would you like us to start?
Ms Jones	As soon as possible. It's pretty urgent, I'm afraid.
Mr Owen	It won't be easy, Ms Jones, we're very busy at the moment, but I'll try and get a team of men together. We can probably start next Monday.
Ms Jones	That's great. Could you give me an idea of how long it will take and how much it will cost?
Mr Owen	Difficult to say. I think it will take about two days to do and will cost no more than £3,000. We'd need a deposit of 50% before we start work.
Ms Jones	Mmm, OK. Right. I'll transfer the money to your bank account today and fax you a detailed list of requirements along with directions to the factory. You can park right outside, by the way. Oh, and I'll post you the keys, too.
Mr Owen	That sounds good. We will, of course, work to the highest standards and we also guarantee that the work area will be kept as tidy as possible.
Ms Jones	That's great. Thanks, Mr Owen. I'll provide all the usual facilities for your workers such as toilets and lunch. Well, good luck. I'll call you on Monday to see how you are getting on. Goodbye.

-------------------------------- fold -------------------------------- fold --------------------------------

2 The following week, Karen Jones went to the factory site. She expected to find the venue ready for the fashion show. Instead, she found a complete mess! Almost nothing was ready. She called Mr Owen to complain. Mr Owen was also not happy.

Work with a partner. You are going to act out the phone conversation. First look at your rolecard to see why your character is unhappy. Then read and continue the conversation.

Ms Jones	Hello. Is that Mr Owen?
Mr Owen	Speaking.
Ms Jones	Mr Owen. This is Karen Jones. I'm afraid I'm very unhappy with your work. You said that you would work to the highest standards. I went there today and the work that you have done is awful!
Mr Owen	Actually, I'm glad you called, Ms Jones. There are some things I'd like to talk to you about, too. You told me that you would …

Student A	**Student B**
You are Karen Jones and you are not happy because …	You are Paul Owen and you are not happy because …
• the work is of a very poor standard.	• Ms Jones sent terrible directions to the factory. Your men got lost for an hour.
• the work isn't finished three days after the deadline.	• there was no parking near the factory.
• the garden next to the factory is covered with litter.	• she didn't send him keys for the factory. They had to climb in through the window.
• the office and catwalk haven't been started.	• there weren't any toilet facilities for the workers.
• the telephones haven't been connected.	• a packet of crisps and one bottle of lemonade is not the 'lunch' they expected.
• Mr Owen never answers his mobile phone.	• the money hasn't been transferred to your account.

18a How wrong can you be?   Jon Hird

1 The experts don't always get it right when it comes to predicting the future. Add *will* and one of the verbs in the box to the incomplete predictions.

> not be able   be used   be (x3)   get
> reach   prove   work   go

1 'There is no reason why anyone would want a computer in their home.'

2 'The bomb _____ never _____ off. I speak as an expert in explosives.'

3 'Television _____ _____ to hold on to any market it captures after the first six months. People _____ soon _____ tired of staring at a wooden box every night.'

4 'The radio has no imaginable commercial value. Who would pay for a message sent to nobody in particular?'

5 'A jet engine, you say? Very interesting, my boy, but it _____ never _____.'

6 'We don't like their sound, and guitar music is on the way out.'

7 'The telephone _____ to inform people that a telegram has been sent.'

8 'There is not the slightest indication that nuclear energy _____ ever _____ obtainable.'

9 'The horse is here to stay, but the automobile is only a novelty.'

10 'X-rays _____ to be a hoax.'

11 'There _____ never _____ a bigger plane built.'

12 'Everything that can be invented has been invented.'

13 'The abdomen, the chest, and the brain _____ forever _____ shut from the intrusion of the surgeon.'

14 'Man _____ never _____ the moon, regardless of all future scientific advances.'

2 Can you match the predictions to who said them?

a ☐ Sir John Eric Ericksen, British surgeon, appointed Surgeon-Extraordinary to Queen Victoria, 1873

b ☐ Decca Records rejecting the Beatles, 1962

c ☐ Admiral William Leahy, US Atomic Bomb Project, 1945

d ☐ David Sarnoff's associates in response to his urging investment in the radio, 1920

e ☐ The president of Michigan Savings Bank advising Horace Rachham (Henry Ford's lawyer) not to invest in the Ford Motor Co., 1903

f ☐ Alexander Graham Bell, Scottish-born US scientist and inventor, 1877

g ☐ Ken Olson, president of Digital Equipment Corporation, 1977

h ☐ A Boeing engineer, after the first flight of the 247, a twin-engine plane that carried ten people

i ☐ Dr Lee de Forest, inventor, 1967 (two years before man landed on the moon)

j ☐ Darryl F Zanuck, head of 20th Century Fox, 1946

k ☐ Albert Einstein, German-born US Physicist, 1932

l ☐ William Thomson, Lord Kelvin English scientist, 1899

m ☐ Professor of Aeronautical Engineering at Cambridge, after being shown Frank Whittle's plan for the jet engine, 1930

n ☐ Charles H. Duell, Commissioner, U.S. Office of Patents, 1899

18b A–Z race

Gina Cuciniello

Work in teams. Correct the sentences which have a grammar mistake. You have a time limit of ten minutes.

A	I'm usually going to work by car.
B	The climate gets warmer because of global warming.
C	My boss stays often in luxury hotels.
D	Could you tell me where is the meeting room?
E	The committee chose the new Financial Director last Tuesday.
F	This Internet search engine developed without the use of advertising.
G	Could you me tell where you live?
H	Food served in British restaurants isn't bad as you think.
I	I have to work much harder in my current job than in my last one.
J	The Chairman said that profits have risen by 5% this year.
K	Have you heard the news? Our competitor went bankrupt!
L	Employees should be punctual for work in the mornings.
M	I'll to take that call if you like.
N	I not have to back up my work. My computer automatically does it for me.
O	I'm absolutely exhausted. I am at my desk since eight o'clock this morning.
P	No, really Carlo. I pay for the drinks. I insist!
Q	What do you do after the conference, Anna?
R	The Marketing Manager told that we should promote it on the Internet.
S	Who you visited when you went to Turkey?
T	She's worked in Tokyo for three years.
U	If we don't leave now, we're late for the Managing Director's presentation.
V	I'm going not to buy any more shares until the market improves.
W	His company is the more profitable in this sector.
X	Shall I to order a taxi for you?
Y	She says everyone she's the manager when she's really only the assistant.
Z	He's the kind of person you can depend on to do a job well.

19 What if …?

Jon Hird

If you were the boss of your company, …?	If you could wear whatever you wanted to work, …?
If you could change one thing about your office, …?	If you were offered the chance to work in another country, …?
If you could change one work decision you made today, …?	If you were annoyed that a colleague was always leaving work early, …?
If it was possible to turn back the clock and start your career again, …?	If you accidentally opened your boss' private e-mail folder, …?
If you had the option to work from home, …?	If you could speak perfect English, …?
If you were offered a job at a rival company, …?	If you discovered that two of your married colleagues were having an affair, …?
If you didn't agree with your boss about something, …?	If you could choose your own working hours, …?
If you could change one thing about your job, …?	If you were asked to work extra hours for no extra pay, …?
If you could have any job in the world, …?	If you woke up with a hangover on a work day, …?
If you could change one work decision you've made in your life, …?	If you found a confidential report on a colleague, …?
If you could choose your own company car, …?	If you could retire tomorrow, …?

20 That's not right!

Mark Powell

Work with a partner. Look at the things you might say during a business lunch. In each pair of sentences, only one is correct. Score out the incorrect sentence each time. Then roleplay the three stages of the conversation with one of you reading the odd numbers and the other the even ones.

1A	So, shall we take a drink at the bar while we wait for our table?	**1B**	So, shall we have a drink at the bar while we wait for our table?
2A	OK. Do you mind if I just have a mineral water?	**2B**	OK. Do you care if I just have a mineral water?
3A	Mineral water, sure. Gassy or flat?	**3B**	Mineral water, sure. Still or sparkling?
4A	On second thought, I'll have a martini.	**4B**	On second thoughts, I'll have a martini.
5A	Good idea. I think I'll join you.	**5B**	Good idea. I think I'll copy you.
6A	Great place, by the way. Do you go here often?	**6B**	Great place, by the way. Do you come here often?
7A	Quite often. Ah, looks like our table's ready. After you.	**7B**	Quite often. Ah, looks like our table's ready. Behind you.

8A	Wow! What a fantastic view of the city!	**8B**	Wow! What a fantastic sight of the city!
9A	Isn't it? Now, this is the main menu and those are the particulars.	**9B**	Isn't it? Now, this is the main menu and those are the specials.
10A	OK. So, what do you recommend?	**10B**	OK. So, what do you guarantee?
11A	Well, you could attempt the rabbit. That's very good here.	**11B**	Well, you could try the rabbit. That's very good here.
12A	Actually, I'm not that keen for rabbit.	**12B**	Actually, I'm not that keen on rabbit.
13A	Well, the veal is also a speciality.	**13B**	Well, the veal is also a specialism.
14A	Mmm, that sounds good.	**14B**	Mmm, that sounds well.

15A	So, are you ready to order?	**15B**	So, are you ready to command?
16A	Yeah, I'm going to have the fillet – I like a good bloody steak.	**16B**	Yeah, I'm going to have the fillet – I like a good rare steak.
17A	OK. And shall we have a bottle of red of the house?	**17B**	OK. And shall we have a bottle of the house red?
18A	A whole bottle? What about this afternoon's meeting?	**18B**	A whole bottle? How about this afternoon's meeting?
19A	Good point. Let's just have a pair of glasses, then.	**19B**	Good point. Let's just have a couple of glasses, then.
20A	Fine. Well, I think this morning's presentation went very well.	**20B**	Fine. Well, I think this morning's presentation came very well.
21A	Mmm, let's hope this afternoon is just as successful.	**21B**	Mmm, let's hope this afternoon is just so successful.

Macmillan Education
Between Towns Road, Oxford OX4 3PP
A division of Macmillan Publishers Limited
Companies and representatives throughout the world

ISBN 0 333 95727 X

Text © Macmillan Publishers Limited 2003
Design and illustration © Macmillan Publishers Limited 2003
First published 2003

Note to teachers

Photocopies may be made, for classroom use, of pages 94–123 and
145–174 without the prior written permission of Macmillan Publishers
Limited. However, please note that the copyright law, which does not
normally permit multiple copying of published material, applies to
the rest of this book.

Text by Helena Gomm

Resource materials by Simon Clarke; Gina Cuciniello; Paul Dummett;
Paul Emmerson; Jon Hird; Mark Powell; Nicholas Sheard; Jeremy
Taylor; Jon Wright

Designed by eMC Design, www.emcdesign.org.uk
Illustrated by Mike Stones icons (research photos Photodisc); Julian
Mosedale p146; Val Saunders p152, 162; Martin Shovel p147, 151, 155
Original cover concept by Jackie Hill at 320 Design
Cover illustration by Mike Stones (research photos Photodisc)

The authors and publishers wish to thank the following who have
kindly granted permission to use copyright material: Extracts in *11a
Nannies* from 'Mary Poppins' Portfolio' by Julie Pitta. Reprinted by
permission of FORBES Global © 2003 Forbes Global Inc.; Extracts
in *11b Top boss?* from 'What type of boss are you?' from
RateYourself.com. Reproduced by permission of RateYourself;
In *14a Unfair dismissal?* 'Man sacked for working too hard wins his
job back' and 'Worker sacked over Bermuda shorts loses case' from
Ananova.com. Reproduced by permission of Orange Multimedia
Operations; Dictionary extract from the *Macmillan English
Dictionary* © Bloomsbury Publishing Plc 2002.

Student's Book acknowledgements

Text © Simon Clarke

Design and illustration © Macmillan Publishers Limited 2003
Designed by Jackie Hill at 320 Design
Illustrated by Mike Stones icons (research photos Photodisc);
Cyrus Deboo pp26, 58; Max Ellis p7; Julian Mosedale pp31, 57, 69, 78
Photo research by Sally Neal

The publishers would like to thank Bob Ratto, Byron, Rome; Angela
Wright, British Council, Rome; Norman Cain, IH Rome; Fiona
Campbell, Teach-In, Rome; Sue Garton, Lois Clegg and Irene
Frederick, University of Parma; Simon Hopson and Gordon Doyle,
Intensive Business English, Milan; Dennis Marino, Bocconi
University, Milan; Mike Cruikshank, Advanced Language Services,
Milan; Christine Zambon, Person to Person, Milan; Fiona O'Connor,
In-Company English, Milan; Peter Panton, Panton School, Milan;
Colin Irving Bell, Novara; Marta Rodriguez Casal, Goal Rush Institute,
Buenos Aires; Elizabeth Mangi and Silvia Ventura, NET New English
Training, Buenos Aires; Graciela Yohma and Veronica Cenini, CABSI,
Buenos Aires; Viviana Pisani, Asociación Ex Alumnos, Buenos Aires;
Claudia Siciliano, LEA Institute, Buenos Aires; Cuca Martocq, AACI,
Buenos Aires; Laura Lewin, ABS International, Buenos Aires; Charlie
Lopez, Instituto Big Ben, Buenos Aires; Alice Elvira Machado; Patricia
Blower; Valeria Siniscalchi; Carla Chaves; Virginia Garcia; Cultura
Inglesa, Rio de Janeiro; Susan Dianne Mace, Britannia, Rio de Janeiro;
John Paraskou, Diamond School, Sèvres; Dorothy Polley and Nadia
Fairbrother, Executive Language Services, Paris; Claire MacMurray,
Formalangues, Paris; Claire Oldmeadow, Franco British Chamber of
Commerce, Paris; Ingrid Foussat and Anne James, IFG Langues, Paris;
Karl Willems, Quai d'Orsay Language Centre, Paris; Louis Brazier,
Clare Davis, Jacqueline Deubel, Siobhan Mla̐cak and Redge,
Télélangue, Paris; John Morrison Milne, Ian Stride, Gareth East and
Richard Marrison, IH Madrid; Gina Cuciniello; Helena Gomm;
Paulette McKean.

The authors and publishers would like to thank the following for
permission to reproduce their material: Adapted extract from
'Customised Greetings Cards Win Stamp of Approval' from *The Times*
16.12.00 copyright © NI Syndication Limited, London 2000, reprinted
by permission of the publisher; Adapted extract from
www.betterdogfood.com, reprinted by permission of the publisher;
Adapted extract from 'Ringing Up The Millions' from
www.brendan.com.au/articles.html, reprinted by permission of
Brendan Walsh; Adapted extract from 'Hotels Play the Global Brand
Game' by Andrew Clark 18.04.01 from
www.guardian.co.uk/Archive/Article/0,4273,4171589,00.html,
copyright © *The Guardian* 2001, reprinted by permission of the
publisher; Adapted extract from 'The 50 Richest in the World' from
Forbes 400 October 2001 and *Forbes Global* March 2002, copyright
© Forbes Inc 2002, reprinted by permission of Forbes Magazine;
Adapted extract from 'The Worm Man' by Lee Stokes from *BMG
Online Magazine* www.bmgroup.co.uk, reprinted by permission of
the author; Adapted extracts and photograph from
www.inditex.com/english/home.htm, reprinted by permission of the
publisher; Adapted extract from 'Wasting Time at Work' by Galen
Black from www.vgg.com/tp/tp_050201_slack.html, reprinted by
permission of (The Van Gogh-Goghs: www.vgg.com); Dictionary
extracts from the *Macmillan English Dictionary* © Bloomsbury
Publishing Plc 2002.

Whilst every effort has been made to trace owners of copyright
material in this book, there may have been some cases when the
publishers have been unable to contact the owners. We should be
grateful to hear from anyone who recognises copyright material and
who is unacknowledged. We shall be pleased to make the necessary
amendments in future editions of the book.

The authors and publishers would like to thank the following for
permission to reproduce their photographs: Action Plus/S.Bardens
p13; Alamy/P.Bowater p5(m), ImageState p12, C.Newham p33(mb),
C.Lewis p38, Novastock p45(b), A.Willett p49(t), T.Tracy p58, R.F
p64(t), Rubberball p75, ImageState p83, R.F p85, H.Sieplinga p87; Car
Photo Library/D.Kimber p35(b); Cartoonbank/M.Maslin p8; Cartoon
Stock/C.Zahn p117, J.Morris p119; Corbis/J.L.Pelaez p4, T.Horowitz
p23(t), W.Tenaillon p23(b), Sygma/D.Lamont p51, R.W.Jones p66(t),
L.Bonaventure p66(b); Eyewire p91; Farabolafoto p67;
Getty/H.Kingsnorth pp10, 89(mb), B.Bailey p14, K.Mori p17(rt),
B.Truslow p17(rb), R.Chapple pp17(b), 45(mb), C.Bissell p20, X.
Bonghi p21, M.Douet p32(t), R.Lockyer p32(b), P.Eckersley p33(mt),
P.Turner p33(b), K.Chiba p34, J.L.Batt p39, M.Goldman p40(l),
C.Franklin p40(m), Chabruken p40(r), K.Biggs p42(t), T.Anderson
p45(mt), M.Douet p53, B.Ayers p56, D.Roth p64(mt), China Tourism
Press p64(mb), D.Robb pp64(b), 89(t), T.Brown p65, B.Erlanson p72,
J.Bradley p77, P.Scholey p81, S.Hunt p86, E.Dryer p88, G.Wade
p89(mt), J.Tisne p89(b), P.Arthur p90, C.Simmons p93; Foodpix
p33(t); Hulton Archive/T.Hopkins p28, J.Kobal p52, Hulton Archive
pp37, 47, 70; ImageState pp9(t), 15, 45(t), 46; Inditex pp42(b), 43;
Maserati/PFPR p35(t); Moonpig p5(t), P.A p24; New Yorker/© 2002
The New Yorker Collection from cartoonbank.com. All Rights
Reserved; Photodisc pp46, 61; Powerstock pp9(b), 29, 60, 63; Private
Eye/K.Smith p27; Remote Lounge/J.Cate p54; Science Photo
Library/Tek Image p5(b); Sporting Pictures/P.O'Connor p49(b);
Topham/A.P p25, Photri p55; Vin Mag Archive p73.

Printed and bound in Spain by Edelvives SA

2007 2006 2005
10 9 8 7 6 5 4